X

SOCIAL THEORY
FOR TODAY

SAGE was founded in 1965 by Sara Miller McCune to support the dissemination of usable knowledge by publishing innovative and high-quality research and teaching content. Today, we publish more than 750 journals, including those of more than 300 learned societies, more than 800 new books per year, and a growing range of library products including archives, data, case studies, reports, conference highlights, and video. SAGE remains majority-owned by our founder, and after Sara's lifetime will become owned by a charitable trust that secures our continued independence.

Los Angeles | London | Washington DC | New Delhi | Singapore

SOCIAL THEORY FOR TODAY

MAKING SENSE OF SOCIAL WORLDS

ALEX LAW

Los Angeles | London | New Delhi
Singapore | Washington DC

Los Angeles | London | New Delhi
Singapore | Washington DC

SAGE Publications Ltd
1 Oliver's Yard
55 City Road
London EC1Y 1SP

SAGE Publications Inc.
2455 Teller Road
Thousand Oaks, California 91320

SAGE Publications India Pvt Ltd
B 1/I 1 Mohan Cooperative Industrial Area
Mathura Road
New Delhi 110 044

SAGE Publications Asia-Pacific Pte Ltd
3 Church Street
#10-04 Samsung Hub
Singapore 049483

Editor: Chris Rojek
Assistant editor: Gemma Shields
Production editor: Victoria Nicholas
Copyeditor: Solveig Servian
Indexer: Judith Lavender
Marketing manager: Michael Ainsley
Cover design: Lisa Harper-Wells
Typeset by: C&M Digitals (P) Ltd, Chennai, India
Printed in Great Britain by Henry Ling Limited,
at the Dorset Press, Dorchester, DT1 1HD

Library of Congress Control Number: 2014948948

British Library Cataloguing in Publication data

A catalogue record for this book is available from
the British Library

MIX
Paper from
responsible sources
FSC   FSC™ C013985
www.fsc.org

ISBN 978-1-4462-0901-1
ISBN 978-1-4462-0902-8 (pbk)

At SAGE we take sustainability seriously. Most of our products are printed in the UK using FSC papers and boards.
When we print overseas we ensure sustainable papers are used as measured by the Egmont grading system.
We undertake an annual audit to monitor our sustainability.

CONTENTS

ABOUT THE AUTHOR

Alex Law is Professor of Sociology at Abertay University in Scotland. His research and teaching interests include the relationship between social theory and social, political and cultural change. His more recent publications include *Key Concepts in Classical Social Theory* (Sage, 2011).

ACKNOWLEDGEMENTS

This book is a result of trying to make sense of social theory over many years. During that time I have benefited from teaching social theory and learning a great deal from students and former colleagues Norman Gabriel, Alex Howson, Peter Kennedy and Mick Smith. Recently, my understanding has been aided greatly by critical discussions with Christos Memos. I am most grateful to Bridget Fowler for reading and commenting on the manuscript and saving me from making numerous errors. John Scott, David Inglis, Neil Davidson, Ian Wall, Duncan Forbes and Eric Royal Lybeck have in different ways contributed to the ideas developed in this book. I owe a huge debt of gratitude to the patience, encouragement and unstinting support of Chris Rojek and Gemma Shields. They understood the often overwhelming demands made on the time and space needed for undivided scholarship by officious managerialism and the many distractions of audit culture. Mostly, I have Jan to thank for inoculating me against tedium and to Daniel as the bearer of unadulterated joy.

INTRODUCTION: THE NARCISSISM OF MINOR DIFFERENCES

The time is out of joint. O cursèd spite, That ever I was born to set it right!

Hamlet (Act 1, Sc. 5)

Ours is a time out of joint – a time of crisis. The sense of crisis seems all-pervasive. A feeling is engendered that the social conditions necessary for a tolerable social existence are in jeopardy. Social suffering has been extended on a vast scale. Politicians demand more and deeper austerity measures. Public services and welfare benefits are scaled back further and commodified wherever possible. Everyday life appears more uncertain. Institutions as different as banks, medicine, journalism, politicians, food producers, undertakers and disc jockeys have lost public trust and respect. Inequalities of wealth and income are at grotesque disproportions. Violence dominates the headlines, with daily reports of wars between states and civil wars within them, terrorist atrocities, popular insurrections and riots, racist brutality, as well as a prurient media interest in sexual and personal violence. A sense of impending disaster is pressed through the culture mill of television, film, novels and computer games in fictional landscapes of survival struggles in post-apocalypse chaos.

Despite increased feelings of insecurity and foreboding, social relations have not automatically collapsed into a war of all against all. Even as the texture of social life becomes more abrasive and threatening, as the great sociologist Norbert Elias explained, today most people, most of the time, do not resort to physical violence, either individually or collectively. They only do so under particular social conditions handed down by the lengthy historical development of specific nations and states. Yet much sociological effort is invested in studying the most immediate, spectacular and violent symptoms of crisis – racism, terrorism, riots, media, poverty, depravity – as if they stood in isolation from the long-term development processes of state societies. This has often been perceived in terms of crises of various kinds – political, cultural, moral, and economic. It is necessary to set our current concerns within the efforts of social theory to represent the crisis of modernity over the past two centuries.

In *Hamlet*, Shakespeare famously compared the crisis of state authority in Denmark to a dislocation, a 'time out of joint'. Yet the meaning of the phrase 'out of joint' is equivocal. It may be a hinge that keeps the world suspended or an 'unhinged' breakdown of the world. It may also refer to a 'world upside down' or a corrupt world of moral decadence. Or it may be the crooked precondition of a just world (Derrida, 1994: 23). Hamlet's curse is that he is destined to set a wrong world aright. Time seemed to stand still as the psychologically tortured and resentful Hamlet prevaricated before the task of repairing the dislocated joint, in the play, to avenge the murder of his father. Hamlet's hesitation was held up by Romantic poets like Coleridge and Wordsworth as an idealisation of political passivity in England following the French revolution (Taylor, 1989: 101–111).

Unlike the Romantic intellectuals, who flirted with the French revolution but could not commit to political action 'at the proper time', Hamlet weighs up the competing demands of a sense of duty, revenge, and his sense of personal integrity, before undertaking decisive action – fighting pirates, killing rivals, pretending to be insane – to resolve social and psychological crises. These crises almost bring Hamlet to the edge of madness. Yet, by feigning madness, fluctuating between rationality and irrationality and back, Hamlet opens up a performative space for personal autonomy and freedom from social convention. Crucially, however, Hamlet's game can only be played because of his position in social space as the Prince, son of the King, next in line to the throne (Heller, 2002: 48).

Social theory often tries to play the role of Hamlet. It also stands aloof from the action, acting as if it is unaffected by the troubles of daily life and its vulgar interests. Only when it is good and ready will social theory deign to advise on the public issues of the day. It weighs up the demands of preserving its own integrity and the responsibility it often feels to make a difference by pointing a way out of the crisis and recommending how society should live. In so doing, social theory often fixes on a single aspect of crisis, for instance, a crisis of over-production of goods, a crisis of identity, a crisis of authority, a crisis of meaning, a crisis of technological systems, and so on.

Social theory presents a special kind of knowledge about social worlds. From the point of view of common sense the language and concerns of social theory can seem remote and arcane, touched by a kind of self-referential madness much like the Prince of Denmark. In this, social theory claims to provide an antidote to common sense. Every student textbook announces that 'common sense' is an inferior type of knowledge. It is charged with naturalising arbitrary beliefs, the root of everyday prejudice, stereotypes, error, bias, and irrationality, the 'what everyone already knows' of exclusionary social identities, the self-evident appeal of last resort of racism, nationalism, and sexism.

Social theory on the other hand is represented as making logical, rigorous and impartial claims about the truth of the social world. It protects itself from contamination by common sense through abstract concepts and systematic forms of logic. As students of social theory also know only too well, social theory rehearses its own semantic style and codes, unfamiliar concepts, pedantic logic and obscure points of reference that place it at a remote distance from the ordinary social world.

Crisis throws such assumptions into doubt. Knowledge about the social world cannot be known, a priori, in all its essentials like the perfect circle described by geometrical knowledge. Social theory concerns itself with the historically variable, equivocal, disparate and ambiguous material of common-sense understandings of the social world. However, this is often dealt with in unreflective, tacit and implicit ways. Two broad (often confused) versions of common sense emerge in social theory: as good, sound judgement (sense) about the practical significance of specific things, *or* whatever is general and widespread (common) in the culture.

On one side, common sense is understood as a precondition of solidarity and social action. Here social theory is viewed as continuous with and an extension of common sense, an 'umbilical cord' that can never be cut but simply needs to be more systematically ordered and controlled. On the other side, common sense is reproached as a constraint on scientific reason and autonomy. Here, sociology strives for a discontinuous reflexive 'break' with the spontaneously given self-evident truths and pre-judgments of ordinary social worlds.

THEORETICAL PLURALISM

What we would recognise as modern social theory only truly emerged as a distinct intellectual tradition in eighteenth-century Europe, first appearing in France and Scotland before spreading to Germany, England and beyond (Heilbron, 1995). It is often assumed that it developed out of a concern to emulate the natural sciences. While rational scientific models of knowledge exerted a fascination for social theory, this was also mixed in with varied approaches to moral philosophy, law, history and political economy, as well as pre-theoretical common sense (Schneider, 1967). Much early modern social theory drew inspiration from the histories, political philosophy and ethics of the classical world of ancient Greece.

The Greek word *logos* can refer to both reason and discourse. Sociological theory refers to this sense of an explanatory logic of the social world. Contrary to popular belief, the specialised discourse of social theory is not mainly due to wilful obscurantism (although a case for a complex and verbose style has been made by some social theorists, such as the abstract, non-linear social theory of Niklas Luhmann (1995; Moeller 2012: 10–15)). One source for over-complex language lies in a continuous history of synthesis and revision of previous theoretical frameworks. Older concepts that manage to survive rarely do so with their original meaning intact. Concepts and theories are altered when they come into contact with revised or new paradigms and changed social conditions. A major example of this recently has been the change to the meaning of 'capital'. Once restricted to refer to stocks of economic resources it was extended by the work of Pierre Bourdieu in the last quarter of the twentieth century to also refer to cultural resources (cultural capital), educational qualifications (educational capital) and social networks (social capital).

Social theory appears to be plagued with contrary approaches to the social world. A profusion of social theories confronts every student of sociology. Every few years or so some particular theory, theorist or school emerges above all others to captivate the field with bold new concepts and themes until it is eclipsed in turn by yet another theory.

For some, sociological knowledge is or should be cumulative in nature, with the latest theory building on and improving previous theories. Theories succeed for a while because they appear to work better than the alternatives. For others, theoretical change is more haphazard and accidental, bearing little relationship to the explanatory scope or descriptive power of theories. Social theories respond to a generational need for novelty and invention as markers of distinction and advantage in intellectual games of succession.

How to make sense of the theoretical pluralism that mushrooms within the single discipline of sociology? Many of the disputes in sociology concern the place of social theory in the constitution of the social world. For some the social world needs to be transformed into a definable theoretical object made up of discrete concepts and definite propositions. For others the social world should be explored subjectively first of all in order to account fully for all its empirical richness and diversity. The battle over social theory in sociology echoes the long-running dispute in Western thought between empiricism and rationalism.

Empiricists tend to be impatient with the specialised language and logic of theory and seek to establish the facts of the matter in the most efficient and reliable manner possible. Empiricism adopts the scientific procedure of *induction* which pictures theory as standing at the end of the research process. Here social theory is something generated by empirical study and only later generalised into universal propositions. From this perspective, theoretical pluralism reveals the chaos that is produced when social theory is not grounded by the stringent test of empirical evidence and is made an autonomous object of study in its own right.

Rationalists tend to be critical of the naivety of empiricism for wishing away the intellectual difficulties and necessity of theoretical effort. Here the scientific procedure of *deduction* places theory at the logical beginning of the explanatory process. Empirical evidence either corroborates or refutes an already established theory at the end of a logical chain of reasoning. From this perspective, theoretical pluralism reflects the lack of a common starting point or axiomatic principle for theory to logically and rigorously build on.

SOCIAL THEORY AND SOCIAL SCIENCE

Within sociology this division came increasingly to be seen as false and artificial. It produced a damaging schism between professional sociologists primarily concerned with empirical research and those primarily concerned with clarifying and refining social theory. Each tends to pursue autonomous and specialised interests divorced from each other. Fifty years ago C. Wright Mills (1959) criticised the separation between 'abstract empiricism' and 'grand theory'. Mills' appeal was not entirely in vain, especially with the flourishing of critical sociology in the late 1960s and 1970s. But neither was it entirely successful. In the 1980s Anthony Giddens (1984) argued that sociology was still beset on one side by 'mindless empiricism' and on the other by 'unconstrained theoretical pluralism'.

Social theory is sometimes viewed as a body of knowledge that bestrides the whole of the social sciences. From this standpoint social theory has no special relationship to sociology. Sociology is only one discipline among others that contributes to and borrows from social theory. Other specialised disciplines like economics, human geography, politics, psychology and anthropology share with sociology an interest in the development of social theory as a common stock of knowledge. Social theory allows separate disciplines to meet on the same ground despite their different interests and problems.

After all, collective human problems are social in nature even if these are not always defined in purely 'sociological' terms. Economics for instance makes assumptions about the social character of interaction when it formulates models of market exchange. Human geography concerns the settlement and movement within and between societies distributed across physical space. Politics studies the role of social relations and governing institutions in struggles for power. Anthropology describes and analyses the cultural expressions of discrete groups. Psychology can seem to be situated at the furthest remove from social theory where it assumes that cognitive processes are first locked up in the minds of individuals and only subsequently enter society as measurable actions. But even here influential schools of psychology have drawn on and developed social theory in recognition of the profoundly social character of the human personality.

SOCIAL THEORY AND PHILOSOPHY

Sociology grew out of a growing dissatisfaction with the limitations of traditional philosophy. Philosophy measured society against ideal principles without recourse to the facts of a pre-given reality. Although it never quite shook free of its debt to philosophy, sociology modelled itself as an empirical science of society. Comte, who coined the term 'sociology', originally called his new science 'social physics' but sometimes alternated this with 'social philosophy', indicating the twin pull of attraction for social theory of science and philosophy. Philosophy has always shared a close interest in the nature of society, even if this was from a detached, ideal standpoint a long way off from the action. Both Aristotle and Plato were concerned to identify the virtues needed for an ideal society and the types of authority that would make the 'good life' possible.

Social theory has found itself entangled in a struggle with philosophy ever since it emerged as a distinctive branch of knowledge. Until the emergence of sociology in the nineteenth century, philosophy occupied a special place as an academic institution authorised by the cultural prestige of philosophers themselves. Professional philosophy protected its autonomy by increased technical specialisation and virtuoso displays of symbolic paradoxes. In many countries it continues to exercise a bewitching spell over other disciplines from an exalted position in the academic hierarchy. An authoritative claim to fundamental truths, clarity and logical reasoning seemed to grant philosophy a final say about what constitutes sound, valid or 'interesting' knowledge.

One reason for theoretical pluralism, it has been claimed, is an excessive preoccupation with philosophical concepts and problems like epistemology, morality, aesthetics or ontology, and borrowings from philosophical traditions like materialism, phenomenology, existentialism, structuralism, Kantianism, and post-structuralism. Social theory often acts as a bridge that allows philosophy to cross over unhindered into territory occupied by sociology (Kilminster, 1998). By making itself dependent on the transcendental categories of philosophy, sociology is deflected away from fashioning an epistemology adequate to social conditions.

Against the abstract demands and prestige of philosophy, a sense of sociological vertigo is felt and theoretical development is abandoned behind the *cordon sanitaire* of empiricism. In the other direction it can lead to the pursuit of formal theoretical systems that imitate prescribed philosophical discourses rather than theorising substantive claims about the social world. One form that this takes is to treat the metaphysical dualisms of philosophy, say individual versus society, or structure versus agency, as defining the central problem for social theory. Social theory then proceeds to resolve or overcome the intellectual puzzle given by philosophy through some third category like structuration.

Of course, the classical social theorists were steeped in Western philosophical culture. They looked to ancient Greek philosophy for examples or analogies with which to address the epistemological, ethical, political and ontological problems of capitalist modernity. Modernity was perceived through the prism of liberal, Enlightenment and Romantic thought, as well as contemporary philosophical currents. While classical sociology set itself apart from the traditional claims of philosophy it arguably let the old metaphysics in by the back door (Kilminster, 1998: 30). However, European philosophical culture was not adopted wholesale or uncritically but was transformed by the classical sociological imagination. The sociological achievements of Marx, Durkheim and Weber brought philosophical stargazing down to earth.

A THREE-WAY BALANCING ACT

The rupture of social theory from philosophy can be traced to Comte. Comte attempted to de-mystify knowledge, though in the process succeeded only in reifying scientific laws. Social theory cannot simply swallow philosophy whole and regurgitate it later as 'philosophical sociology'. Social theory provides sociology with a conceptual framework for approaching the social world as a scientific object. It delineates the social content of physical, cultural, political or economic forms. Its relationship with philosophy is therefore a tense, estranged one between incompatibles. At least this was how Marcuse, dialectically straddling critical theory and 'negative' philosophy, saw things in 1941 (375): 'Sociology does not "negate" philosophy, in the sense of taking over the hidden content and carrying it into social theory and practice, but sets itself up as a realm apart from philosophy, with a province and truth of its own.'

Sociology certainly narrowed the room for manoeuvre for philosophy, which responded in turn by retreating further into the abstract void of conceptual games or by recasting social theory in the static language of eternal categories. Social theory often repays the compliment and tries to stay on good terms with the seemingly more profound categories of philosophy. Social theory is not separated from philosophy by its object of study, since both may be concerned with 'society' at some level, but by how the object is constructed. For the sake of simplicity the relationship between social theory, sociology and philosophy may be summarised in the following way:

1. Social theory
2. Social philosophy
3. Sociological theory

In the first case, philosophy informs social theory but does not dominate it. It frames the problems, procedures and results of sociology by borrowing concepts and logic selectively from philosophy. Social theory continues to rely on philo- sophical categories like alienation or ontology. Sociological problems are posed in terms of philosophical dualisms, such as structure and agency, self and society, idealism and materialism, and so on. Social theory acquires the function of a 'second-order' activity, removed from but guiding the 'first-order' discipline of empirical sociology.

In the second case, social philosophy is framed within the terms of and accepts the priority of philosophy. Social philosophy is divorced from substantive entan- glement in empirical sociology. Sociology depends on philosophy to determine the terms of its fundamental problems, ultimate values or scientific rigour. Social philosophy addresses more fundamental problems of being, essence and appear- ance, thing in itself, relativism and realism, justice, freedom and so on. Working from philosophical concepts and logical inferences, backed by scatterings of examples and illustrations, social philosophy flits between intellectual fashions for science (positivism, materialism, functionalism, structuralism) or 'life' (existen- tialism, vitalism, phenomenology, idealism) as the cultural mood changes.

Finally, in the case of sociological theory, sociology is seen as a discrete science wholly or largely independent of philosophy. As part of sociology, theory develops in close contact with empirical processes. It has no particular need for philosophy, either as epistemology or ontology, or as ethics. Sociological theory refuses to be ensnared in what it sees as endless, futile debates, such as how social theory might overcome the division between structure and action, or reality and language. As a practising empirical science, sociological theory keeps a respectful distance from problems of ultimate values or formal logic. These are distractions from the explanatory function of theory in a normal science. Indeed, since it carries so much philosophical baggage, the term 'social theory' should probably be replaced with 'sociological theory' as more appropriate to the theoretical condensate of an autonomous empirical science.

Even where it borrows from philosophy much social theory is in fact 'socio- logical theory'. At one end, social theory excludes the empirical content of the social world to construct ideal models of what is specifically 'social' about the world. Early German sociology and phenomenology, for instance, were prepared to leave the diverse contents of the social world to other empirical disciplines while logically isolating what they took to be their specifically 'social' form. At the other end, substantive sociological theory argues that theory cannot be isolated in an autonomous way from empirical content (Holmwood and Stewart, 1991). Theory and evidence must always bear the closest relationship to each other and construct more modest, empirically specific theories instead of large-scale theorising. Social theory should be determined principally not by its inner logic but by its fit with empirical content.

THEORY-BAITING

Theoretical texts seem to take on an independent life of their own as part of an autonomous canon operating under its own logic. Abstract theory runs the risk of becoming a purely scholastic exercise in intellectual history: interesting background perhaps, but largely irrelevant to the practical needs of professional sociology today. Yet social theory today would be greatly impoverished if it simply covered up what it has inherited from the past. Study of earlier forms of social theory is not an interesting diversion from social theory today but is a precondition of its vitality. As Adorno argued in the extreme case of religious dogma, this was always an attempt to:

> recoup the price of progress, by taking account of what has been lost, and noting what was once present at least as an approach, a conception ... this over-eager assertion of the mistrust of the obsoleteness of a phenomenon without indicating precisely in what respect it is out of date is almost always a means of nipping in the bud, or of covering up wounds which continue to exist in such theoretical conceptions. (2000: 96)

Adorno gives the example of Herbert Spencer (1820–1903), one of the most ridiculed and caricatured nineteenth-century sociologist in the twentieth century. Spencer, Adorno claims, left a wealth of ideas and perspectives that would be impossible for the more specialised sociology of today. Despite the condescension of social theorists like Talcott Parsons (1902–1979), much social theory in the twentieth century, from Durkheim on, remained deeply indebted to the scope and depth of Spencer's original ideas like 'integration' and 'differentiation'.

Almost all types of social theory are subject to codification and caricature by their opponents (sometimes by their allies as well). Take the routine othering of 'positivism'. Positivism is said to stand outside of society in order to generate unbiased knowledge about it in the form of either 'rationalism' (by developing logical and crystal-clear concepts that mirror reality) or 'empiricism' (by acquiring facts from pure sense experience and clear-headed perception). This model typically states that, first, positivism as the dominant method of social science makes the metaphysical assumption that reality exists as an object independent of the perceptions or actions of any subject. Second, that objective reality can be known scientifically, that is, without distortion or bias, through a neutral methodology of value-freedom and transparently clear forms of communication. Third, this method generates facts as objective data that reflect objective reality. On the basis of the absolute certainty of objective facts, theory can begin to be constructed.

Whether this is an accurate model of any particular positivist method – Hume, Comte, Spencer, Mill, Durkheim, or Neurath – is, to say the least, open to question as later chapters indicate. Nevertheless, it functions as a convenient fiction with which to contrast 'critical' social theory. This neglects the extent to which the various historical forms of positivism saw themselves as contributing to a self-critical social theory, however unsatisfactory they may have been in other respects. It is essential, therefore, to try to present social theories in their strongest light and refrain from relying on adversarial polemics or over-simplified composite models of rival theories.

Within social theory a temptation arises to wage intellectual disputes as partisan, win-at-all-costs ideological struggles. In such cases theoretical disputes proceed along the lines of a courtroom prosecution or a combat sport. Aggressive polemics open up against adversaries deemed to be a danger to the new theoretical 'turn'. Satisfaction is taken in the inclination to theoretical aggression, which helps bind together insiders and purge outsiders. In the context of nationalist and religious conflict, Freud (1991b: 305) called this phenomenon 'the narcissism of minor differences'. In social theory deep-seated differences become entrenched as dominant theories acquire a greater degree of autonomy and protection not only from rival theories but also, more significantly, from substantive studies of the social world.

Against gratuitous theory-baiting, Antonio Gramsci (1971: 343–4) recognised that theory should not be subjected to 'a process at law in which there is an accused and a public prosecutor whose professional duty is to demonstrate that the accused is guilty and has to be put out of circulation'. As Gramsci suggests, the adversary in any theoretical dispute may well be expressing a real problem or identifying a blindspot that needs to be addressed rather than simply demolished by polemical critique.

In law, war and politics, Gramsci argued, the enemy is destroyed by attacking them where they are weakest, to gain a decisive and lasting victory. In intellectual disputes, by contrast, opponents need to be engaged where they are strongest, represented by the most reputable scholars, where each 'victory' is hard won through scrupulous accuracy of representation and intentions, and can only ever be considered temporary and never definitive:

> A new science proves its efficacy and vitality when it demonstrates that it is capable of confronting the great champions of the tendencies opposed to it and when it either resolves by its own means the vital questions which they have posed or demonstrates, in peremptorily fashion, that these questions are false problems. (Gramsci, 1971: 433)

A desire to detect the real significance of the adversary rather than the impulse to obliterate their perspective might encourage social theory to escape from what Gramsci calls 'the prison of ideologies'.

Theoretical disputes must assume that interlocutors are competent experts and are resistant to appeals to authority or emotion. Without the proper theoretical propriety, petty polemics replace scientific endeavour and 'facile verbal victories' are secured against second-rate adversaries. If we assume with Gramsci (1971: 439) that 'the end proposed is that of raising the tone and intellectual level of one's followers and not just the immediate aim of creating a desert around oneself by all means possible', then it is vital to try to understand what intellectual opponents really mean and to avoid simplistic caricatures of rival perspectives.

Yet theory-baiting is difficult to contain. Even Gramsci's (1971: 421) respect for intellectual culture conflicted with his view elsewhere that Marxism can only be conceived 'in a polemical form and in the form of perpetual struggle'. Because of the tradition of caricaturing opposing theoretical perspectives in the polemical game of what might be called 'theory-baiting', this book aims to dispel some of the most obdurate myths about the losers in social theory rather than simply parading the victors anointed by the canon of social theory. Theoretical disputes are too often excited by petty polemics and easy victories against cartoon-like versions of opponents such as 'positivism', 'realism', 'structuralism', 'Marxism', 'modernism', and other 'losers' in the game of theory-baiting.

Over the past few decades some post-modern critics caricatured 'modernism' as a unified object of ridicule that represented all that was stale and decaying in social theory. So-called 'modernist' dogma was alleged to have entertained 'humanist' illusions about universal emancipation based on the false closure of absolutist theoretical systems grounded by unshakeable conceptual foundations and transparent language, resulting in the certainties of 'universal truth'. This disregard for local, heterogeneous discourses and theoretical 'modesty' conceals social differences and power struggles over the practical and moral consequences of social theory. It also justified the worst excesses of European ethnocentrism and totalitarian dictatorships.

WHAT FOLLOWS

Such simplifications may satisfy a craving for invective but they do little to aid the process of self-understanding. Large, sweeping assertions aimed at subject-less constructions like 'modernism' or 'humanism' result in Pyrrhic victories at the level of rhetoric. Unlike worldly ideologies, theoretical constructions do not possess the kind of causal efficacy ('totalitarian') assigned to them. This book will attempt to show that the story of social theory is more complex than an absolute 'modernist' demand for solid foundations and universal truth indifferent to social suffering. This is why some of the most caricatured social theories are examined, in the chapters that follow, with a little more attention than is usual. Approaches as different as that taken by Comte, Bukharin, Neurath, Lefebvre, and Borkenau were marginalised as social theory took another of its regular 'turns' towards alternative critical perspectives. Such theorists are more often re-presented through the polemics of their opponents, Gramsci, Lukacs, Horkheimer and Adorno, among others, who in turn were themselves subject to caricature as modernists, elitists and dogmatists, by more recent social theory adopted by the pragmatic, cultural and post-modern turns.

The approach here aims to overcome some of the faddishness that, in a kind of sociological amnesia, forgets that contemporary theories are shaped, in part, by past struggles. This means that social theory for the present is the product of past struggles over social theory. One result of the seemingly permanent crisis of social theory is not only an expanding palette of theories to chose from but also a restricted focus on favoured theoretical perspectives. Judgments have to be formed about which perspectives in social theory most illuminate the problematic nature of social crisis. This means that some currently favoured theoretical perspectives are barely touched on, while space is devoted to less celebrated or half-forgotten perspectives. It is hoped that this historical approach will help support the recovery from sociological amnesia that is currently underway.

- Given that the social world today is beset with perceptions of crisis, Chapter 1 examines some of the ways that social theory has engaged with the relationship between crisis, risk and critique.
- Chapter 2 looks a bit closer at the first major attempt by modern social theory to address the problem of crisis. Auguste Comte argued that a new science of society was necessary to deal with crisis, inaugurating 'the sociological turn'.
- Chapter 3 outlines the thorny relationship of Marxism to sociology. Marx developed a theory of crisis without developing a social theory of transformation, something that has vexed Marxist theory since, including one of the few Marxists that attempted to produce a (much criticised) sociological theory, Nikolai Bukharin.
- Chapter 4 introduces the classical social theory of Max Weber and Georg Simmel, often seen as an alternative to Marxist theory (although they themselves thought that their forms of sociology were complementary with historical materialism). In different ways, both engaged with the critical anti-modernist philosophy of Friedrich Nietzsche, often recognised as one of the founders of modern social theory, alongside Marx and Freud.
- Chapter 5 examines the alternative Marxist theories of Antonio Gramsci and Georg Lukacs. They placed an emphasis on political and cultural agency and the problem of ideology. In contrast to Bukharin, aspects of this more-philosophically inclined Marxist social theory were critically assimilated by non-Marxist social theory.
- Chapter 6 shows how social theory took a 'reflexive turn' as a way out of the crisis of the 1930s in the perhaps surprising form of the much-derided empiricist approach of Otto Neurath. Neurath represents almost the polar opposite of the typical (mis-) representations of positivism.
- Chapter 7 outlines the critically celebrated social theory of Walter Benjamin together with the rather less celebrated but no less pioneering cultural sociology of Siegfried Kracauer. For them theory was subordinate to the empirical materials of their various studies into history, popular culture and urban space.
- Chapter 8 covers the emergence of critical theory of what became known as 'the Frankfurt School', principally Theodor Adorno and Max Horkheimer. Theirs was social theory conceived in a social philosophical idiom, engaged in a struggle against what they saw as the positive complicity of empirical social science with a corrupt social world.

- Chapter 9 traces the increasingly negative turn in critical theory. As crisis and barbarism came to be viewed as endemic to modernity, Adorno and Horkheimer developed a more sociological version of Nietzsche's 'will to power' as a counter to the dominance of positivism. Against this 'negative turn' in critical theory Jurgen Habermas later advanced a normative ideal of consensus with his communicative theory of action.
- Chapter 10 concentrates on the theory of everyday life developed over 50 years by Henri Lefebvre and its relationship to modernity, crisis and moments of intense living. Theoretical creativity enabled Lefebvre to resist the pessimism of critical theory and the idea that crisis is necessarily catastrophic for society.
- Chapter 11 covers phenomenology, a wide and disparate field of philosophy, social theory and sociology. It concentrates on the theory of Maurice Merleau-Ponty, who restored the human body to the centre of social theory in what later came to be called 'the corporeal turn'. This is preceded by a sense of how the phenomenologist Edmund Husserl delineated the crisis of European culture in the 1930s.
- Chapter 12 surveys some of the ways in which the philosophy of pragmatism entered social theory in the US. It shared some of the same territory with phenomenology in the social theories of G.H. Mead, Erving Goffman, and ethnomethodology, to more recent feminist theories of Judith Butler, Iris Marion Young and Dorothy Smith.
- Chapter 13 outlines the renewed importance of culture and social creativity in the context of crisis in social theory in France and Britain. In France, Michel de Certeau, Jean Baudrillard and Cornélius Castoriadis produced different theories of cultural resistance and transformation. In Britain, the crisis was explicated through the synthesis of structural and cultural theories carried through by Stuart Hall, indebted to Gramsci, and developed by Paul Gilroy. With his theory of 'structuration' Anthony Giddens similarly tried to synthesise the problem of structure and agency.
- Finally, Chapter 14 charts the 'relational turn' represented by Norbert Elias and Pierre Bourdieu. Both were concerned with how symbolic power emerges over time by emphasising practical social relations. Both also saw theoretical *synthesis* oriented to substantive problems as the beginning of a solution to crisis in sociological theory.

1

SOCIAL THEORY AND CRISIS

Crisis is a process, not a fixed condition. It suggests a decisive moment of limited duration. Yet crisis has come to be understood as operating at different levels (psychological, institutional, national, planetary), extending over different time periods and spaces, and with different degrees of intensity. Instead of a moment of exception precipitating a turning point, crisis becomes a normalised, semi-permanent condition. As something latent to modernity, the signs of crisis may be faint enough that they don't register in public discourse and only become manifest as political and economic crises break through the surface of social life at a certain trigger point. Latent crises are rendered visible by theories that make intelligible underlying processes, structures and relations. The difficulty is that the abstractions of theory transform the dynamics of crisis as a process into crisis as a fixed condition.

THE ROOTS OF CRISIS

Terminologically, crisis is closely related to 'critical', 'critique' and 'criticism', *Kritik*, of coming to a decision or judgment (Koselleck, 2006). From the ancient Greek term *krisis*, the modern term 'crisis' has three sources: medical, legal-political and religious. Medically, crisis refers to the turning point of a pathological condition identified by the expert judgement and decision making of a medical practitioner. When a body is said to be in a critical condition, it is in mortal danger unless careful prognosis and diagnosis allow the patient to recover. Crisis requires critical knowledge to reverse trauma and entropy.

In terms of legal, social and political crisis the term took on a double meaning: on one side, it refers to the theoretical criteria to diagnose objective conditions; and on the other side, the pathology of illness rests on an ideal of healthy normality to be restored or end in death. Finally, this was translated into the Christian worldview of apocalyptic visions of the Last Judgement that only a decision to seek salvation can remedy.

As the historian Reinhardt Koselleck (2006) argues, the modern meaning of crisis broke from the classical sense of crisis as forcing a change in life. It began to be used less as a concrete diagnosis than as a metaphor in the social sciences in the context of revolution and war. A crisis of social relations is different in kind from a medical crisis. Critically, the concept referred ambiguously to both a chronic, more or less permanent and long-term condition and a more limited, cyclical process. Such ambiguity gives crisis its unique semantic power.

When it was extended to also cover economic imbalances and shortages of trade, finance, consumption and production, 'crisis' became a central concept in the lexicon of everyday life. The new modernist historical sensibility recast 'crisis' as a break with both blind optimism in human progress and an eternal cycle of change that follows a predetermined historical pattern. Economic crises were reassuringly viewed as cyclical, short-run phenomena from which recovery could soon be expected.

Crisis is redolent of drama, decision and deed. It is not only normative – improving the condition of social suffering by outside intervention; it is also dramaturgical – when human groups actively identify with the power of recovery and renewal and overcome the mythic power of fate with collective resources of their own making. This is when decisions have to be taken 'for or against' in legal, political, social and moral judgements. This sense of crisis entered the English language during the English civil war of the 1640s and acquired its modern sense in the French enlightenment of the 1780s (Koselleck, 1988). Connotations of illness, legal judgement and catastrophe lend crisis a considerable metaphorical power to measure the present against some future perfect state. Crisis became the authoritative judgement on historical time. History is pictured as one long crisis or, punctuated by crises, history is forced to take a decisive change in direction (Koselleck, 2006: 371).

Perceptions of the end of an epoch and a transition to a new one can be measured by an increased use of the term 'crisis'. Crisis authorises a leap into the future based on prophecy, as much as prognosis, to redeem any number of fantasies, hopes and anxieties. When crisis is announced it is cast as the final one, at least once an ultimate decision has been taken to make the future something entirely different from how it had been conceived previously. Increased usage of the term is accompanied by a sense of bringing the old things to an end, whether with triumph or regret (the end of history, the end of ideology, the end of class, the end of modernism, the end of neoliberalism) and the start of the new ('new times', 'new realism', new social movements) and a move beyond, signified by the transcending prefix 'post' post-modernism, post-structuralism, post-history, post-colonialism, post-Fordism.

CRISIS AND CRITIQUE

Crisis itself seems to be so self-evident as a category that it is rarely interrogated by social theory while its counterpart *critique* is subject to endless commentary. While there is a crisis of critique there is rarely a critique of crisis as a concept. Yet in an important sense, social theory itself is only made possible by crisis. Crisis allows competing theories to identify critical points of dissonance in other theories and in social and political life. Today, however, contemporary critique induces crisis in social theory, not in social or political life itself. Without crisis it seems necessary for social theory to invent one.

Crisis becomes the occasion for social theory to renew itself. This standpoint was stated most famously by Alvin Gouldner in *The Coming Crisis of Western Sociology* (1971). As far as Gouldner was concerned, ideological disarray rather than empirical anomalies tends to lead sociologists to substitute the more comforting games of Grand Theory for political action. Plato only turned to philosophy after his political ambitions were already in tatters; early positivists like Auguste Comte in France turned to social theory when excluded from political influence; Karl Marx retreated to intensive theoretical study after the defeat of the revolution of 1848; Max Weber's failed bid for political office resulted in deeper specialisation in theoretical and methodological studies.

By the late 1960s the dominant strand of American, or 'Western', sociology, as Gouldner put it, was an elaborate theoretical system called 'functionalism'. Developed by Talcott Parsons under conditions of crisis in the 1930s as an intricate theoretical edifice, functionalism emphasised the self-correcting stability and equilibrium of the 'social system' as always able to absorb and nullify the chance emergence of social and political crises, conflict and disorder. For Gouldner and other radical sociologists of the period, Parsons' construction of a grand theoretical system merely disguised a hidden premise: that social theory's role is to stabilise any crisis of legitimate authority of the kind experienced in the 1930s and later in the 1960s. In trying to 'professionalise' social theory, Parsons aimed 'in the midst of the Great Depression to mend the rift between power and morality and to find new bases of legitimacy for the American elite' (Gouldner, 1971: 154).

Social theory changes, Gouldner argues, not only through 'internal' technical or formal developments within theory itself but also as a result of 'external' changes in the social and cultural 'infrastructure' that supports the practical life and tacit assumptions of social theorists. When social theory takes on the appearance of a technical 'finished' system it no longer depends directly on the support of its social and cultural infrastructure. In turn a more fundamental critique is developed by the infrastructure heralding a crisis of the once-dominant social theory.

In the 1960s this discontent came from the radical culture of young student activists known as the New Left, many drawn to the promise of sociology as an enemy of self-serving illusions. At the same time the rapid expansion of the post-war welfare state supported the enlargement of academic sociology to address social problems and conflicts that functionalism consigned to merely secondary importance in this orderly, best of all possible worlds.

Not only functionalism but also a crisis of theory deeply affected orthodox Marxism as the official ideology of the Soviet Union and its satellites. This was expressed by the proliferating varieties of Marxist theory, some versions coming close to the 'finished' system of functionalism, while others stressed the more open-ended possibilities of praxis and cultural sociology. Theoretical proliferation is for Gouldner further evidence of intellectual crisis.

As a way out of professional and theoretical crisis Gouldner advocated what he called 'reflexive sociology', a self-conscious sociology of sociology. Unless sociologists take steps to avoid being burdened with doomed social theories and professional conformism they will fall into the tragedy of wasted, life-sapping efforts. All that the sociologist can do is to make a Pascalian wager:

> When sociologists commit themselves compulsively to a life-wasting high science model they are making a metaphysical wager. They are wagering that the sacrifice is 'best for science'. Whether this is really so, they cannot confirm, but they often need no further confirmation than the pain that this self-containment inflicts upon them. (Gouldner, 1971: 506)

The tragedy of social theory can only be overcome, Gouldner claims, by an appeal to the robust individualism of the engaged scholar. Here sociologists ought to follow their own 'inner impulses', 'special bents or aptitudes', and 'unique talents'.

Yet the crisis of social theory will not be resolved by placing a bet on the metaphysics of an 'authentic' self playing the role of sociologist. For one thing, sociology has and is becoming more 'worldly' and integrated with the heterogeneous demands of the neoliberal university and beyond in policy making – the alternative apparently estrangement and irrelevance. In the face of this a determined effort has been made to establish a broader role for 'public sociology' and 'critical' sociology (Clawson et al., 2007).

SCIENCE AND CRISIS

Gouldner's style of reflexive sociology as a tough-minded independence of thought and intuition is familiar enough from the image of radical American sociologists like C. Wright Mills as 'outlaws' fearlessly speaking truth to power. Such calls are symptomatic of what Raymond Boudon (1980) identified as the 'epistemological uncertainty' that results from sociology's dependency on external social influences and abrupt theoretical change through periodic crisis rather than cumulative empirical results. A predictable symptom of latent crisis, Boudon argues, is the profusion of epistemological and methodological disputes in sociology, for instance, in the exaggerated opposition between micro-sociology and macro-sociology, or that between quantitative and qualitative research methods.

It is instructive to compare the crisis of social theory to theories of crisis in the natural sciences. Most famously, Thomas Kuhn (2012) in *The Structure of Scientific Revolutions* identified a crisis in science as occurring when problems or 'anomalies' encountered by a dominant 'paradigm' mount up, reaching a point where they can no longer be ignored. A paradigm for Kuhn not only concerns the formal or explicit propositions of theory but also includes the underlying assumptions, practices and tacit understandings involved. Paradigms restrict 'normal science' to routine problem-solving activities or 'puzzles' without needing to address anything more fundamental. In normal conditions paradigms are robust enough to displace, marginalise or eliminate problems and discrepancies, what Kuhn calls 'anomalies'. With its variety of theories and methods, sociology lacks one dominant paradigm (in Kuhn's sense) that would structure the discipline as a unified field.

Paradigms will protect theories for relatively long periods of time from failure by sacrificing empirical accuracy for increased theoretical complexity. As theories become more and more baroque and increasingly unable to solve routine puzzles they also become vulnerable to critique from rival paradigms. What were once considered routine puzzles may from a rival viewpoint become a source of crisis. An acute sense of explanatory failure and a proliferation of novel theories are what Kuhn recognises as a 'crisis' of theory: 'All crises begin with a blurring of a paradigm and consequent loosening of the rules for normal research' (2012: 84). As theories proliferate, crisis relaxes the grip of the dominant paradigm and opens a space for alternative theories to not only emerge but also to be more widely recognised and shared as a valid standpoint. With divergent theories, the scientific field is no longer structured by a common source of authority. Attention is increasingly focused on the 'trouble spots' of theory.

Outside of crisis conditions novel theories are singularly ill-equipped to challenge dominant paradigms so long as they continue to solve problems that they themselves establish as the core business of scientific practice. Indeed, paradigms structure the very worldview that makes 'facts' possible in the first place and are only surrendered after a protracted crisis. Theoretical invention is a more painful process than factual discovery, requiring a severe crisis of theory to conquer normal science. Much more than factual anomalies are needed for a revolution in science to occur. Theories are not discarded lightly and cannot be falsified all in one go by a factual anomaly, as Popper (1992) would have it. Crises either, first, result in the restoration of the dominant paradigm through solving recalcitrant problems, or, second, the problem is put aside and suspended for a later generation; finally, the revolutionary establishment of a new paradigm solves the crisis in a novel way.

CRISIS OF SENSATE CULTURE

Since sociology is not subject to paradigms in the manner of Kuhn's model of the natural sciences it makes more sense to locate theoretical crisis in historical context. A grand attempt was made by Pitirim Sorokin (1992) to situate crisis in a large-scale social theory. Amassing huge quantities of historical data for his multivolume *Social and Cultural Dynamics* (1985), Sorokin divided all societies into three stages of knowledge – sensate, ideational and idealistic. A 'sensate' epoch in history occurs when the sensible bodily experiences of the empirical world predominate culturally; an 'ideational' epoch refers to the predominance of supersensory cultural values; finally, 'idealistic' culture is a rational synthesis of the other two. Essentially, Western culture has passed back and forward between these epochs of knowledge since ancient Graeco-Roman culture. From the thirteenth century sensate culture has predominated as the pace of technological invention and scientific discovery intensifies, stimulating empiricism in philosophy, nihilism in culture, and materialism in society.

By the twentieth century, 'sensate culture' was in serious crisis. Theoretically, Sorokin claims, sensate culture abandoned the distinction between truth and error, and knowledge was reduced to expedient arbitrary constructs based on the principle that whatever works is useful. Sorokin (1992: 100) protests against the disenchantment that sensate culture produces, making all knowledge and values relative, genius an object of mockery, and moral integrity something to be suspicious about. Sorokin was scathing about the mediocrity of his contemporaries in social theory: 'Since Comte and Spencer, Hegel and Marx, Le Play and Tarde, Durkheim and Max Weber, Simmel and Dilthey, Pareto and de Roberty [1843–1915, Russian positivist], there has hardly appeared a name worthy of mention in sociology' (1992: 104). Intellectual decline was taken as evidence of the crisis in the theoretical system of sensory knowledge. Despite the resources lavished on economics the dismal science singularly failed to prevent recurring crises and declining measures of happiness and security. Sorokin pile up the symptoms of mid-twentieth-century crisis resulting from the empiricism of sensate dogma – war, revolution, crime, suicide, mental illness, tyranny, exploitation, fraud, force, and so on.

Behind the welter of data, Sorokin adopted the role of a prophetic sociologist. Sensate sociology needs to be tempered by ideational sociology. Crisis had put Western culture at a crossroads – either further decline and decadence of human values or the restoration of ideational or idealistic human culture. From his comparative historical analysis of the rise and fall of cultures, Sorokin (1992: 260) delivered a theory of revolution through what he claimed was a 'sound sociological induction', summed up in the formula 'crisis-ordeal-catharsis-charisma-resurrection'.

Initially, the crisis is drawn out as material prosperity declines and the 'ordeal' of a brutal, violent period is endured under failing attempts to reform sensate culture. As cultural failure appears irreversible to many people, a collective sense of 'catharsis' places greater faith in a higher, eternal spiritual culture in contrast to the ephemera of material culture. This is consolidated by a 'charismatic' phase organised around a more stable belief system based on altruism, duty, norms and universal solidarity. Society is 'resurrected' as an 'integral', stable system that promises a long period of security and belonging. Yet it is not so easy, Sorokin laments, for society to learn from the medical metaphor of crisis and to enter recovery without first experiencing the fiery ordeal of violent disintegration. Sensate cultures stubbornly cling to 'momentary pleasures' even as 'an infinitely greater catastrophe' awaits (1992: 263).

A late-twentieth-century follower of Sorokin, theoretical physicist Fritjof Capra (1982), in his book *The Turning Point*, captured the spirit of the alternative ideational system to the ongoing crisis of sensate culture. Numerous symptoms of crisis persist, including nuclear arms, large-scale hunger, toxic pollution, social disintegration, violent crime, suicide, income inequalities, and other social pathologies. Like Sorokin, Capra takes a long-term, dynamic perspective of crisis as a process of transformation. Modern transformation is more dramatic than any before, because the rate of change in society is faster, more extensive, and on a planetary scale, with several changes happening simultaneously. In the case of the latter, Capra notes three major transitions: the decline of patriarchy, the end of fossil-fuels, and a shift away from sensate culture. This transition will be 'fundamental', 'deep', 'thorough' and 'profound', Capra prophesises, with limited need for the kind of struggle and conflict that Marxists typically anticipate. Instead of class struggle Capra appeals to the ideational knowledge of the ancient Chinese book of wisdom, the I Ching (Book of Changes), as complementing Sorokin's model of continuous cyclical fluctuation between the archetypal polar opposites of the yin and the yang. It is not a choice of isolating one or the other, Capra argues, but of finding the dynamic balance between extremes of rational knowledge (yang) and intuitive wisdom (yin). In the absence of an 'idealistic' solution, the crisis of sensate culture has, if anything, deepened. The question is why.

CRISIS AND HISTORY

Historians traditionally use the term 'crisis' in a self-evident way, for instance to denote a 'general crisis' of politics, war or society. Crisis allows historians to balance between patterns in historical development and the uniqueness of historical events. This leaves a great deal of scope for historians to speculate on the meaning of crisis. Randolph Starn (1971) argues that 'crisis' is twice-removed from the historical evidence. It is first removed from what crisis intends to signify and it is at a second-remove because it is a metaphor borrowed from biology and medicine. This does not necessarily count against using the term so long as it adequately describes what it sets out to. How well crisis functions as an explanatory or descriptive concept depends on the cogency of the narrative in which it is embedded. However, with the crisis metaphor of sickness and malaise a danger lurks that social pathologies may be looked for everywhere to the neglect of more mundane, unexceptional processes: preoccupied with the sickness, theorists neglect the patient (Starn, 1971: 21). A focus on crisis may also lock social theory into the present and the short term and neglect long-range developments.

Crisis may also be experienced as a threat to traditional normative and cultural values. For the historian of the Renaissance, Jacob Burckhardt (1818–1897), the long crisis of the nineteenth century and the disorderly effects on the individual of democracy, socialism, revolution, and technology confirmed the decadence of modernist culture (Hinde, 2000). In his 1870 lecture on crisis Burckhardt (1979) mystically found in the idea of crisis the possibility for history to sweep away everything that was mediocre and demeaning to the human spirit and to prophesise catastrophe and chaos for the twentieth century as technology, war and revolution produced mass destruction and individual demoralisation. Such anti-modernist sentiment was given an even more dramatic expression by Burckhardt's great admirer, the philosopher Friedrich Nietzsche, who looked to crisis as the last chance for European culture to raise itself out of the hypocritical morass of modernity.

Other historians see the source of crisis less as a result of too much political activity but of too little as politics becomes separated from the greater appeal to moral critique. For Reinhardt Koselleck (1988), as for Comte a century earlier, uninhibited moralistic critique of political authority and utopian fantasies pre-cipitated the crisis of the French revolution by fatally weakening the political authority of the pre-revolutionary absolutist state. Koselleck's theory of crisis built on the philosophical critique of the Enlightenment theory as totalitarian devel-oped by the critical theory of Max Horkheimer and Theodor Adorno under the influence of Nietzsche as well as Marx. A later critical theorist, Jurgen Habermas (1989: 267) challenged Koselleck's account of modernity's first crisis, pointing to early capitalist rationality in politics and economics, but acknowledged Koselleck's 'outstanding investigation' as a major influence on Habermas' own, more famous, model of the bourgeois public sphere.

Klaus Eder (1993) broadly accepts Koselleck's location of crisis in the moralistic sidelining of politics. Moral critique introduces a radical break between past and future. Critique sees the future as open, not closed by absolute state authority. It stimulates a heightened consciousness of history and invests events with unique significance. Nothing is immune from critique except the right of critique. However, this also makes critique vulnerable to unattainable utopian fantasies unless it is rooted in the contradictions of modernity.

> Without such 'contradictions' modern society runs into crisis for two reasons: (1) because such societies are not able to react to their systematic problems; and (2) because they are not able to correct pathogenic learning processes. (Eder, 1993: 194)

Eder's crisis theory is critical of a political culture that refuses to recognise that class contradictions are constitutive of modernity. Instead, society produces con-tradictory knowledge about itself. This generates the need for a 'reflexive turn' in social theory to address the way that a society that masks its own contradictions necessarily blocks knowledge about itself (Eder, 1993: 185).

Like Comte and Eder, Piet Strydom (2000) identifies the enduring sense of crisis with the inability of modern society to regulate the course of its own devel-opment. Ever since the early modern period, through what Strydom calls the 'consequent pathogenesis of modernity', the discourse of modernity has taken the form of a discourse of crisis. Strydom advances a specifically sociological account of crisis rather than reducing it to a problem of moralist or political critique alone. Crisis is generated by social relations and a failure to take collective action to resolve collective problems. Illusory ideals about a fully rational society and civic moralism were proposed by the main groups in the French revolution, republi-cans and Jacobins respectively. Such ideal solutions to crisis denied that society is inherently divided and conflictual, leading to escalating cycles of repression and disorder.

A failure to recognise conflict in a divided society remains for Strydom the source of crisis today: 'the core of the persistent crisis of modern society has been and remains to this day the absence of a participatory politics of conflict, contesta-tion and compromise and, supporting it at a more fundamental level, a culture of contradictions' (2000: 266). Specifically, Strydom claims, crisis discourse raises three sets of problems, or 'societal semantics', that predominate in different periods: violence, poverty and nature (see Table 1.1). Early modern crisis took a violent form with states facing the constant prospect of wars and revolution. As the new state stabilised its rule, internal crises of social justice and economic systems predominated. Most recently, crisis discourse identifies nature as the main threat to human survival. Such three-stage models of development are popular in social theory. At the outset of sociology, August Comte identified three stages of theology, metaphysics and science, while Sorokin's three stages of culture – sensate, ideational and idealistic – was developed a century later to account for crisis.

Table 1.1 *Changes in crisis discourse from the 16th century to the present (Strydom, 2000: 286)*

16–18th century	Late 18th–20th centuries	Late 20th century–present
Violence	Poverty	Risk
State	Economy	Ecology
Order	Growth	Sustainability
Constitution	The social	Nature
Rights	Justice	Responsibility
Law	Money	Knowledge

RISK AND CRISIS

In recent years, social theory has preferred to talk about 'risk' rather than crisis. On 26 April 1986, an explosion at the Chernobyl nuclear plant in Ukraine released radioactive material over a wide geographical area, as far as the Scottish Highlands and Wales, spreading public fear across Western Europe. This helped to popularise the idea that people now live in a 'risk society', developed in the mid-1980s by the sociologist Ulrich Beck (1992). A risk society is one that is organised around the need to identify and manage future threats of catastrophe that the process of industrial modernisation both makes possible but also aims to control. Because of increased global interdependencies, risk is not limited to nations or states.

Crisis has become cosmopolitan and the risk of crisis has become permanent. Bauman and Bordini (2014) argue that 'liquid modernity' has fundamentally transformed the nature of the crisis in important ways. Crisis is a result of the uncertainties and insecurities of the transition from the 'solid modernity' of mass bureaucratic society founded on a rigid work ethos, to a still dimly-perceived 'liquid modernity' of a fragmented market society composed of isolated and morally indifferent individual consumers (Bauman, 2007).

Subjectivity is now determined by the gratifications enjoyed from 'pure relations'. In a pure relation each individual treats the other as a 'thing' divested of the moral attachments of mutual commitment and empathy. Individual relations are increasingly 'adiaphoric', cut adrift from the pressures of moral evaluation by the dominance of the pure exchange model of consumer–commodity relations (Bauman and Bordoni, 2014: 153). Individuals are joined-up as aggregates in networks rather than being founded in coherent communities. Economic, political or environmental problems are dispersed from the centres of power and wealth for states and localities to resolve. What Manuel Castells terms 'the space of places', especially big cities, are called upon to resolve problems created elsewhere by the 'space of flows', a process captured by Castells' hybrid term 'glocalisation': '"Glocalization" means local repair centres servicing and recycling the output of the global problem industry' (Bauman and Bordoni, 2014: 125).

Crisis is a result of profound long-term secular change, of which the financial crisis of 2007–8 is a symptom not a cause. Financial crises merely reinforce the main trend identified by Bauman (2000a) of shallow and utilitarian social relationships of 'liquid modernity'. A crisis of democratic agency results from a divorce between politics and power, where politics is understood as the right to take decisions, and power is the ability to effectively carry them through. Politics are emptied of substantial content as globalisation processes weaken the capacity of the state to dominate economic processes. Politicians are unable to protect citizens from crisis, undermining further the legitimacy of the liberal democratic state. For instance, the ecological crisis is not limited to the boundaries of any one or group of nation-states.

With the unification of Germany after the collapse of Stalinism, European elites, especially France, wanted to integrate Germany economically through the Eurozone to prevent any risk of a new European catastrophe in a re-run of German state power of the 1930s. However, the anticipation of crisis resulted in the unintended consequence of what Beck (2013) calls 'German Europe' based on economic logic not military logic. Along with other social theorists, Beck argues that a Europe founded on fear of catastrophe, rather than the free association of citizens, will not survive crisis-ridden globalisation.

As the unintended effects of globalisation are felt and conflicts over expert knowledge become apparent, say over climate change, population, health, or finance, ontological crises are induced that need to be further regulated by disciplined self-reflexivity. Yet this has the character of a never-ending Sisyphean labour in what Beck (1992) calls 'reflexive modernisation' as a heightened discourse of 'world risk society', and Bauman (2000a) calls 'fluid' or 'liquid' modernity where consumer capitalism results in more uncertain and fragile social bonds. Beck refers to the unintended effects in the present of the automatic logic of autonomous modernisation processes of 'industrial society' of the past. As an ideology of economic, technological and scientific progress, modernity feeding upon modernity – not 'post-modernity'– is overrunning all pre-modern hierarchical institutions, like the family, that previously militated some of the worst excesses of modernity. As wealth is pursued more recklessly, greater risks result, such as global warning, nuclear disasters, and energy depletion (Giddens, 2013).

Risk is not the same thing as catastrophe (Beck, 2009). Risk anticipates catastrophe and tries to avert it or at least manage its imagined consequences.

Catastrophe occurs when perceived risk becomes an actual event. Risk imagines or 'stages' catastrophe in order to avert it. At the same time, imagined risk feels more real. In this sense, risk is a 'self-refuting prophecy' because it wants to prevent what it predicts as possible. For instance, the global 'staging' of the threat of terrorist actions by the media and security industries curtail the civil rights and freedoms that they purport to protect. And the star terrorist is brought onto the world stage by the global anticipation of risk in the so-called 'war against terror'.

Every aspect of society – economy, politics, intimacy, family, science, education – finds itself at a decisive turning point. As industrial modernity imposed order and control on people and nature, the more insistently that uncertainty and insecurity returned. Beck (2009) argues that 'crisis' is both the correct and the incorrect term for the ambivalences of the new risk consciousness. 'Crisis' is the wrong term if by that is meant the end of modernity or its supercession by 'post-modernity':

> All the 'crisis phenomena' with which countries of the West are struggling – reform of the welfare state, falling birth rates, ageing societies, loss of definition of national societies, mass unemployment, not to mention the self-doubts of science and expert rationality, economic globalization and advances in individualization that undermine the foundations of marriage, the family and politics, and, finally, the environmental crisis which calls for a revision of industrial society's exploitative conception of nature – can be understood in terms of the distinction as transformations of basic institutions in which the basic principles of modernity retain their validity. (Beck, 2009: 231)

It is the global dominance of industrial modernity, not its failure, that undermines taken-for-granted institutional certainties. The continuing force of the principles of 'more-modernity' – ambiguity, loss of certainty, and increased personal reflexivity – leads to discontinuities in the institutions of the industrial forms of modernity – family, politics, economies, and nations. Crisis rightly focuses attention on the dissolution of the taken-for-granted certainties of the first, *industrial* modernity and the new inequalities that are threatened by the second, *reflexive* modernity. With the rampant disorientation and uncertainty that crisis produces, anti-modern forces are encouraged that threaten science, liberty and democracy.

Beck calls this 'reflexive modernisation'. Triumphant modernity can only refer back to itself since there are no longer any pre-modern institutions that it still needs to overcome (Beck, Giddens and Lash, 1994). There is nowhere that exists outside reflexive modernity that might function as a fixed point of orientation, theoretically, socially or politically. All justifications and legitimations must come from within the resources of modernity itself. Beck goes back to the seventeenth-century political theorist Thomas Hobbes (1588–1679) to establish a grounding principle with which to resist the threat of self-annihilation posed by the staging of the ecological crisis. Hobbes argued that people have the right to challenge powerful institutions like the state wherever they threaten the conditions of life. Beck (2009) translates this into the principle that the life-threatening risks confronting humanity can be averted by political action on behalf of endangered humanity against the limitations of the state form. Only the perceived anticipation of catastrophe will be able to galvanise a fully cosmopolitan human community.

Science, not class, becomes the new site of social struggles. Paradoxically, Beck argues, as science and technology become more completely globalised the more that the authority of expert systems is challenged by lay knowledge. Until recently, Beck assumed that welfare states had replaced material poverty and acute class inequalities with individualised claims based on identity and status. Class domination has not gone away but its effects are experienced at an individual level. This requires personalised plans to rationalise and manage global risk, not collective organisations like trade unions. More recently, recession and austerity have tempered some of the claims about reflexive individualisation and material abundance, and forcibly returned the structuring role of class relations to the concerns of sociology.

FROM CAPITALIST CRISIS TO IDEOLOGICAL CRISIS

A social theory of crisis has been traditionally associated with various strands of Marxism, starting with Marx (1818–1883)himself, through to critical theory, notably Jurgen Habermas' and Claus Offe's theories of the crisis of state legitimation in the 1970s and 1980s. Marx developed the first social theory of system-wide crisis. This inverted the philosophy of Hegel that viewed crisis as, in essence, a crisis of ideas into a crisis of social and material conditions. In the Hegelian philosophical system, crisis results from a contradiction between thesis and antithesis that is reconciled in a new, higher synthesis. For Marx crisis consists of unresolved contradictions of social and economic structures, especially the conflict between social knowledge embodied in the forces of production and its private appropriation in the form of wealth by unequal social relations of production. People experience crises in the threat that private appropriation of social labour in the form of wealth or weapons poses to their social and material survival.

Marx derived from his philosophical milieu, the Young Hegelians, a critique of the gap between dominant representations of reality – freedom, equality, justice, cooperation, public good, love of humanity – and reality itself, where the representations were found to be inverted – servitude, extreme inequality, injustice, self-interest, inhumanity. In this gap, social, economic and political crisis festered. Marx saw economic crisis in terms of a structural logic that operates in defiance of the wishful thinking of the bourgeoisie that capitalism represents the best of all possible worlds. Like the sorcerer's apprentice, the bourgeoisie conjures up forces beyond its control – the collective means of production. The accumulated social knowledge stored in the forces of production 'revolts' against private ownership in periodic crises: successive crises 'put on trial, each time more threateningly, the existence of the entire bourgeois society' (Marx and Engels, 1998: 41). Society is suddenly thrown back into a state of 'momentary barbarism', creating misery and fear on a large scale.

Disorder defines bourgeois society and threatens its survival. Every crisis is a crisis of over-production. Too much is produced, not too little, for the market to absorb at the going rate of profit and to allocate the social product proportionately between autonomous units of production, distribution and consumption. Large amounts of the productive forces therefore need to be destroyed, creating larger, more centralised and concentrated units of capital among the survivors. These units become so large and integrated that their destruction threatens the social conditions of survival, as today when the largest banks are said to be 'too big to fail'. By failing to eliminate less productive activities like finance, the way is paved 'for more extensive and more destructive crises, and by diminishing the means whereby crises are prevented' (Marx and Engels, 1998: 42). As workers are made unemployed or real wages decline the bourgeoisie are further unable to sell their goods for a profit. Here Marx marries an economic theory with a theory of revolution. In the absence of revolution, crisis became a staple of social theory. Collapse is not automatic since Marx's 'pure model' of capitalism neglects the many countervailing tendencies that may serve to moderate crisis today, above all, state intervention.

A more recent emphasis in social theory on the crisis of belief in authority marks a departure from Marx's systemic theory of crisis. To illustrate this shift, Jurgen Habermas (1976: 17–24) describes the different tendencies of various societies (see Table 1.2). First, 'primitive social formations' are relatively undifferentiated and so do not enter crisis as a result of internal problems but only as a result of external causes like war, conquest or exchange leading to demographic inter-ethnic change. Second, 'traditional social formations' based on political domination enter crisis owing to internal contradictions of rising exploitation coupled with weakening ideological legitimation producing class struggle and revolutionary change. Third, the crisis of 'liberal-capitalist social formations' expresses the impersonal relations of capital and wage labour in the autonomous economic cycle of boom, crisis and recession. Problems of competitive accumulation affect the entire system, not merely individual states.

Table 1.2 *Habermas' typology of crisis (1976: 24)*

Social formations	Principles of organisation	Social and system integration	Type of crisis
Primitive	Kinship relations: primary roles (age, sex)	No differentiation between social and system integration	Externally induced identity crisis
Traditional	Political class rule: state power and socio-economic classes	Functional differentiation between social and system integration	Internally determined identity crisis
Liberal-capitalist	Unpolitical	System integrative	System crisis
	Class rule: wage labour and capital	Economic system also takes over socially integrative tasks	

From its roots in 'economic steering problems', the crisis of system integration in liberal capitalism threatens to engulf social integration of the lifeworld. To begin with, the middle class are integrated by the market. Legitimation is founded on an economic ideology of equal exchange. Institutionalised by the labour market, class relations are taken out of the sphere of formal political competition. Political dependency is replaced by wage dependency. Wage labour has the double character analysed by Marx. On the production side, private exchange value is created at the same time as social use value. On the market side, social labour is allocated by the private medium of money exchange at the same time as the power balance between labour and capital is institutionalised.

Marx's social theory analysed both the steering principle of a market economy and the ideology of class society. Marx exposes the ideology of bourgeois political economy by demonstrating that equivalents are not exchanged. Instead of equal exchange between agents in the market, civil law secures the private appropriation of the surplus social product. Periodic crises are a result of transforming the contradiction of class interests into a contradiction of system imperatives. Crises are endemic to a market society because cyclical difficulties of economic growth endanger social integration.

> With the persistent instability of accelerated social change, periodically recurring, socially disintegrating steering problems produce the objective foundation for a crisis consciousness in the bourgeois class and for revolutionary hopes among wage laborers. No previous social formation lived so much in fear and expectation of a sudden system change, even though the idea of a temporally condensed transformation – that is, of a revolutionary leap – is oddly in contrast to the form of motion of system crisis as a permanent crisis. (Habermas, 1976: 25)

So long as class contradictions go unrecognised by its members, ideology helps to justify asymmetrical relations of power. Any open conflict between classes is explained ideologically in terms of the hostile intentions of the subjects rather than the structural contradiction of social interests. Where conflicts are understood in terms of ordinary language as immediately empirical then they have no relation to 'truth' as such. Habermas restricts 'truth' to the conceptual language of communications theory since only it can reveal an 'immanent relation to logical categories' (1976: 28). In this situation of the non-truth of ordinary common sense, social theory acquires a special value for bringing to light the deep logic of crises, or at least the relationship between logical categories that reveal the underlying roots of crisis. Paradoxically, theoretical 'truth' is available to the theorist but not the subjects taking meaningful action.

'POST-STRUCTURALISM' AND CRISIS

Theorists labelled as 'post-structuralist' like Michel Foucault, but also structuralist theorists like Louis Althusser, take a different approach from Habermas and Beck. For them crisis is productive since it exposes the limitations of knowledge and power. In such accounts crisis presses the arbitrariness of norms and regulation to the discursive limits of truth, prompting further critique. Foucault (1997) called this critique 'a limit-attitude' to the crisis. Criticism is not transcendental or universal but, in Foucault's terms, 'archaeological' in its methodical concentration on a specific history and 'genealogical' in the efforts of theory to work from the contingencies that have selectively made us what we have become and what we can no longer be. Critique attempts to 'cross over' the limits of crisis:

> In what is given to us as universal, necessary, obligatory, what place is occupied by whatever is singular, contingent, and the product of arbitrary constraints? The point, in brief, is to transform the critique conducted in the form of necessary limitation into a practical critique that takes the form a possible crossing-over [*franchissement*]. (1997: 315)

Global critiques, Foucault argues, must be replaced with specific, local and practical critiques, for instance of sexuality, insanity, authority, or illness, if the mutual development of individuals are not to be dominated by the 'technologies of power'. What Foucault proposes is less a theory as such than a concrete problematisation of history, ethics and ontology.

Epistemological crises arise when theory acquires an objectivist mask and forgets its origins in non-theory. Foucault describes the decision of the institutional knowledge of psychiatry and medicine to segregate the socially useless and transform them into objects of knowledge. Only with modernity does madness become a crisis, because of an inability to work, requiring special powers of confinement and segregation. Medicine, psychiatry, penal justice and criminology enter into crisis when they are forced out of a self-referential system of knowledge that validates itself, essentially by turning subjects into objects, and being made to confront what Foucault calls the 'power-knowledge' nexus.

What were purely epistemological questions of truth and classification are always for Foucault simultaneously social, political, and economic issues of power. With the liberal critique of too much state interference, externally imposed discipline is displaced by 'governmentality' or self-regulation of conduct. Neoliberalism adapts the technology of self-governance more completely to market compulsion as a coming to power of economic will. By restricting the space for state support for the economy through social policies (housing, health, education, social insurance) neoliberalism aims to extend 'the rationality of the market, the schemes of analysis it proposes, and the decision-making criteria it suggests to areas that are not exclusively or not primarily economic' (1997: 79).

Sharing some affinity with post-structuralism, in her book *Anti-Crisis* Janet Roitman (2014) argues that crisis is a post-hoc term, mobilised after the fact to organise disparate events. In the absence of firm beliefs in religion or reason, crisis serves as a 'transcendental placeholder' by signifying contingency and the possibility that things could be 'otherwise'. This narrative function assumes that crisis is history's way to bring justice to the world. Crisis is a judgement that defines reality in a certain way while obscuring other definitions. In the absence of any absolute grounds for knowledge, for 'post-structuralist' theory, Roitman refers to Foucault and Judith Butler, crisis exposes the limits to what is known. More than that, it also invites critique by speaking about what has not been heard until now: 'crisis is productive; it is the means to transgress and is necessary for change or transformation' (2014: 35).

For Roitman (2014), glossing Niklas Luhmann, crisis is not an empirical concept available to 'first-order observation' but a 'second-order' logical observation. In other words, crisis is a distinction that confers meaning. Concepts, in this approach, cannot be true or false since they constitute 'self-referential systems' that empirical investigation is premised upon. Crisis cannot be explicated in itself since it is always a crisis of something else: capitalism, finance, politics, culture, society, subjectivity, identity. Social movements that emerge to contest crises will never establish an alternative to crisis and anti-crisis narratives because they already operate on and are constituted by the terrain of crisis and anti-crisis. Systemic, structural, and moral failures are claimed to typify crisis. These are the hidden possibilities that are made manifest by crisis.

Roitman (2014: 24) takes issue with Koselleck's account of the crisis of modernity for making too many absolute distinctions, between the modern and pre-modern, politics and morality, theology and history. Koselleck's account of crisis does not depend on what Roitman calls 'a truth correspondence theory of history'. Only weakly empirical, Koselleck primarily provides a thematic account of private morality as the site of critique rather than the public interest where, for instance, Habermas grounds critique.

On the contrary, Roitman (2014: 93) argues, crisis is purely contingent, a convenient way to repackage debt from something positive to something toxic, but not something 'intrinsic to a system'. It fulfils a 'hope' that 'we can perceive a dissonance between historical events and representations of those events' (2014: 65). Narratives of crisis fail to take into account specific networks and forms of technical expertise, crucially, the technical assemblage supporting the financial instruments blamed for the current crisis. Although light on primary empirical materials and relying in places on conjecture and counter-factual 'what ifs', Roitman is similarly disposed to find the dissonance of crisis between events and representations. As a second-order category, 'crisis' is ambiguously perched by post-structuralism somewhere between systemic contradiction, the sociology of error, the unintended consequences of local decisions, and political, moral, and ideological failure.

THE FUTURE OF CRISIS

Social theory cannot take the measure of itself from both a future that is not yet known and knowledge that is determined by the past. While it cannot gamble recklessly on prophecies, theoretical perspectives that once seemed utopian or irrelevant can acquire a new salience in changed conditions of crisis. Marx was plucked from the margins of social theory in the 1970s where he had been derisively consigned or turned into a monolith by Cold War ideologies. That he became relevant to students and scholars alike is not unconnected to the social and political crises of the 1960s. In the context of an emerging neoliberal political consensus in the 1980s, Marxism fell just as quickly out of intellectual fashion. On the other hand, some of its key ideas like alienation and ideology had been assimilated by the 'cultural turn' while others like class seemed less promising in a situation of apparent class decomposition. Perhaps the Marxist concept of class may (or may not) become a central concern of social theory in the future while today's exciting discourses about fluidity or risk or identity may seem like old hat that obstruct the future development of sociology. It is difficult for social theory to exercise foresight even about itself with any precision. This is especially the case when seismic shifts are taking place in the tectonic plates of social relations. If it is to exercise control over the satisfactions of theory-baiting that underlies much of the recurring crises in social theory, then account needs to be taken of the longer-term patterning of the theoretical field.

2

POSITIVIST TURN: AUGUSTE COMTE

For a long time 'positivism' has been something of a swearword in social theory. It is often introduced to students of social theory as a simple-minded curiosity or an accusatory slight aimed at 'applied' social research's concern to uncover 'objective' facts, numbers and laws. Its founding figure, Auguste Comte (1798–1857), has long been disparaged as a self-deluded prophet suffering from a Bonaparte complex. He was damned with faint praise by the liberal philosopher Isaiah Berlin:

> His grotesque pedantry, the unreadable dullness of his writing, his vanity, his eccentricity, his solemnity, the pathos of his private life, his insane dogmatism, his authoritarianism, his philosophical fallacies, all that is bizarre and utopian in his character and writings, need not blind us to his merits. (Berlin et al., 1964: 4)

And this was meant as a qualified defence of Comte at a lecture series named in his honour! Comte experienced a number of intellectual personal crises that have caused some to view his social theory, especially his later 'religion of humanity', as the bizarre ravings of a madman (Manuel, 1962: ch. VI). From early on, Comte rebelled against his lower-middle-class family and found himself expelled by royalist authorities from his elite school for his part in student protests. He broke violently from his mentor Saint-Simon, married, separated, suffered a mental breakdown, attempted suicide, won and lost supporters, and survived in precarious financial circumstances.

Perhaps it is not surprising that Comte's voluminous output has been left to moulder in contemptuous neglect, much derided but rarely read. Yet such neglect has meant that students of social theory barely recognise its origins or are introduced to a caricature that bears little resemblance to Comte's own theory or purpose. The mythical version of Comte's social theory asserts that, among other things, he imagined that society was subject to 'laws' in exactly the same way as nature, that social theory should imitate the methods of physics or biology, that sociology should collect and organise facts, and that society can be studied 'objectively' regardless of cultural or historical context.

Closer inspection of Comte's social theory reveals a very different approach from the myths of 'positivism' (Pickering, 1997; Ray, 1999). Comte understood science not as an eternally valid doctrine of linear progress as is often assumed but as a historically relative process. Comte's importance for social theory lies not only in the fact that he founded modern social theory or that this was conceived on an ambitious scale, nor that it was an attempt to mobilise social theory to resolve the first crisis of modernity, the social and political disorder in the wake of the French Revolution. Its main claim for our attention today is based less on the (often derivative) substantive claims of his social theory, the value of which has been a matter of acrimonious debate for almost two centuries, so much as the way in which Comte conceived the central role of social theory in establishing sociology as a distinctive new science.

This has not gone entirely unrecognised in recent social theory. As Norbert Elias, in an attempt to rehabilitate Comte, put it: 'Yet if we put aside the fads and eccentricities and trouble to blow away the dust, we encounter ideas in Comte's work which are virtually new, that have been forgotten or misunderstood, and are in their own way no less important for the development of sociology than those of Marx – who would turn in his grave if he knew that he and Comte could even be mentioned in the same breath' (1978: 33). More recently, Comte has been given more serious consideration in textbooks like Larry Ray's (1999) *Theorizing Classical Sociology*. Chris Shilling and Philip Mellor's (2001) *The Sociological Ambition* draws attention to Comte's achievement in attempting to construct a social science that would resolve crisis through moral action. Similarly, Mike Gane concluded his fresh reassessment of Comte – 'Today Comte's conception of humanity can provide for a sociological defence of the idea of society against a new biological reductionism' (2006: 134). Comte's importance for Anglophone social theory today has been aided by the authoritative three-volume biography of Comte by Mary Pickering (1993, 2009). There are now no excuses to mindlessly parrot obvious falsehoods or baseless clichés about Comte's social theory.

This chapter does not seek to rehabilitate for social theory everything that Comte attempted. It selectively outlines his contribution to major areas of interest for social theory today: first, the relationship between social theory and crisis; and second, how social theory was understood by Comte in its triangular relationship to philosophy, science and common sense. Before that, Comte's sociology needs to be placed briefly in intellectual context.

COMTE'S SOCIOLOGY

Although the term '*philosophie positive*' formed part of the social theory of Henri Saint-Simon (1760–1825), it is with Comte, his former assistant (from 1817 to 1824), that positivist social theory decisively confronted the pretensions of traditional philosophy. In their different ways, both Marx and Durkheim credited Saint-Simon, not Comte, as the founder of modern social theory. For Durkheim

(1962, 1964), Saint-Simon's utopian socialism sought to progressively reform society by first transforming it into an object for scientific study. The crisis of industrial, social and political 'anarchy' for Saint-Simon, as for Comte, was that it lacked a coherent social theory to resolve it (Saint-Simon, 1975). To organise the industrial apparatus on a more orderly, equitable and humane basis, philosophical speculation needed to be replaced by a reliable social theory. Saint-Simon hoped that a convincing social theory would help persuade industrialists and politicians of the need for a more rational and stable social order.

Comte was a trained, disciplined scholar, able to impose coherence and system on his mentor's muddled ideas (Pickering, 1993). In an act of bad faith, Comte later denied any public recognition to what he borrowed from his master, even defaming Saint-Simon as 'a depraved juggler' (Pickering, 1993: 239). Rather than reduce social development to a single law, as Saint-Simon had attempted, Comte devised his famous 'law of three stages' in his *opuscule fundamental* of 1822, precipitating the break with Saint-Simon (1998: Essay 3).

As a hypothetical 'law' the three stages should not be confused with the actual historical sequence of events in any empirical society. Theoretically all societies pass through three stages of intellectual development: theological, metaphysical and positive. First, the theological stage was based on belief in supernatural forces like gods, power was exercised by priests (spiritual) and warriors (temporal); with wealth acquired by violent conquest. Second, the metaphysical stage represented a transitional stage where abstract rationality replaced superstition; power was exercised by philosophers (spiritual) and lawyers (temporal); and wealth acquired by competitive production. Finally, the positive stage is reached: science replaces speculation; power is exercised by sociologists (spiritual) and industrialists (temporal); and wealth is created through cooperative production.

Comte coined the 'monstrous' neologism 'sociology' to announce the emergence of a new science of society, distinct from the natural sciences in theory, method and object. It is not always clear if sociology forms the presupposition or the logical conclusion of Comte's hierarchy of the sciences that he builds progressively from mathematics to biology. Comte may have synthesised an existing body of theory, but he was the first to frame the relative autonomy of social theory as a scientific enterprise. Science can only be grasped in its relationship to historically formed societies. This cannot be comprehended until sociology, as the last science, reveals retrospectively the pattern of development of the sciences, including itself (Wernick, 2001: 31). Sociology is logically necessary for society to know itself and so bring social and political chaos to an end.

To the extent that Comte concentrated on thought and knowledge, he remained bound to the idealism of traditional philosophy. To the extent that he emphasised society as a relatively autonomous object requiring a distinctive, historical form of social theory, he represented a break with the fixed categories and eternally valid logic of philosophy. Comte's social theory also served a social and moral purpose – love, progress and order – in its aim to become a sound basis for common sense.

Comte attempted to fuse the diametrically opposed perspectives of, on one side, radical theories of progress (or 'social dynamics') found in Condorcet (1743–1794) and Saint-Simon, and, on the other side, conservative theories of tradition and order (or 'social statics') found in de Maistre (1753–1821) and de Bonald (1754–1840). This concoction was also mediated by the broader social theory of the Enlightenment beyond France, particularly the Scottish social philosophy of David Hume (1711–1776), Adam Smith (1723–1790), Adam Ferguson (1723–1816) and William Robertson (1721–1793) in Scotland, as well as his, albeit defective, familiarity with German 'scientific' philosophy of Herder (1744–1803), Kant (1724–1804) and Hegel (1770–1831) (Pickering, 1993: ch. 6). As it happens, Comte misinterpreted the critical Scottish–German enlightenment as endorsing his view that a positive epoch of science and social peace was opening up in Europe. Nonetheless, the search for a 'scientific' philosophy emboldened Comte in his quest for a social theory capable of understanding and resolving social and political crisis.

CRISIS IN LONG-TERM PERSPECTIVE

An overwhelming sense of crisis led to the invention by Comte of what he termed 'sociology' on 27 April 1839 (Pickering, 1993: 615). To his mind, sociology was needed urgently to reorganise society on a more orderly basis. Two 'social systems' contradicted each other: an old, declining social system spreading disorder every-where, and a new, rising social system heralding political stability and moral order: 'A social system which is dying, a new system whose time has come and which is in the process of taking definitive shape, this is the fundamental character which the general course of civilization has assigned to the present age' (Comte, 1998: 49). Comte held the old 'Catholic-feudal' social system responsible for the 'profound moral and political anarchy' that characterised the 'grand crisis' of post-revolutionary France. As far as Comte was concerned, it was high time to bring the revolutionary crisis to a close (Baker, 1989).

Positivism offered a utopian vision of social stability. By realising an orderly social function, Comte imagined that positivism would unify 'almost all minds, from the highest to the commonest' and dispense with the 'anarchy' of 'vague and mystical conceptions': 'It is time to complete the vast intellectual operation begun by Bacon, Descartes, and Galileo, by constructing the system of general ideas which must henceforth prevail among the human race. This is the way to put an end to the revolutionary crisis which is tormenting the civilized nations of the world' (Comte, 1858: 37). Comte contrasted the 'critical doctrine', essentially negative and destructive, with his own 'organic doctrine', essentially positive and constructive.

While answering the call of the crisis, Comte assumed considerable analytical distance from the daily political goings-on around him in Paris and across France between the 1820s and 1850s. From his earliest writings, he adopted an extended long-term perspective of the crisis and painted it in the most general theoretical terms. Comte set the crisis of modernity within a time span of 1,400 years, from the establishment of Christianity in Europe and the decline of the Roman Empire around the third and fourth centuries. By the eleventh and twelfth centuries, both feudalism and the papacy were at the zenith of their respective social and religious powers. However, even at the height of Catholic and military-feudal rule, alternative sources of power were germinating. As Comte (1998: 10) put it, Catholic-feudal 'splendour rested on a minefield' of science and industry. Scientific knowledge was introduced into Europe by Arab philosophers around this time, while riches began to be acquired through industrial activities by those Comte termed collectively as 'the communes', a class of independent artisans, artists and scientists.

The twin development of industrial capacity and scientific capacity over time undermined the feudal-Catholic universe and prepared the ground for its eventual overthrow. Whereas the industrial process developed peacefully within the feudal order, aristocratic wealth required violent force. So long as the communes remained outside the orbit of the nobility they could not be drawn into a violent conflict that they had no chance of winning. Their victory, unknown to them at the time, depended on playing the long game.

A three-century-long process of revolution destroyed the basis of the old social system: two 'partial' revolutions were followed by a 'general' revolution – the Reformation of the sixteenth century, the revolutions against feudalism in England and France of the seventeenth century, and the 'general revolution' against the old social system as a whole of the eighteenth century.

> The final result of all this great commotion [in France] was the abolition of privileges, the proclamation of the principle of unlimited freedom of conscience, and finally the establishment of the English constitution, bestowed by royal power itself. (Comte, 1998: 18)

First, the Reformation established freedom of thought (*Liberty*) as a principle, and exposed blind adherence to superstitious belief to critical examination and rational demonstration. This was taken to its ultimate conclusion, Comte (1858: 666) argued, by the American Revolution, which, for him, sanctioned the worst excesses of free-thinking critical doctrines by creating a 'universal colony' lacking any overall social purpose. Second, the absolutist regime of Louis XIV (1643–1715) annulled the political power of the feudal nobility in France, while in England the revolution of 1688 restored royal power all the better to confine aristocratic privilege and erode traditional relations of social position (*Equality*). Its revolutionary height was attained for Comte by the democratic forces led by 'the lofty genius' Oliver Cromwell in the 1640s. Finally, scientific progress and criticism of the decadent social system in France by the communes led to the 'general' revolution of 1789 against the old military–theological regime in the name of the sovereignty of the people (*Fraternity*). The most advanced revolutionary expression of the national sovereignty of the communes was demonstrated by the Dutch defeat of the mighty Spanish monarchical regime.

Yet, though profoundly depleted, the old system persisted. An English-style constitutional monarchy was installed in France 1814 since, Comte argued, no fully formed alternative existed that could replace the old regime in one fell swoop. This failure to complete the 'general revolution', Comte claimed, led directly to the crisis of modernity in nineteenth-century Europe. After three centuries, the new society could not be born while the old would simply not die. On one side, the decay of the old regime; on the other side, the arrested development of the new.

For Comte the crisis consisted of a declining system clinging by its fingernails to bare survival, a caricature of its former glories, alongside an ascending system almost but not quite able to complete the process of reorganising society. 'The revolutionary crisis assisted and confirmed the advance by completing the secular destruction of the ancient hierarchy, and raising to the first social rank, even to a degree of extravagance, the civic influence of wealth' (1858: 754).

But the new wealth of industrial employers failed to provide moral leadership for society. Instead they acted like old feudal chiefs, though without the same paternal obligation to provide subsistence for workers, who were now subjugated by the naked economic and technological power of capital. This crisis of social bonds could not be resolved piecemeal by reforms but only by a broad theoretical understanding of the blocked sources of social and moral integration.

France had been placed at the head of a general revolutionary movement across Europe but merely spread the crisis elsewhere. In its initial revolutionary phase it leapt from Catholicism to critical theory without being detained by Protestantism, which had diverted the American Revolution into a quagmire of theological and metaphysical speculation. Moreover, critical theory was more rational than either English empiricism or German idealism. France was also at the forefront of scientific advances, and second only to Italy in artistic developments (though it was soon to be the seat of avant-garde modernism). The revolutionary crisis produced courageous military and civic leaders, supported heroically by the people while religious doctrine lost any claim to moral leadership. Its greatest problem was a 'vicious philosophy' that relied on an abstract model of principles drawn from ancient Greece:

> That philosophy, by its very nature, represented society to be wholly unconnected with past events, and their changes destitute of rational instigation, and indefinitely delivered over to the arbitrary action of the legislator. It passes over all the intervening centuries to select a retrograde and contradictory type in the ancient form of civilization, and then, in the midst of the most exasperating circumstances, appealed to the passions to fulfil the offices of reason. (Comte, 1858: 743)

Comte reserved particular invective for the philosophical system of Jean-Jacques Rousseau (1712–1778), who looked to ancient civilisation as a model to found the world anew from original abstract principles.

When such philosophical artifice was applied to the practical problems posed by the revolution it only unleashed disorder and undermined the theoretical and creative power of science and art. Excessive negative critique threatened temporal power 'by destroying the subordination of the working classes to their industrial leaders, and calling the incapable multitude to assist directly in the work of government' (Comte, 1858: 744). Negative theory was indeed necessary as a blunt revolutionary instrument but later had a demoralising effect that left society vulnerable to the dictatorship and military adventurism of Napoleon Bonaparte (1769–1821), clothed suitably in feudal and theocratic garments, followed closely by the (limited) return of the monarchy.

SOURCES OF ORDER AND PROGRESS

To 'close the revolution', Comte claimed, moral and theoretical order needed to be deduced from scientific principles. His understanding of the term 'crisis' derived from its use in medicine, where the body can be repaired only if external intervention observes the living body's spontaneous forces of recovery, its innate vital strength (*force vitale*) (Canguilhem, 1994: 248). This has direct lessons for social and political crises. Crisis is a pathological condition that even as it deviates from 'normal' development, it reveals something of the underlying course (law) of nature or civilisation. Here it is unclear if the crisis itself represents for Comte a (necessary) 'normal' or (aberrant) 'pathological' stage of development (Gane, 2006: 42).

Comte drew on contemporary developments in the science of teratology, the study of biological abnormalities, to condemn political 'monstrosities' that ran counter to the long-term, 'normal' development of social organisation. Progress does not develop in a straight line but follows a fluctuating path of the social body's resistance to crisis. These fundamental forces of resistance to crisis need to be discovered, otherwise political action, however daring and imaginative, will prove futile, even self-defeating and 'monstrous'. A 'politics of imagination' will founder if it attempts to invent on a purely empirical basis practical remedies without general observation of the disease (Comte, 1998: 86ff). Imagination must be made subordinate to a 'politics of observation', one that discovers the forces of recovery inherent to the whole organism and prudently removes obstacles to the 'natural resolution of the crisis'.

Comte arrived at the conclusion that crisis was a transient effect of moral disintegration. This 'moral interregnum' was derived from a theoretical assumption that social systems can be divided into two parts, 'spiritual powers' and 'temporal powers', reflecting the binary operation of Comte's social theory (see Table 2.1). Spiritual power refers to general theoretical and moral principles that serve to organise and unify social relations. Temporal power refers to the practical relations of power, the mode of distribution of power resources, force and governing institutions. From the eleventh century until the eighteenth century, spiritual-theoretical power was theological, represented by the papacy, while temporal-practical power was founded on military force, represented by feudal nobility.

Table 2.1   *Binary organisation in Comte's (1998) social theory*

Power	Spiritual	Temporal
Domain	Theoretical	Practical
Form of rule	Opinion	Force
Institution	Education	Government
Knowledge	Generalist	Specialisation
Object	Whole	Parts

Power	Spiritual	Temporal
Theory	Synthetic	Analytical
Doctrine	Organic	Critical
Focus	Ends	Means
Motivation	Principles	Interests
Scope	Universal	Particular
Population	Diversity	Similarity
Relations	Civic	Political
Stage 3 (positive)	Science	Industry
Stage 2 (crisis)	Metaphysics	Lawyers
Stage 1 (theology)	Religion	Military
Condition	Normal	Pathological

In the eighteenth century, theology was replaced as French society's theoretical power by 'the critical doctrine' of metaphysics while military force was supplanted as society's practical or civil power by industrial property. Despite the fact that every European state controlled a large military apparatus and war seemed to be threatened constantly, Comte contended that this was mainly for domestic repression – suppressing anarchy and insurrection at home – rather than meeting the demands of warfare between states.

It was the special genius of the Catholic church that it had secured an autonomous realm for spiritual power separate from the temporal power of individual governments. Similarly, the reorganisation of society must begin from the autonomy of spiritual, theoretical and moral power, not from passing, day-to-day exigencies of temporal power. On the one hand, spiritual power sows illusions in the absolute power of theological or philosophical constructions and, on the other, temporal power seeks to remedy the crisis piecemeal or immediately with legal reforms or political revolutions, combining lofty phrases in words with base self-interest in practice.

Although fundamentally separate, the powers mutually serve each other, though temporal power must be made subordinate to spiritual power. For instance, political domination cannot be servile when it is legitimated by the spiritual power of moral authority, and neither is dissent, within certain limits, necessarily a hostile act (Comte, 1998: 188). In this Comte sought to subordinate (temporal) political practices to (spiritual) social theory, following a strain in Enlightenment social theory that privileged civil society over political power. In practice, society and government are inseparable. The precise shape of the 'general order' is determined by the effect of the whole (spiritual and temporal combined) on the parts. Spiritual power is exercised by a special class of thinkers and proselytisers 'charged with the cultivation of theoretical knowledge' (Comte, 1998: 206). Their function is to establish and maintain the principles that govern different social relations and spread these throughout society by education and symbolic reminders in daily life. In this way, society acquires a moral unity and a social purpose, without which it could not be said to really exist.

THEORY IN CHAOS

Comte's main concern had been that excessive criticism and scepticism weakened political legitimacy, thus perpetuating the crisis. Initially critique played a progressive, anti-theological role as a logical, systematic method. Essential for destroying theological dogma, freedom of conscience descended into a blanket rejection of any moral or intellectual community. Inured by three centuries of intellectual struggle, criticism became a corrosive habit that proved disruptive of all social order and progress. From an initially justified reaction to religious dogma, critical theory had by the seventeenth century become an automatic reflex that spread across Europe the following century.

Here Comte summarises one of the major problems of modernity that has exercised social theory ever since: the absence of a unifying moral centre around which society might cohere. Politics now came under a corrupting form of 'administrative despotism' based on pure exigency and detailed calculation, lacking any broader theoretical perspective of all-round social development. At the European level, state rivalry prevented the development of continent-wide social and moral integration.

Negatively, the constant attack on every kind of spiritual power left modern society with a theoretical and moral hole, producing a general restlessness and discontent that Durkheim would later term 'anomie'. Deepening intellectual fragmentation, private morality and personal interests were advanced by liberal critique as prior to the general good.

> Through this dual influence [of instrumental action and private morality], each individual is gradually led to make himself the centre of the great social relationships, and as the notion of private interest alone remains wholly clear amidst all this moral chaos, pure egoism naturally becomes the only motive with enough energy to direct active existence. (Comte, 1998: 197)

The spiritual void nourished grievances against social and political constraints and fuelled insurrectionary crises. Social disintegration was countered in part, Comte claimed, by the practical, temporal power of industry, work discipline, and, anticipating Norbert Elias, 'the universal softening of manners resulting from the progress of civilization' (Comte, 1998: 197).

Following Smith and Ferguson and anticipating Durkheim, the division of labour for Comte (1998: 209) had a universalising tendency that could embrace the whole of humanity, but it also had a fragmenting tendency since specialised functions endlessly divide once-unified practices of social labour. Without theoretical generalism and a common morality guiding government action the fragmentation process would spontaneously overwhelm the integrative one.

PHILOSOPHY AND SOCIAL THEORY

Knowledge is a practical process, not a cognitive decision. Theory must base itself on observed facts but, at the same time, observations must be guided by theory.

Otherwise, Comte contends, facts would be 'desultory and fruitless'. Nor can facts be perceived in the first place without the guiding hand of theory. In establishing his own branch of social theory, Comte thought that science, with sociology ensconced at its summit, would definitively and finally supersede traditional philosophy. This might seem surprising at first blush. After all, Comte saw the new phase of intellectual growth as one of 'positive *philosophy*', which attempted to remove intellectual speculation about logical concepts and to construct what might be clumsily called a 'historical sociology of knowledge'. Comte's idea of philosophy was limited to discovering a key to classify successive systems of knowledge: theological-fictitious knowledge; metaphysical-abstract knowledge; and positive-scientific knowledge.

By making philosophy 'positive' Comte also made it 'scientific'. Although the idea of a scientific philosophy is obscure, Comte's aim was to overturn the arid abstractions of Enlightenment rationalism. This required a historical theory of knowledge that allowed different types of thought a relative autonomy from other kinds. Philosophy, for Comte, pulled the entire history of science together to reveal its underlying logic. Comte recognised that each science develops distinctive theories and methods appropriate to its particular object of study.

Comte dispensed with idle speculation about 'first and final causes' or 'origins and purposes' in order to formulate a theory or hypothesis that could be compared or tested against the 'observable facts'. Philosophical speculation only resulted in fanciful notions about social forces as the arbitrary repetition of the same underlying essence in different conditions. The radical experience of the French Revolution, transferring the scientific spirit to politics, demonstrated conclusively that universal, eternal categories were illusory. Society and politics were to be transformed by a modern conception of progress first glimpsed, Comte (1858: 441) claimed, at an intuitive level by Blaise Pascal (1623–1662): 'The entire succession of men, through the whole course of ages, must be regarded as one man, always living and incessantly learning.'

In support of his contention about intellectual progress, Comte (1858) developed a history of social theory from Aristotle (384–322BCE) to early 19th century political economy. Despite Aristotle's sophisticated metaphysics of political constitutions, it was simply not intellectually possible for ancient philosophers to rise to the level of a positive science of society. Later, Baron de Montesquieu (1689–1755) was able to provide some general precepts about social progress and invariant laws against the dogmatic conviction that political authority could shape society at will (Montesquieu, 1949). Next, Condorcet provided the first scientific conception of social progress, though execution fell somewhat short due to the prevailing conceit of the Revolution as realising the highest form of reason (McLean and Hewitt, 1994) .

Excepting the 'social philosopher' Adam Smith, 'who made no pretension to found a new special science' (Comte, 1858: 446), political economy represented for Comte the final, 'critical' stage of metaphysical speculation before it would be replaced by sociology. Metaphysical sophistry bound political economy to the pedantic abstractions of free market dogma. Finally, Comte briefly considered the contribution of historical studies to the emerging sociological science. While history outlines empirically definite patterns of development it nonetheless suffers from an over-literary and descriptive style of thought that fell well short of Comte's theoretical science of society.

QUEEN SOCIOLOGY

Social theory must first construct its object in theory if it is to avoid 'the fallacy of misplaced concreteness' or become distorted by the demands of powerful social and political interests. An overarching social theory of the history of knowledge seemed necessary for Comte to furnish social science with laws of intellectual development. By 'laws' Comte did not mean absolute, universal or uniform rules of development but provisional claims or hypotheses about observable patterns to be verified empirically. Even though it assumes that nature is knowable because it evinces orderly patterns, science is always relative to the historical state of social knowledge.

Antecedent sciences were understood as being both simpler than and a precondition for the scientific study of society in its complexity, differentiation and diversity. But Comte's social theory of knowledge also required that sociology be conceived as both the positive result and presupposition of the antecedent sciences. As the study of the most complex object in all the sciences, sociology is also the most dependent on other disciplines. It is therefore impossible for sociology to formulate an absolute epistemological break from the natural sciences even as it struggles for relative autonomy. At best, sociology can establish a qualified autonomy for itself, both from other sciences and from the social world.

Against the common miscomprehension that confuses Comtean positivism with naïve empiricism, Comte gave theory, social theory above all, a determining function for positive science. Against the exclusion of theory by empiricism on the grounds of objectivity, Comte argues that 'all isolated, empirical observation is idle' (1858: 475). A vast collection of facts is essentially meaningless and practically useless if it is severed from the most intimate contact with theory. As Comte argued, 'Those who expect that the theory will be suggested by the facts, do not understand what is the course necessarily pursued by the human mind, which has achieved all real results by the only effectual method – of anticipating scientific observations by some conception (hypothetical in the first instance) of the corresponding phenomena' (1858: 525).

All the same, Comte did not therefore adopt a rigid method of deduction from first principles. It was 'incontestable', Comte argued, that as a more advanced stage of knowledge, science was based on observed facts but, equally, at earlier pre-scientific stages, knowledge necessarily springs in the first place from more general conceptions.

As the study of the most complex object, society, sociology would need to deploy a multi-method approach – observation, experiment, comparison and history – on a pragmatic basis as the object permits. Philosophical scepticism and empiricism had cast doubt on the reliability of human observation and testimony as part of the revolutionary assault on the *ancien régime*. Now, however, for the most complex science, sociology, to emerge the rational method of empirical observation guided by theory had to leave behind philosophical paradoxes of first and final causes. Comte recognised that the only way out of 'the vicious circle' was to make a start towards a science of society by relying on admittedly makeshift data and flawed precepts.

First, Comte's observational method was informed by a sociological disposition to study 'apparently insignificant customs, the appreciation of various kinds of monuments, the analysis and comparison of languages, and a multitude of other resources … almost all impressions from the events of life' (1858: 476). Second, experimentation was possible in the form of pathological disturbances to the normal course of social order. As we have seen, crisis conditions and the irrational political experiments that followed the Revolution provided the raw material for the experimental study of pathological disorders that Comte expected would characterise sociology. Third, comparison could profitably be made with non-human animals. Even if it made a negligible contribution to understanding human society a comparison with non-human animals might dislodge the absolute anthropocentric assumptions of critical theory (1858: 480).

SCIENCE IN THREE STAGES

Progress is traced along an ascending curve by Comte from the first theological stage as a necessary point of departure for human understanding, through the metaphysical stage as a transitional phase, before arriving at the positive scientific stage as final, fixed and definitive knowledge. Both the theological and metaphysical stages realise their inherent potential for knowledge to the fullest extent before they are displaced by science, the next, more advanced stage. Finally, sociology absorbs the lessons of the natural sciences, though is not fixated on the methods of any particular science, before striking out on its own distinctive course as the highest branch of positive, scientific knowledge dealing with the most complex known phenomena – human societies.

Comte's 'law of the three states' was not particularly innovative. It had been in circulation since at least 1750 with Turgot's (1727–1781) sketch of the linear progress of human intellect, a model of progress filtered through Condorcet and Saint-Simon. Although Comte (1858: 523) was generous in recognising his intellectual precursors, he considered that he alone had thus far been able to demonstrate the positive evolution towards social theory: 'Social science has, with all its complexity, passed through the theological state, and has almost everywhere fully attained the metaphysical; while it has nowhere yet risen to the positive, except in this book.' All the major sciences – astronomy, physics, chemistry, biology – succeed each other at ascending levels of complexity, according to Comte, only after successfully negotiating the theological and metaphysical stages. At its highest, scientific stage of development each discipline prepares the ground for the emergence of the succeeding one in a hierarchy of complexity.

I. Theology

Theological knowledge represented for Comte a fundamental revolution in human history. It not only provided society with a set of organising principles in collective values and political attitudes. It also introduced a rupture between theory and practice that made possible the emergence of a 'speculative class' with the leisure and authority to develop theoretical conceptions of the natural and social worlds. For Comte this separation represented a lasting achievement for human culture upon which all subsequent theoretical understanding depends. As 'primitive philosophy' theology encouraged human society to spontaneously puzzle over the essential nature of animate and inanimate things and to look for first and final causes in the movement of objects. Gradually the most distant things, the stars, supplanted what was nearest, earthly things like changes in the weather, as objects of veneration. Routine experiences of the social and natural world become weighed down by habit and repetition as something separate from religious cult.

A speculative class or priesthood emerged as gifted intermediaries able to give meaning to the worship of mysterious objects like stars. Astrolatory was not only inaccessible to ordinary mortals but, since the stars in the sky display a regular pattern, they helped stimulate the formulation of general propositions. Earlier 'pure fetishism', a singular belief in magical fetishes, gradually passed over to a stage of polytheist beliefs in multiple gods responsible for separate domains. Here affective passions predominated over the rational intellect to personify and deify even the most inert objects. This in turn was supplanted by a theological dogma about a single God as the creator of all things.

The most advanced species of philosophical monotheism for Comte was mediaeval Catholicism. Its fundamental dogma educated lay believers in a rudimentary sense of history and imparted a universal morality that raised adherents beyond the narrow material concerns of immediate social conditions. Monotheism also encouraged the idea of separate domains – 'Render unto Caesar the things which are Caesar's, and unto God the things that are God's' (Mathew, 22:21). The social world appears to be so mundane that it is not recognised as part of that special world animated by the arbitrary will of a supernatural agent and is relegated by the theological worldview. This separation of spiritual and temporal powers by monotheistic philosophy provided for Comte 'an intellectual as well as a social service because it separated at the same time social theory from practice, and thus laid the foundation of social science in distinction from mere Utopias' (1858: 631).

Spontaneous theology is therefore the distant ancestor of disciplined social theory. The lasting achievement of the theological inversion is that it raised a new hierarchy of knowledge that subordinated what was most practical and immediate to the esoteric secrets revealed by universal abstractions. The theological worldview establishes in society a general need to discover universal laws about the invisible origins of things. Moral and intellectual strength was derived from theological fictions. Theological inquiry was stimulated by practical considerations that promised 'the powerful charm of unlimited empire over the external world – a world destined wholly for our use, and involved in every way with our existence' (Comte, 1858: 27). By encouraging the idea that humans had access to supernatural power, expectations were also raised that natural forces could be first understood as a prelude to confronting and overcoming physical limitations and suffering.

Theology cut through the vicious circle of either collecting facts to form a theory (induction) or forming a theory to observe facts (deduction). It transposed the banal facts of the social world behind ultimate questions about the most sublime mysteries, the nature, origin and purpose of inaccessible things. This theological conception of knowledge persisted in the pre-scientific chimeras of astrology and alchemy, which themselves stimulated the observations and experiments of the 'positive' scientific disciplines of astronomy and chemistry. Against the damning indictment of mediaeval knowledge by leading Enlightenment thinkers like Condorcet, Comte hailed theological philosophy – that 'masterpiece of human wisdom' represented by Thomas Aquinas, Albertus Magnus, Roger Bacon, and Dante – for reaching great heights under feudal conditions as knowledge advanced towards metaphysics, though it could progress no further.

II. Metaphysics

Institutional Catholicism was unable to fully incorporate scientific reason under its own auspices, though Comte credited it with creating the extrinsic conditions that sheltered nascent positive philosophy. Comte dates the ascendancy of the metaphysical or philosophical state from the fourteenth century when Catholicism entered into an epoch of crisis lasting five centuries, the start of a cycle of heresy and violent repression. This coincided with a crisis of theology's social basis in feudalism. For two centuries the challenge of critical metaphysics was spontaneous and unsystematic. Beyond that, as the decay of Catholicism mounted, critical metaphysics became a more rigorous, abstract and negative doctrine. With the strict separation of temporal and spiritual powers, the ambition and centralisation of military authority and Papal authority were bound to breach the boundaries of their respective domains even as they underwent internal crisis of purpose and authority.

By interposing a metaphysical state between theology and science, Comte went beyond the established dichotomy of much post-revolutionary thinking. Comte saw the metaphysical stage as a transitional one, cushioning the decline of theology and preparing the way for positive science. Fated to pass away, Comte gave the metaphysical state only a cursory role in his system compared to theology or science. Metaphysical philosophy absorbed the speculative method of theology, substituting its supernatural character with an abstract rationalism. Because it lacked any real social power, metaphysics adopted a critical standpoint to temporal and religious power that became increasingly speculative, abstract and convoluted.

III. Science

Comte was active in a scientific field rent with struggles for legitimacy and prestige, principally between inanimate sciences of mathematics and physics and the
emerging life sciences. Arguably, Comte's most distinctive contribution is that his
historical theory of science refuses to reduce science to a single, universal principle of validity and refuses to take any single science like mathematics as an
exemplary model for all others to follow (Heilbron, 1995). Comte recognised that
each field of science develops in relative autonomy from the others in line with
the distinctive demands posed by the specific character of its object of study.
While astronomy and physics remained compatible with a mathematical worldview, the organic phenomena studied by chemistry and biology, although
dependent on physical properties, were more differentiated. Their laws of development applied across a lower range of generality.

All sciences develop historically from what is most simple to what is more complex in their given object of study. Comte (1858: 44) classified the relationship
between phenomena with his formula of 'increasing complexity/decreasing generality'. This means that, first, the more simple a phenomenon is, then the more
general it will also be and, vice versa, the more complex that it is, then the more
particular it will also be: 'for whatever is observed in the greatest number of cases
is of course the most disengaged from the incidents of particular cases' (1858: 44).
Astronomical phenomena are the most general, because they are the simplest and
most independent of human activity; sociological phenomena are the most specific because they are the most complex, composed as they are of interdependent,
historically formed individuals and groups, dependent for their existence on
working on nature.

Study must begin therefore with the more simple and general before proceeding
progressively to the more particular and complex. Each science bases itself on the
preceding one, connected to it but also divided from it. This also implies a relationship of dependency, with the more complex phenomena dependent on the
more simple. The more general any phenomena is then the further removed it is
from the complex flux of everyday life. Finally, study of general phenomena therefore requires a more rational and detached perspective than the spontaneous
immediacy produced by the swirl of everyday life.

In some sciences what is easiest to grasp is the elementary unit, for instance
primary numbers in mathematics. Other, more complex objects appear as an
already unified totality, the body in biology or collective knowledge in sociology. Sciences of inanimate objects, mathematics and physics, develop
inductively from specific properties to general laws, while sciences of animate
objects, biology and sociology, could only develop deductively from the general
to the particular. Comte's theory of science, of classifying disciplines according
to the principle of increasing complexity and decreasing generality, prepared
the ground for the rise of social theory. This process would culminate ultimately in the struggle for disciplinary legitimacy waged on behalf of sociology
by Durkheim half a century later.

ANALYTICAL AND SYNTHETIC THEORY

Comte detailed numerous gains in scientific advances but also recoiled at the narrowing of scientific specialisation by the *savants*. Here the analytical theory of science, proceeding from an accumulation of detailed studies, ought to have been a necessary preparatory stage for the development of synthetic theory, of a general science of science, culminating in social science. Comte bristled that 'the spirit of generality' was still not at this stage in charge of 'the spirit of detail'. Specialisation in matters of analytical detail served merely as instrumental means for the practical interests of temporal power divorced from the social ends of synthetic theory. Both analytical theory and synthetic theory were essential to each other, mutually reinforcing detailed and general knowledge. On the analytical side, the specific differences of phenomena – their division and sub-division – form the object of study, while on the synthetic side, resemblances and interconnections between phenomena are arranged in a general system.

Lacking the guidance of synthetic theory, Comte argued, 'the *savants* of each section acquire only isolated fragments of knowledge, and have no means of comparing the general attributes of rational positivity exhibited by the various orders of phenomena, according to their natural arrangement' (1858: 759). Mediocre talents, jealous of superior intellects (like Comte's presumably), resent every form of theoretical generalism that intrudes onto their own narrow field of preoccupation. Instead, they seek to extend their own special analysis, for example geometric or biological, in imperialist fashion to other fields in a flatly reductive fashion.

Specialisation without generalism proves disastrous since the 'elevation of soul and generosity of feeling can hardly be developed without generality of ideas, through the natural affinity between narrow and desultory views and selfish dispositions' (1858: 760). Beholden to narrow industrial interests, the *savants* formed an intermediary 'equivocal' class between the abstract speculation of philosophers and the specialisation of engineers and were therefore doomed to extinction, most passing into technical engineering with only a few of the most able being trained in the generalist doctrine, led at its highest point by social theory.

For its part, philosophy departed further from science, developing abstract moral and social theories that lacked any relationship to empirical research based on a secure method or theory. Instead, modern philosophy parodies the observational method of science by appealing to 'interior observation' (Scharff, 1995: 24–34). 'Reason' reasons about its own innate capacity for reason. In this, philosophy absorbed the logical method of inorganic science, which was only provisionally valid in any case. Against the arid doctrines of modern philosophy, the need for theoretical generalism was, for Comte (1858: 762), simply the new common sense of the age. Science, with social science at its head, provided the only basis for a philosophy determined to counteract social and moral disorganisation by giving theoretical form to Comte's twin goals of order and progress.

COMMON SENSE AND SOCIAL THEORY

Yet the subjective synthesis leading to moral order and social progress seemed as far away as ever. In the aftermath of the 1848 revolution Comte's growing impatience with the open-ended nature of the crisis led him to attempt to short-circuit the process by announcing a positivist 'religion of humanity', or what Thomas Huxley called 'Catholicism minus Christianity' (Pickering, 2009: 60). Rather than wait on the slow work of science to heal the social wounds, a secular church would transform positivism into the new common sense of society by providing it with a universal doctrine (*dogme*), legitimate moral authority (*regime*), and an institutional system (*culte*) (Wernick, 2001: 2–4).

First, the comprehensive positivist regime constructs a 'positive ethic' through a life-long moral commitment to the progress of 'humanity' instilled in the present at home, school and secular rituals, as well as reform of work and government. Second, spiritual leaders would construct theoretical doctrines to diminish egoism, immorality and material conflict, while forging spontaneous alliances with marginalised and credulous but functionally important social groups, primarily the working class and women. Because the working class and women occupy marginal social positions in the structure of temporal power, Comte considered them 'better disposed than their employers to broad views and to generous sympathies, and will therefore naturally associate themselves with the spiritual power' (1998: 384). Third, the positivist cult would mobilise devotees in rituals and habits of devotion, worship and celebration of humanity. In this way, ideas (doctrine) are transformed into sentiments (cult) as a guide to action (regime) to produce a self-reinforcing cycle of love–order–progress, a thickened form of moral sense, and so bring the crisis to a close.

This marked a shift in emphasis from Comte's earlier objective synthesis to the 'subjective synthesis' of the 1850s. And with this shift the underlying metaphysical split between the object (society) and subject (science) of Comte's social theory was transformed into one of totality and praxis. Knowledge is not only intellectual and individual, it also affective and collective. At this stage, sociology was to be subordinated to morals at the apex of the hierarchy of knowledge; the intelligent, self-conscious, feeling and active subject takes precedence over the passive object of social theory. Love, altruism (another term Comte invented), sympathy, solidarity and other sentiments of human relations together constitute the subjective synthesis far beyond the narrowly intellectual cognitions of social theory. This has made the later Comte appealing to some forms of post-modern theory (Gane, 2006). Ultimately, positivism embraced the whole person as a conduit to the whole of humanity. Through the subjective synthesis humanity will finally progress to the habits and feelings of 'the normal state' in a higher moral order.

Common sense as a form of 'public reason' arises out of a community of feeling and principles which positive social theory actively cultivates. Social sympathy provides the spiritual basis for social, political and personal morality. Before social institutions can be reformed, common sense itself needs to be reformed by adopting the general principles adumbrated by Comte's philosopher-priests. First, 'the practical value of social principles' will acquire 'the imposing weight of theoretical truth [that] ensures their stability and coherence by connecting them with the whole series of laws on which the life of man and of society depends' (Lenzer, 1998: 353). Second, since the role of pure reason in human nature tends to be exaggerated and egoism underestimated, 'the strong reaction of all upon each is needed, whether to control selfishness or to stimulate sympathy', through social cooperation and association in clubs, unions and meetings, especially prevalent among the working class. Third, practical life can only be shaped by common sense when it comes under principles established by doctrine and interpreted by educators trained in positive theory. The reform of common sense in the interest of order and progress depends on 'one ultimate condition: the formation of a firm alliance between philosophers and proletarians' (1998: 355).

CRITIQUE AND DEVELOPMENT

After Comte's death, sociology made little headway in Europe as an academic discipline. Nonetheless Comte arguably bequeathed to social theory a contribution of lasting significance. First, he established the general precepts of science by experiment and observation and distilled these into hypothetical verifiable propositions. Second, by bringing the major sciences into a general relationship with each other, social theory exercised a generalist pedagogical function that overcomes one-sided specialisation. Third, positive social theory respected the relative autonomy of individual sciences required by the distinctive properties of their object of study. Fourth, Comte exposed the illegitimacy of positing a formal ideal, an 'ought', to explain an empirical fact, an 'is'. Finally, positive social theory was not a neutral intellectual exercise but aimed to combine moral order, social progress and love of Humanity.

Traditional philosophy is premised on the image of the solitary individual who does all the hard thinking within the limits of a single mind. Instead, Comte insisted that all knowledge is dependent on a long-run, cumulative and collective social process of knowledge production lasting thousands of years, what Marx (1973: 706) slightly later termed the 'general intellect'. Comte recognised that scientific knowledge derives from non-scientific knowledge. He refused to relegate pre-scientific thought as inherently inferior to theoretical knowledge or to adopt an absolute criterion of objective validity. He broached the problem of the relationship of scientific knowledge to other, more spontaneous forms of knowledge. Knowledge is an emergent property of the practical life of all human societies.

Comte's epistemology was not, as is often supposed, founded on abstract generalities about laws of development. It was buttressed by detailed knowledge of major scientific developments. Comte demanded that valid knowledge be restricted to 'positive' hypotheses about observable empirical phenomena. For Comte there could be no universal, single or absolute scientific method, only particular sciences. More complex sciences like biology and sociology cannot be reduced to the closed symbolic logic of mathematics and physics. What was specific to sociology as a science for Comte was the progress of social knowledge – uneven certainly, but conforming nevertheless to the general sequence that all sciences were fated to pass through.

Sociology must develop as a relatively autonomous science in distinction from the natural sciences. Comte was perfectly clear that social processes, relations and structures can be reduced to neither physics nor biology. That Comte formulated the necessity for sociology remains a singular debt. Payment cannot be avoided simply because of Comte's personal crises, arcane language, premature prognoses of social order, or lack of empirical corroboration. He anticipated that specialisation in a narrow branch of science artificially isolated knowledge from the general intellect and buried it under increasingly meaningless detailed information. Comte's solution to crisis was specialisation in a generalist social theory of science.

3

MARX'S TURN

Social theory first acquired its specifically modernist sensibility with Karl Marx. At the heart of Marx's image of modernity is a world in perpetual crisis. This alarming prospect seemed to be confirmed in 1848, the year that a wave of revolutions broke across the European continent. A few weeks before the spread of revolutionary contagion Marx and Engels published an obscure little pamphlet, *Manifesto of the Communist Party* (see Marx and Engels, 1998, for a contemporary version). The two events were not connected in any direct way. Marx anticipated the temper of the times through an acute diagnosis of the social dynamic of new historical classes alongside a sweeping political prognosis of impending revolutionary transformation. This process of constant crisis and transformation was expressed not in the bone-dry language of traditional theory but through the enlivened language of modernity (Berman, 1983). In memorable imagery, Marx famously characterised modern capitalism as unstable, dynamic and revolutionary:

> Constant revolutionizing of production, uninterrupted disturbance of all social conditions, everlasting uncertainty and agitation distinguish the bourgeois epoch from all earlier ones. All fixed, fast-frozen relations, with their train of ancient and venerable prejudices and opinions, are swept away, all new-formed ones become antiquated before they can ossify. All that is solid melts into air, all that is holy is profaned, and man is at last compelled to face with sober senses his real conditions of life, and his relations with his kind. (Marx and Engels, 1998: 38–9)

What was being transformed were the social relations and forces of production, social conditions, and traditional ideologies. No longer bewitched by the magic of religion or the grandeur of monarchy, Marx believed that people were at long last being forced to soberly confront the social relations that structure their lives.

Yet far from soberly approaching the social world, later Marxists argued that the working class had become so intoxicated and numbed by the commodities and ideologies produced by capitalism that social revolution was literally unthinkable. If Marxism is the theory of social revolution, then the absence of working-class revolution represents a formidable dilemma for Marxist theory. If, as Marxists claim, theory can only be confirmed by changing society in practice, then the experience of the past two centuries has severely tested the credibility of Marxism as a predictive science or philosophical prophecy. As it attempts to explain and predict social and political change (or its absence) Marxism itself is plunged into periodic crisis. At one point an exasperated Marx is reported to have complained, 'If anything is certain, it is that I myself am not a Marxist' (Engels, 1882: 353).

Since Marx's death in 1883 social theory associated with his name has been subject to constant revision and dispute, not only from ideological opponents but also among those theorists and philosophers who identify themselves as 'Marxists'. Seemingly perpetual 'crises of Marxism' are tied as much to political success and failure as to its cognitive value as theory. It is a 'crisis theory' in that it is itself subject to patterns of critique, innovation and renewal, a cycle of decline and recovery that raises Marxism repeatedly from its dogmatic slumbers. In this cycle, Marxism has alternately emphasised philosophical critique and science, with various attempts in between to transcend the philosophy–science divide by appealing to 'praxis'.

The course of the tension between science and critique can be crudely sketched. First, down to the *Communist Manifesto* and revolutions of 1848, Marx was engaged with an essentially philosophical critique. Second, nineteenth-century Marxism developed as a general theory of 'scientific socialism', culminating in *Capital* (first published in 1867). Third, later 'revisionist' followers of Marx broke this conceptual unity into separate economic, political and ideological spheres and severed the link between scientific theory and social practice. Marxism was treated in a purely theoretical way, divorced from the shifting dynamics of class struggle. Fourth, with the upsurge of revolutionary struggles after 1917 philosophical Marxism once again re-emphasised the active, subjective side of class struggle over the objective force of social and economic structures, characterised by the so-called 'Western Marxism' of Bloch, Gramsci, Korsch, Lukacs and Lefebvre.

Fifth, in the 1960s and 1970s Marxism was split between structuralist and analytical theory on one hand and cultural theory on the other, as opposing ways to explain the absence of working-class revolution. More recently, Marxist theory has revived as philosophical critique and economic analyses following the collapse of the Soviet Union and the crisis of neoliberal capitalism (Harvey, 2005; Carchedi, 2011). This has been accompanied by various kinds of 'post-Marxism' that draw on the intellectual legacy of Marx without allowing any more, and usually considerably less, analytical priority to class than gender, ethnicity, religion, nationality, and sexuality as forms of identity.

No single chapter could possibly summarise the multiple varieties of 'Marxism'. This chapter is therefore limited to outlining some of the main features that distinguish Marx and Marxism as social theory. These include the role of method, the relationship between theory and practice, the notion of crisis, and the fraught relationship between Marxism and sociology. It does this by outlining the social theory of Karl Marx and the later attempt to construct a Marxist sociology by Nikolai Bukharin, one of Marxism's most tragic figures. As Marxism was transformed into a state dogma in the 1930s it had terrifying consequences. Bukharin, one of the most loyal Bolsheviks, was executed in 1938 after a grotesque show trial in which his 'mistakes' in social theory were absurdly claimed to have led to political betrayal of the Soviet Union (Cohen, 1980).

Against the prevailing view that Marxism was an omniscient philosophical system, Bukharin tried to develop a materialist sociology in an attempt to steer Marxism between the poles of theoretical science and political agency. This chapter describes how Bukharin was influenced by mainstream sociological perspectives of the period, which Bukharin overlaid with Marxist concepts and suppositions. Bukharin was sharply criticised by Marxist theorists of the stature of Lukacs, Korsch and Gramsci and, more crudely, by Stalinist apparatchiks. This hostility set the tone for Bukharin's neglect by social theory.

KARL MARX AND CRITIQUE

First of all, Marx's social theory is *critical*. Contemporary society was understood by Marx as a specific transitory phase of a long-run historical process. From this perspective, Marx adopted a critical theoretical and practical standpoint. Marx made his purpose clear in the titles of his studies at different stages in the development of his social theory:

- *Critique of Hegel's Philosophy of Right* (1843–4) (Marx and Engels, 1975)
- *The Holy Family, or Critique of Critical Criticism* (Marx and Engels, 1844)
- *The German Ideology: Critique of Modern German Philosophy* and *Volume 2: Critique of German Socialism* (1845–6) (Marx and Engels, 1975)
- *A Contribution to the Critique of Political Economy* (1859)
- *Capital: A Critique of Political Economy* (Marx, 1976)

A critique of contrary standpoints, their hidden assumptions and explicit propositions, is a necessary stage in the development of social theory. Critique distinguishes Marxism from all attempts to construct positive theoretical systems whether in philosophy or political economy.

But critique is not an end in itself. In his early polemics of *The Holy Family* Marx satirised 'critical criticism' of hair-splitting theorists who went round and round in a self-referential circle of ideas, critical of still other ideas but making little contact with human practice. Marx poured scorn on the abstract metaphysical 'standpoint' of critical models, the '*judgment from the standpoint of the standpoint*', as merely 'warming up old speculative trash'. Purely theoretical criticism by radical intellectuals merely turns everything into a self-conscious 'standpoint', collapsing the gap between theory and practice.

[T]here is a world in which *consciousness* and *being* are distinct; a world which continues to exist when I merely abolish its existence in thought, its existence as a

> category or as a standpoint; i.e., when I modify my own subjective consciousness without altering the objective reality in a really objective way, that is to say, without altering my own *objective* reality and that of other men. Hence the speculative *mystical identity* of *being* and *thinking* is repeated in Criticism as the equally mystical identity of *practice* and *theory*. That is why Criticism is so vexed with practice which wants to be something distinct from theory, and with theory which wants to be something other than the dissolution of a definite *category* in the *'boundless generality of self-consciousness'*. (Marx and Engels, 1844: 193)

By attributing to the idealised proletariat the universal standpoint of human society, the gap between being and consciousness was obliterated philosophically but not practically. Any fusion of theory and practice in the worldly 'realisation of philosophy' remains 'mystical' and premature, according to Marx, so long as capitalism is able to reproduce itself as an actually-existing totality. Theory can only become a social force when it practically transforms objective reality.

Marx considered the classical phase of German philosophy of Kant and Hegel and the classical phase of political economy of Adam Smith and David Ricardo as the highest expression of critical social theory possible within bourgeois society. Yet despite registering some of the conflicts and contradictions of class society, the greatest bourgeois thinkers could not go beyond the assumption that capitalism seemed to be a permanent rather than a historically specific form of society founded on exploitative social relations. All earlier societies such as ancient Rome were viewed through the prism of bourgeois society on the assumption that the present is merely a more perfect version of the past.

This led Marx to break decisively with Hegel's speculative philosophy, which both mystified social existence (as a problem of consciousness) and uncritically justified the Prussian state (as the end-point for human culture or 'world-spirit'). Marx (1976: 102) inverted the 'mystical shell' of Hegel's dialectic to uncover its 'rational kernel' and abandoned its apologetic function for the existing social order.

> My dialectic method is, in its foundations, not only different from the Hegelian, but exactly opposite to it. For Hegel, the process of thinking, which he even transforms into an independent subject, under the name of 'the Idea', is the creator of the real world, and the real world is only the external appearance of the idea. With me the reverse is true: the ideal is nothing but the material world reflected in the human mind, and translated into forms of thought.

Marx effected an inversion of Hegel's philosophy, not its extension as is sometimes claimed: from bourgeois theory to proletarian theory, from ideal consciousness to materialist practice, from the end of history to social processes, from philosophical system to substantive social theory.

Critical philosophy was renounced by Marx because it demanded that the social world realise the truth of formal philosophical categories as an essentially cognitive process. Philosophical categories obscured Marx's specifically *social* theory. Contemporary German philosophers failed to understand the significance of Marx's early breakthrough because it was clouded with philosophical verbiage and so they attempted to assimilate it as a modern version of the old 'worn-out' speculative metaphysics.

> Where speculation ends, where real life starts, there consequently begins real, positive science, the expounding of the practical activity, of the practical process of development of men. Empty phrases about consciousness end, and real knowledge has to take their place. When the reality is described, a self-sufficient philosophy *[die selbständige Philosophie]* loses its medium of existence. (Marx and Engels, 1975: 37)

There is no human or historical 'essence' or unchanging 'species-being' to be found in any particular individuals, states or nations outside of the 'ensemble of social relations'. When philosophers eventually identified social relations as the 'essence' of humankind they turned the banal premise of all human existence into a conclusion. As Engels argued:

> Philosophy has reached a point when the trivial fact of the necessity of intercourse between human beings – a fact without a knowledge of which the second generation that ever existed would never have been produced, a fact already involved in the sexual difference – is presented by philosophy at the end of its entire development as the greatest result. (Marx and Engels, 1975: 12)

Hence, by the mid-1840s Marx considered that it was time to put misleading speculation about 'essences', 'species-being' and other philosophical 'phraseology' aside and to develop a materialist theory of 'actuality', 'which is *not without premises*, but which empirically observes the actual material premises as such and for that reason is, for the first time, *actually* a critical view of the world' (Marx and Engels, 1975: 236). With his emerging social theory, Marx was concerned to repudiate his own earlier use of philosophical jargon.

By inverting Hegel's dialectical method Marx was able to reconstruct the specific laws of motion of capitalist society. However, parts of *Capital*, his scientific opus, still flirted with the terminology of 'that mighty thinker', Hegel. This was because Hegel's dialectic contained a sting in the tale unpalatable to bourgeois social theory. As well as a positive apology for the existing order, Hegel's dialectic was also critical: 'because it regards every historically developed social form as being in a fluid state, in motion, and therefore grasps its transient aspect as well; and because it does not let itself be impressed by anything, being in its essence critical and revolutionary' (Marx, 1976: 103).

The problem with earlier social theory was that it treated bourgeois society, the state, culture and economy, as the end goal of all previous human development. By justifying the necessity of a state to keep order over a society that would otherwise break out into a 'war of all against all', Hobbes lacked a critical theory of mid-seventeenth-century England. This competitive struggle within society was extended by Darwin in the nineteenth century into the competitive struggle within nature.

While Marx found in Saint-Simon a utopian rationale for socialism, he cast Comte as an uncritical apologist for the social order. Marx famously adopted Saint-Simon's slogan to characterise the future stateless society: 'The government of men would give way to the administration of things'. In contrast, Marx

(1866: 289) dismissed Comte's encyclopaedic 'la synthèse' out of hand as inferior to the philosophical system of Hegel. Engels later damned Comte as a plagiarist of Saint-Simon, who applied a mathematical formula to scientific developments:

> How little Comte can have been the author of his encyclopaedic arrangement of the natural, which he copied from Saint-Simon, is already evident from the fact that it only serves him for the purpose of *arranging the means of instruction* and *course of instruction,* and so leads to the crazy *enseignement intégral,* where one science is always exhausted before another is even broached, where a basically correct idea is pushed to a mathematical absurdity. (1954: 331)

While Comte developed his theoretical system to resolve the social crisis, Marx's theory of crisis aimed to bring philosophy to a revolutionary conclusion. As a critical social theory of capitalism Marx romantically thought that he had detected in social reality a possibility that the dependency of the working class on capital, for acquiring the means of life through wage labour, could give way to free and transparent human interdependencies.

Critique does not only mean criticism of other social theories; it also refers to criticism of social conditions. This shifts the burden of critique from cognition to ethics. The problem here is that Marx famously rejected morality as a basis for critique, although he and Engels clearly took a normative standpoint against the inhuman conditions of the impoverished working class under capitalism. He assumed that social contrasts would deepen and class antagonisms become more intense. Little account was given by Marx of the possibility of the rising living standards of workers and decreasing social contrasts between the classes. Neither have the many crises of capitalism since 1848 to the present led to the 'inevitable' proletarian revolution predicted by Marx.

MARX'S METHOD

At no point did Marx equate knowledge with a formal method called 'dialectical materialism' or 'historical materialism'. While registering its historical importance, Marx was critical of traditional materialist philosophies. He referred to his 'dialectical' method as 'rational', never as materialist. Rather than a formal or universal method, Marx recognised that social theory always adopts a standpoint from some definite position in social space. For Marx, previous social science took the standpoint of 'civil society' or 'the society of free competition'. Economists like Adam Smith tended to assume that the totality of social relations was an unintended side-effect of countless individuals pursuing their own private interest. As Marx saw it, this neglects the standpoint of human society as a whole, as a 'totality': 'The standpoint of the old materialism is "*civil*" society; the standpoint of the new is *human* society, or socialised humanity' (1845: 145).

What is essentially human, for Marx, is not some abstract quality to be found in individual people but is formed by 'the ensemble of social relations' (1845: 145).

By this he meant that the social system as a whole necessarily precedes and makes possible private interests and public indifference in the first place. In this, knowledge is never neutral. Under capitalism, knowledge accumulated as science and technology over many generations in the form of social labour is stored as privately controlled capital (even if state-owned) to generate greater value than originally obtained at the start of the process. As recent sociologists have emphasised, knowledge is always a stake in the struggle in social relations of domination (Bourdieu, 1990; Postone, 1993).

Marx therefore reserved an independent role for social theory. Clearly, the theoretical presentation of material in Marx's major study *Capital* is organised on different lines from the practical observations on which it was based (Marx, 1976: 102). Only after the material was assembled and analysed (dialectical induction) could the actual movement of social reality be re-presented theoretically (dialectical deduction) (Carchedi, 2011: 44–7). Marx assumed that the outer appearance of things do not coincide with their inner reality. If they did coincide, then all science would be 'superfluous' (1959: 817). However, since they also form part of reality, appearances need to be taken seriously and not simply dismissed as trivial.

In a society dominated by commodities, appearances are necessarily deceptive. Marx called commodities 'social hieroglyphs' because they contain secret meanings concealed behind their reified appearance. Commodity-hieroglyphs have to be deciphered as outward signs of particular kinds of social relations. Science only belatedly deciphers the secret of the 'social hieroglyph' after the commodities take on an objective life as impersonal things concealing the work of human labour that stands behind them. In *Capital*, Marx attempts to reveal that the economic category of 'value' is a 'pure social relation' between people cooperating in production, not a relation between things – although that is how it appears in reality.

Theory rises from the abstract to the concrete, from relations between things (the money form) to social relations between people. Marx began *Capital* with an analysis of the commodity rather than labour, the practical source of surplus value, because the commodity, including labour power, now represents the fundamental dualism that characterises capitalist society: use value and exchange value. From the commodity as the elementary social form of capitalism, Marx progressively examines an increasingly complex chain of concepts – value, the exchange process, money, capital, labour-power, surplus value, the working day, division of labour, technology, wages, capital accumulation, early history of capitalism, and colonialisation.

At this stage it may well appear as if the conceptual order is deduced by an abstract a-priori ideal model rather than according the underlying principles of capitalism itself. The sequence of concepts in Marx's social theory presupposes that the subject – society – is always present as the historically specific conditions that make certain kinds of social theory possible, providing its characteristic problems and ways of thinking:

> therefore this society by no means begins only at the point where one can speak of it *as such;* this holds *for science as well* ... In all forms of society there is one specific kind of production which predominates over the rest, whose relations thus assign

rank and influence to the others. It is a general illumination which bathes all the other
colours and modifies their particularity. (1973: 106–7)

It is a mistake therefore for social theory to begin with the most general categories, say, time and space, human or non-human nature, or generic ideas about
work, technology, freedom, or greed, and to gradually build from these apparently more basic, elementary phenomena to arrive later at more complex,
multifaceted explanations.

However, 'misplaced concreteness' is equally mistaken. To begin inductively
with the concrete and the real, say, population or classes, Marx argued, would
result in a 'chaotic conception of the whole'. This ignores a whole series of preconditions. Population and classes presuppose wage labour and capital, which
presuppose exchange, division of labour, money, and so on. The concrete is a
complex totality of interdependent relations – 'unity of the diverse' – therefore
it must form the result of empirical theory, not its starting point. 'As a rule, the
most general abstractions arise only in the midst of the richest possible concrete
development, where one thing appears common to many, to all' (1973: 104).
Even though detailed observation of the concrete is always the starting point for
empirical research, Marx considered that the most valid procedure for social
theory is to begin from the most characteristic *social form* – the commodity
form for capitalist social relations – rather than the most general form, such as
labour or wealth.

Social forms express the empirical movement of society, what kind of processes
and relations necessarily constitute it, and, given this, what possible directions it
can take in future. Capital not only presupposes the definite social form of wages,
profit and rent but must also reproduce the social relations of production and
distribution as the precondition of its survival (Marx, 1959: 879). Marx's theory of
social forms overcomes the static philosophical dualism of subjective agency and
objective structure. The structure–agency dualism, Marx famously noted, con-
ceives reality 'only in the form of the object or of *contemplation*, but not as *human
sensuous activity*, *practice*, not subjectively' (1845: 143).

However, social theory is not simultaneous with social practice but always
takes place after the event (*post-festum*), working from the finished social form
rather than actual course of social evolution (Marx, 1976: 168). Gramsci argued
in this vein:

A structural phase can be concretely studied and analysed only after it has gone
through its whole process of development, and not during the process itself, except
hypothetically and with the explicit proviso that one is dealing with hypotheses.
(1971: 408)

Because bourgeois society represents the most complex historical organisation,
the categories which express its social relations provide an insight into earlier
social formations like antiquity. As Marx put it, 'Human anatomy contains a key
to the anatomy of the ape' (1973: 105). This retrospective principle reverses the
assumption in much social theory, as in Durkheim, that simple, 'primitive' tribal

units hold the key to later, more complex social divisions of labour. This does not mean for Marx that later social forms can be projected back onto earlier social relations in the manner of Weber's ideal-types or Simmel's social forms.

The principle of historical specificity requires that knowledge of a later social form may illuminate an earlier one without being made identical to it. When socio-historical problems are posed concretely, scholastic point-scoring about the precise relationship between concepts – say, between base and superstructure – loses its force. For instance, contrary to the fixed base-superstructure model, Marx (1973: 110–1) recognised that art often exercises considerable autonomy from social development. Formulated in a general way, art (superstructure) can easily be made the prisoner of social conditions (base) or escape them almost entirely (absolute autonomy).

Conceived in an abstract way, little is understood of how art develops under its own aesthetic concepts and problems and how the field of art is related to the wider social forms of development. As soon as this is posed in concrete terms, however, the specific relationship of art and society becomes more explicable. So while Greek art and epic poetry are associated with ancient forms of social development, what needs to be explained is why they are held up as aesthetic ideals by completely different forms of society. For Marx (1973: 111), the continuing pleasure afforded by Greek art lies in what 'the historic childhood of humanity' reveals about the needs of contemporary society: 'Does not the true character of each epoch come alive in the nature of its children?'

COMMODIFICATION AS A SOCIAL PROCESS

Marx did not describe capitalism in its step-by-step historical development. Throughout *Capital* he makes the assumption that long-run historical processes are concentrated in a specific form of social domination – the commodity form. Where classical political economists like David Ricardo began with the abstract concept of 'value', Marx begins *Capital* with the commodity as the specific form of wealth peculiar to capitalism. Only when this specific form becomes generalised does the relationship between things – money, commodity, capital, machines – dominate and conceal relations between human beings.

When the commodity becomes a general social form, concrete phenomena can only be approached as a 'real abstraction'. Social relations are turned into an abstraction by commodity exchange. Here the specific quality of things is dominated by the 'universal equivalence' of money relations. Therefore, the concrete must be the result, not the starting point, of analysis. Marx revealed that the commodity is a '*real* abstraction' arising from practical social relations in the labour process rather than a *formal* abstraction locked inside theoretical philosophy or political economy (Sohn-Rethel, 1978).

Social theory ought not to speak about 'labour' or 'capital' or 'class struggle' or 'technology' in general but only as specific forms of social relations under distinctive conditions. It is the specifically bourgeois form of property, freedom, individuality, work, the state, family, 'national interests' and morality that Marx sought to over-come, not some eternal point of principle about wealth and work inequalities. Commodity fetishism, for instance, was simply not possible in any previous society since power relations were based on direct forms of *personal dependency* between, say, slaves and slave-owners or peasants and lords. In this situation of direct, inter-personal domination, the objects of labour could not assume a life of their own (Marx, 1976: 170). In contrast, as social labour becomes abstract, quantifiable and interchangeable under capitalism, power relations take the necessary social form of *impersonal interdependencies*.

Generalised interdependency through exchange value is the result of a long-term historical process, Marx argued. First, relations of *personal dependence* are the earliest social forms possible in conditions of isolated human labour. Second, relations of *personal independence* are founded on the 'objective' dependence of family, clan and community to generate universal human needs and capacities. Third, dense relations of *social interdependence* in an advanced division of social labour subordinate the community to private individuality. Individuals now pro-duce for society but their production is not 'directly' social. It is no longer a direct relation of independent individuals but an indirect relation mediated by things (commodities):

> Exchange, when mediated by exchange value and money, presupposes the all-round dependence of the producers on one another, together with the total isolation of their private interests from one another, as well as a division of social labour whose unity and mutual complementarity exist in the form of a natural relation, as it were, external to the individuals and independent of them. (Marx, 1973: 158)

As society became dominated by exchange relations, direct relations of personal dependency were replaced with impersonal relations of many-sided dependence on other producers. Reciprocal dependence of all on all is expressed by the con-stant imperative for exchange to take place. Social interdependencies are mediated by the power of money: 'The individual carries his social power, as well as his bond with society, in his pocket' (Marx, 1973: 157). In conditions of universal exchange, social relations appear as alien and objective, dominating individuals as an independent coercive force.

Specific processes and relations therefore need to be studied in their concrete development, not deified by fixed concepts like 'class' or 'value'. Each form of society – ancient, feudal and capitalist – must be studied according to the relations and processes specific to it as transitory and contradictory social forms. Even the most universal forms of 'pure thought' presuppose specific social forms. What is specific to capitalism is that human labour, which occurs in all societies, is trans-formed into 'labour power', a special form of commodity, experienced as the universal compulsion for work to take the form of wage labour (Marx, 1976: 275, n.4). In *Capital*, for instance, Marx focused on the economic form, the production of commodities (products) by commodities (labour power), as the distinguishing feature of the capitalist mode of production, and relegated economic forms that predominated in earlier societies, such as trading capital and lending capital.

Previous forms of exchange and distribution are transformed by capitalism into radically new forms like 'finance capital'.

THEORY OF CRISIS

For Marx, crisis is the 'normal' social condition of capitalism. Crisis is built into the accumulation imperative of capitalism and constantly threatens to devastate the bases of social existence. Capitalism as a socio-economic system cannot escape its inner tendency towards crisis, bringing in its wake destructive human costs, general insecurity and stunted lives. In contrast, social theory from Comte to Durkheim to Parsons pathologised social crises as abnormal deviations from the regular, stable functioning of society. As the theory of universal crisis, classical Marxism was not particularly concerned with the appearance of social stability and order in bourgeois society but with its tendency to general breakdown and instability (Korsch, 1971).

Crudely stated, Marx (1959) argued that as capital became more technologically intensive, the more it displaced labour as the real source of surplus value. A lower proportion of labour relative to capital produces a tendency for the rate of profit to fall across the system. The result is periodic crises of overproduction and mass unemployment. Marx's theoretical analysis of the inner 'law of motion' of capital predicted deepening and more frequent crises.

Crisis theory deduced capitalism as a system that functions under an absolute imperative to be inherently wasteful, destructive and fragile. The only way out of the crisis within capitalism, at least for a period, is for sufficient quantities of capital to be physically destroyed through bankruptcy, rationalisation or global warfare. Without the widespread destruction of capital the system will struggle to reproduce itself. Such hypotheses seemed to be borne out by the 1914–1918 world war, the 1929 stock market crash, state dictatorships, the 1939–1945 world war, fascist genocide, colonial wars, and nuclear warfare. Marx's theory of crisis was given a more optimistic gloss by the non-Marxist economist Joseph Schumpeter (2010: 73–5), who claimed that capitalism needed periods of intense crisis to slough off inefficient units of production and allow a new phase of technological dynamism, a process he termed 'creative destruction'.

On the basis of Marx's theory of economic crisis, later Marxists predicted that the objective trajectory of capitalist development would result in catastrophic breakdown and collapse. In 1913 Rosa Luxemburg (2003) argued that collapse was only averted because capitalism could still expand into the 'non-capitalist spaces' of countries under imperialist domination. Once capitalism became a truly 'universal system' that covered the entire globe, however, the logic of capital accumulation would plunge world society into catastrophic decline and 'barbarism'. In 1920 Nikolai Bukharin (Bukharin and Preobrazhensky, 1969) thought that the inevitable process of collapse would be hastened by the downward spiral of the productive forces as military spending consumed the social surplus on a colossal scale, producing nothing but waste and destruction. In 1929 Henryk Grossmann (1992) in *The*

Law of Accumulation and Breakdown of the Capitalist System located crisis within the disproportions that necessarily emerge within the labour process between the exploitation of labour power (exchange value) and the cooperation of labour (use value).

In their different ways, these were deductions from Marx's closed economic model of capitalism. However, it is not only that the economy, narrowly conceived, enters periodic crisis; the condition of crisis is endemic to capitalist society in the form of universal self-alienation. Scientific, technological, cultural and intellectual progress gives life to material forces that come to dominate, haunt and brutalise human life. Technological development, Marx declared, is a more dangerous force for social stability than the most subversive revolutionaries:

> On the one hand, there have started into life industrial and scientific forces, which no epoch of the former human history had ever suspected. On the other hand, there exist symptoms of decay, far surpassing the horrors recorded of the latter times of the Roman Empire. In our days, everything seems pregnant with its contrary. (1856: 577)

Marx reached for obstetric metaphors – pregnancy, birth pangs, womb – to express the living forces of the new society whose potential, he believed, was being nurtured within the carcase of the old one. Although he outlined a historical series of modes of production – ancient, feudal and capitalist – Marx recognised that history never develops in a straight line. Bourgeois society may be afflicted by a universal crisis of human existence but progress to a higher form of civilisation – socialism or communism – was far from inevitable, notwithstanding rhetoric by Marx and Engels to the contrary.

One problem for crisis theory is that while the logic of crisis may undermine the legitimacy of capitalism it cannot by itself effect a transition to socialism. For that, society needed to create a force with a motivation and the potential power to replace capitalism. Marx deduced that this force of social transformation could only be the working class. Given its poverty, numerical size, democratic spirit and central position in the production process the working class had nothing to lose but everything to gain by gambling on revolutionary change, thus liberating the whole of society from the distortions to human potential inflicted by capitalism.

Generations of Marxists wrestled with the gap between Marx's closed theory of endemic crisis alongside the reality of the enduring structures of capitalism. Revolutionary social theory was forced to account for non-revolutionary reality. For the Polish Marxist Rosa Luxemburg (1903) the problem was that Marx's theory outstripped the practical needs and understanding of the working class in their day-to-day struggles. Marxist theory therefore develops separately from working-class conditions. From a subordinate position in class relations, workers cannot create by their own efforts an intellectual culture independent of bourgeois culture.

> Although certain 'socialist' professors may acclaim the wearing of neckties, the use of visiting cards, and the riding of bicycles by proletarians as notable instances of participation in cultural progress, the working class as such remains outside contemporary

culture. Notwithstanding the fact that the workers create with their own hands the whole social substratum of this culture, they are only admitted to its enjoyment insofar as such admission is requisite to the satisfactory performance of their functions in the economic and social process of capitalist society. (Luxemburg, 1903: 149–50)

Luxemburg concluded that because practical struggles do not demand much from theory, Marxist theory is prone to stagnation. Once Marx had deduced the agency of proletarian revolution from the source of surplus value (labour) and its preconditions from the increasing socialisation of production (capital) there was little impetus for further theoretical development.

BUKHARIN'S SOCIOLOGY

An initial attempt to extract the sociological kernel in Marxist theory was made by Nikolai Bukharin's 1921 popular textbook *Historical Materialism: A System of Sociology* (2011). Merely by mentioning sociology in the title of his book, Bukharin scandalised the metaphysical system of 'dialectical materialism'. Bukharin made the bold claim that historical materialism is not primarily a methodology that can be applied to concrete events, as some Marxists understood it. And neither is it a superior type of political economy or history. Instead, historical materialism is 'the general theory of society and the laws of its evolution, i.e., sociology' (2011: 15). History describes events at a particular place and time. Sociology locates these within a more general theory of social processes, relations and structures. An abstract social theory is necessary, Bukharin argued, to identify causal processes and patterns behind the chaos of events.

However, Bukharin rejected teleological explanations of historical development. Teleology pictures society as conforming to some mysterious purpose or plan devised either externally, by a God or world-spirit, or 'immanently', by the steady development or inner 'progress' of phenomena, to realise a predetermined end goal. Social theory can only describe the general tendency of social-historical processes. It cannot predict specific phenomena like crises, wars, and revolutions. Such 'disturbances' are a result of social contradictions that are tending towards either 'gradual development' (evolution) or 'sudden leaps' (revolution), or a transitional situation (crisis).

At a certain point in social development the incremental accretion of changes reaches a point where any additional change suddenly produces a qualitatively new situation. Bukharin (2011: 81) illustrates this typical Marxist statement of dialectical change of quantity into quality with a fable by Tolstoy (1962: 37–8). A hungry peasant ate three large rolls, one after the other. Still hungry, he wolfed down a pretzel. Suddenly he felt satiated. The peasant reasoned that eating the rolls had been a complete waste since it was the pretzel that appeased his hunger. Tolstoy's lesson, for Bukharin, is that theory cannot isolate the last phase of a process but must account for the preceding conditions that make a sudden change possible.

Another way to see Bukharin's point is through the distinction made in philosophy between insufficient and necessary conditions. Causes (rolls) are 'Insufficient but Necessary' conditions that produce some further condition (satiety), which is realised by an 'Unnecessary but Sufficient' effect (pretzel) (Mackie, 1965). Here the 'rolls' exemplify historical necessity, for without them the pretzel alone could not have satisfied the peasant's hunger pangs. While the rolls were necessary causes they were not in themselves sufficient ones, and while the pretzel was a sufficient cause it was not a necessary one.

In reality the relationship between causal necessity and sufficient effects is rarely so clear cut (von Wright, 1974). As Bukharin emphasises, in any dynamic system, cause and effect constantly change places. Nothing in the world is immutable. Continual motion, becoming, and transformation are the hallmarks of the dialectical method, even where reciprocal effects and change are not observed directly: '*In the first place, therefore, the dialectic method of interpretation demands that all phenomena be considered in their indissoluble relations; in the second place, that they be considered in their state of motion*' (Bukharin, 2011: 67).

SOCIAL REPRODUCTION

Yet by reputation *Historical Materialism* adhered to a crude mechanical model of economic causes that generate various social, political, and ideological effects in a one-way process and dogmatically dismiss other social theories. Bukharin's theory of equilibrium is not quite the static model of society that his many critics assume (Tarbuck, 1989). It is a relational theory that emphasises the dynamic, mutual constitution, and process character of social phenomena. Against fatalistic theories of historical inevitability, Bukharin (anticipating his critics) asserted that the role of human agency in 'social equilibrium' is 'indissoluble' from all other relations. Bukharin transposed the Comtean distinction between static and dynamic social relations into a Marxist binary of socio-technological *stagnation*, where everything seems permanent, and socio-technological *dynamism*, where everything seems temporary and contingent.

Equilibrium is understood by Bukharin as a process, not a stable condition. Social relations have a tendency to be reproduced on the whole rather than to simply disintegrate, even in crisis conditions. If this tendency to equilibrium did not operate, then the social world would disintegrate. So while contradictions abound in class society, 'society and certain groups within it continue their relatively permanent existence' (Bukharin, 2011: 157). Society was defined as a system by Bukharin because it is founded on the survival and reproduction of mutual interactions – what Marx called 'unity of the diverse' – that endure over relatively long periods of time. Since capitalist society is in perpetual motion, social equilibrium was not conceived by Bukharin as a stable state of rest but as a state of disturbance. Social forces are balanced only exceptionally, if at all. Stable equilibrium was viewed as a purely 'imaginary' ideal by Bukharin (2011: 76). Conflict and contradictions are concealed by a stable equilibrium but are forced to the surface by any disturbance to the equipoise.

As an ideal model, Bukharin helped to translate the tripartite formula of Hegel's dialectic into a social system – thesis (equilibrium), antithesis (disturbance) and synthesis (new equilibrium) – while jettisoning the metaphysical baggage of the 'organic' social theories of Comte and Spencer that 'reconstructs society as a huge fabulous beast' (Bukharin, 2011: 88). Society's internal structure and external environment change together in ways that determine whether the system has a tendency to grow ('positive' unstable equilibrium), decline ('negative' unstable equilibrium), or stagnate (stable equilibrium). First, between society and nature a necessary process of social reproduction occurs if society is not to collapse. Human society adapts itself to and mediates external nature through social technology. This is not a teleological or anthropomorphic view of nature: 'nothing could be more incorrect than to regard nature from the teleological point of view: man, the lord of creation, with nature created for his use, and all things adapted to human needs' (2011: 104). As Marx argued, in changing external nature, people change their own natures and create for themselves new needs and desires (Geras, 1983).

Second, society is structured internally by the interdependency of people, things, and ideas. Together, these cohere to produce a historically specific 'system' of social technology. This system depends on the mutual position of classes in society, their function in the division of labour, and changes in socio-technical organisation overall. Social relations between classes are conditioned by their unequal power to 'distribute' people and things. The distribution of products in the market relies on the prior distribution of the means of production and the distribution of people as waged labour. In contrast, labour lacks the unilateral power to 'distribute' capital or the technical means of labour. From the standpoint of labour the means of production take the form of an external 'thing' outside their control, what Marx called the 'capital fetish', the necessary correlate within the production process of the 'commodity fetish' in the market distribution of goods and products.

Bukharin viewed the contradiction between system and environment as more fundamental than structural contradictions within the system. Internal structural equilibrium depends on and is a function of external environmental equilibrium (Bukharin, 2011: 79). This emphasis on social environment over individuals paralleled Durkheim's social facts. However, Bukharin charged Durkheim with retreating from the 'materialist' implications of social morphology by turning 'moral density' into a wholly separate phenomenon 'incapable of explanation' (2011: 93). Even when people set out with a conscious purpose to achieve some preconceived end, as in the 'external' moral regulation of social relations through laws, institutions, or ideology, account is still needed of interdependent relations of cause and effect. Since cause and effect are not fixed properties, in mutual process they change places – effects become causes and vice versa (2011: 228). Although in their actions people pursue certain ends, the results are rarely those originally planned. Bukharin predicted that 'blind social forces' would give way to collective foresight of social necessity: 'Freedom is the recognition of necessity' (2011: 42).

Dominant social norms, manners and customs, what Bukharin called 'social ideology', are the preconditions of equilibrium. Social ideologies prevent internal contradictions from destroying the social system. Following Simmel, Bukharin (2011: 209–10) argued that the common forms of *social* ideology become lodged in the mental life of individuals through their mutual interaction in society. He offered Simmel's 'brilliant' example of the 'double function' of fashion as a social ideology holding a group together while simultaneously distinguishing it from other groups (2011: 203). A specific class psychology, distinct from class interests but closer to later sociological ideas of 'habitus', takes hold of individuals from a definite, shared position in the social system. Social ideologies systematise the almost imperceptible dispositions of class psychology and often lag behind them. As examples of social ideologies Bukharin pointed to contemporary sociological studies by Weber and Sombart on the 'spirit of capitalism' as expressing the collective psychology of the entrepreneur as a social type. As Durkheim also noted, as the division of labour in society increases, 'ideological labour' becomes an increasingly independent and specialised function (2011: 217).

CRITIQUE AND DEVELOPMENT

In the case of Bukharin's sociology a consensus developed among Marxist intellectuals that it was deeply flawed. Some found that it was too 'mechanistic' and did not leave scope for human action, such as class struggle. Bukharin was accused of over-simplifying, even for the purposes of a popular textbook, social and political processes into formulaic schemata. Lukacs had little sympathy for Bukharin's theory of sociology as a 'historical method' since it threatened to set up a rival science in competition with the 'dialectical method':

> The dialectic can do without such independent substantive achievements; its realm is that of the historical process as a whole, whose individual, concrete, unrepeatable moments reveal its dialectical essence in the qualitative difference between them and in the continuous transformation of their objective structure. The *totality* is the territory of the dialectic. A 'scientific' general sociology, on the other hand, if it does not surpass itself into a mere epistemology, must have its own independent achievements allowing one type of law. (1972: 140)

Lukacs has in mind the construction of theoretical systems premised on a single principle like the law of equilibrium applied to both natural and social phenomena.

Bukharin's 'essential error' was to adopt the 'false objectivity' of technological determinism in place of a theory of social relations that Lukacs saw as essential to Marxism. To make social and economic development dependent on 'technique', as Bukharin does, is to turn it into a self-sufficient 'fetish'. Against vulgar Marxism, Lukacs appealed to Max Weber to argue that social organisation based on relations of slavery, not technology as such, hindered development in the ancient world: 'Slavery is not made possible by a low level of technique; rather slavery as a form of the domination of labor makes the rationalization of the labor process, and hence a rational technique, impossible' (1972: 138). The superstructure cannot be reduced to the economic base in any direct way as Bukharin tends to assume. Against claims that the same class dominates both the economy and the state Lukacs allows for a range of possible relationships: 'For it is perfectly possible that a balance of economic power between two classes in competition may produce a state apparatus not really controlled by either (if it must secure many compromises between them) so that the economic structure is by no means simply reflected in the state' (1972: 135).

Lukacs claimed that Bukharin explained the inability of social science to predict the precise timing of social processes as a result of imperfect statistical knowledge rather than the unevenness of social processes themselves. Since social processes are determined by human practice not abstract laws, no absolute predictions about the future are possible. Differences in social phenomena demand that a qualitative distinction be made between statistically determined natural laws of development and the social tendencies of the historical process overall.

A similar criticism was made by Gramsci (1971: 438) that predictions about the future are made without being affected by practical human action or the 'collective will', which cannot be know with any definiteness in advance: 'one can "scientifically" foresee only the struggle, but not the concrete moments of the struggle'.

However, Bukharin recognised only a general *tendency* towards social reproduction or 'equilibrium'. In fact, the mere possibility of society, Bukharin (2011: 93) argued, is 'conditional' on 'a very complicated system of mutual interactions between the various persons, ... interactions [that] are extremely varied in quality and quantity'. The problem of prediction for Bukharin was one of social complexity and the curve of general tendencies of development, not imperfect statistical data, as Lukacs asserted.

For Karl Korsch (1970), Bukharin fell into one side of two falsely opposed 'deformations' within Marxism: philosophical theory and 'general sociology'. Both tendencies substituted a 'purely theoretical critique' of bourgeois society for 'revolutionary practice'. In the case of Bukharin, 'the fluid methodology of Marx's materialist dialectic freezes into a number of theoretical formulations about the causal interconnection of historical phenomena in different areas of society – in other words it became something that could best be described as a general systematic sociology' (Korsch, 1970: 56). When Korsch's (1938) later book, *Karl Marx*, appeared in a London-based series on 'Modern Sociologists' he gave no quarter to the founders of sociology, Comte and Spencer. Later sociology was forced to confront the limits to positivism's evolutionary model of social progress to take account of the crisis of social relations under capitalism (Korsch, 1938: 204).

By the late 1930s, Korsch (1938: 47) accepted that classical German sociology developed out of a dialogue with Karl Marx and that the contemporary social theory of Tönnies, Weber, Scheler, Mannheim, and Sombart had been 'modified' by a 'mutual interaction' with Marxism. Marxism was part of the received wisdom of German sociology. Moreover, Korsch denied that Marx had established a general theory applicable to all of society. Korsch argued that Marxism was a social science that describes the specific nature of bourgeois society, which, 'being a strictly empirical investigation into definite historical forms of society, does not need a philosophical support' (1938: 169). Hegel's contribution to

Marx's development was not the dialectical method but an empirical science of the history of 'civil society' (1938: 179).

As a social science Marxism inductively applies observational research methods rather than deduce prescriptions from general concepts of an uncertain validity:

> An exact science cannot form its general concepts by the simple abstraction of certain more or less arbitrarily chosen traits of the given historical form of bourgeois society. It must secure the knowledge of the general contained in that particular form of society by the exact investigation of all the historical conditions underlying its emergence from another state of society and by the actual modifications of its present form under exactly established conditions. Only thus can social research be transformed into an exact science based on observation and experiment. (1938: 79)

In this way, Korsch argued, it might be possible to control sophistical worldplay about 'materialism' and refused to entertain the 'crude thesis' of a sociology of knowledge reduced to 'material' class.

Marxist social theory must allow a degree of mediated autonomy between class position, class interests, and ideologies. Indeed, Korsch drew increasingly away from a speculative philosophy of praxis and came closer to the scientific viewpoint of the Vienna Circle, writing on the methodology of sociology and psychology for their journal, and favourably acknowledging the work of leading logical empiricist Philipp Frank (Korsch, 1938: 227; Lewin and Korsch, 1939). In his work with the social psychologist Kurt Lewin emphasising the relationship of theory and practice, Korsch contributed to the development of 'action research' as a research method (van Elteren, 1992).

Marx thought that he had settled his accounts with philosophy. Not so. An entire tradition of philosophical Marxism emerged in the stormy years of the 1920s to assert the subjective agency of the working class rather than submit to the objective contradictions of capitalism. Yet at the moment of its highest political achievement Marxism was exposed to multiple and conflicting re-interpretations. In some quarters, Marxism was transformed into a pure, self-sufficient source of theoretical authority, its fundamental framework right in all essentials just so long as the correct 'dialectical' key is applied to the social mechanism. Others kept Marxism open to wider developments in philosophy and social theory and avoided the stagnant dogmatism assumed by Marxist 'purity'. With the revival of revolution in the first decades of the twentieth century, Marxist theory once again became revolutionary and shed some of its scholastic shell. And as the prospects of revolution receded Marxism again took the form of an abstract critical theory.

Marxist theory does not limit itself to theory for its own sake but aims to clarify what precisely is revolutionary from the standpoint of the proletariat. Marxists, like Korsch (1970) and Lukacs (1971), understood Marx's social theory as the theory of the revolutionary process. Gramsci (1971) called Marxism 'the philosophy of praxis' to emphasise that philosophy and revolutionary practice are mutually defining. Korsch argued that philosophy, as it had been understood traditionally and adopted by 'vulgar Marxism', needs to be abolished. Marxism itself needs to be understood not as a timeless methodology or finished theoretical system but as an expression of specific socio-historical processes, 'the only really "materialist and therefore scientific method"' (Marx, 1973: 50).

While Lukacs and Gramsci attempted to reformulate Marxist theory, Korsch came to see the roots of the crisis in Marxist theory increasingly in the isolation of 'pure theory' from historical and theoretical development. Marx and Engels developed their social theory at a certain point in the history of capitalism and the class struggle. Marx achieved a double theoretical innovation. First, Marx criticised the class society of his time from the standpoint of the working class and the theories of the utopian socialists like Saint-Simon and Charles Fourier. Second, and often neglected, Marx also criticised utopian theories and working-class movements by applying the more advanced methods of 'bourgeois science'. In the crisis conditions of the 1870s, Marx's theory, developed in the previous period, was uncritically absorbed into the workers' movement in a purely formal and theoretical manner. Theory became an abstract and passive 'scientific system', limited to uncovering objective laws of social development, with revolution postponed indefinitely. From Marx's category 'value' a Marxist economic theory was deduced as more scientifically rigorous than that of classical bourgeois economics.

However, the red thread of Marx – the scourge of formal theory, ideological criticism, and morality – was broken. Without an orientation on revolutionary practice, Marxism became simply another critical theory of society, a theory of passing conjunctures rather than structuring processes. Without the strategic agency of the proletariat the world-defining function of Marxism is gone. Marxism became an ethical rather than a sociological critique of capitalism, placing moral appeals to a higher vision of freedom, justice or equality before the concrete analyses of social forms and processes. Marx claimed that no new society can be born before the old one has exhausted all its possibilities. Capitalism continues to expand unevenly as a worldwide system. It is this process of social reproduction that a critical theory of society would seek to explain.

Social theory does not exist in empty space. In the first decades of the twentieth century, like the first decades of the twenty-first, a world economy and a world culture were emerging alongside the possibility of a world society. Yet this prospect remained, then as now, perilously divided by the concentration of military and economic power of rival states that periodically sends society 'whirling in the mad hurricane of world wars' (Bukharin, 1972: 158). In his critique of the Austrian school of economic theory, Bukharin (2011: 8) identified not only its sociological significance as a new, ahistorical theory of the subjective individualism of consumers, corresponding to a new leisure class (*rentiers*) living purely on financial investments far removed from the world of production, he also argued that it is necessary to deconstruct theory *as* theory as well as reconstructing its sociological context:

A sociological characterization of a certain theory, therefore, does not relieve us of the responsibility of waging war against it even in the field of a purely logical criticism. (2011: 8)

Bukharin assumed that the state of social theory in the present provides the highest point from which to judge all previous theory. Yet if, as Hegel claimed, 'the rational is real and the real is rational', then taken in its historical context earlier theory was just as valid in its own time and performed a necessary social function for the groups that needed it (Gramsci, 1971: 449).

4

NIETZSCHE'S TURN: MAX WEBER AND GEORG SIMMEL

From different starting points Simmel, Weber, and Durkheim were united in the quest for a general sociological method as a response to the wider crisis of European culture between 1890 and 1920 (Hughes, 1958; Liebersohn, 1988). Modernity had earlier been criticised by the poet Charles Baudelaire in France and the philosopher Friedrich Nietzsche in Germany as banal and lacking in heroic virtues, experience and personality. Confidence in the positive progress of science, culture and society was badly shaken by the time of the catastrophe of the 1914–1918 war. While social theory in *fin de siècle* Europe emerged as part of the response to a wider 'revolt against positivism' and the democratic demands of political modernity (Hughes, 1958), Durkheim, Weber, and Simmel refused to accept that the 'tragic' or 'anomic' condition of modernity would inevitably destroy individuality, erode morality, and debase culture.

In 1914 Durkheim, Simmel, and Weber supported the war aims of their respective states as a way of unifying fractured national societies. Yet crisis took a distinct shape in different state-societies. First, the states of Germany and Italy, created as recently as fifty years ago, were exposed as fragile and unstable authoritarian entities, placing in jeopardy what Weber viewed as the rational sources of legitimate authority in the judicious statecraft of enlightened bourgeois elites. In France, republican ideologies of patriotism were undermined by the infamous Dreyfus affair that rumbled on between 1894 and 1906 when a Jewish officer, Captain Alfred Dreyfus, was framed for treason. Durkheim demanded a public mobilisation of the intellectuals to counter the 'deep moral crisis' and to re-affirm humanist universalism and social justice that Durkheim identified with the French Republic (Fournier, 2013: 285–308).

Second, by the 1890s socialism had developed as a mass working-class movement alongside the appeal of Marxism as an explanation for social suffering, state authoritarianism and economic crises. In different ways, Durkheim, Weber, and Simmel engaged critically with Marxism, which they tended to see as too crudely

fixated on economic explanations for social phenomena. Weber formed a relationship with a bohemian community of 'ethical anarchists' while Simmel participated
in the German feminist movement (Whimster, 1999; Simmel, 1984, 1997: 270–4).
Meanwhile, Durkheim (1962) addressed the socialist tradition in France established by Saint-Simon and the revival of religious movements in protest against
the rule of science.

Third, large-scale, impersonal organisations, urbanisation, and technological
change fragmented public life and undermined liberalism's ideology of the sovereign individual. The crisis of modernity was conceived by Durkheim (1933: 28) in
terms of an 'abnormal' division of labour that produced the 'veritable sociological monstrosity' of 'pathological' forms of restless individualism that he termed
'anomie'. For Durkheim the crisis of anomie in France found a response in the
demands of socialism, religious revival, and the development of sociology. To
address the crisis of anomie a fully fledged science of society was needed to displace an increasingly discredited liberal economics.

Sociology appeared necessary in a situation where shared morality and meaning was no longer produced spontaneously by the social order: 'because our social
state is abnormal, because the unsettled collective organization no longer functions with the authority of instinct – for that [crisis] is always what determines the
rousing of scientific thought and its extension to a new order of things' (Durkheim,
1962: 284). While there was undoubtedly a nostalgic longing in social theorists
like Ferdinand Tönnies (2002) for an integrated, organic community or association (*Gemeinschaft*) against a fragmented and impersonal modern society
(*Gesellschaft*), Durkheim, like Simmel and Weber, recognised that there could be
no return to pre-modern, collective forms of society based on what he called
'mechanical solidarity'.

Fourth, the development of modernism as an artistic movement threw down a
challenge to traditional cultural values. While this alarmed social and cultural conservatives, Weber and Simmel were more sympathetic towards the avant-garde
(Leck, 2000). More widely, impatience with the diligence demanded by science as a
means to end moral disorder, the emotional satisfactions of middle-class culture and
religious cults provided more immediate responses to public and personal crises.
Cultural solutions to crisis are easier to absorb than the laborious detour of social
theory. In their haste to resolve moral crisis, Durkheim argued that religion and
socialism put things the wrong way round: 'The problem must be put this way: to
discover through science the moral restraint which can regulate economic life, and
by this regulation control selfishness and thus gratify needs' (Durkheim, 1962: 285).

One major strand of European theory would have rejected Durkheim's moral
diagnosis of the crisis out of hand: the philosophy of Friedrich Nietzsche
(1844–1900). Although he was familiar with Marxist theory, Durkheim (1982:
167–74) was far less captivated by the Marx–Nietzsche poles of social theory
than his German counterparts. As a social reformer, Durkheim aimed to overcome the crisis of anomie by recourse to moral regulation in a way that Nietzsche
would have viewed as part of the sickly decadence of modernity.

This chapter concentrates on how Simmel and Weber's generation were
entranced by the temper, if not the letter, of Nietzsche's critique of modernity.

From Nietzsche, Simmel and Weber took different but overlapping approaches to social theory. Although they shared certain themes about modernity, Nietzsche's theory could not be readily translated into the kind of methodologically rigorous sociology demanded by Max Weber. The more philosophically inclined Simmel engaged more directly with Nietzsche to develop a type of theoretical relativism or 'perspectivism', what David Frisby (1992) called 'sociological impressionism', and left behind his earlier positivist-influenced social theory. Lacking absolute foundations, Simmel's social theory took an aesthetic turn, rightly or wrongly, as the only adequate way to capture the fleeting experiences and fluid social relations of modernity.

NIETZSCHEAN SOCIAL THEORY

By concentrating on the crisis of human qualities wrought by capitalist modernity, the uncompromising but ambiguous philosophy of Friedrich Nietzsche, along with Marx and Freud, fundamentally restructured social theory (Love, 1986; McNally, 2001). Indeed, Jurgen Habermas (1987) identifies Nietzsche as the 'turning point' in social theory that made possible 'post-modernity' in the late twentieth century. However, it may be overstating things to say with Stauth and Turner (1988: 101) that Nietzsche provides the 'absent centre of Weberian sociology and this argument could be extended to modern social science as a whole where ... Nietzsche's themes of language, morality and reason form the framework for modern analysis of the character of modernism and post-modernism.' Certainly, Nietzsche's critique of modernity resurfaced in response to the inter-war crisis in Europe, for instance in Horkheimer and Adorno's *Dialectic of Enlightenment* (1972). But while post-structural and post-modern social theory share Nietzsche's playful embrace of desire and his trenchant critique of modernity, they tend to neglect Nietzsche's demand for elite superiority, domination over inferiors, the severe command of self-discipline, and the value of science, honesty, and truth as human achievements (Antonio, 2001).

Sam Whimster (2004: 299) memorably compared Nietzsche to a 'sadistic dentist' stabbing at the roots of European culture. Nietzsche saw the European crisis as a never-ending repetition of the newness, nothingness, and meaningless of modernity, a condition he termed 'nihilism' (Goudsblom, 1980). This is expressed by Nietzsche as the crisis of 'will' in modernity. Human subjectivity or 'will' is driven inwards and the personality dominated by external constraints such as the state, education, markets, science, and liberal ideology. Paradoxically, in modernity the 'ascetic ideal' requires a will not to will:

> this hatred of the human, and even more of the animal, and more still of the material, this horror of the senses, of reason itself, this fear of happiness and beauty, this longing to get away from all appearance, change, becoming, death, wishing, from longing itself – all this means – let us dare grasp it – *a will to nothingness*, an aversion to life, a rebellion against the most fundamental presuppositions of life; but it is and remains a *will*! ... man would rather will nothingness than not will. (Nietzsche, 1995: 189)

Modernity demands that human beings forget that they alone are the authors of their own world. Modern civilisation curbs outward signs of emotion and spontaneity by individuals. Christianity placed the blame on individuals for their own emotional and moral suffering using the language of sin and guilt. Due to a lack of resolute action to uncover the truth of human self-determination, Nietzsche predicted that Europe was hurtling towards a violent catastrophe in the next century. Disaster could only be averted by the emergence of a self-willed 'superman' or 'overman' (*Übermensch*) able to rise above mass banality.

Nietzsche is like a modern Hamlet making a 'heroic' commitment to overcome personal and social crises that bordered on madness. For Nietzsche the body has its own drives, needs, and desires that human cognition can never fully comprehend or control (McNally, 2001: 29). Notoriously, Nietzsche valorised the self-sufficient male body alongside a misogynist fear of women and the reproductive body, as well as ignoring bodily frailties despite his own failing physical and mental health. The denial of (male) bodily instincts is, for Nietzsche, a denial of the self.

Self-denial is the basis of the herd morality in modern culture. Both bourgeois society and socialism express the decline of civilisation since both systems level human beings into an undifferentiated mass. Bodies are homogenised by the state and the market and lost to the self. The mediocrity and servility of the disembodied masses produce only resentment against the 'little things' of everyday life, its desires, pleasures, generosity, and beauty (Stauth and Turner, 1988). However, there is little sense in Nietzsche (or Foucault more recently) that the frailty of the body, all too humanly evident in disease, sickness, hunger, pain, and ageing, produces a collective need for the protection provided by social solidarity that is more than the endless play of power struggles (Turner and Rojek, 2001).

In this Nietzsche embraced nihilism as the unavoidable truth of a world without meaning (Goudsblom, 1980: 20). Nietzsche held on to an idea of 'veracity' even though he disparaged it in others who noisily promoted their deepest-held 'convictions' as 'truth'. He demanded radical veracity against metaphysical 'lies' through a harsh and consistent attitude to theory, truth, and values, what he called 'philosophy with a hammer', even if that meant celebrating cruelty, inequality, violence, and 'the will to power'. At the same time, he adopted a 'pathos of detachment' in order to unmask the mediocrity and complacency that modernity breeds (Stern, 1978: 65). Nothing is believed more passionately than the conviction of demagogues overcome by their own belief in themselves. Knowledge unconstrained by the need to serve human development is just as dangerous as blissful ignorance. Unrestrained pursuit of knowledge is an illusion that needs to be unmasked.

For Nietzsche, modern values function as masks for lies that need to be exploded. Nietzsche saw himself as a 'destroyer' of myths, as Norbert Elias (1978) later defined the role of sociology, and demanded a 'revaluation of all values', a thoroughgoing self-examination of humanity and the exposure of all unexamined 'truths'. Above all this meant rejecting the Christian morality of humility, self-denial, asceticism, benevolence, pity, and altruism and the language of 'spirit' and 'soul' as a denial of the body and its material-sensual need for nourishment, shelter, and health. Christianity's life-denying ideal survives in secular modernity in the nihilistic form of ascetic rationality. Once this is exposed 'all power structures of the old society will have been exploded – all of them are based on lies' (Nietzsche, 1995: 229).

Unlike Weber, Nietzsche's interpretative strategy refused to develop a methodical scientific theory of social processes and structures. Instead, Nietzschean sociology adopted an aphoristic style of presentation because, as Runciman argues, 'It is the least self-deluding way of talking about the pursuit, distribution and exercise of power in a world, including an intellectual world, which anyone of good intellectual conscience must acknowledge to be a "disenchanted" one' (2000: 13). Nietzsche viewed the scientific aspirations of early German sociology as symptomatic of the decadent culture of modernity:

> Even the ideals of science can be deeply, yet completely unconsciously influenced by decadence: our entire sociology is proof of that. The objection to it is that it knows only the form of decay of society, and inevitably it takes its own instincts of decay for the norms of sociological judgment. (Nietzsche, 1967: 33)

Yet the lure of truth led Nietzsche deeper into the snare of nihilism (Goudsblom, 1980: 36). Nihilism is true because it is a denial of a truthful world, a claim taken up later by Adorno's 'negative turn' in critical theory. Nietzsche glamorises deprivation and suffering in a nihilistic transvaluation of metaphysical ideals of scientific 'progress'. He declared that his own 'fundamental innovations' supplanted a scientific theory of society with an aesthetic critique of culture: 'In place of "sociology", a theory of the forms of domination. In place of "society", the cultural complex, as my chief interest' (Nietzsche, 1967: 255).

Nietzsche's aesthetic 'sociology of sociology' arguably forces sociology to take a more reflexive, self-critical perspective as embedded in a world of bodies and language that it simultaneously seeks to analyse but also presupposes. No social theory of power can be valid for all eternity, although some hard-won insights may stand the test of time. Since there is no shared criteria to form judgements, Nietzsche's theory formed its own self-sustaining justification, apparently oblivious to competing perspectives (Solms-Laubach, 2007: 25).

Yet while Nietzsche (1995: 228) aimed to found a valid theory by his own 'will to power' – 'I am dynamite ... the first to discover the truth by being the first to experience lies as lies' – his insights were not meant to be confined to him alone. Nietzsche expected, rightly, that his type of philosophy would structure the concerns of social theory in the century ahead. He demanded agreement from his readers for his austere value judgements that, paradoxically, appealed to an ideology of bourgeois individualism that he so despised. After all, any refusal of Nietzsche's ambiguous and contradictory judgements meant being cast into the oblivion of inferiority, decadence, and servility of the homogenous masses.

MAX WEBER AND POST-NIETZSCHEAN THEORY

Unlike Nietzsche's wandering aphoristic style, Max Weber was concerned to develop a systematic empirical sociology. While Weber's debate with the 'ghost of

Marx' is widely recognised, more contentious is his debt to Nietzsche. Weber himself is reported to have commented:

> Today a scholar's honesty, and especially that of a philosopher, can be measured by his attitude toward Nietzsche and Marx. Whoever does not admit that he could not have accomplished crucial parts of his own work without the contribution of these two men deceives himself and others. Our intellectual universe has largely been formed by Marx and Nietzsche. (in Bendix and Roth, 1971: 21; Radkau, 2009: 167)

Whatever the precise nature of Nietzsche's influence on Weber they both shared a concern with a moral critique of capitalist modernity (Stauth and Turner, 1988). Weber was concerned that the *fin de siècle* generation had falsely assimilated Nietzsche as an unprincipled anti-modernist, making them vulnerable to political fanaticism in the name of a struggle against decadent cultural values (Antonio, 2001: 164). Weber rarely referred to Nietzsche (or Marx) directly, though his influence is apparent in Weber's appeal to 'heroic pessimism', personal conviction, and resolute critique of illusions.

Yet, as a post-Nietzschean, Weber was also aware that the achievements of his own 'will to power' would be overtaken at some point by other 'wills to power' whose precise shape he could not yet conceive from his particular perspective. It is impossible for social theory after Nietzsche not to address the problematic established by the 'will to power'. Both Weber and Nietzsche accept that there can be no single, absolute 'truth', only particular 'perspectives' from certain vantage points that create order out of the chaotic flux of the world. It is often claimed that they shared a 'tragic pessimism' about modernity. For Weber individuals were imprisoned in the 'iron cage' of instrumental rationality while Nietzsche thundered against the meaningless nihilism of modernity (Vandenberghe, 2009: 130). Yet this summary verdict of shared pessimism fails to allow that both anticipated that history may be prised open in unexpected ways by charismatic individuals (Weber) or supermen (Nietzsche).

However, crucial differences also flow between Weber and Nietzsche. Weber departed from Nietzsche in his commitment to academic authority, his distance from Romanticism and his 'materialism'. Instead of reviving Romantic illusions about the authenticity of an aesthetic life, Weber defended the fastidious discipline of rationality imposed by science as a vocation in a way that Nietzsche would have rejected. While Nietzsche and Weber fearlessly pursued intellectual honesty wherever it led, Weber developed a rigorous methodology of value-free 'ideal-type' models in the name of detached understanding or *Verstehen*. Neitzsche's rejected *Verstehende Sociologie* as too passive and indiscriminate. *Verstehen* timidly refuses to judge what is truly of human value. In contrast, Neitzsche's 'intellectual honesty' (*Redlichkeit*) ruthlessly ranked things of human value and disposed of inferior rankings (Eden, 1987: 406).

For such reasons Runciman (2000: 7) defined Weber as both a sociologist *and* a Nietzschean, but not a 'Nietzschean sociologist'. Despite his echo of heroic pessimism in images of disenchantment, rationalisation, and the 'iron cage', Weber was no nihilist. Individuals would cope with the collapse of a unified meaning system under modernity by adopting a disinterested 'ethic of responsibility', precisely the self-comforting bourgeois asceticism that Nietzsche despised (Stauth and Turner, 1988: 107).

VALUES AND IDEAL-TYPES

Weber's resolutely anti-philosophical sociology aimed to release empirical social science from the tutelage of speculative metaphysics. For Weber, value judgements cannot be validated by science and need to be banished from research since they risk introducing arbitrary suppositions and interpretative errors into the construction of theories. Science cannot reconcile theory and values. It is unable to verify the kind of world that we ought to live in, only the kind of world that we find ourselves in. All it can do is to outline the logic and consequences of different moral choices in particular historical conditions. By placing value judgements outside of the scope of science, Weber, unlike Nietzsche, was prepared to tolerate – though not endorse – values irreconcilable with his own liberal nationalism and ethic of responsibility, including anarchism, pacifism, and socialism.

As a Nietzschean *and* a sociologist, Weber, like every other scholar, wanted to impose on his readers a social theory of power acquired from his particular cultural perspective as a bourgeois liberal nationalist. His 'ideal-types' derived from the inescapable values provided by his own subjective cultural position. They functioned as a 'regulative principle', a heuristic device that makes sense of experience but does not constitute it. Weber ruled out any further judgement about the objective validity of values. This derives from the epistemological position of Kant. Kant separated theoretical validity and moral value into autonomous spheres, autonomous both from each other and from empirical reality.

Neo-Kantianism aimed to specify the underlying cognitive conditions that make an object possible (Oakes, 1987). These, it was assumed, transcend and are not derived primarily from empirical observation or experience. Since there is no direct access to the object being studied, it can only be approached subjectively from a particular viewpoint. It is the theorist who subjectively constructs ideal-type models of the object, which can never be truly known 'in itself'. Ideal-types arrest the stream of events because they isolate what has meaning and significance for the theorist, not because they exhaust all the qualities that might be known about the event.

Weber's famous ideal-type of charismatic authority, for example, was indifferent to the values that it served so long as followers believed that the individual was truly an extraordinary personality. After all, 'one need not have been Caesar to understand Caesar' (Weber, 2012: 65, 274). Charisma stands in such sharp contrast to the social order in Weber's model that it further dramatises the domination of modern rationality over authentic individuality. Pure charisma is not explicable in terms of social conditions but of subjective will alone. Under the impersonal rationalisation of capitalist modernity individual charisma became a sheer test of willpower. Weber (1946: 77–156) reminded students in his famous lectures of

1918 and 1919 on science and politics that only a determined individual suited to a particular 'calling' could make an impression on an impersonal contemporary world, either through the obsessive scholarship needed to overcome today's indifferent educational factories or as the committed politician leading the bureaucratic machine (Liebersohn, 1988: 122).

A major difficulty for ideal-type constructions is the distance between concept and reality that Weber inherited from neo-Kantian epistemology (Oakes, 1987). If reality is independent of its concept, then it will remain unintelligible. It is therefore not possible to compare ideal-types with reality but only with some other ideal-type. Weber's demand that ideal-types need to be verified by a comparison with reality is logically impossible within the neo-Kantian framework. Nietzsche's critique of Kant's formal rationality exposed the intellectualist trap that Weber entered.

A second problem is the distance of Weber's sociology from everyday life. Stauth and Turner (1988: 108) have argued that, in contrast to Nietzsche's concern for the 'little things' of everyday life, Weber's ideal-types of social action are disconnected from the everyday world. His two main ideal-types of instrumental-rational action and value-rational action are essentially purposeful, self-conscious, rational, and meaningful. His other two ideal-types – traditional and affective action – are marginal cases since they are pre-rational, emotional, and habitual, exactly the kinds of routine practical-sensual action that characterises everyday life.

In such ways *Verstehen* is restricted to an elevated level of cognition beyond the everyday social world. Weber presents an unnecessarily limiting conception of sociology restricted to the interpretation of (ideal) rational action that can never approach reality as the ground of conceptual verification. Nietzsche, on the other hand, adopted the standpoint of the 'little things' in the habitus of everyday life and was scathing about the 'imaginary' perspective of Christianity and Kantian philosophy as a denial of living human processes.

SOCIOLOGY OF RESENTMENT

Parallel to Nietzsche's genealogy of modernity as the survival of Christian asceticism, Weber (1930) famously uncovered the origins of the 'capitalist spirit' in Protestant rationality. Weber's liberalism was tinged with the Protestant ideal that he so evidently admired in his famous essay, *The Protestant Ethic and the Spirit of Capitalism* (1930). Calvinism produced self-reliant and ethically responsible charismatic individuals who refused to yield to the demands of secular authority. Once capitalism established itself as a socio-economic system, however, it had no need for the Protestant ethic of responsibility or the individual driven to choose a world-defining 'calling'. Weber therefore charged capitalist modernity with the 'disenchantment of the world', an echo of Nietzsche's critique of nihilism after the 'death of God'.

Without a belief in God to ground a moral politics of compassion no unifying centre for social ethics is possible. All attempts to unify morality by values of authenticity, pleasure, moderation and so on are illusory and self-defeating. But where Nietzsche worked to destroy public morality as false, Weber advocated the public toleration of moral differences. Weber wanted to extend democracy, and came to appreciate the virtues of the working class, whereas Nietzsche despised all forms of social levelling and mediocrity.

Weber rejected Nietzsche's sociology of resentment as a theory of social ethics. Tolerance, mercy and solidarity were viewed by Nietzsche as a 'slave revolt in morals'. Modernity now imposed this 'slave morality' on a restrained, mediocre ruling class at the expense of the highest human values. Where once a negative evaluation of suffering allowed the privileged to feel that their fortune was rightly deserved, the impersonal duty to serve and work had become a social ethic of repressed retaliation, producing an ascetic resentment against the leisurely evasion of work and necessity.

Against Nietzsche, Weber maintained that the positive ethic of salvation ought to be treated as a separate historical development from the negative force of class resentment. The religious glorification of suffering and justice gave rise to the idea of a messianic redemption for both the community and individuals. Weber (1946: 277) argued that 'satiated' elites had less need of being saved by prophets and priests than the lowest social groups, whose social dignity can be secured only by a special ethical imperative: 'Resentment has not been required as a leverage; the rational interest in material and ideal compensations as such has been perfectly sufficient.'

A more general theory of resentment that drew on Nietzsche (and the phenomenology of Edmund Husserl) was also developed by the philosopher Max Scheler (1874–1928). Scheler rejected Nietzsche's critique of Christianity as a slave morality. For Scheler, since Christianity was founded on the grace of the few it was far from an egalitarian doctrine. Resentment, he contended, arises from the psychological repression of 'natural' human emotions behind distorted feelings of revenge, hatred, envy and spite.

Lacking empirical support, Scheler arbitrarily asserted that the underlying biological basis of resentment finds vicarious expression among certain groups, primarily the lower classes, petty bourgeoisie, women, the elderly and Jews. While Scheler considered that resentment was prevalent among dominated individuals and groups it also typified the utilitarian culture of bourgeois society and humanitarian ethics (Scheler, 1994). It does seem perverse, however, to argue that the humanitarian ideal to prevent suffering, torture and violence is merely an expression of resentment while the wilfully cruel Nietzschean anti-humanitarian attitude has nothing whatsoever to do with the resentments that arise from an uncertain position in social space.

A more sociological approach to resentment was developed in the 1930s by the Danish sociologist Svend Ranulf (1964). Examining Weber's claim that moral restraints are imposed out of practical necessity rather than general feelings of resentment, Ranulf argued that the lower middle class made a virtue out of necessity in their hostility to the undeserved leisure and luxury of the aristocracy. Feelings of misery caused by a never-ending struggle to acquire wealth through hard work and pious sobriety gave rise to group resentment disguised as moral indignation to see the wicked punished.

As moral indignation rises in intensity, so moral inconsistency becomes more frequent, a trait Ranulf (1964: 198) found in the life conditions of the lower middle classes more than other groups: 'the disinterested tendency to inflict punishment is a distinctive characteristic of the lower middle class, that is, of a social class living under conditions which force its members to an extraordinarily high degree of self-restraint and subject them to much frustration of natural desires'. Not living in conditions of misery the upper bourgeoisie lack the appetite of the disposition for disinterested moral indignation and impersonal punishment.

A Nietzschean theory of resentment along similar lines was also proposed by Werner Sombart's (1998: 340–1) study of the petty bourgeois ethic. All grapes had a sour taste for downwardly mobile groups in their struggle to retain the 'respectability' of a bourgeois citizen. Everything about the aristocratic way of life, its hunting, nepotism and immorality, looked contemptible to the petty bourgeois. 'Self-righteous jealousy' transformed exclusion from the secretly desired upperclass lifestyles into spurned riches.

What Ranulf (1964: 50) called 'plausible guesses' in social theory need to be rejected unless they can be made subject to detailed empirical study along the lines proposed by Durkheim and not passed off, in the manner of Scheler's guesswork about biological heredity, as sufficient in itself as the basis of group resentment. Ranulf's own study of pamphlets, sermons and newspapers from the English Civil War showed that Puritan propaganda in its indignant denunciation of its enemies inconsistently condemned the behaviour of others but justified it when carried out by themselves. Puritans proudly boasted about the atrocities that they committed against Catholics and the Irish as keeping with God's work while the Royalists were less prepared to admit of crimes that they accused Puritans of committing.

While resentment forms one aspect of the compensatory theodicy of suffering, for instance that the wicked are condemned to an eternity of suffering, asceticism cannot be deduced from a general theory of class power such as Nietzsche proposed. Nietzsche's general theory of class power lacks the tension that Weber identified for the middle class, between the ethic to specialise in an 'inner calling' of professional values and the inchoate revolt of bourgeois youth against capitalist rationality and worship of aristocratic 'natural' superiority. However, Weber's critique fails to do justice to Nietzsche's theory of resentment as a more general alienated condition beyond repressed class revenge (Stauth and Turner, 1988: 112). Weber psychologised resentment as intellectual rationality in a way that obscured Nietzsche's critique of impersonal duty and obligation, which Weber's idea of the 'calling' sanctifies.

Such an individualistic 'ethic of responsibility', for Weber, pointed to a way out of the crisis. Weber's diagnosis of the German crisis indicted the German middle class for singularly failing to raise itself into a class fit to exercise power in the national interest. Instead, it subordinated itself to and adopted the decadent mores of the military and political castes controlling the authoritarian German state apparatus.

Based on Weber's understanding of class resentment as repressed revenge, Liberalism succumbed to the interests of business and military elites rather than advancing a national programme of social reform and opening up a public sphere for democratic expression. In the 1890s, Weber (1946: 384) saw national danger for a Germany internally divided into an urban industrial society in the west, and a rural society in the east controlled by a landlord class (the Junkers), increasingly reliant on cheap migrant labour that undermined the individualist ethic and eroded stable social relations in the region. This social fracture weakened Germany in the face of the threat of more advanced industrial and military nations on its borders and eroded the capacity of the middle class for national leadership and personal responsibility. Weber anticipated that the German bourgeoisie's surrender to authoritarianism would have dire consequences for the whole continent of Europe in the decades ahead.

GEORG SIMMEL AND CULTURAL CRISIS

Rather than its consequences for European state power, for Georg Simmel (1997) the crisis of turn-of-century modernity consisted in the 'tragic' quality of its culture. In language reminiscent of Marx and Nietzsche, the 'tragedy of culture' for Simmel consisted in human alienation from cultural products. It is a 'tragedy' that individuals are compelled to become mere 'bearers' of the inexorable logic of 'objective culture'. Young people in particular experienced a profound disorientation from traditional cultural values that made them vulnerable to the illusory attractions of brutal egoism.

> The rapid extension and diversification of life, of interests and activities, that Germany experienced after 1870 had loosened an extraordinary number of ties that were of a conservative and beneficent character – had in particular weakened the reverence of our youth for the principle of authority; and with this there were, of course, bound up, as in all emancipations that are not entirely justified from within, a proportionately blinder imitation and suggestion of new gods and new idols to adore. (Simmel, 2008: 180)

An increase in the material conditions of the middle classes went alongside the primacy of technical rationality, not just in industry but also in the natural and human sciences, painting, music, and poetry. Things, not individuals, are perfected by improvements in technique.

Although Germany was unified politically as a state in 1870 it was still subject to numerous cultural and material divisions. In his 1902 essay on 'Tendencies in German life and thought since 1870', Simmel (2008) sketched the contours of cultural crisis. He noted two main social developments in Germany: on the one hand, increased social contrasts, and on the other, a relative levelling between social groups. In the case of the women's movement, middle-class women wanted a role outside the home in contrast to working-class women who wanted a role outside the factory: 'the woman of the proletariat has not, as has the middle class woman, too little, but on the contrary too much social freedom – however badly it may stand with her individual freedom' (Simmel, 2008: 186). As women entered public life a new dynamic of gender difference and equalisation was unleashed, captured in the slogan 'Not of the same kind but of the same worth' (Simmel, 2008: 189). Church and state were subject to increased centralisation as they mediated between the demands of 'externalisation' of life in material objects and the needs of 'spiritualisation' in an attachment to higher values of God and patriotism.

In both science and art, positivism was in retreat by the turn of the century. Art was also subject to a 'transcendental impulse' as individuals searched for a release from a fragmented social existence in protest against domination by scientific rationality. Even here the positivist attitude supported a 'naturalist' reproduction of the visible, as with Impressionist painting capturing fleeting, insignificant and 'ugly' details as evidence of optical realism and truth. Within science, a revolt was underway against the positivist concentration on physical material directly available to the senses that proceeded without any need to reflect on the deeper meaning of life processes.

> In science the mere assemblage of facts and the avoidance of higher and more general points of view denote a stage of naturalistic externalization – the deification of experience, of which it has been justly said that it may be had the more cheaply and safely, in as much as there is now no one who does *not* admit that experience is important and indispensable. (Simmel, 2008: 197–8)

In reaction to the 'superficial' reproduction of appearances rather than uncovering their deeper meaning, a renewed understanding was underway of Kant's lesson that objective knowledge was not pre-given by sense-data itself but was imposed on the 'meaningless chaos' of disconnected sense-impressions by the working hypotheses of theory. This reversed the materialist assumption that matter must be explained by material causes, not as a product of consciousness. Science therefore rests upon a metaphysical and a spiritualist basis. It does not simply reflect material reality but creates ideas about things, aesthetics and morals.

As part of the 'rapid development of external civilization' brought about by large-scale industry, Germany experienced 'the outbreak of the greatest popular movement of the century': socialism (Simmel, 2008: 171). The socialist ideal proposed a rational future of economic centralisation and equal rights, following the model of large-scale factory organisation that the working class were so well acquainted with. Sections of the middle class were attracted to socialism on purely verbal grounds. Unedifying types of what Simmel called 'parlour-socialism' provided sections of the middle classes with an exciting 'revolutionary' diversion from the general meaninglessness of culture.

Schopenhauer's philosophy also expressed for some the post-Christian experience of a lack of any ultimate meaning in life except a never-ending human will that is unable to realise itself in some final object. More widely, practical, ethical, and theoretical interests coalesced in a heightened consciousness of social interdependencies:

> For, all at once, it was seen that it was society, the sum of all social groups, from which we derived every inner and outer good as a loan, that the individual was but the crossing-point of social threads, and that he, by a devotion to the interests of all, merely discharged an obligation of the most fundamental character – by a devotion

that had as its primary object the most oppressed and undeveloped portion of society, which, nevertheless, through its labor supported the whole. (Simmel, 2008: 176)

Popular support grew for social reforms to protect the sick and the elderly. From around 1890 a different tendency emerged that promoted inequality and selfish egoism against any idea of the social good, often as a result of a mistaken understanding of the philosophy of Nietzsche, the enemy of egoism and individualism, as well as altruistic social reform. Nonetheless, Nietzsche's doctrine had deleterious consequences: 'The phrases "superior nature" [and] "distance from the multitude" became a standard under which were concealed countless arrogant, brutally selfish, and obscure tendencies' (Simmel, 2008: 180).

OBJECTIVE AND SUBJECTIVE CULTURE

Such tendencies derived from a culture torn between an 'objective culture' of things, technology, machines, science, institutions, and economics, and a 'subjective culture' of creative individuality (Simmel, 1997: 45). One part, objective culture, predominates over the other part, subjective culture, outstrips it and leaves it languishing far behind. An immense mass of objects were becoming so sophisticated, intellectual, refined, and opaque that individuals could not possibly assimilate them in a meaningful cultural relationship.

> There thus emerges the typical problematic condition of modern humanity: the feeling of being surrounded by an immense number of cultural elements, which are not meaningless, but not profoundly meaningful to the individual either; elements which have a certain crushing quality as a mass, because an individual cannot assimilate every individual thing, but cannot simply reject it either, since it belongs potentially, as it were to the sphere of his or her cultural development. (Simmel, 1997: 73)

Relations between cultural means and cultural ends are blurred by increasingly complex intermediate relations of an opaque division of labour: 'The long strands of means and ends, which transform life into a technical problem, make it completely impossible to remain clearly aware at every instant of the terminus of each strand' (Simmel, 1986: 3). People and things can only live indirectly through functional relations. In the process, the development of singular individuality is lost as the true purpose of culture.

Cultural value, Simmel argued, resides exclusively in its capacity to develop or 'cultivate' the purposive human personality rather than in the accumulation of things as such. Simmel identifies culture with 'the creative dynamism of life [as it] produces certain artefacts which provide it with forms of expression and actualization, and which in their turn absorb the constant flow of life, giving it form and content, scope and order: for example civil laws and constitutions, works of art, religion, science, technology and innumerable others' (Simmel, 1997: 76). Objective culture is the historical accumulation and reproduction of knowledge – the culture of things remains a human culture. Great art only has cultural value in so far as it cultivates human development, even though it may have other non-cultural values such as price, technical criteria or institutional status.

Cultural value is not somehow innate to human beings as a pre-formed bio-logical drive or as the pre-existing mental structure of the discriminating personality. It is imparted by the relation between thing and individual in the development of a personal habitus, as sociologists might say today. In order for human subjects to develop they must pass through the material products of objec-tive culture, an interrelated process that Simmel termed 'an objectification of the subject and a subjectification of the object' (Simmel, 1997: 58). Without such interweaving, culture becomes merely formal and technical. However, the flow of culture from subject through objects and back to subjects was now arrested at the objective pole. Objective material culture, a means to realise the higher goal of subjective human culture, had increasingly become an autonomous goal in its own right. Thus the ideal of eighteenth-century pedagogy as the cultivation of the internal capacity for human self-development was replaced in the nineteenth-century by the concept of 'education' as the transmission of a body of objective knowledge and behaviours (Simmel, 2011: 449).

Objective culture imposes its products on individuals ill-prepared to meet the challenge, overwhelmed as they are by the unlimited quantity of cultural objects. Individuals are not developing as rapidly or as widely as things. For instance, although their conditions of life diverged radically, middle-class and working-class women were subject to domination by technological culture:

> Both phenomena belong equally to those typical cases which represent the entire suffering of the present day: the fact that the development of objective conditions has progressed faster than the development and adaptation of individuals. The cul-ture and technology of things poses requirements and develops consequences that no longer coincide with the historically evolved living conditions of the people. (Simmel, 1997: 273)

Just as the commodity form in capitalist society assumes the form of a 'fetish', so the contents of culture more generally take on an independent life of their own. This also has lessons for intellectual productions divorced from the wider dev-elopment of human culture. As scholarship is increasingly identified with 'methodologically faultless knowledge', itself validated by an abstract conception of knowledge, it finds itself 'alienated from the general purpose and meaning of all research' (Simmel, 1997: 71). A scholastic fetish of 'method' legitimates even the 'most inconsequential studies' that otherwise fail to serve the development of culturally meaningful knowledge.

Paradoxically, the 'tragedy of culture' was moderated for Simmel by the 1914–1918 war. As the problem of personal survival became a mere means for the ends of military strategy, war raised metaphysical paradoxes to a higher level beyond its basis in European inter-state rivalries for markets and colonies. Simmel argued that the shock caused by the wartime devaluation of life would force a changed relationship to what counts as significant and what is secondary in subjective culture, even if the change was only temporary. Its chief consequence was to have produced a unified form of subjective culture, albeit at a terrible cost: 'the disintegration and perversion of cultural life has reached an extreme, and life has risen in revolt against it in the shape of this war, with its unifying, simplifying and concentrated force' (Simmel, 1997: 101). Simmel rightly feared that war merely deflected but would not prevent the return of cultural crisis. Individuals remained singularly incapable of comprehending the effects of objective culture as an end in itself, set apart from subjective culture.

MONEY AND VALUE

As technical means become ends in themselves the purpose and meaning of human culture becomes increasingly distant from individuals. This is most apparent when the most abstract of all means – money – becomes the supreme end of life (Simmel, 2011). Money has no cultural meaning except that it allows any product of objective culture to be possessed as a commodity for consumption. As a pure means, money spreads everywhere and transcends all other values. All value ultimately depends upon a qualitative judgement about the relative difficulty of acquiring an object. Money, however, reduces the value of social relations to one of quantity. 'How much money?' replaces the question of 'how much effort?' is needed to acquire something perceived as valuable.

Possession of money removes all obstacles to the acquisition of desirable objects without demanding personal sacrifice, discipline, hardship, stress, and deprivation, the basis of all value for both Simmel (1986: 167) and Nietzsche. Money stimulates only a weak-willed, hedonistic and debased individualism. Fully human qualities are not to be found in the pleasure of consumption or egoism but only in 'the severest inner discipline, through the greatest rigor exercised towards one's self, through the complete renunciation of every enjoyment for enjoyment's sake' (Simmel, 2008: 182).

For money to function as the medium of transaction it requires the mutual adjustment of numerous individuals to each other as buyers and sellers. In modernity, means predominate over ends, or rather ends become means, in ever-extending social networks or webs of relations and functions. In this process, the calculating rationality of universal exchange dominates the subjective culture of a singular individuality. As fields like art, science, philosophy, and religion become more specialised and distant from each other, their incommensurability prevents them from entering a direct relationship. Specialised, partial fields can only be approached from the perspective particular to them. For this reason, technical expertise acquires the character of an absolute worldview.

Money is opposed to cultural value, argues Simmel, because it mediates between diverse things on the basis of being featureless and infinitely interchangeable. It is well known that pre-capitalist prohibitions on the nobility maintained a rigid boundary that separated them from market transactions as degrading to the honour and distinction of their social position. Qualitative judgements of cultural value, like aesthetics, are indifferent to quantitative evaluation. Money value destroys the essence of cultural value. In a money economy all things are measured in common and are made equivalent and interchangeable: 'all float with the same specific gravity in the constantly moving current of money' (Simmel, 2011: 392).

Objects are levelled by money. By making an exquisite object available to all who can buy, money gains by its association with the object while the object itself is degraded in value by its loss of independence: 'The production of cheap trash is, as it were, the vengeance of the objects for the fact that they have been ousted from the focal point of interest by a merely indifferent means' (Simmel, 2011: 394). An interest in the price of things dominates an interest in the individual qualities of the object. In contrast, when an object stands outside the levelling effect of the money relationship, Simmel argues, its only distinction is that of being valued for its own inherent qualities.

DISTINCTION AND NOBILITY

Yet domination by objective culture and money was not the end of the matter for Simmel. Cultural domination also calls forth resistance, a response that Simmel (2011: 389ff), echoing Nietzsche, termed 'distinction'. In *Schopenhauer and Nietzsche*, the work that Simmel (1986: 162) considered his lasting achievement, distinction or nobility defined in terms of an individual's 'dignity' is expressed not by their social position but through 'formal conduct which characteristically unites a resolute personality and a lucid objectivity'. What matters is the inherent superiority of the person, not worldly success. As Simmel summarised it, 'If we grant that there are strong and weak, wise and stupid, refined and vulgar, beautiful and ugly men, and that the annihilation of these differences is but the dream of a child, then the worth-accent in the life of mankind can rest only upon its highest examples' (2008: 179).

As ever with Simmel, distinction is multi-dimensional. It sets apart individuals on the basis of personal qualities of reserve and detachment independent of the general run of things. On the other hand, the 'positive exclusion' of distinction cannot be reduced to a mere 'relationship of difference' that invites comparison to others. In intellectual matters, distinction is characterised by scrupulous objectivity: 'the hallmark of a noble spirit is to treat an opponent's opinion objectively, to argue fairly, and not to be drawn into the tempest of subjective passion' (Simmel, 1986: 162).

As Nietzsche recognised, the loss of distinction is the 'tragedy' of the levelling process of modernity. A money economy pulls down the higher level further than the lower level can rise. Higher achievements can only meet lower ones on the grounds of the latter. A similar principle applies when specialists in different fields attempt to find common grounds to communicate. They resort to a more general, impoverished language than their field of expertise usually demands. A more rounded personality is able to adjust their language, feelings, sensibilities, knowledge, and so on to the level of the less developed, but not vice versa. This is because the lower, more general ground is common to both but the higher is more exclusive and reserved: 'Apart from certain exceptions, the base of common interests and actions among the higher and lower elements can be accomplished only if the higher elements are able to disclaim their individual superiority' (Simmel, 2011: 392).

Simmel's concern with the loss of distinction derived from Nietzsche's claim that the 'pathos of distance' is the source of human striving and achievement (Liebersohn, 1988: 141). Social distance is central to Simmel's sociology of relations between insiders and outsiders, domination and subordination, fixity and mobility, breadth and narrowness, and other aspects of social space. Distinction requires the cultivation of an inner distance from social inferiors. Society touches only on the external action of individuals, not their inner qualities. Therefore it is right for Nietzsche that the masses suffer so that a single individual may rise to a new evolutionary level. Self-responsibility makes life more trying and severe as the evolutionary level rises. It is experienced at higher levels as the crushing pressure of responsibility that is unavoidable and permanent, as in Nietzsche's idea of 'eternal recurrence' (Simmel, 1986: 170–1). This concept is not an empirical one but a regulative ideal that allowed Nietzsche to mediate history between bounded events and unceasing processes and to root it in earthly life in opposition to the transcendental ideals of traditional philosophy. By creating a higher consciousness of living historically, eternal recurrence compels great individuals to always take personal responsibility at every moment.

While Simmel recognised 'a certain aura of nobility' in Nietzsche's doctrine of distinction, he was far from uncritical about Nietzsche's appeal to the natural evolution of higher qualities like honesty, beauty or power. This ignored the fact, as Simmel pointed out, that evolution also and more frequently produced the opposite qualities. It is Nietzsche's illusion to imagine that evolution culminates only with higher faculties of distinction as the demiurge of disinterested natural necessity. His appeal to distinction as natural grace is thereby divorced from his conception of distinction as a purely ethical ideal. 'For him, by logical necessity, interest in society is destroyed by interest in mankind: the value of the individual is bound to a dominating, surging, and all-consuming distance' (Simmel, 1986: 159).

By dismissing the concept of society in preference for the human essence of life Nietzsche loses any sense of the immense tragedy of the total picture and the prospects for a more human life in changed social circumstances. Simmel (2008: 184) recognised Nietzsche's axiom 'that which elevates lower groups lowers the higher' as a 'tragic relation' contradicted by the ethic of social justice demanded by the working class. Instead, life appeared to Nietzsche as a logical deduction derived from the axiomatic premise of his rigid social geometry which held that height is always obtained at the expense of breadth. This would also mean recognising that the possibility for distinction relied on forms of social distance only made possible by the impersonal social relations of modernity rather than some pre-social condition of natural grace. As Harry Liebersohn notes, 'Absolute personal autonomy offset the social order only by internalizing its logic, creating, to be sure, a style that set the bearer apart, but doing so only through a pattern of radical repression. This was the price one paid for turning the modern fate into a personal destiny' (1988: 143).

A SOCIOLOGY OF RELATIONS

Simmel's theory of forms is the precondition for the possibility for social theory to emerge. Although they are always bound together in practice, sociology strips out social forms from their empirical content to construct them as purified analytical abstractions. Only in this way is a science of society possible for Simmel (2009). Simmel's dualist sociology is constructed around the way that social forms – secrets, money, poverty, metropolis, fashion, gossip, sociability, and so on – hold in tension or balance two opposing but inseparable tendencies that presuppose each other. Such dualities include the poles of inside and outside, distance and proximity, unity and division, superordination and subordination, object and subject, conflict and cooperation, individual and group, idealism and materialism. All social forms are subject to conflict and tension between the opposing poles. This produces a dynamic process, a movement now in one direction, towards the pole of objective culture, now in another direction, towards the pole of subjective culture.

Simmel's sociology concentrates dialectically on the point of interaction rather than on the individual units that precede interaction (Schermer and Jary, 2013). Sociology is distinguished from other social sciences by relations rather than substances. An abstract conception of 'society' can too readily be reified as existing as an independent substance-like thing over and above interaction (Frisby and Sayer, 1986). Society, however, acquires a more or less intense expression with each defined form of interaction, in every shared feeling or conversation, divisions of cliques, rulers and ruled, gossip and secrets, dressing up or dressing down, and so on. Individuals are pulled into a higher unity by processes of association and they are pushed into association by living interests, economic and ideal, warlike and erotic, religious and charitable, in workplaces, neighbourhoods, states, church, clubs, and family (Simmel, 1997: 120).

Individuals are the presupposition and the consequence of social relations. However, individuality is never exhausted by 'society'. Something individual is always left over and kept in reserve in ways that cannot be accounted for by social functions, relations and structures. Individuals therefore are both inside and outside society at the same time. Society exists only through the interaction of countless 'social threads'. Since society appears all-powerful it might be thought that sociology should study every conceivable thing ever said and done by human beings. After all, social interaction underlies everything in history, art, culture, morality, politics, religion, technology, philosophy, language, and so on. Only when individuals mutually and reciprocally condition each other in the process of social interaction does the motivating content of life become 'society'. Even conflict involves the mutual influence of the protagonists. Reciprocity is also found in highly unequal power relations, such as Hegel's master–slave dialectic where not only the master but the slave also conditions the nature of the relationship (Schermer and Jary, 2013: 141).

In this Simmel (2009: 24) opposed the inductive approach of 'naïve naturalism' which allows 'mere data' to dictate analytical concepts. Instead, theoretical concepts of social forms must be verified in two ways. On the one hand, the same social form will be found across diverse social and historical contents and, on the other hand, the same social content will be discovered in different social forms. The abstract forms taken by social interaction do not cause 'society'; they *are* society. Society in the strict sense used by Simmel is the overall abstract concept for the combined forms of social interaction. Simmel began from the most basic and broadest image of 'society' conceivable: 'society exists where several individuals enter into interaction' (2009: 22). Individuals have all sorts of reasons to interact with each other: friendship, animosity, obedience, devotion, hunger, profit, and so on. But individual motivation is far less important to Simmel than the fact that every type of interaction creates a new unity, a 'society'.

Simmel (2009: 27–8) makes an analogy with geometry. Different materials can take the same geometrical form, say a circle, while the same material, say water, can take different spatial forms. Sociology stands to the empirical social sciences as geometry stands to the empirical sciences of physical nature. Geometry restricts itself to the study of abstract spatial forms through which diverse empirical materials take on definite shape; sociology is limited to abstract social forms through which diverse social materials acquire their unity. This allows sociology to discover relational patterns across countless empirical instances. These occur at a descending level of precision, from: first, the widest and most common principles of social interaction, such as the formation of classes, nations, and circles, or inner cohesion as a product of external opposition to an enemy; to, second, more specific forms, such as the influence of numbers on group processes; and, finally, even more complex processes, such as the effect that standing at the intersection of various social circles has on the individual personality.

As an analogy, however, geometry is of limited value. Sociology cannot decompose complex social processes into a few ideal forms like circles or polyhedrons. For instance, the same social content, say a religious group, will include different forms of social interaction such as domination and subordination, competition, imitation, inclusion and exclusion, and so on, but the same religious content might also take a wide range of different social forms, from a bureaucratic church to a free commune of believers.

MORE THAN LIFE

Unable to assimilate objective cultural forms, modern life can appear, especially to young people, to be 'formless' or lacking in the need for conventional forms. *Life*, the vital spontaneity of subjective being, is condemned to constantly result in its presumed opposite, *form*, a fixed and enduring objective culture. This is the 'tragedy of culture' as Simmel (1997: 94, 103) sees it. Life cannot be expressed except in forms that take on an independent existence and meaning. All self-enclosed theoretical systems are abandoned as out of touch with life itself in the same way that objective culture represses authentic individuality. This includes the rejection of formal religion for formless mysticism of every kind. Inner impulses are sanctified at the expense of external forms. Such 'intuitions' result in crisis because sooner or later they will take on a more or less stable form, which was the initial source of restlessness and rebellion.

In Simmel's time the protest against forms as restricting personal authenticity led to the idealisation of the unrestrained flow of 'life' as the highest value of culture (Simmel, 2010). War excited a 'positive' cultural concern with the vitality of life. This found intellectual expression in *Lebensphilosophie*, a philosophy of life associated with Nietzsche and with the 'vitalist' philosophy of Henri Bergson (1859–1941). Life is a single process that pushes beyond itself in two ways. It is a self-perpetuating process, an 'experience' of living that Simmel (2010: 13–14) calls 'more-life'. Nietzsche's philosophy comes to a standstill at the limits of individual volition against domination by social forms. Life can only be conceived in terms of an 'absolute unity' of subjective individuality and objective form (Simmel, 2010: 13). More-life produces objects that transcend their human author, what Simmel calls 'more-than-life'. Simmel's two-sided idea of life – 'more-life' and 'more-than-life' – replicates philosophically his dualist conception of culture as objective product and subjective process (Weingarter, 1960).

'Life', for Simmel, fulfilled the function of a governing principle that would lead beyond a culture perceived to be in crisis. Until the twentieth century, old forms were destroyed by the demand for new forms. Previous European eras revolved around one core idea – being (ancient Greece), God (middle ages), nature (Renaissance onwards), individual ego (eighteenth century), and society (nineteenth century). In each case, Simmel (1997: 78) claims, the core governing concept gave form to intellectual culture. Today there is no shared governing concept around which a new form could be mobilised. In modernity, 'life' is proposed in opposition to all (dead, exhausted, eroded) forms like society, machine, science, or individual. There are only the specialised interests of a fragmented objective culture. Modern art, for instance, claimed to serve as the expression of authentic emotions, not formal technique or tradition. Van Gogh's paintings were popular because they elicited 'this incandescent, palpable spontaneous vitality' that so informs the mood for spontaneous processes over conventional forms (Simmel, 1997: 83).

In philosophy, rather than the traditional idea of theory as governed by its own autonomous rules and conventions of internally consistent argumentation, more recent theories such as pragmatism and 'vitalism' were legitimated by the values of life: 'This theory answers the question of knowledge in terms of an "intuition" which transcends all logic and all the operations of the intellect and directly apprehends the essential inner truth of things – which means that only life is capable of understanding life' (Simmel, 1997: 85). Life, after all, is not a form of something else but is its own self-sufficient value. Neither is it possible to come down definitively on one side of the classic philosophical dualisms such as agency and structure, absolute and relative, truth and error, essence and appearance, form and content. Conceptual logic imposes such an unduly restrictive form on life that it is impossible to decide between alternatives unless a third term appears to resolve the dilemma. It is necessary, Simmel contends, to go beyond the 'either/or' form of theory, for instance of a forced choice between *either* absolute free will *or* mechanical necessity.

Life processes already form a unity. Kant divided this unity into two conceptual parts 'in order to mediate between the conflict of the concepts' (Simmel, 1997: 106). For instance, the physical and the psychological will form a duality from a certain perspective and a unity from another perspective. Kant's 'great solution' placed necessity with the perceived phenomenon, or appearance, and freedom with the unknowable 'thing-in-itself', or essence. But this merely evaded the problem of the relative relationship of freedom (or agency) and necessity (or structure) as a unified process. It is necessary, Simmel argued, to try to work from living processes, even if this is based only on a vague intuition to begin with. Life cannot be resolved or even posed adequately by purely logical constructions.

AMBIGUITY AND SOCIAL THEORY

More than other classical sociologists, Simmel allowed for ambiguity and ambivalence (Levine, 1985). His entire conception of sociology arose from the argument that scientific knowledge emerges from a practical sense about how to survive the primordial threat posed by external nature and other people. Over time knowledge became autonomous from the exigencies of immediate necessity. Science began to take on an abstract form that made it possible to comprehend 'the totality of things'.

As a distinctive science, sociology reorganises the knowledge produced by other disciplines like history by pursuing a theoretical interest 'beyond the superficial collection of facts' through a specific focus on 'the practical balance of power' in society. Theory brings together and makes connections between things that were previously separated and divided. By producing 'a new abstraction and ordering', sociology constructs 'society' as a dense substance that previously lacked coherence and singularity. Sociology is defined 'not by its object but its way of looking' (Simmel, 2009: 26). Uniquely, sociology places the totality divided up into individual human sciences under the organising power of theoretical abstraction.

In developing his social theory Simmel eliminated many things in order to concentrate on what he considered really significant for understanding. In writing the cultural history of artists like Rembrandt or the philosophers Schopenhauer and Nietzsche, Simmel (1986, 2005) did not re-describe a full biography of their lives as it was actually lived. Instead 'an ideal interpretation' was formed corresponding to the aim of the study: 'one must select from the totality of the philosopher's utterances those that form a coherent, uniform and meaningful context of thought – and it does not matter if the totality also includes contradictions, weaknesses, and ambivalence' (Simmel, 1986: liv). It may be possible to select passages from Nietzsche's writings that contradict Simmel's interpretation, yet this would not refute it. So long as a theoretical interpretation reconstructs the original core of Nietzsche's own writings, selectively shorn of sensational claims or over-burdened turns of phrase, then it would retain its validity for Simmel. Social theory must concentrate on what is essential, not on what is ephemeral, of secondary importance or isolated individual parts.

For Simmel the purpose of social theory is not to remain bound up within metaphysical terms. Neither is it to elevate the mundane to the level of 'philosophical nobility'. The whole point of theoretical knowledge is to make sense of the reality of human meaning: 'to lower a plumb line through the immediate singular, the simply given, into the depths of ultimate intellectual meanings' (Simmel, 2005: 3). Simmel attempts to transcend the classical divide between physical reality and metaphysical theory. The movement from subjective perception to objective forms is the dialectical ground for Simmel's social theory (Schermer and Jary, 2013: 44). Simmel's dialectical theory is not arbitrary. Only through social forms can the subject be absorbed into the object, as when subjective emotions are objectified by musical forms or subjective perception is objectified by artistic forms. Similarly, subjectively experienced social life is objectified and given definite form by social theory.

Objective truth can only be established by the closest relationship between a sound epistemology and its object. For Simmel a sound epistemology derives from the active process of concept formation, an intellectual debt that can be traced to Kant (Wolff, 1974: 35–6). Only through active creativity, not passive reception of an object, might access to the truth of social existence prove possible for Simmel: 'We are really ourselves, therefore, when we act' (in Helle, 2001: 34). Social practices produce subjective interests which force people to form objective relationships with each other. Knowledge is not contemplative and disinterested but active and interested.

Simmel took from Kant a cyclical image of knowledge production. He accepted Kant's premise that theoretical knowledge cannot be a copy of reality given directly to sensory perception but must be logically a priori, that is, available before any experience of the flux of perceptible reality. Kant's solution is that the intellect structures the a-priori categories necessary for understanding ordinary experience. What Kant calls the 'thing-in-itself' cannot be known from its surface appearance but must be mediated by the a-priori concepts of practical knowledge.

> No sense perception or logical derivations can directly assure us of a reality. Rather, they are only conditions that evoke the supra-theoretical feeling of affirmation, of agreement or whatever one may call this rather indescribable sense of reality. (Simmel, 2011: 452)

However, Simmel rejected Kant's claim that a-priori categories exercise a universal claim on all individuals equally. Instead, Simmel (1997) saw the highest ethical and epistemological ideal being realised only in a unique, fully developed individuality, able to make subjective judgements because it had absorbed objective culture as part of the process of overcoming alienation.

EPISTEMOLOGICAL IDEALISM

Historical materialism had come closest to a theoretical synthesis of the human sciences, Simmel claimed, despite its tendency to reduce cultural forms to the economic base. In his pioneering study *The Philosophy of Money*, Simmel (2011: 56) developed a subjective theory of value in order to 'construct a new storey beneath historical materialism'. Simmel (1977: 185–200) argued that although historical materialism is narrowly based, it is the first theory to explain historical change through psychological factors such as hunger, pain, and suffering. By introducing a 'spiritual' conception of the world, historical materialism provides a necessary corrective to the dominant conceptions of crude utilitarianism.

Historical materialism for Simmel is, ironically, a classic model of Kantian epistemology. It established the economic region as a theoretical norm which it transposed into reality through action (2011: 451). 'History', like 'sociology', is a theoretical construct made possible in the case of historical materialism by the a-priori ideal of economic forces. Economic processes perform a constitutive role as a heuristic device for historical materialism. As such, they cannot be considered a naturalistic description of the interwoven complexity of the social fabric. It is not the object itself that theory is after but knowledge of it. Theory is not the same thing as the totality of human life.

Economic interests are central to historical materialism because it is motivated by the politics of socialism. Socialism is the 'axiological' value principle that makes the materialist conception of history possible and is not simply the logical consequence of an objectively 'realist' theory of history. From the political and moral perspective of socialism, only economic interests can concentrate the largest masses of otherwise disconnected individuals, now redefined by the concept of 'class' as the elemental variable in history. Concrete individuals may be different from each other in all sorts of ways but everyone belongs to the abstractions of an economic category. Socialism aims to radically level social distinctions by eliminating unjust forms of inequality. Since differences in personal qualities cannot be levelled out, an egalitarian reduction is possible only in the sphere of material production and consumption.

Historical materialism then is not a self-sufficient epistemology but the 'logical articulation of an interpretation of history based on a final and ultimate meaning' (Simmel, 1997: 196). This does not mean, however, that it is 'idealist' in the sense that history is caused by ideas like freedom or equality. Historical materialism opposed 'historical idealism' because it conflated the idea with the cause of historical development. However, as Simmel argues, ideas can have real consequences, as religious, liberal and nationalist ideologies prove. Historical idealism shares similar methodological principles with historical materialism; only it sees ideas, not material conditions, as the sole efficacious force of history as it really happened. Hence both are really forms of 'realism' since they purport to accurately describe reality in transparent ways.

Against both philosophical materialism and 'historical idealism' Simmel (1977: 199) defends what he called 'epistemological idealism'. By this he meant that history is a cognitive construction made possible by theoretical categories. That is why, for Simmel, historical materialism, notwithstanding its opposition to ontological or historical idealism, can be conceived as a form of epistemological idealism: it organises the historical process by higher abstract concepts into a distinctive theoretical construction. 'Historical materialism is an attempt to discover the meaning that history must have in order to conform to our epistemic categories that are based on the idea that existence has a meaning' (Simmel, 1977: 199–200). Historical materialism, of course, fails to recognise that the theory of material interests is first and foremost an epistemic theory animated by political and moral values. It itself constructs the developmental process theoretically that it hopes to change, a problem that the next generation of 'Western Marxists', many influenced by Simmel, were forced to confront.

POST-NIETZSCHEAN SOCIAL THEORY

While Simmel was a contemporary of Durkheim and Weber, his social theory has been rather less celebrated over the past hundred years. Yet Simmel initially had a wide influence on the development of sociology in Germany, France, and America and his social theory shares affinities with some recent developments in cultural sociology. As a pioneer in social theory, Simmel's contemporaries were initially sympathetic to his project, followed typically by more critical reconsiderations, outright rejection and, finally, indifference (Levine, 1985: 94). They were each shaped in important respects by the epistemological idealism of Kant, as has much subsequent sociology, wittingly or unwittingly (Rose, 2009).

Simmel (2008: 200) felt that the task of theoretical synthesis beyond individual empirical studies had not been fulfilled, even in Germany, 'the classic land of the *theory of knowledge*'. Despite, or because of, his emphasis on fragmentary interactions of modernity, Simmel considered theoretical generalisation beyond the empirical details of disconnected experience as essential. Both Durkheim and Simmel were concerned with social differentiation and integration. However, Durkheim evolved his concept of 'social morphology', by which he meant population size and density across space and their connectedness through communications networks, as part of his growing critique of Simmel's theory of forms (Levine, 1985: 92).

Durkheim (1964: 355–9) rejected the idea that social forms, understood as 'the most general form of social relation', can be detached from their specific content as 'arbitrary'. There are not two kinds of reality, form and content, but only 'social facts' at different levels of abstraction. Durkheim contrasts the priority that he gave to social facts *sui generis* to Simmel's 'completely indeterminate' individual interactions (even though Simmel had criticised such a conception of sociology and defined society as 'a unity *sui generis*' in the first issue of Durkheim's journal (Fournier, 2013: 280). Simmel disregards the moral character of social forms that Durkheim identifies as central to social facts, and fails to show how abstract forms necessarily correspond to 'the nature of things' (Durkheim, 1982: 191).

In terms of Durkheim's (1982: 237) attempt to rescue sociology from 'the tute-lage of philosophy', Simmel arrested the development of a specialised science founded on reliable methodological principles. Simmel's philosophical intuitions neglected the need for critical analysis and 'regular proof' leading to 'an integral scientific system'. In a review of *The Philosophy of Money*, considered by many as Simmel's masterpiece, Durkheim (1980: 98) castigated Simmel's unmethodical approach as neither fish nor fowl: 'we confess not to place great value on this type of bastard speculation, whereby reality is expressed in necessarily subjective terms, as in art, but abstract, as in science, since for this reason it cannot give us the vital and fresh objects that the artist enlivens nor the clear notions that the scientist's inquiry seeks to define.'

In other places, however, Durkheim (1983: 3) distanced speculative Nietzschean judgements from pragmatist philosophy. Nietzsche claimed that theories are 'fic-tional' constructions that only survive because they serve a useful human function, not because they are 'true' as such. As a form of 'radical empiricism', pragmatism limits theory to the world as it directly appears to us. In contrast, Nietzsche adopted an 'artistic critique' of reality that required inspiration and intuition to go beyond the world of appearances and the 'useful' fictions of theory. Here Durkheim joins Nietzsche in a form of social theory that attempts to uncover a deeper truth of real-ity veiled by surface representations and symbols (Meštrović, 1991: 82).

But this is a different 'truth' in each case. In the shift from what Durkheim called 'mechanical solidarity' to 'organic solidarity', the size and complexity of society increases while morality becomes less and less binding across disparate but functionally integrated social groups. For Nietzsche, in contrast, mutual self-restraint and common civility are indicators of decline and decadence. In Nietzsche's case, individual value arises by limiting the boundaries of society, while for Durkheim shared value is limited by the enlargement of social bounda-ries (Bull, 2011: 53).

While Weber and Simmel were on warm personal and professional terms, they made little explicit mention or criticism of each other's work (Frisby, 1987). Before Weber entered into the new field of sociology around 1900, Simmel had already made a number of significant contributions to the subject. Although a critical reading of Simmel's *Philosophy of Money* may have stimulated Weber's *Protestant Ethic* (1930) essay, Weber is quite at odds with Simmel's claim that money imposed a capitalist mentality, insisting instead that the role was played by the sacred 'calling' of Calvinism. Money merely had a 'congruence', or what Weber would call an 'affinity', with marginal groups like Quakers and Jews who are denied regular means of social reproduction like political rights (Simmel, 2011: 222).

Nonetheless, Simmel's emphasis on the rationalisation function of money resurfaces in Weber's analysis. Both were concerned to round out Marx's ana-lysis of capitalism to take into account sociological and psychological factors. Weber also developed Simmel's insight that what began as a final goal can become a means, and vice versa (Whimster, 2007: 41). Weber developed his sociological theory of social action from Simmel's psychologistic premises of instinctual and purposive action, although he would also criticise Simmel for neglecting to distinguish between purposively intended meanings and objectively valid meanings (Weber, 2012: 60–1). And despite recognising Simmel's mode of expression as 'nothing short of brilliant' and overflowing with an abundance of 'new ideas', Weber (2012: 419) found great difficulty with Simmel's delicate mode of arguing from analogy. Weber's main methodological debt was to Simmel's (1977) *Philosophy of History* as a key source for his famous method of 'understanding' or *Verstehen*. Simmel distinguished between the objective *understanding* of the meaning of a statement and the subjective *interpretation* of the motives of the speaker. In Simmel's sense, to 'understand' is 'to take a stand concerning the "objective" *meaning of a judgement*' (Weber, 2012: 60). Weber famously (2012: 65, 274) adopted Simmel's (1977: 94) example, 'one does not have to be Caesar to understand Caesar' – although he pointedly rejected Simmel's reduction of understanding to psychological processes.

While Weber and Durkheim had some idea of each other's work and both shared common substantive concerns – above all the sociology of religion – they managed to ignore the steps that each was taking to establish professional sociology in radically different ways (Giddens, 1987a). Perhaps this is not surprising since, although they shared a critical relationship to Kantianism, they adopted contrasting methodological principles (Jensen, 2012). Weber advocated what is now known as 'methodological individualism', where analysis starts from the rational perspective of individuals. In contrast, Durkheim began from 'social facts', by which he meant the external, collective and constraining moral forces that act on individuals. Durkheim attempted to demarcate sociology as an exclusive discipline by establishing explicit rules of methodology. Weber was much less convinced about limiting sociology to a prescriptively demarcated method since it was closely related to cognate disciplines like history and economics. Durkheim was concerned with symbolic forms of moral power. Collective representations enable society to imagine itself and allow social intercourse between individuals. Weber, in contrast, was concerned with the legitimate monopoly of the means of violence that characterised state power.

CRITIQUE AND DEVELOPMENT

Later social theorists as different as Walter Benjamin, Theodor Adorno, Martin Heidegger, Georges Bataille and, more recently, Gilles Deleuze, Jacques Derrida, and Michel Foucault, were captivated by Nietzsche. Influenced by Nietzsche's *Genealogy of Morals*, Foucault developed a distinctive type of 'genealogy' that aimed to objectify historical processes by which power comes to be objectified as knowledge. For Foucault (1984), genealogical analysis has the advantage of rupturing complacent notions of unlinear progress for a more fragmented, recursive, and contingent idea of 'descent' and 'emergence' as a never-ending game of domination over bodies that takes different forms at different times. Later Foucault would highlight from classical texts the various ways that the body was worked on by 'technologies of the self': 'technologies of the self ... permit individuals to effect by their own means, or with the help of others, a certain number of operations on their own bodies and souls, thoughts, conduct, and way of being, so as to transform themselves in order to attain a certain state of happiness, purity, wisdom, perfection, or immortality' (1997: 225). Clearly, this concept shares an affinity with the Nietzschean superman ideal of 'self-making' or overcoming.

This Nietzschean strain of social theory from Adorno to the later Foucault was criticised by more rationalist philosophical approaches. Jurgen Habermas defended the potential for rational critique and objectively valid truth in opposition to the Nietzschean artistic critique of modernity. If all knowledge functions in the interest of power, as the Nietzscheans claim, then there can be no grounds for a rational, disinterested theory or the universally applicable criteria of validity of the sort that Habermas proposes with his theory of communicative action. While sociology is concerned with structures of power, it cannot be reduced *deus ex machina* to the will to power. More centrally, sociology is concerned with tensions and contradictions in social relations of domination *and* cooperation, human interdependencies *and* institutions, reciprocity *and* enmity, group belonging *and* exclusion, trust *and* suspicion.

Habermas takes Foucault to task for what he sees as a self-defeating critique of rationality. As far as Habermas is concerned, Foucault's genealogy produces an unsustainable ambiguity for social theory. On the one hand, genealogy functions as an empirical social theory of specific power technologies, for instance penology or medicine, but, on the other, it is engaged as a 'transcendental-historicist' concept that 'emerges' in different forms at all times and places. 'In his basic concept of power, Foucault has forced together the idealist idea of transcendental synthesis with the presuppositions of an empiricist ontology' (Habermas, 1987: 274).

If power always precedes truth claims and gives rise to them, then Foucault's truth claim must also be a mask for some play of power. For Habermas the exercise of power always depends on some criteria that would let subjects know if their actions proved to be a success or a failure. Habermas finds Foucault's genealogy 'incoherent' as an objective historical analysis of power. First, Foucault's self-knowing perspective reflects the interests of the present even though objective genealogy was meant to disqualify current meanings from historical analysis. Second, all knowledge, practical or theoretical, subversive or conformist, is fated to find a place in a hierarchy of power. Even the knowledge of marginal groups that resist domination by official knowledge will, if their struggle is successful, form yet another dominant knowledge-power regime. Such relativism is inevitable because of Foucault's refusal to establish 'neutral' criteria about what would count as valid as a propositional truth claim. Foucault needs to specify a mechanism, Habermas (1987: 287) argues, to connect local power struggles to stabilised institutional power.

In his general theory of the capillary effects of power through modern forms of surveillance technology suggested by the panopticon architectural model, Foucault fails to address the rights of the formal legal subject and the difference that this makes to the power balance. Legal rights, for Habermas, grant modern subjects an ambiguous gain in freedom that is more than the disciplinary effect of power. For Foucault (and Nietzsche) legal and normative rights are functional effects of power relations. Justice is always a stake in social struggles, not for its own sake but in order to acquire or contest power. As Foucault at his most 'Nietzschean Marxist' put it in a discussion with Noam Chomsky:

> I will be a little bit Nietzschean about this: in other words, it seems to me that the idea of justice in itself is an idea which in effect has been invented and put to work in different types of societies as an instrument of a certain political and economic power or as a weapon against that power. But it seems to me that, in any case, the notion of justice itself functions within a society of classes as a claim made by the oppressed class and as justification for it. (1974: 184–5)

Foucault is upbraided for neglecting what Habermas considers central to a certain kind of social theory, while Foucault believed that he was engaged in a deeper critique of institutional power.

Given their different historical contexts, philosophical influences and substantive interests, from classical sociology through to more recent developments, Nietzschean-inspired social theory was unable to bequeath a coherent tradition of cumulative social theory. Nonetheless, and whatever its shortcomings and aporia, Nietzschean social theory from Simmel and Weber to Foucault placed the development of a relational theory of power at the heart of the concerns of sociology today.

5

IDEOLOGICAL TURN: ANTONIO GRAMSCI AND GEORG LUKACS

Sociology has had a bad reputation among Marxists. While sociology cut its teeth on the social theory of Karl Marx, academic sociology barely registered with Marxism (Hughes, 1958). Sociology was placed under suspicion as 'bourgeois sociology', an ideological reflection of the standpoint and interests of the dominant class. Since it emerged in societies where capitalist social relations prevailed, Marxists argued that sociology, as the science of society, cannot help but to serve the dominant social interests. In contrast, Marxist social theory assumed that it could transcend the narrow, one-sided horizon of sociology because it represented universal human interests through identifying with the working class and its struggles. Based on the claim that contrasting class standpoints inevitably shape social theory, some Marxists ventured to claim that a distinctive sociology is possible only from the standpoint of the working class. 'Bourgeois sociology' may assume that capitalism is permanent but 'proletarian sociology' (Marxism) knew that it was temporary. Capitalism has been 'temporary' since the mid-nineteenth century.

A sophisticated form of Marxist theory was developed by Antonio Gramsci (1891–1937), who furnished Marxism with a differentiated socio-historical account of cultural and institutional processes shaping the social relations of classes, groups and nations. For Gramsci (1971: 426–7), sociology presupposes and is subordinate to a general 'conception of the world' established by philosophy. Georg Lukacs and Antonio Gramsci tried to explain developments in the first few decades of the last century. More than a contingent theory of economic crisis, Marxist theory extends to what it sees as a wider crisis of human relations. In the twentieth century this was given a distinctive emphasis by Georg Lukacs' theory of reification, which set the course for the emergence of critical theory and 'Western Marxism' (Anderson, 1976). As some Marxists like Karl Korsch became more receptive to sociology Lukacs became increasingly hostile, while Gramsci argued that his conception of Marxism as a 'philosophy of praxis' subsumed sociology in a wider, open-ended critique. Finally, Lukacs, whose Marxism was formed out of intimate contact with the sociology of Simmel and Weber, constructed a crude anti-sociology as the price of political compromise with the Soviet dictatorship.

REIFICATION AND SOCIAL THEORY

For Lukacs a deeper source of passivity and fatalism than hegemony was the structuring of everyday reality by the commodity form. Where Marx identified the commodity fetish as the characteristic form of alienation of capitalist society, Lukacs was also influenced by the theory of reification in Georg Simmel's (2011) *Philosophy of Money*. As a relation between things, the commodity structure, not ideology, represents 'the central structural problem of capitalist society in all its aspect' (Lukacs, 1971: 83). Only in capitalist society does the commodity perform the universal function of exchange and, following Tönnies' distinction between *Gemeinschaft* and *Gesellschaft*, breaks the personal bonds of earlier 'organic' communities. Instrumental rationality, following Weber, and calculability, following Simmel, suffuse every aspect of life.

Social relations between people are hidden by the immediate commodity relation. Therefore immediate perception and consciousness misrecognises reality and conflates the abstract character of the commodity relation with authentic human relations. Social theory expresses the creeping bureaucratisation of knowledge when it constructs an essentially contemplative formal system in 'an ever-increasing remoteness from the qualitative and material essence of the "things" to which bureaucratic activity pertains' (Lukacs, 1971: 99). Bureaucratic 'conscientiousness' and impartiality merely solidify the reified structure of consciousness.

The reified solidity of reality only begins to be dissolved when the intensity of everyday life is heightened by crisis. Crisis has a tendency to intensify reification at the same time as the crust of fixed, reified categories begins to crack open, exposing its 'inner emptiness' (Lukacs, 1971: 208). In a crisis the social sciences discern only chaos without a pattern. Crisis throws an element of chance and contingency into the mix. 'In its unthinking, mundane reality *that* [reified] life seems firmly held together by "natural laws"; yet it can experience a sudden dislocation because the bonds uniting its various elements and partial systems are a chance affair even at their most normal' (1971: 101). Echoing Weber, while isolated systems are subject to strict rationalisation the total process is relatively irrational: specialised functions are rationally controlled while totality is ruled by chance. Social sciences, like economics, that take isolated functions as fixed 'datum' are unable to comprehend the overall tendency to systemic crises: 'it is the very success with which the economy is totally rationalised and transformed into an abstract and mathematically oriented system of formal "laws" that creates the methodological barrier to understanding the phenomenon of crisis' (1971: 105).

With science and philosophy distorted by the all-encompassing power of reification only the proletariat, self-conscious of its function as a commodity, can break its hold over human society. Lukacs argues that labour's role in the production process enables it, ideally, to recognise practically that social facts are not objects but relations between people and that 'facts are wholly dissolved into processes' (Lukacs, 1971: 180). The worker sells their only possession, the ability to labour, not as a whole person but as a limited function interchangeable with other rationalised things. Labour typifies the social process as whole: 'this transformation of a human function into a commodity reveals in all its starkness the dehumanised and dehumanising function of the commodity relation' (Lukacs, 1971: 92).

From the perspective of the most extreme form of reification, humans as functional objects, workers can pass beyond the immediacy of their condition. From being a mere quantity in calculations about profit and efficiency, labour is forced to confront its own qualitative capacities in the moral, physical, emotional, and intellectual life of the whole person (Lukacs, 1971: 166). Because labour suffers from the degradation of absolute reification, only it can transcend these conditions in practice. If confined to the level of social theory, Marxism becomes merely a deductive 'theory of praxis.' It can only become a 'practical theory' of social transformation through an uneven process of self-conscious class conflict (1971: 205).

Lukacs first sets up the problem of reification as total domination of social relations by things and then abolishes it with a theory of ideal forms of class consciousness. Ideal or attributed consciousness exists only as a speculative philosophical construction not found in any empirical individual, group or class. The French Marxist Henri Lefebvre argued that while appearing to abolish the split between theory and practice Lukacs restored the prestige of philosophy:

> Lukacs substitutes a philosophy of the proletariat for classical philosophy. His philosophy delegates philosophical authority, the power of representing and systematizing reality, to one thinker. This perpetuates the risks and dangers of classical systematization even – and more than ever – when the thinker becomes the collective thinker! (1968a: 36–7)

Lukacs' abolished philosophy philosophically. In contrast, Marx had argued that philosophy will come to an end only when it is finally realised in practice. By this Marx meant that philosophy will uncover the truth of reality as the ensemble of social relations only by transforming social conditions that suppress the truth of social interdependency. Philosophers merely interpret reality when the point is to change it, as Marx famously declared.

MARXISM AS METHOD

No Marxist arguably did more to reduce Marx's social theory to a philosophical 'method' than Lukacs. For Lukacs (1971) the method of totality alone is what distinguishes Marxism as social theory. This philosophical claim ensures that Marxism would remain valid even if all the substantive results of Marx's theory of capitalism were found to be false. Totality requires a shift in perspective from what is immediately given towards the mediation of the present by the historical process (Lukacs, 1971: 158). Only from the point of view of totality can all the antinomies of bourgeois theory that reflect a fractured bourgeois society – subject and object, form and content, facts and values – be overcome.

Taking the standpoint of the social ensemble or totality appears to be the only way to grasp the dense movement of social interdependencies. If totality is 'the standpoint of human society', then it can only be known by transcending every fixed point in social space. Such a standpoint is open to relatively independent intellectuals, like Marx, who possess the leisure and education to adopt a universal perspective (Mannheim, 1936). Marxist intellectuals like Lukacs ascribed the universal standpoint to an idealised proletariat who, as the exploited class in society, have no particular interest in the survival of capitalism and so represent the universal interest in human freedom. For Lukacs, the proletariat can only understand its own class position if it comprehends the whole of society and it alone can unify theory and practice from its social position in the relations of production: 'From its own point of view self-knowledge coincides with knowledge of the whole so that the proletariat is at one and the same time the subject and object of its own knowledge' (Lukacs, 1971: 20).

But in what sense is the proletariat the subject and object of 'its own knowledge'? After all, social theory is not given spontaneously by social conditions. Moreover, a small group of professional intellectuals, not proletarians, developed the theory of totality and the dialectical method.

In many respects, Lukacs' Marxist method demonstrates a continuing affinity with Max Weber's ideal-types (Liebersohm, 1988; Perkins, 1993). This intellectual debt profoundly shaped Lukacs' journey from the tragic pessimism of German sociology to the revolutionary optimism of Marxism (Lukacs, 1971: ix; Lowy, 1979). Concrete reality cannot be approached directly from the immediacy of empirical relations and actual consciousness of discrete individuals or classes. It can only be grasped in terms of 'objective possibility', a term that Lukacs borrowed from Weber, given by a model of the social whole. Lukacs deploys a Weberian ideal-typical perspective that 'infers' or 'imputes' class consciousness as the rational response of people to basic types of 'objective situations':

> By relating consciousness to the whole of society it becomes possible to infer the thoughts and feelings which men *would have* in a particular situation *if* they were able to assess both it and the interests arising from it in their impact on immediate action and on the whole structure of society. (1971: 51, emphasis added)

Lukacs' (1971: 149) model overcomes the subject–object dualism of 'bourgeois' social theory by the ideal methods of 'bourgeois' Weberian sociology. In Lukacs' ideal-type the working class is simultaneously an *object*, constructed by and dependent on capital's possession of the means of production, and a *subject*, collectively struggling against capital for its own emancipation. In the process of practical struggle the working class acquires 'true' consciousness of its universal function in ending human self-domination. Only by taking theoretical distance from empirical reality, Lukacs argues, might 'true' class consciousness be derived and the 'objective possibility' within totality discovered for social action.

Periods of crisis present the ideally class-conscious proletariat with the 'objective possibility' of moving beyond capitalism. Without this attributed historical consciousness, the crisis would remain permanent (Lukacs, 1971: 76). As the last class in history, the proletariat must abolish capitalism armed with full consciousness of its historical task. Revolutionary praxis attempted to abolish capitalism in reality after it had already been abolished as an 'objective possibility' established by an ideal-type model of the social whole for dialectical theory. Political action guided by ideal theory would, Lukacs argued, fulfil Marx's injunction for revolution to abolish philosophy by realising it in reality.

HEGEMONY AND CRISIS

For many Marxists, stubborn faith in the eventual final crisis of capitalism was a source of defiance against objective circumstances of defeat and demoralisation since the 1920s. Gramsci described faith in mechanical determinism as 'a tremendous force of moral resistance, of cohesion and of patient and obstinate perseverance … fatalism is nothing other than the clothing worn by real and active will when in a weak position' (1971: 336–7). However, even in the depths of ideological retreat Gramsci argued that faith should always be challenged by reason.

Gramsci gave crisis a more differentiated social and political significance than purely economic models. He followed Marx in assuming that no society breaks down unless it has exhausted it potential for further development. An important distinction was made by Gramsci between an '*organic*' and 'relatively permanent' structural crisis and an episodic and passing '*conjunctural* crisis'. The former raises profound criticism of the social order while the latter involves relatively minor criticism of politicians and parties.

> A crisis occurs, sometimes lasting for decades. This exceptional duration means that incurable structural contradictions have revealed themselves (reached maturity), and that, despite this, the political forces which are struggling to conserve and defend the existing structure itself are making every effort to cure them, within certain limits, and to overcome them. (Gramsci, 1971: 178)

No social formation accepts that it has been superseded and so continues to struggle on the conjunctural terrain to try to salvage the situation. Opposing social forces, meanwhile, struggle on the organic terrain to overcome the old social structures before the crisis plunges humanity more completely into catastrophe. The problem that Gramsci identifies is that organic crisis and conjunctural crisis are too often confused, giving rise to arbitrary political judgements about the nature of the process.

Politically, a patient 'war of position' is appropriate for 'conjunctural crises' while a rapid 'war of movement' is appropriate to 'organic crises'. Yet political leaders and movements often adopt a war of position (reforms) in an organic crisis that demands urgent action, or engage in a disastrous war of movement (insurgency) in a conjunctural crisis. In modern states, economic and political conjunctural crises prevail over organic social crises. This is because 'civil society' is complex and highly resistant to crises, even when these prove economically catastrophic: 'The superstructures of civil society are like trench-systems of modern warfare' (Gramsci, 1971: 235). In the case of the Russian Revolution of 1917, the state proved vulnerable to insurrection because its civil society was weakly developed under the oppressive weight of a centralised autocratic state, making it relatively defenceless against the 'organic crisis' of war and hunger.

The most profound crisis for civil society is a 'crisis of hegemony'. By hegemony Gramsci meant that the ruling class 'leads' society ideologically rather than merely dominating it through physical force alone. Gramsci refused to invent a new terminology but re-fashioned existing concepts like 'hegemony', already widely used by intellectuals and political leaders to address the balance between state power and coercion (Ives, 2004). Gramsci brought the concept of hegemony into contact with a host of related, distinctively Gramscian terms – common sense, good sense, passive revolution, civil society, intellectuals, war of position and war of movement – enriching its meaning and theoretical possibilities.

A crisis of authority occurs when the traditional ideas are no longer able to prescribe the limits of popular discourse. At the same time, however, alternative forms of ideological authority are fragmented and dispersed. This is a dangerous situation since all manner of solutions to the crisis of authority are entertained, including the wildest fantasies and illusions: 'The crisis consists precisely in the fact that the old is dying and the new cannot be born; in this interregnum a great variety of morbid symptoms appear' (Gramsci, 1971: 276). Since in the interregnum nothing is fixed, the crisis may be resolved by mass physical violence and terror: 'either the old society resists and ensures a breathing space, by physically exterminating the elite of the rival class and terrorising its mass reserves; or a reciprocal destruction of the conflicting forces occurs, and a peace of the graveyard is established, perhaps even under the surveillance of a foreign guard' (1971: 185).

Social and political competition over ideological leadership raises the problem of the role played by intellectuals. Gramsci (1971: 7) distinguished between 'traditional intellectuals', a privileged group of autonomous thinkers independent of dominant social groups, and 'organic intellectuals', a group of thinkers practically aligned with a class, either through conviction, as when bourgeois intellectuals like Marx and Engels take the side of the working class, or when a class throws up intellectual leaders from within its own ranks. So while everybody is an intellectual of some sort by virtue of their self-conscious existence, not everyone is a professional intellectual.

In their everyday dealings, Gramsci argues, people are already 'spontaneous philosophers'. They use conceptual language, move between 'common sense' and 'good sense', and inhabit popular folklore. Philosophy coincides with the widely held practical wisdom of 'good sense', which gives some coherence and unity to the taken-for-granted, diffuse assumptions of 'common sense'. Common sense underpins the uncritical, tacit assumptions that make the ideological hegemony of the dominant class possible. Sense-making is a constant process of practical experimentation and observation of reality.

A challenge to the received nostrums of common sense is not only possible in theory but is already underway in everyday life. When common sense absorbs theoretical advances it inches closer to 'good sense', though there is no rigid division between one and the other:

> Common sense is not something rigid and immobile, but is continually transforming itself, enriching itself with scientific ideas and with philosophical opinions which have entered ordinary life. 'Common sense' is the folklore of philosophy, and is always halfway between folklore properly speaking and the philosophy, science, and economics of the specialists. (Gramsci, 1971: 326, n.5).

Here Gramsci avoids fixed ideal-types of class consciousness and attempts to understand the processes constantly shaping the social forms of popular sense. So while Marxism is a critique of common sense, since everyone is already a philosopher (or sociologist) Marxism is itself premised on common sense, which it in turn renovates and makes 'critical'.

Intellectual progress is not measured in small literary or scientific coteries but with the widest possible spread of theoretical consciousness. A theoretical culture strengthens the critical-active side of what Gramsci calls 'contradictory consciousness' against its uncritical-passive side. In this way, theory is united with practice to become a political and ethical force (Gramsci, 1971: 365). On the other hand, professional intellectuals lead organisations and parties, requiring that 'the theoretical aspect of the theory-practice nexus [be] distinguished concretely by the existence of a group of people "specialised" in conceptual and philosophical elaboration of ideas' (1971: 334). Where intellectuals are divorced from the rest of society, fateful costs are imposed on both knowledge and common sense. The working class experience a popular sense and feeling for the situation but cannot explain its sources; intellectuals possess formal knowledge but have little feeling for the experiences of ordinary life (1971: 418).

GRAMSCI AND SOCIOLOGY

With Lukacs and Korsch, Gramsci similarly rejected the idea, often attributed to Marxist theory, 'that every fluctuation of politics and ideology can be presented and expounded as an immediate expression of the [economic] structure, must be contested in theory as primitive infantilism' (1971: 407). Under conditions of fascist prison and censorship, Gramsci used Bukharin's popular sociology as an opportunity to ruminate on sociology and Marxism, or what he obliquely called 'the philosophy of praxis'. Gramsci excluded sociology as a valid theoretical domain. 'Theory' for

Gramsci meant 'philosophy'. When Gramsci called Marxism the 'philosophy of praxis' he understood by this a theory of political action, not sociology.

For Gramsci sociology was founded on the evolutionary positivist model of natural science. As such, sociology presupposes a philosophical conception of the world, a 'naive metaphysics'. An arbitrary suppression of philosophy allowed sociologists like Bukharin to confine problems only to those of 'immediate political and ideological order' (1971: 427, 436). In the nineteenth century, Gramsci claimed, sociology began to supplant political science. As parliamentary government came to be seen as a process of 'natural' evolution, sociology took over the traditional subject matter of political science:

> If political science means science of the State, and the State is the entire complex of practical and theoretical activities with which the ruling class not only justifies and maintains its dominance, but manages to win the active consent of those over whom it rules, then it is obvious that all the essential questions of sociology are nothing other than the questions of political science. (1971: 244)

Therefore Gramsci argued, Bukharin ought to have specified the nature and purpose of sociology, qua political science, its relationship to Marxism, and its 'scientific' character.

Since Gramsci's critique is often regarded in social theory as a decisive refutation of Bukharin's 'positivism' it is worthwhile examining in a bit more detail. Unfortunately, Gramsci's critique of Bukharin falls short of his own strictures about the necessity for intellectual fidelity, and misrepresents the spirit and content of Bukharin's book (Gramsci was, after all, writing in prison mainly from memory). For instance, he claims that Bukharin 'contains no treatment of any kind of the dialectic' because of his capitulation to the 'peremptory certainties' of vulgar common sense (1971; 434–5). In fact Bukharin's theory of equilibrium attempts to popularise the dialectical method as a scientific model. In a chapter called '*Dialectical* Materialism' Bukharin (2011: 74–5) translated the standard Marxist tripartite dialectical formula (thesis–antithesis–synthesis) to explain the role of contradictory forces in the historical process.

Gramsci called Bukharin's philosophy 'positivistic Aristotelianism' because it attached formal logic to the methods of natural science. According to Gramsci (1971: 437) the result is a metaphysical materialism that reduces everything to a single, final cause of 'regularity, normality and uniformity'. In this way Gramsci depicts Bukharin as reifying 'society' as something qualitatively distinct from the individual quantities that compose it. Such a mechanical idea of development renders revolutionary praxis impossible and blocks the dialectical passage from quantity to quality (Gramsci, 1971: 426). On the contrary, Bukharin argued that quality and quantity are not binary elements formally opposed to each other but stand on a dynamic continuum of relative difference. Neither did Bukharin propose an absolute evolutionary 'law', as Gramsci claims. He constructed a theoretical model of 'tendencies' in social reproduction, not that dissimilar from Gramsci's (1971: 401) own 'law of tendency in large numbers' or Marx's 'law of the tendency of the falling rate of profit'.

Gramsci (1971: 468) went so far as to attribute to Bukharin the view that scientific theory drives historical change, even though Bukharin (2011: 161–2) repeatedly insisted that 'every science is born from practice ... practice created theory'. If anything, far from changes in science causing social change, Bukharin failed to allow scientific theory sufficient relative autonomy from class interests. As Gramsci (1971: 457) notes, progress in science cannot be reduced to its technical apparatus, not even as the last instance of a lengthy causal chain. As the central technical instrument in geology, the hammer undergoes no material progress even though geological science makes theoretical progress.

While Bukharin's system is unduly formal and schematic, it did not reduce everything to a single cause, technological or economic, that mechanically produces predetermined outcomes. True, Bukharin outlined the relationship between philosophy and material conditions in a causal schema that may have made Comte blush (perhaps) – where philosophy (or art or religion or language) presupposes science, which presupposes social psychology, which, finally, presupposes social technology. Again, Bukharin (2011: 226) categorically denied that Marxism reduces the ideological superstructure to the economic base as the only active factor in the system or as lower in the scale of relative importance. After all, he reasoned, the economy would cease to exist without the mutual activities of state, science, language, or ideologies.

LANGUAGE AND THEORY

While Gramsci's critique of Bukharin and sociology more generally is riddled with inconsistencies and inaccuracies, it also contains a number of important precepts and hypotheses. If it wants to attract non-specialists, Gramsci asserted, popular sociology should begin with a critical examination of common sense. Bukharin's 'first mistake', therefore, was to begin with the traditional philosophical concepts of intellectual culture. Because Marxism can 'only be conceived in a polemical form and in the form of perpetual struggle' as it attempts to create a higher theoretical culture among the working class, its 'starting point must always be that common sense which is the spontaneous philosophy of the multitude and which has to be made ideologically coherent' (Gramsci, 1971: 421).

Contradictorily, Gramsci (1971: 425, 431) also argued that Bukharin should have begun with a general theoretical discussion of philosophy to justify his claim that historical materialism is Marxist sociology. Without a critical discussion of philosophy, Gramsci claimed, there can be no sociological 'theory' as such. Because Bukharin did not clearly pose the problem of what 'theory' actually is he was unable, in Gramsci's (1971: 427) view, to present 'a realistic historical judgment of past philosophies, all of which he presents as pure delirium and folly'.

Remote from common sense, philosophy is experienced negatively by dominated groups as an external imposition of cultural elites. It is therefore futile, Gramsci argued, to appeal, as Bukharin did, to the common-sense view that the world exists as objective reality, and then ridicule 'subjectivist' philosophers who hold that the world is a creation of human spirit, an idea that the general public finds laughable (1971: 442). What is really required, Gramsci asserted, is to recognise that human knowledge is always relative and to assimilate active subjectivity to Marx's theory of superstructures. There is no absolute, external position from where the 'objectivity' of the world might be definitively established. There is only a human process, a process of 'historical becoming, knowledge and reality are also a becoming and so is objectivity, etc.' (1971: 446). Even in the experimental method of the natural sciences 'objective' theory is controlled by subjective practice, trial and error, theoretical testing and revision.

Conceptual language forms part of the historical process. As concepts are renewed, social theory is also renewed. Hence an effort must be made to translate between different theoretical domains of philosophy, politics and economics. Marx translated immanence as a speculative concept of German philosophy into a 'historicist form with the aid of French politics and English classical economics' (Gramsci, 1971: 400).

> The new 'metaphorical' meaning spreads with the spread of the new culture, which furthermore also coins brand-new words or absorbs them from other languages as loan-words giving them a precise meaning and therefore depriving them of the extensive halo they possessed in the original language. Thus it is probable that for many people the term 'immanence' is known, understood and used for the first time only in the new 'metaphorical' sense given to it by the philosophy of praxis. (Gramsci, 1971: 452)

Metaphors like 'immanence' acquire a new meaning when they form part of a new theoretical synthesis. This renewed idea of 'immanence' also transforms the conceptual meaning of 'teleology', a term rejected as metaphysical by Bukharin (see Meikle, 1985). Social processes develop 'teleologically' in the sense that they are restricted to a finite number of directions and not others, due to the 'immanent' possibilities permitted by intrinsic kinds of social relations, without any necessary end goal – the cork tree exists for its own purposes, not to provide bottle stoppers (Gramsci, 1971: 471).

Concepts inherited from an earlier period can have their meaning transformed by coming into contact with a new constellation of social theory. For example, Gramsci challenges Bukharin's (2011: 26) anti-teleological dismissal of the word 'immanence' as merely a metaphorical expression of Marx while 'materialism' continued to be used in its literal nineteenth-century sense of objective physical matter. An excessive emphasis on 'materialism' in Marxism, Gramsci (1971: 461) argued, rested on 'the baroque conviction that the more one goes back to "material" objects the more orthodox one must be'. Here physical matter is given unwarranted priority over historical processes and social relations. Vulgar materialism hypostatises 'matter' by turning it into a fixed, objective 'quality', 'that is to say, an arbitrary abstraction rather than a process of analytical distinction necessary for explanatory purposes' (1971: 469). Material forces are simultaneously objective *and* subjective sides of social processes: 'The ensemble of the material forces of production is at the same time a crystallisation of all past history and the basis of present and future history: it is both a document and an active and propulsive force' (1971: 466).

Gramsci wanted to reclaim the term 'orthodoxy' for his brand of Marxism from those, like Bukharin, that he considered crude materialists. By orthodox Marxist theory, Gramsci meant a self-sufficient culture: 'a total and integral conception of the world, a total philosophy and theory of natural science, and not only that but everything that is needed to give life to an integral practical organisation of society, that is, to become a total integral civilisation' (1971: 462). Marxist theory should not be reduced to its various sources in politics, philosophy and political economy.

With this scope of revolutionary ambition Marxism saw itself as wholly autonomous theory, incomparable to other theories, which were in any case rooted in a disappearing culture. A wholly new way of conceiving theory opened up by Marx and Marxism as a living doctrine was beginning to establish its own independent hegemonic credentials over traditional culture. In such ways, Gramsci allowed the second, activist, part of his famous aphorism, 'Pessimism of the intellect, optimism of the will', to dominate the first, the positivist discipline of scientific culture.

LUKACS' CRITIQUE OF 'IRRATIONAL' THEORY

As some Marxists like Korsch inched closer to sociology to account for crisis, Lukacs, who was steeped in classical German sociology, moved even further away. This process culminated in the early 1950s with *The Destruction of Reason* (1980), his major survey of modern German philosophy and sociology over the last hundred years. Lukacs' main claim is that modern philosophical and sociological theories substitute for an objective theory of history arbitrary theories of subjective essences, 'vital life-forms' or situated knowledge. This provides the philosophical 'comfort' of illusions about personal autonomy and cultural superiority, allowing Western intellectuals to veil their dependence on imperialism. As 'decadent self-knowledge', intellectuals placed the dominated masses at the bottom of the scale of human values.

To reveal the social genesis and function of social theory, Lukacs (1980: 5) undertook the interpretative strategy of an 'immanent critique', what Lichtheim (1970: 109) called a 'transcript theory of cognition' and Rockmore (1992) an 'interactionist' theory of knowledge by which the objective world enters into thought processes behind the back of the theorists' intentions, which in turn acts back on the social and political context. Textual analysis by a critic like Lukacs reveals social theory as a distorted mirror of a misrecognised reality that has unintended political effects.

By reading closely a number of texts considered to be characteristic of the previous century, Lukacs aimed to reveal their hidden and unconscious affinities with the 'irrationality' of capitalist crisis, imperialism and fascism. Sociologists and philosophers always adopt some particular standpoint relative to their social situation, sometimes explicitly, more often implicitly. Lukacs' takes this standpoint as a benchmark with which to critique hidden assumptions about power and class relations. As a defensive but largely unacknowledged reflex against Marxism, philosophy embraced 'irrationalism'. In different ways, the 'irrationalist' theories of phenomenology, existentialism, vitalism, and pragmatism denied any dialectical conception of human progress. These theories, Lukacs argued, rejected historical processes and froze 'authentic' human life into a timeless ontology of 'being'.

Essentially, Lukacs argues that the failure of the 1848 Revolution and the Paris Commune of 1871, followed by aggressive imperialist expansion and world war (1870–1920), marked the general decline of bourgeois intellectual culture in increasingly defensive struggles against Marxism, particularly in Germany. In its ascendant phase during the Enlightenment, bourgeois philosophy challenged and destroyed the premises of feudal ideology. Hegel was the last bourgeois thinker to view philosophy, specifically the dialectical method, as the servant of historical development, a positive process culminating in his glorification of the Prussian state. Since the mid-nineteenth century, however, philosophy lacked any self-conscious motivation about the historic role of rationality. When it came to Marxism, scholars no longer conscientiously acquired detailed knowledge of source material but merely repeated, second hand, superficial phrases and polemics.

Irrationalism was given its fullest expression in the philosophy of Nietzsche. Intellectuals without a social function beyond self-interest became fascinated by Nietzsche's stock of witty aphorisms, scandalous assertions and rebellious aristocratic gestures as a substitute for rational knowledge about the world. Behind Nietzsche's aphoristic fragments lay a hidden 'system'. Nietzsche's 'transvaluation of all values' corresponded, for Lukacs, to 'complacent, narcissistic, playful relativism, pessimism, nihilism':

> Nietzsche's philosophy performed the 'social task' of 'rescuing' and 'redeeming' this type of bourgeois mind. It offered a road which avoided the need for any break, or indeed any serious conflict, with the bourgeoisie. It was a road whereby the pleasant moral feeling of being a rebel could be sustained and even intensified, whilst a 'more thorough', 'cosmic biological' revolution was enticingly projected in contrast to the 'superficial', 'external' social revolution. (1980: 317)

As a young man, Nietzsche had opposed the Paris Commune in his 'revolutionary' rejection of social levelling in favour of domination by a ruthless elite. Nietzsche substituted the myth of will-power in the earlier 'irrational' philosophy of Schopenhauer with the myth of the will-to-power. Through the idea of 'eternal recurrence', humanity is condemned by Nietzsche to endlessly repeat the violence of imperialist crisis.

Although Nietzsche showed little interest in Marxism, he acquired 'an anticipatory sensitivity to what the parasitical intelligentsia would need in the imperialist age' – the need to combat Marxist theory philosophically lest intellectuals lose their privileged positions vis-à-vis the working class. A purely intellectual 'revolution', confined to a critique of culture beyond economics and politics, secured the privileges enjoyed by dominant groups, intellectuals most of all, while expressing the violent pathos of a barely repressed fear of socially dominated masses. As intellectuals experience the meaningless of life the attraction of positivism, the scientific ideology of the competitive phase of capitalism, waned while irrationalism and nihilism waxed as the cultural ideology of the imperialist phase.

IRRATIONAL SOCIOLOGY

Sociology emerged, Lukacs argued, in response to the twin crises in classical political economy in Britain (Ricardo) and utopian socialism in France (Saint-Simon and Charles Fourier) in the early nineteenth century. Comte and Spencer had looked for the scientific roots of universal progress beyond economics in comprehensive accounts of the historical development of societies. But as sociology became a specialised, detached discipline the fundamental problems of capitalist civilisation were dissected and deferred, passed from one isolated sub-specialism to another, preventing anything like a comprehensive understanding of the issues. So long as capitalist development in Germany stalled, the bourgeoisie could not lead society and settled for a treacherous compromise with the old feudal-military regime.

Only after the 1870s did sociology begin to emerge in Germany. It began as a critique of positivism as a metaphysical philosophy of history, surrendering any pretensions to a unified theory of historical progress to purely empirical, specialised studies. Intellectually, sociology was made possible by the Austrian School of economics since, having 'refuted' Marx in the economic sphere, they cleared the way for sociology to answer historical materialism in the social sphere emptied of 'economics', with the aim of moderating class conflict within a nationalist framework. Instead of causal explanations of capitalism, sociology contented itself with purely formal analogies and ideal-types of rationality, exchange, association, bureaucracy, charisma, action, and so on, valid across different places and times.

Well acquainted with the facts of modern capitalism, Weber, Simmel, Sombart, Tönnies and Mannheim – Lukacs argued – stood the capitalist economy on its head and abstractly prioritised the surfaces of calculation and rationality over the development of the productive forces, producing 'false answers to questions that were justified, because [they were already] posed by reality itself' (1980: 614). Lukacs (1980: 593) placed Tönnies in 'the classic German tradition' and closer to 'the progressive scientific learning of Western Europe' than later sociologists. But Tönnies remained a 'Romantic anti-capitalist' at heart, limited to a backward-looking, negative critique of capitalism as part of the bourgeois intellectual disaffection with imperialist culture. Yet the critique remained 'irrational', Lukacs argued, a distorted reflection of the contradictions of capitalist reality. He relied on a mysterious idea of subjective 'will' to bring about his famous contrast between the 'essences' of 'organic' community and 'mechanical' society. This antithesis inflated the binary opposition between 'civilisation' (progress in science, technology, economy) and 'culture' (decline in art, philosophy, spirituality) in later sociology.

Irrational Simmel

Influenced by Nietzsche and vitalism, as well as Kant and positivism, Simmel was representative of irrational social theory. Objective reality was simply unknowable except from the subjective viewpoint of 'life', a third term that allowed Simmel to bypass the old philosophical dualism of being and consciousness (Lukacs, 1980: 443). A subjective or constructed emphasis on the forms of life, not objective reality, was developed by Simmel from the concerns of vitalist philosophy (*Lebensphilosophie*) as he increasingly abandoned a positivist concern for the methods of science. Knowledge is always relative to cultural standards of truth for Simmel. Relativism like Simmel's, Lukacs claimed, opened the door to the genocidal racism of fascism since each theory stands on its own without any measure of objective criteria in the external world.

While Simmel moderated the nihilism of Nietzsche he retreated from reality into a 'tragic' worldview. Simmel confronted the problems of capitalist civilisation, such as money, alienation and modernity, that Marx had first critiqued, going so far as an anti-capitalist cultural critique that formed the young Lukacs' own starting point (Lowy, 1979). Yet Simmel's sociology was limited to the most abstract relational forms of social life and neglected their social content. Every sociological content became simply another manifestation of the 'eternal tragedy of culture' arising from the tension in the domination of subjective culture by objective culture. All that intellectuals like Simmel could do was to adopt a haughty standpoint of detachment. Objective culture reserved for inner life ('soul') an autonomous sphere where a unique personality could take refuge.

By appealing to this deeper realm of inner life, Simmel distracted attention away from concrete social and economic problems: 'From a mixture of purely theoretical radicalism and absolute conformity, in practice, to conditions which could never have stood up to criticism, there came about this sapping of the thinking personality even in such lively and gifted men as Simmel' (Lukacs, 1980: 459). For instance, if religion is one of life's vital forms then, paradoxically, declarations by Nietzsche that 'God is dead' can only assume the form of a 'religious atheism' (1980: 449). By using myth (of the soul and life) to corrode the scientific basis of philosophy, Lukacs hyperbolically claimed, Simmel prepared the way for the intellectual culture for fascism.

Irrational Weber

Although Weber was an avowed 'rationalist' in his explicit statements, for Lukacs he was unconsciously irrationalist. In his struggle for scientific rationality Weber succumbed to a higher form of 'irrationality': 'Even here, with the German scholar who, in his subjective aims, made the most honest and rigorous effort to pursue his discipline purely objectively, to found and translate into praxis a methodology of pure objectivity, the imperialist tendencies of pseudo-objectivity proved

stronger' (Lukacs, 1980: 613). For Weber the rise of capitalism was only secondar-
ily a matter of economic forces and first of all an ideology of rationality, nurtured
inside a religious ethos. Weber reduced sociology to a series of pure mental constructs, 'ideal-types' that allowed for a 'rational casuistry' of irrational social
developments.

Since all values were purged as 'irrational' pre-judgements by Weber, all that
sociology might offer is a 'technical critique' of the relationship between means
and ends, not the end goal itself. Weber defined as irrational all value judgements
imposed from outside the circumscribed rationality of technical critique. As
Weber (2012: 351) argued in his lecture 'Science as vocation', there is no rational
criterion to resolve the conflict between the warring gods of competing values;
something may be beautiful without being good or true or sacred. This is evidence
for Lukacs that Weber lapsed into the 'religious atheism of the imperialist age',
caught between a belief that democracy could provide the only effective basis for
modern German imperialism while equating democracy and capitalism with an
abstract 'disenchantment'.

Irrational Mannheim

Karl Mannheim represented for Lukacs the final stage of 'irrational' sociology
before fascism. Mannheim's sociology of knowledge was a backhand 'capitulation'
to the Marxist idea that being determines consciousness. Yet despite rejecting 'relativism', Mannheim equally denied that knowledge could be 'objective'. All knowledge
was 'relational' for Mannheim – 'situation-bound', depending on its context. While
Mannheim may have derived his sociology of knowledge in part from Lukacs'
earlier theory that ascribed specific forms of consciousness to specific classes,
thirty years later it looked to Lukacs like another form of irrational relativism that
broke the concrete link between the economic foundation and ideology, and made
it impossible to distinguish 'false consciousness' from 'true consciousness'.

Only a socially sensitive, detached intelligentsia, Mannheim claimed, has the
chance to transcend 'situational bound' knowledge from the standpoint of the
total situation. Democracy multiplied the possibilities for irrationalism and so
needed to be managed by a rational intelligentsia. From this Lukacs leapt to the
conclusion that Mannheim's brand of liberal sociology saw democracy, not fascism, as the cause of irrationalism: 'Since they had always contested democracy
out of a fear of its social consequences, they seized on the case of Hitler with
delight and satisfaction in order to camouflage their old, unchanged rebuttal of
democracy as a battle against the Right and reaction' (1980: 638).

As Mannheim turned to the problem of post-war social planning he could no
longer be considered 'irrational' in Lukacs, terms, given his own support for the
'planned' economies of the Soviet Union and its satellite states, except that
Mannheim failed to address the socio-economic basis of imperialism in 'monopoly
capitalism', and continued 'formalistically' to treat 'as equivalents fascist dictatorship and the dictatorship of the proletariat, revolutionary and counter-revolutionary
violence' (1980: 639). Failing to challenge the role of British imperialism, Lukacs
found Mannheim complicit with imperialist reaction after the war.

FROM FARCE TO TRAGEDY

Lukacs' apologia represents a strange journey in the anti-sociology of Marxism, starting as a farce and ending in tragedy. Genuine knowledge about German sociology is combined with ludicrous exaggerations. German sociology led Lukacs to Marxism, yet it also supposedly led to fascism (Perkins, 1993: 96). By the 1950s Lukacs rejected the formal construction of ideal-types that he had inherited from Weber in his models of class consciousness of that 1920s (Meszaros, 1995: 339). The main issue here is that cultural sociology represented a clear challenge to the explanatory priorities that Lukacs attributed to historical materialism. All non-Marxist theory was deemed to be irrational since reason itself was made identical to Marxism (Kolakowski, 2005: 1014). In denouncing liberal sociology Lukacs was unable to express openly any of the problems or crimes, let alone the irrationalism, that the Soviet dictatorships committed in the name of the proletariat. Three years later, farce would become tragedy with the brutal suppression of the Hungarian Revolution in 1956 by Soviet military force.

While Adorno (1977: 152) dismissed *The Destruction of Reason* (Lukacs, 1980) as revealing 'the destruction of Lukacs' own' under 'the most threadbare clichés of the very conformism that social criticism once attacked', Aronowitz (2011) broadly endorses the main thrust of Lukacs' critique of philosophy, especially Nietzsche's nihilism and pessimism and Heidegger's ontological essence of Being as superior to the so-called 'Ontic' realm of everyday life and the privileging of the struggle for an 'authentic' self against caring for other beings. However, the claim of irrationalism for the sociology of Simmel and Weber is a hollow one that, for Aronowitz, smacks of 'sour grapes and tendentiousness':

> Simmel and Weber were keen observers of the vicissitudes of modern life: the triumph of bureaucratic rationality that accompanied the rise of capitalism; the ironies of everyday life that defied rationality; and, for Simmel, the role of the unconscious in the reproduction of the commodity form. (2011: 63)

Although some see Lukacs' analysis as 'a knowledgeable, closely reasoned, almost academic discussion' (Rockmore, 1992: 179), its crude 'reflectionist' thesis relies on a polemical shortcut between materialist premises (capitalist irrationality) and idealist reflections (theoretical irrationality) leading to murderous conclusions (fascist irrationality).

If theoretical 'irrationalism' reflected 'the age of imperialism', then presumably it should have been more widespread in Europe and the US and not limited to Germany (Lichtheim, 1970: 112). If irrationalism is theory that falls short of 'objective reality', then all theory must be irrational since absolute knowledge of the plenitude of reality is a non sequitur. Neither is it obvious why only a rising class has reason on its side or that the bourgeois classes have been in decline since 1848. Moreover, Lukacs fails to convince that Nazism is the result of rather disparate philosophical and sociological theories (Rockmore, 1992: 194). Finally, if, as Lukacs argues, theoretical reason and unreason mirror the practical needs of the class position of intellectuals, then theoretical rationality, including Marxism, would seem to be an impossible, even 'irrational,' illusion. Even intellectuals need to eat.

What remains useful in *The Destruction of Reason* (Lukacs, 1980) beyond its polemical excesses is its underlying pedagogical purpose. Against the irrationalist mythology of Nietzschean 'epistemological aristocraticism' (1980: 174), where knowledge is given intuitively to naturally gifted elites, therefore deserving of group privilege, for Lukacs dialectical theory can be learned only if prior conditions of accessibility and legibility are established. Aronowitz (2011: 51) claims that Lukacs' critique of philosophical theory anticipates the social theories of Adorno and Bourdieu and that the pedagogical problems raised by Lukacs remain contemporary ones. Indeed, Bourdieu's (1991: 105) socio-analysis of the texts of Heidegger's 'pure philosophy' echoes Lukacs' symptomatic reading, albeit without the same dogmatism: 'It is perhaps because he never realised what he was saying that Heidegger was able to say what he did say without really having to say it.' Where Lukacs trades in 'vulgar' abuse and bloated extrapolations from a predetermined schema, Bourdieu deliberately 'vulgarises' the philosophical field as relatively autonomous from social conditions, rather than something wholly determined by the needs of imperialism.

Kadavany (2001) advances a more sympathetic textual reading of Lukacs' study. Just as Lukacs attributed a hidden structure of irrationality to non-Marxist texts, Kadavany argues that Lukacs constructed an implied critique of the irrationalist orthodoxy and personality cults imposed by the repressive Stalinist elite, under which Lukacs struggled to simply stay alive: 'burying an acute philosophical description of a tyrannical regime among hundreds of pages of dross is an effective covert strategy' (2001: 308). To evade political opponents, Lukacs was forced to adopt ruses and analogies just as Gramsci deployed Aesopian language to escape the prison censor. If, as Lukacs maintained, no theory is politically innocent and that it cannot evade distortion and caricature by 'epistemological aristocraticism', then this also applies to the misappropriation by authoritarian elites of social theory formulated for other emancipatory purposes, as was the case for the misuse of Marx by Stalinist dictatorship.

CRITIQUE AND DEVELOPMENT

In the last decades of the twentieth century, Marxism had an increasingly tenuous relationship to contemporary social theory. Seemingly refuted by the collapse of the Soviet Union in 1991, Marxism was no longer an ideology that decided the fate of millions across the globe. It had become an irrelevance and a bit of an embarrassment, something that could be taken or left according to one's taste. If theory is embedded in specific cultural contexts, then it cannot be evaluated from some ideal point in abstract space as a universal formula to be applied to all places in all times. All that can be done is to recognise that both theory and the cultural context are contingent, and modestly adopt a pragmatic theory.

Social theory 'after Marxism' combated what it saw as various failings of economism, reductionism, determinism, statism, and simplistic binaries of class in traditional forms of Marxism. Against these weaknesses, post-Marxism emphasised pluralism, fluid identities, the public sphere, language games, and situational politics as the characteristic features of neoliberal global capitalism (Therborn, 2008). 'Post-Marxism' was part of a wider withdrawal from theory as a self-contained logic of abstractions that the post-modern theorist Jean-Francois Lyotard (1984) called 'the crisis of grand narratives'. Lyotard mainly had Marxism in mind as the exemplar of theoretical crisis.

By the 1980s, then, Marxism was *passé*, no longer relevant to the shift in social theory towards burgeoning problems of language, culture and identity. This shift was asserted most emphatically by Ernesto Laclau and Chantal Mouffe's (2001) *Hegemony and Socialist Strategy*. Their answer to the crisis of Marxism was to develop Gramsci's concept of hegemony, itself a response to an earlier crisis of Marxist theory. With the concept of hegemony, Gramsci tried to resolve theoretical crisis by linking economic relations of class to political and ideological consciousness; Laclau and Mouffe now tried to resolve theoretical crisis by using Gramsci's concept of 'hegemony' to separate politics from class. With the rise of new social movements since the 1960s, politics became radically detached from the 'single unifying principle' of class (2001: 69). Politics was conceived as a linguistic construction, not the reflection of objective class conditions. Linguistic practices 'articulate' a new 'historic bloc' of diverse groups to fashion democratic demands that are, temporarily, shared in common. Hence Gramsci's concept of hegemony remains useful so long as 'essentialist' assumptions about class are given up. This also means giving up the concept of 'society' since it assumes a level of order and coherence that underpins the discursive construction of plural identities.

Needless to say, post-Marxism brought forth a sharp rebuke that Marxism had been caricatured and simplified by the exaggerated deployment of vague generalities, ramshackle logic and dubious assertions (Geras, 1990; Wood, 1986). If social theory was now decidedly 'post-Marxist', it required a good dose of theoretical amnesia to erase the traces of what it inherited from earlier crises of Marxism. Post-Marxist theory-baiting forgot that Marx insisted on the historical specificity of social, economic and political relations and rejected all attempts to construct trans-historical theoretical systems. As Terry Eagleton sardonically put it, 'The earlier generation of thinkers had been post-Marxist in the sense of both distancing and drawing upon it; the new generation was post-Marxist in the sense that David Bowie is post-Darwinist' (2003: 43).

A notable attempt was made to overcome the divide between 'the linguistic turn' and Marxism by the leading theorist of 'deconstruction', Jacques Derrida (1930–2004). Deconstructionism is a literary theory or a 'science of writing' that reveals the binary oppositions in a text to undermine any fixed meaning or privileged hierarchy of 'reality' (Norris, 1982). Language depends on differential relations that reach beyond the text or even the author's intended meaning. Whatever is present in a text (words on a page) depends on what is absent from it (its context). To destabilise the text and dispel the illusion of self-sufficient presence, Derrida (2001) focuses on something apparently marginal to the text, a footnote or a passing example, to develop his critique of the self-contained text as the main support of Western metaphysics. This procedure allows the peripheral and the repressed elements of wider context to make a surprising reappearance.

In this vein, Derrida (1994) aimed to 'radicalise' Marx by pointing to the 'spectres' and ghost-like afterlife that Marxist theory made possible: 'As a rule, I analyze and question the fantasy of legitimate descent (father, sons and brothers, et al., rather than mother, daughter and sister), attempting to throw it into crisis ...' (Derrida, 1999: 233). Derrida compared Marx to the ghost in Hamlet as not quite fitting in a 'time out of joint', a phrase that for Derrida opens Marx up to multiple readings and signifies the contested inheritance ('the fantasy of legitimate descent') of Marxism. Deconstructionism, which Marxism had generally seen as a kind of post-modern evasion of radical politics, had all along been conceived by Derrida in 'a certain spirit of Marxism', out of time, disjointed, dislocated, not quite what was expected. In response, the Marxist conflation of deconstructionism with the post-modern critique of grand narratives ignored Derrida's frequent denials that the science of deconstruction has much in common with the vague generalities of post-modernism (Sprinker, 1999).

Attempts to produce a critical sociology in the spirit of Marx did not fare well. It is no accident that Bukharin's sociology appeared at the point when the tide of revolution was already ebbing away but which the 'Western Marxism' of Korsch, Lukacs, Bloch, and Gramsci were doing their theoretical best to extend as 'legitimate heirs'. Marxist criticism of sociology derives in part from political considerations and in part by its association with scientific 'positivism' that Bukharin seemed to exemplify. Instead, Western Marxists emphasised the active, subjective side of class struggle over the 'objective' social structures of capitalism. Science cannot be completely divorced from politics in so far as it transforms people's beliefs and practices on a 'rational' rather than an 'arbitrary' basis (Gramsci, 1971: 244).

The prospects for Marx's 'legitimate heirs' were mixed. Korsch came to accept some of the appeal of a theoretical science of society, while Lukacs proceeded to denounce the classical German sociology of his youth as 'irrational'. In his conception of 'orthodox Marxism', Lukacs was far more concerned about staying faithful to 'the dialectical method' that he found in Marx than in examining the substantive claims that Marx had made about the social dynamic of capitalism. It may well be the case that there is a concealed critique of Stalinist ruling elites in Lukacs' later work. This raises the issue of whether social theory needs to be judged primarily on what is literally stated, to avoid the danger of 'reading in' something that the reader might find more palatable than the actual words used. As Lukacs, Gramsci, and Korsch recognised, the deconstruction of social theory also implies the reconstruction of its context. This is what Derrida recognised as the absent presence or 'ghost' of social theory and why he looked so closely in the texts between the lines and in the margins for clues about missing presuppositions.

6

REFLEXIVE TURN: OTTO NEURATH AND EMPIRICAL SOCIOLOGY

A different kind of positivism emerged in the 1920s among a group of eminent philosophers and scientists known collectively as 'the Vienna Circle' after their 1929 manifesto of the same name (Neurath, 1973: 299–318). The Vienna Circle shared with Comte and Spencer a deep distrust of metaphysical speculation. They wanted to restrict science to logical statements about empirical observations. Sometimes called 'logical positivism' or 'logical empiricism', they practised a type of philosophy or meta-theory that aimed to clarify the language used in science and consign anything not couched in empirical or logical terminology to the rubbish heap of nonsensical 'pseudo-statements'. The group discussed major strands in the philosophy of science and social sciences, including positivism, empiricism and utilitarianism of Hume, Bentham, Comte, Mill, Spencer, and Marx, among others (1973: 304).

Even within such celebrated company the sociologist Otto Neurath (1882–1945) cut a most remarkable figure. He was not an academic but a publicly engaged and radical social scientist. This commitment distinguished Neurath from most others in the Vienna Circle, even its 'left wing', like the philosopher Rudolf Carnap.

All of us in the Circle were strongly interested in social and political progress. Most of us, myself included, were socialists. But we liked to keep our philosophical work separated from our political aims. In our view, logic, including applied logic, and the theory of knowledge, the analysis of language, and the methodology of science, are, like science itself, neutral with respect to practical aims, whether they are moral aims for the individual or political aims for a society. Neurath criticized strongly this neutralist attitude, which in his opinion gave aid and comfort to the enemies of social progress ... He would deride those purist philosophers who sit on their icy glaciers and are afraid they might dirty their hands if they were to come down and tackle the practical problems of the world. (Carnap, 1963: 23)

Far from playing the role of a detached philosopher Neurath was directly involved in the political and social crisis wrought by the First World War, the revolutionary Bavarian workers' council of the early 1920s; he was arrested for 'high treason' in Munich in 1919, and led the radical housing and allotment movement of Red Vienna (Cartwright et al., 1996; Neurath, 1973). To communicate sociological and economic knowledge on a wider basis Neurath founded the Museum of Economy and Society in Vienna and developed the ISOTYPE (International System of Typographical Picture Education), a unique form of visual sociology or 'picture statistics' (Vossoughian, 2008).

In great personal danger when arrested during the counter-revolution in Bavaria, the sociologists Max Weber and Otto Bauer testified on Neurath's behalf. In his testimony Weber described Neurath as an unusually accomplished scholar in the economic history of antiquity (one of Weber's own specialist areas) but 'too easily carried away by a utopian scheme'. Bauer described him as an apolitical 'authoritarian' concerned purely with the socio-technical problems of a planned economy (Cartwright et al., 1996: 54–5). Disillusioned with Soviet communism, Neurath narrowly escaped the Nazi seizure of power in the 1930s, which, as a Marxist (of a curious sort), forced him into wartime exile in The Hague and England. This culminated in Neurath's (1973: 432) appeal in 1942 for a global *societas societatum*, a utopian society of societies that would end crises as a prelude to a 'world commonwealth'.

As a positivist (of a curious sort) Neurath shared with Comte and Spencer their sense of social mission, albeit without Spencer's individualism or Comte's religious cult. The whole point of social science for Neurath was to raise the 'conditions of life', the cultural and material level of the whole community, the working class and women most of all. Conditions of life for these groups were threatened constantly by crisis and insecurity that necessitated socialist planning or 'orchestration'.

Neurath's alternative economic sociology argued that the economy be 'socialised' to overcome crises of overproduction and poverty in concrete ways (Neurath, 2004). Socialisation was famously opposed by the ideal market models of Max Weber, Ludwig von Mises and Friedrich von Hayek (Uebel, 2004). Socialisation required an alternative economy-in-kind where workers would transfer wages to each other. This would force individuals and groups to consider the wider effects of a rise or fall in wages on the general condition of the working class. Women who perform the socially necessary work of child-rearing would be paid like other full-time workers.

One way to combat the conditions of crisis that gave rise to fascism, Neurath contended, was to unify science as a collective labour in order to banish mythology – including philosophical speculation, from the social sciences and, by extension, eliminate fantasy from common sense. Neurath rounded on the pretensions of philosophy and adopted an 'anti-philosophical' meta-theory of science. This did not mean that social theory should not be reflexive about itself. If anything, because it shouldered a responsibility to steer humanity out of crisis conditions, social science needed to be more explicitly reflexive about its way of arguing (Zolo, 1989).

Now largely, and unjustly, written out of social theory as an unspeakable 'empiricist', Neurath rejected any conception of science that opposed theory to empirical research. An Neurath said: 'there are only theoretical sciences' (2004: 271). Statements by themselves cannot determine whether science is practical or theoretical. Neurath was on intimate terms with the sociology of Tönnies, Weber, and Simmel. Social science in Germany before 1914 was consumed by struggles of self-clarification over the proper role of values in sciences (the *Werturteilsstreit*) and the proper relationship of method and theory in social science (the *Methodenstreit*). On the issue of value-freedom Neurath gave qualified support to Weber, while on the issue of the method called *Verstehen* he opposed Weber.

This chapter outlines the meta-theory of Neurath. It focuses particularly on its relevance for social theory's current concerns with the relationship between theory and practice, values and science, language and utopia. In surprising ways, Neurath can be seen as a precursor of the anti-foundational 'linguistic turn', post-positivism, and post-modernism in philosophy and relational sociology (Reisch, 1997).

NEURATH'S BOAT

Imagine sailors, who, far out at sea, transform the shape of their clumsy vessel from a more circular to a more fishlike one. They make use of some drifting timber, besides the timber of the old structure, to modify the skeleton and the hull of their vessel. But they cannot put the ship in dock in order to start from scratch. During their work they stay on the old structure and deal with heavy gales and thundering waves. In transforming their ship they take care that dangerous leakages do not occur. A new ship grows out of the old one, step by step – and while they are still building, the sailors may already be thinking of a new structure, and they will not always agree with one another. The whole business will go on in a way that we cannot even anticipate today. That is our fate. (Neurath, 1970: 47)

Neurath returned repeatedly to his now famous simile of the boat. Unable to refit the boat on firm ground Neurath created an image of knowledge as active reconstruction. By replacing the original materials with bits and pieces as they come to hand the entire reconstruction job is improvised collectively, all the while skilfully keeping the boat afloat. This striking image blows out of the water any idea of absolute foundations for scientific 'truth' or 'certainty' (Cartwright et al., 1996: 91–4).

Social theory is no fixed hulk, securely fastened by timeless concepts and logic that can be relied on for safe passage through every storm it encounters. It is lashed together not because it provides a safe passage to reality but by rational decisions made in concrete conditions. In so far as social theory is rational, it admits freely of its own limitations. In so far as it refuses to recognise its own empirical conditions, it is non-rational and metaphysical. And in so far as social theory is placed under constant reconstruction the scope for consensus and cumulative progress is curtailed.

Social theory (the process of reconstruction) cannot begin from nowhere. It must begin from the non-science of common sense and ordinary language ('the boat'). Social theory is a raft of interconnected statements that cannot simply be isolated and tested one by one as true or false (Uebel, 1996). Both theory and evidence rise together and are inherently revisable. Without this revisionist history of theoretical 'turns' and 'breaks', social theories deteriorate into timeless fetish objects, useful as a scholastic ritual perhaps but not for elaborating empirical statements.

Neurath applied the anti-foundational philosophy of Pierre Duhem (1861–1916), theorist of thermodynamics, and the physicist Henri Poincaré (1854–1912) to the social theory elaborated by Simmel, Tönnies and Weber (Cartwright et al., 1996: 115–24). Within the rules of logic Duhem allowed considerable scope for decisions governed by 'good sense' (*bon sens*) to sustain a theoretical statement (1996: 117). Theories are both 'indeterminate' and 'underdetermined'. Because everyday life and science operate within different domains, the relationship between vague language of practical facts and more precise language of theoretical statements must remain 'indeterminate'. Because they are part of a larger 'holistic' group of theories, theories are 'underdetermined' by results. Theories need not be rejected by any single result if scientists decide to shift the focus away from the disputed theory to a related hypothesis. In contrast to the 'Duhem principle' that facts provide the infallible test for theory, according to the 'Neurath principle' *both* theory and data are fallible, not merely theory alone.

A selective process of concept formation is essential. At some point a concrete decision about how to proceed has to be taken. This requires a force of a 'social will', an idea familiar to Neurath from Tönnies. A decision cannot be arrived at by pure thought itself. This was the problem of absolute forms of relativism, especially the mystical form propounded by Oswald Spengler in *The Decline of the West* (1991). Spengler argued that 'cultures' were absolutely incomprehensible to each other. Such baloney was anathema to Neurath (1973: 158–214), who aspired to a 'scientific world conception' no less (1973: 299–318). For one thing, how could Spengler know anything about other cultures when he claimed to be shut out from them? Yet, like today's anti-multiculturalists, cognitive ignorance did not prevent Spengler from proclaiming about the absolutely 'alien' ways of non-Occidental cultures. Against Spengler's pronouncement, 'What is true for us is false for another culture: this holds ... [for] every result of scientific thought', Neurath countered rhetorically: 'Are ancient mechanics and geometry false for us? Were they false for the Arabs? Would our physiology be false for Aristotle? Is it false for the Chinese?' (1973: 204). Something held in common is implied as soon as people begin to communicate with each other. People learn to recognise the signs being used by each other the more regularly that dialogue takes place.

ANTI-PHILOSOPHY

Neurath objected to 'pseudo-rational' philosophy for denying the very meaning of rationalism as disclosing the empirical limits to knowledge. Philosophy creates artificial foundations for theoretical system-building. For Neurath, the theoretical system builder 'is a born liar' (in Cartwright et al., 1996: 128). Ideal concepts that emerge deductively from intuition or pure theory, like Kant's a-priori system, are unlikely to have much explanatory empirical value. Idealist deductions like Hegel's 'world spirit' are created first in pure thought and only later 'realised' or discovered in empirical reality, if at all. While Hegel placed history on 'the earthly plane' of geography and human action his system remained in all essentials a mysterious spiritual process (Neurath, 1973: 336).

In some ways the Vienna Circle continued the tradition of sceptical empiricism established by David Hume (Kolakowski, 1972). For Hume all that we can be certain about are logical relations between ideas, which tell us nothing about the world itself, or matters of fact, claims that can be subjected to an empirical test. All other claims, Hume argued, 'contain nothing but sophistry and illusion' (2007: 114). Hume's critical philosophy denied that empirical facts can ever be known with absolute certainty since observations are bound to be affected by the contingent understandings derived from human senses.

Like Hume, the Vienna Circle rejected vague non-empirical generalities and 'philosophical' pronouncements in favour of logical analysis of empirical statements. They aimed to eliminate the last traces of metaphysics from science through the logical analysis of empirical statements. Neurath insisted on calling his theory of science an 'anti-philosophy': 'philosophy does not exist as a discipline; the body of scientific propositions exhausts the sum of all meaningful statements' (1959: 282). It made no sense to Neurath to construct a philosophical theory of knowledge, an 'epistemology', as an exercise to ground science in categorical abstractions separate from the practical formulation of empirical hypotheses. Epistemology hands down apodictic rulings about proof and validity even before science begins.

On the contrary, science is formed by concrete judgements about inter-subjective connections of empirical statements. Neurath's 'reflexive epistemology' was premised upon collective and pragmatic negotiation of how science proceeds in particular situations (Zolo, 1989). Knowledge of society can only ever be approximate and conditional. This emphasis separated Neurath's positivism from the biological positivism of Spencer and the historical positivism of Comte. For the Vienna Circle 'pure' logic must be tautological: what is inferred as a conclusion in any chain of logic must already have been present in the premise. Philosophical or theological statements about God or morality or essence express certain feelings and tones which are unquestionably part of life. But these are properly expressed in art, poetry or music, not social theory.

> If a mystic asserts that he has experiences that lie above and beyond all concepts, one cannot deny this. But the mystic cannot talk about it, for talking implies capture by concepts and reduction to scientifically classifiable states of affairs. (Neurath, 1973: 307)

Neurath (1973: 362) declared the classic moral problem of 'free will' a 'pseudo-problem', irrelevant to the spatio-temporal processes of empiricist science.

Metaphysics commits two basic mistakes. First, it commits the error of *substantialisation* by following too closely the way that ordinary language treats qualities ('hardness'), relations ('friendship'), and processes ('sleep') as thing-like substances ('apple'). This 'substantialist' conflation of relations and processes with things and states continues to plague social theory (Bourdieu, 1984; Elias, 2012). Second, metaphysics imagines that *thinking* by itself produces new knowledge without any empirical content or that new content can be inferred logically from first principles.

SOCIOLOGY AMONG THE SCIENCES

Neurath (2004: 265) shared Comte's 'prophetic vision' to unify the study of individual sciences as a specialised field study in itself. However, Comte's construction of a fundamental taxonomy of the sciences – 'putting those sciences at the top that deal with the least determined objects, then moving on to the ones whose objects are more and more determined' – had for Neurath become even less plausible for twentieth-century science, not least the traditional division between natural and social or 'moral' sciences.

John Stuart Mill (1971: 174) placed social science, the 'moral sciences', on a continuum with the natural sciences while accepting Comte's argument that the object is more complex due to human action and consciousness. Moral science must be deduced from first principles determined by human nature and self-examination. Despite his metaphysics of 'human nature', Neurath (1973: 355) viewed Mill as fumbling towards empiricist theory in his subordination of selfish motives as an explanation for 'the social feeling of members of a class'. By contrast, in Germany the complexity of human society and feeling gave rise to debates about the autonomy of social sciences from natural sciences. The significance of this for Neurath was that metaphysical sociology proved all too amenable to the ruling class whereas an anti-metaphysical sociology destroyed mystical illusions about power.

Neurath returned to Simmel's founding problem of what constitutes the object of sociology. Is it to be found in the interaction of many people? Is sociology distinct from history? Neurath (2004: 268) gave the example of Wilhelm Wundt's (1832–1920) attempt to demarcate sociology from history by allocating to history the study of development, and to sociology the systematic study of 'the less important stages of the historical development'. For Wundt the whole point of abstract theory was a more precise definition of concepts without any detailed consideration of empirical problems.

Such classifications impose arbitrary distinctions on science. Any classification of sciences by neat boundaries has limited value unless it exposes the interrelationship between things. Disciplines like sociology acquire proper names solely for the purposes of orientation rather than as logical exercises in classification (as Comte, Spencer, and Mill supposed). Indeed, any hierarchical idea of a scientific pyramid founded on physics should be abandoned as irrelevant to sociology:

> The development of physicalistic sociology *does not mean the transfer of the laws of physics to living things and their groups,* as some have thought possible. Comprehensive sociological laws can be found as well as laws for definite narrower social areas, without the need to be able to go back to the microstructure, and thereby to build up these sociological laws from physical ones. (Neurath, 1983: 75, my emphasis)

To avoid an unwarranted standardisation of complex conditions Neurath (1970: 33) preferred to talk about 'social silhouettes' as a starting point for analysis. By this he meant beginning in a less categorical way from a mixture of different qualities that are present in individuals and in groups to varying degrees at any one time and place.

Neurath proposed that all the sciences be unified into a single science of cosmic history, dealing with everything from stars, earth, plants, animals, humans, forests, tribes, nations, families, and so on. The kind of sociology that Neurath had in mind was cosmic in scope. Rejecting binary dualisms such as society and environment and asymmetrical cause–effect phraseology, Neurath spoke about interrelated statements of 'different cosmic aggregations', changeable in space and time, for instance grouping together human groups, animals, houses, streets, fields, and swamps:

> Peoples, states, age groups, religious communities, all are complexes built up of single individuals. Such composite groups have certain interconnections which are ruled by laws, and they have a definite 'physiognomy'. The separate features of these complexes are not independent of each other but are related. (1983: 387)

In contrast, arguments about causation separate out 'random' variables by using *ceteris paribus* phrases about background constancy, such as 'everything else being equal' or 'given the same conditions'. Speaking of 'mutual causation' where one factor asymmetrically affects another that in turn re-influences the first factor plays havoc in sociology.

Neurath preferred a more developmental language of emergent properties, of 'growing out of' or 'arising from', as when educational institutions 'grow out of' a definite social aggregation. Neurath (1970: 49, n.41) noted the 'very stimulating' way that the scientist James Clerk Maxwell discussed sociology. With echoes of Comte, Maxwell distinguished between two kinds of knowledge, which he termed 'dynamical' and 'statistical'. The statistical method groups people according to some characteristic, the raw material needed to 'deduce general theorems in sociology' (Campbell and Garnett, 1882: 438). The dynamical method observes individuals, learns their history, analyses their motives, and compares their expectations of how they will act in practice. Although the dynamical method lacks precision it is the method proper to sociology. On the other hand, the statistical method loses sight of individual cases and assumes an average type from 'which we may estimate the character and propensities of an imaginary being called the Mean Man' (1882: 439). Individual molecules are entirely different from the body as a whole, even though the body consists of an enormous number of such molecules.

SOCIOLOGY AS A VERBAL TRADITION

Any scientific discipline represents a 'systematized transfer of a verbal tradition' (Neurath, 1970: 39). Unless guided by reflexive self-understanding, this transfer carries the danger of passing on the 'old folklore' of the verbal habits of non-scientific institutions. Neurath gave the example of economics. There the institutional language of book-keeping – 'cost', 'profit', and 'investment' – is used routinely. At the same time political economy concerns itself with human happiness. Within this 'hybrid' discipline, however, the principles of book-keeping dominate the problem of human happiness, not the other way round. Economics perpetuates the 'old folklore' of univocal institutional language which holds human welfare as an accidental side-effect of the market. Similarly, in the discipline of jurisprudence (and its hybrid cousin criminology) the 'old folklore' imports unrevised institutional terms like 'crime', 'punishment', and 'justice' into science.

For sociology the problem is especially acute since it deals directly with 'old folklore' in the language of everyday life, magic, theology, criminal justice, politics, pedagogy, and so on. There is simply no 'neutral' position of 'extra-territoriality' from which to judge sociology sociologically.

> There is no exterritoriality [sic] for sociologists, or for other scientists, and this is not always sufficiently acknowledged. Sociologists are not only outside their scientific field in arguing, deciding, and acting like other human beings; they also argue, decide, and act like other human beings within their scientific field. (Neurath, 1970: 46–7)

Here Neurath argued for a reflexive sociology in terms not dissimilar from, though less famously than, Pierre Bourdieu four decades later (Nemeth, 1994).

Social theory is damaged by conceptual over-simplification or precision, which impoverishes rather than enriches its vocabulary. Science is inherently dialogical. It takes the form of argument and negotiation. Science is potentially universal whereas other forms of knowledge are local and particular.

> What we call science may be regarded as the typical branch of arguing which human beings of all nations, rich and poor have in common. Discussions on the sun, moon, stars, anatomy, geography, pleasure and pain, may be carried out in any civilization: whereas theology and legal terms are mainly local. (Neurath, 1996: 251)

All statements, theoretical and empirical, are connected with all other statements about the world and with the previous history of all our concepts. Concepts and their interrelatedness therefore vary according to the demands made on them in time and space. Observation statements about social relations index rich and fuzzy relations of space and time. Excessively precise language can obscure the lack of a 'critical attitude' that Neurath argues is essential for social science. A book on racism, for instance, may be written in a plain empiricist style while avoiding a critical stance.

NEURATH AND MARX

Neurath transfigured the verbal tradition of social theory, above all of Marx and Weber, as well as Tönnies and Simmel. Never a conventional Marxist, Neurath managed to offend both allies and enemies in equal measure. He distrusted claims for dialectical logic, whether Hegelian or its Marxist transposition, compared to the empirical value of symbolic logic (Carnap, 1963: 24). Neither could Neurath accept the Kantian–Marxism fusion proposed by Austro-Marxists Max Adler, Otto Bauer, and Karl Renner. His Marxist credentials were also under suspicion for the influence exerted on the Vienna Circle by the historical-critical philosophy of Ernst Mach (1838–1916). Although Mach's philosophy rejected philosophical wordplay his followers were denounced as 'reactionary' by Lenin in *Materialism and Empirio-Criticism* (1909), which became the orthodox Marxist standpoint after the Russian Revolution.

For Neurath, vague talk by Marxists about 'materialism' was burdened with metaphysical assumptions about matter. It was 'less ambiguous to speak of Physicalism and of the "materialist foundation"' (1973: 359). 'Physicalism' describes concrete events ordered in space and time processes (Neurath, 1959). Physicalism emerges dialogically from everyday life rather than from a predetermined metaphysical system.

> 'Physicalism', as I suggested it, starts from everyday language, which avoids elements which the various peoples on earth do not have in common. The assumption is that Melanesian tribes and European explorers can start to talk on cows and calves, pains and pleasures without difficulties, whereas difficulties appear when expressions like 'cause', 'punishment', 'mind', etc. enter the talk. In this part of our everyday language which physicalism acknowledges one formulates questions with 'where, when, how'. (Neurath, in O'Neill, 2007: 84)

By 'physicalism' Neurath did not mean that sociology should imitate physics or become a science of the purely physical, merely that sociology confine itself to statements about the spatio-temporal order.

For Neurath, Marx's study of capital represented the clearest example of physicalist sociology. With Marx, 'history and political economy becomes part of an inseparable unit, sociology' (Neurath, 1973: 359). A new social order is deduced by Marx from the old one, which inevitably produces crises of human conditions.

Prediction is an odd business in social science since there are always multiple active elements in play. No theory could predict an event as unique as the mass murder of European Jews by the Nazis (Neurath, 1970: 26). Neurath distinguished self-fulfilling prophecies that proclaimed 'there is no alternative' from the explanatory possibilities released by scientific activism:

> Perhaps the penetrant doctrines dealing with the 'iron laws of history' and of the 'evidence which dictates that some attempts are hopeless from the start' belong to the family of augury, omens, and palmistry. (1970: 44)

As Thomas Uebel (2004: 63–4) notes, Neurath's concern with self-realising prediction was written well before its more famous formulation in sociology by Robert Merton's 'self-fulfilling prophecies' and the pithy theorem attributed to W.I. Thomas: 'If men define their situations as real, they are real in their consequences' (Merton, 1995).

Other Marxist ideas like class 'consciousness', as a non-physical process, looked to Neurath very much like disguised metaphysics. Neurath was also troubled by the 'base–superstructure' phraseology of Marxism as an instance of muddled cause–effect asymmetry. Marx used the language of ideology 'arising' out of socio-economic relations. But the process whereby the superstructure 'grows' empirically from the base is not shown; it is simply imputed as the logical effect of a prior cause. Marx's formulation needed to be 'delimited' by an empirical hypothesis

> by specifiable spatio-temporal objects (thus, on the one hand, of the state as an aggregate of men, streets, houses, prisons, rifles, factories, etc., and, on the other, of works of art, buildings, pictures, sculptures, religious books or speeches, scientific books or lectures, facial expressions, gestures, behaviour in love, etc.) without first delimiting groups of concepts, about whose adequacy one cannot decide before-hand, but only later within the framework of a strictly physicalist system. (Neurath, 1973: 353)

Neurath remained dissatisfied with the causal asymmetry embedded in Marx's hypothesis. Knowledge about the mode of production cannot be induced from knowledge of law and art. What can be stated is that knowledge of production relations can lead to knowledge of art and law in a certain time and place by means of induction (Neurath, 1970: 22). 'Holistic' knowledge needs to take pro-duction relations and art and law together. Neurath accepted with Simmel and the Austrian economists that value is determined subjectively by the relationship between human wants and the supply of goods, and kept a diplomatic silence about the objective alternative, Marx's labour theory of value (Uebel, 2004: 53).

All this was heretical for orthodox Marxism. Neurath was closer to the 'total process of life' (historical monism and social complexes) in the Marxism of Georgi Plekhanov and Antonio Labriola (Cartwright at al., 1996: 236–43). Like them, Neurath emphasised the fundamental interdependent density of social relations and institutions as an entire process: 'What cannot be expressed in terms of rela-tions among elements cannot be expressed at all' (1959: 294).

Although Neurath (1973: 349) detected a metaphysical phraseology in Marxism this did not necessarily invalidate it as an activist theory of history. As a 'strictly scientific unmetaphysical physicalist sociology', Marxist sociology 'lies on the earthly plane':

> The cultivation of scientific, unmetaphysical thought, its application above all to social occurrences, is quite Marxist. Religious men and nationalists appeal to some feeling, they fight for entities that lie beyond mankind. To them the state is some-thing 'higher', something 'holy'. Whereas for Marxists everything lies on the same earthly plane. (1973: 295)

From the perspective of a 'world history without names' the fate of individuals can be deduced from class relations so long as 'no unstable conditions' interfere. By bringing into existence a new revolutionary class, the proletariat, the bourgeoisie are the unwitting tool of historical conditions, a process of inversion captured for

Neurath by Goethe's Mephistopheles: 'part of the power that would ever do the Evil, and ever does the Good' (1973: 348).

Neurath looked back to the ancient philosophy of Epicurus, the subject of Marx's doctoral thesis, as well as forward to a utopian future (which was not for him a pejorative term): 'Theory best serves practice when it is unrealistic in a certain sense: when it is ahead of reality, not just following it' (2004: 310). Any restriction of the sociological imagination to known conditions of 'the given' excludes the not-yet-known history of the rise and fall of social orders whereby 'the utopias of one period often become the trivialities of the following' (Neurath, 1970: 31).

Instead of individual judgements about happiness, 'social Epicureanism' would end the fear and insecurity that comes from an indifferent economic system and replace it with the purposeful rule of empirical science and human morality. Decisions and values are communicated from shared premises of common experience. Moreover, this undermines any sharp division between values and empirical judgements. Against liberal conceptions of an abstract language of rights as providing a minimal basis for dialogue and democracy, Neurath's physicalism insisted that particular social groups ('who') in the concrete conditions of life ('where', 'when', 'how') form the basis for moral and political action (O'Neill, 2003).

NEURATH AND WEBER

Limited to physicalism, Neurath seemed confined to local, situationally embedded statements rather than the world conception of unified science that he proposed. A 'middle way' was needed to steer between the 'art of not knowing' and the 'courage to err', demonstrated for Neurath (2004: 114) by Max Weber's economic interpretation of ancient history. Neurath rejected Weber's interpretative sociology but accepted, with qualifications, Weber's fact–value distinction.

The wager of *Verstehen*

Weber gave personal expression to the difficulty of combining metaphysical social theory with a strong empiricist bent. Most famously Weber explained the rise of capitalism by a non-materialist appeal to 'the spirit' of religion. Neurath doubted whether Weber's claims about the efficacy of 'the rational ethos' could be transformed into physicalist statements about social behaviour. The main problem is that ideal-types of 'Protestantism' or 'the capitalist spirit' are radically divorced from statements about specific historical and geographical relations: 'There are Protestants, but there is no Protestantism' (Neurath, 1973: 358).

Empiricist sociology aimed to produce a controlled description of behaviour at a certain time and place to investigate how new habits emerge historically. For Neurath the literal words of religion have to be subordinated to statements about observed action: on the one hand, Christ's words of love, self-sacrifice and poverty; on the other hand, a papacy that built magnificent monuments to itself while living in the lap of luxury. Without much further ado, Neurath rejected Weber's *Verstehende* sociology:

> Empathy, understanding (*Verstehen*) and the like may help the research worker, but they enter the totality of scientific statements as little as does a good cup of coffee which also furthers the scholar in his work. (1973: 357)

By securing for human culture a special position among other animals, interpretative sociology performs an anthropomorphic function. In contrast, Neurath's physicalism investigated human cultures in the same manner that other sciences treat animals, plants, and stones.

Taking an empathetic standpoint relies on a process of inferring the feelings and attitudes of other people from visible signs of behaviour, such as chopping wood in Weber's and Schütz's example, and attributing to them an ideal motive that any rational human would feel if placed in the same situation. In such ways, hermeneutics smuggles the old metaphysics back in. It transcends observation statements of inter-subjective spatio-temporal action to arrive at the (ideal) inner life of (ideal) individuals from an (ideal) rationalistic vantage point. This does not mean that all attempts at interpreting the meanings that people have about their actions should be abandoned in favour of statements of purely physical description. It merely means that the idealist assumptions built in to the hermeneutic method need to be translated into 'physicalist' language or dropped as unsubstantiated speculation.

Values and valuation

In the *Werturteilsstreit* Neurath accepted Weber's fact-value distinction. Science is limited to descriptive statements of 'means' and leaves normative and political 'ends' to be determined in some other way. Yet, Neurath argued, if science describes matters of fact, then it also has to describe the good or bad effects of the facts. The relationship between right values and right action is less strict than supposed by Weber. People may be merciful, tolerant and considerate without subscribing at all to any 'ultimate values'. On the other hand, they may equally

> be intolerant, may persecute one another, and may be interested only in good food and nice clothes. But persecution, intolerance and appreciation of food and clothes have also been found in societies which promoted 'eternal values'; indeed, even in societies which promoted love as an important item within their commandments. (Neurath, 1970: 45)

Any 'wishful thinking' on the part of sociologists is constrained by the 'thinkful wishing' of social theory in its reflexive decisions, construction of hypotheses, comparison of observation statements, and ways of arguing.

> People full of 'thinkful wishing' may present the same scientific material as people of other habits but may combine it differently. In this way a sociologist may support scientifically some decision without becoming unscientific. (Neurath, 1970: 43)

Judgements of value cannot be simply opposed to judgements of experience. Every value judgement is also an empirical judgement at some level.

While Neurath saw social science as guided by values these intrude on empiricist theory as little as a touch of toothache:

> When I say: 'I feel pleasure when as few people as possible are unhappy, and I am glad about a restriction of competition, because this reduces misery', I have asserted a value judgement about a value judgement, but there is nothing metaphysical in that. Whether I have a feeling of pain because of the social order or a toothache comes to the same thing. (Neurath, 2004: 283)

Neurath addressed Weber's ethical paradox of the relationship between scientific disenchantment and religious duty. If religion is correlated with a way of life that is habitually tolerant and trusting, and the scientific attitude weakens religious faith, then the increase in the general level of intolerance will in turn erode the conditions for science itself.

In such a situation, both science and religion have an interest in tolerance independent of their separate institutional interests. Like today's ultra-rationalists they become '"unscientific" when they maintain that their decisions, their propaganda, are based on far-reaching experiential statements' (Neurath, 1970: 46). Where there is a general increase in intolerance, weapons are always ready to hand; first verbal weapons that elevate petty differences to demonise other people, followed later by physical weapons, as Neurath knew from firsthand experience.

Scope must be allowed for judgements of value – valuations – in concrete situations so long as certain scientific controls are met, above all, reasoned and intelligible scrutiny of statements:

> The term 'valuation' dealing with the state of a person may be useful, since it leads us to communication and social relations, whereas terms such as 'value' very often slide into unphysicalist language with metaphysical man-traps and then the antagonism 'internal world' and 'external world', and other dangerous reduplications frequently appear. (Neurath, 1970: 16)

Valuations enter into science in two ways (Neurath, 2004: 297). First, as empirical examination of specific relations of pleasure and pain and, second, as an evaluation of the social and institutional order that produces pleasure and pain. In the first case, concrete study takes account of moral indignation caused by domination as well as the poverty that results from domination. In the second case, the institutional order that causes social suffering can be evaluated by comparing different orders against an agreed principle, say a more equal distribution of goods. In neither case would the scientific basis of political economy be harmed: 'Political economy is being "ethicised" by this just as little as chemistry is being "hygienised" by attempts to make an hygienic assessment of certain chemical compounds' (Neurath, 2004: 298).

Weber dismissed Neurath's vision for an economy in kind not simply on value grounds but for what he saw as its flawed technical and descriptive analysis

(Uebel, 2004: 45–8). For Weber, the formal rationality of market-allocated goods operated efficiently through the price mechanism, indifferent to all considerations of value rationality. An economy in kind can only be asserted as a value but cannot be defended scientifically. By accepting the fact–value distinction and remaining on the ground of rationality Neurath's alternative welfare economics appeared to be skewered.

From Neurath's pluralist conception of theory, Weber's assumptions about formal rationality are unacceptable. Empiricism does not begin from one fixed principle like 'rationality':

> 'Pluralism' leads to an 'orchestration' of statements in any case, leaving many things open to 'choice' and 'decision', which even many of our scientific friends want to handle by means of a univocal calculus. (1983: 553)

Weber is like a gambler who has rigged the game beforehand in favour of formal rationality: 'What would you think of a gambler who declares that he will start with some fantastic theory which teaches him definitely how to win in any case?' (Neurath, 1970: 44). Just as a gambler weighs up all relevant factors in making a wager, so social theory cannot rely on a single failsafe guiding rule.

NEURATH AND REFLEXIVE SOCIOLOGY

The need to reflexively examine epistemological foundations through a logical analysis of concepts and empirical adequacy applies to social science as much as any other branch of science (Zolo, 1989). Here the process of eliminating the residue of metaphysical assumptions from social theory has not gone as far as physics. This may be due to the fact that social theory is more closely tied to the ordinary language of everyday life. Common-sense concepts like war and peace, or import and export, or family and nation, provide people with a relatively secure orientation in their immediate perception.

Sociological statements should not be too narrowly construed. They belong to a large family of statements about the pattern and behaviour of different individuals, groups and institutions, including animal groups. Neurath shared with Tönnies a preoccupation for the difference that language makes to social theory. He sought to expunge everyday language of its non-physicalist elements in the process of creating a 'universal jargon' (Neurath, 1940–41). Attempts by epistemology to establish the truth-conditions for knowledge 'behind or before language' are futile (Cartwright et al., 1996: 159). Social theory does not begin from clear-cut 'sense data' or first principles or precise concepts, as is often attributed to positivism. Neurath talked about starting from the vagaries of ordinary language, with 'a full lump of irregularities and indistinctness, as our daily speech offers it' (1970: 18). Later a process of refinement and regularisation will turn the lumps or 'clots' (*Ballung*) into more defined statements without entirely eliminating imprecision.

Theoretical statements are elaborated in ways that shake loose historically formed relations and interconnections. Scientific theory logically describes the structure of things, the 'form of order' not their 'essence'. This order of concept formation formalises and disciplines the intuitive inferences of common sense. Any kind of claim is allowed so long as it is phrased in a language that allows empirical analysis in a double sense. First, in an empiricist and positivist sense, subjectively experienced qualities like pleasure are not in themselves knowledge yet knowledge can emerge only from experience in the world. People are united in language by 'structural formulae' which frame the content of common knowledge. This places definite limits on the scope of science. Second, in a logical and analytical sense, the meaning of any concept must allow a logical reduction step-by-step to other more basic concepts, arriving ultimately at empirical concepts.

From this method of logical reduction all concepts can potentially be arranged to produce a 'constitutive theory' that can be examined by 'protocol-statements' consisting of all the conditions involved in making an observation statement. In natural science a 'protocol' record of observations is made by a named person (Otto) at a specific time and place (3.15) and encompasses in descending order, first, verbal thought, which encompasses, second, perception, which encompasses, last, a physicalist fact (table in the room).

A complete protocol sentence might for example be worded like this: 'Otto's protocol at 3.17 o'clock: [Otto's speech-thinking at 3.16 o'clock was: (at 3.15 o'clock there was a table in the room perceived by Otto)]'. (Neurath, 1983: 93)

Carefully formed protocol statements not only record physical observations, they also regulate the construction of more general theoretical statements or clusters. Theory and observation do not constitute distinct claims about reality but emerge together. In this sense, protocol statements are already rich in theory. A first step for the protocol is to chase metaphysical terms from ordinary language, which always overlaps with the terms of science.

ERROR AND JUDGEMENT IN THEORY

Neurath adopted a pragmatic and conventional approach to science. A generation earlier than Kuhn's (2012) concept of 'paradigms' (perhaps the most used term in social science), Neurath referred to 'encyclopaedias' as clusters of overlapping statements that are relatively impervious to the failure of discrete theories or hypotheses. Any justification of what scientists do can only come from how it 'fits the whole pattern of personal life of which we approve' (1973: 249). This did not mean that science is completely arbitrary or that any hypothesis is acceptable so long as it conforms to the demands of protocol statements.

With any theory, difficulties will be encountered that cannot be known in advance. Simply because a statement makes empirical observations says little about how a hypothesis might be supported. Neurath (1970: 23) set out possible relationships between statements, hypotheses, and empirical testing (Neurath uses 'assaying' due to the mechanical connotations of 'testing'). Although every relationship must be kept available, induction is prioritised by science. It is futile to impose fixed rules or a calculus for induction, since there is always more than one possibility in a sociological aggregation. At some point a 'decision' has to be made that allows 'again and again' for a margin of error.

> As social scientists we have to expect gulfs and gaps everywhere, together with unpredictability, incompleteness, and one-sidedness of our arguing, wherever we may start. (Neurath, 1970: 27)

Given the inherent fallibility of hypotheses, a pluralistic willingness to start over again must be adopted. Hypotheses can be 'corroborated' or 'shaken' – but not decisively verified or falsified:

> 'Supporting' hypotheses by means of material suitable for hypotheses is based on decisions: we are selecting material; 'corroborating' hypotheses and 'shaking' them by means of 'positive instances' and 'negative instances'; but no *experimentum crucis* may invalidate any single hypothesis. (Neurath, 1970: 25)

Scientists do not automatically discard a hypothesis when it has been badly shaken by a negative instance, such as a contradictory observation statement. Neurath rejected 'the asymmetrical refutation-verification scheme', a calculus of weighing negative and positive instances made famous by Karl Popper (Cat, 1995; Uebel, 1992).

Popper (1992) outlined a deductive 'logic of discovery' for science rather than an inductive reconstruction of the empirical practices of scientists. For Popper, the proper business of philosophy is to spell out the criteria for justifying science, not to report the empirical practices of scientists. Popper turned his 'logic of discovery' into the 'discovery of logic'. All theory can do is to deduce hypotheses to be submitted for a logical test which they could fail as a principle of scientific scruple.

In contrast, Neurath argued that the positive corroboration of hypotheses is the backbone of success in the social sciences. Neurath's appeal to the space-time contingency of protocol statements was denounced by Popper (1992: 75) as 'psychologism' for apparently reducing science to the phenomenal experiences of individual scientists. Neurath's proposal to drop protocol statements where they contradict observation statements simply opened the door for Popper (1992: 79) to every kind of unruly and arbitrary system.

In fact, psychologism represented the exact opposite of Neurath's own views. When something like psychologism in the private language of individual scientists was proposed by his friend Carnap, Neurath (1959: 206, 290) seized on it as 'methodological solipsism' – 'an attenuated residue of idealistic metaphysics' beyond the public, inter-sensorial and inter-personal 'physicalist' language of science. Most observation statements will be physical statements rather than phenomenal statements about 'ego', 'mind', or 'personality'.

Philosophy has no business acting as the final court of appeal for science. Popper's principle of falsification was for Neurath a 'pseudo-rationalisation' because it traded on an abstract metaphysical model divorced from the messy language of scientific practice.

> Pseudo-rationalism is inclined to treat everything as calculable, whereas strict science comes to admit the multiple interpretations of its systems, and to leave the unitary character of life to other factors, above all to common agreement on decisions. (Neurath, 1973: 407)

Popper's deductive theory closed in on itself so that science might be purified by philosophy, and politics and social science made to submit to the strictures of the purified scientific method.

Neurath was content to pragmatically emphasise empiricism at the expense of 'logic'. Such pragmatism kept the goal of social and political efficacy on the horizon of science. Neurath (1983) favoured description against Popper's prescription, empirical theory against 'pure theory', indistinct concepts against precise definitions. Science cannot be conceived as a closed logical system founded on general methods of testing and principles of failure. It must always explicitly set out ('assay') its methods in detail and in relation to theoretical systems within the 'scientific conception of the world'. Negative instances may indeed 'shake' the confidence of scientists in a favoured theory without at the same time destroying it.

UTOPIA AND CRISIS

In the years before his death Neurath worked on the nature of the relationship between metaphysics and persecution (Reisch, 2005: 37). Western totalitarianism was traced by Neurath to Plato's absolute doctrine of a higher reality accessible only to metaphysical adepts. In contrast, much like George Orwell (1968) on 'The English People' written around the same time, in letters to friends Neurath commented on how deeply impressed he was by the antimetaphysical, the common-sense habits of the people he encountered in wartime England:

> It is impressive to listen to plain people here, how they avoid boasting and over-statements in daily matters. I collect 'expressions' eg fire guard leaders explaining how people should get a feeling to be sheltered by their neighbours etc and then explaining what is needed to act 'quickly', to be 'calm', and to have the 'usual common-sense'. I like this type of habit much more than the continental one, with 'highest duty', 'national community', 'self-sacrifice', 'obedience', 'subordination', etc. 'eternal ideals' whenever you give a chance to open the mouth. (in Reisch, 2005: 199)

Neurath hoped that because of its regard for the empirical conditions of a plural 'common sense' for 'other people's happiness', empiricism would prevent complicity in 'anti-human' violence:

empiricists on an average are less prepared to become merciless persecutors, and not so frequently the enthusiastic followers (for the higher glory of THE transcendent nation, ideal etc. or something else) because they are not prepared to sacrifice their own end and other people's happiness to something 'idealist' and anti-human. The common sense leads back to human happiness. (in O'Neill, 2003: 588)

Neurath is a bit too sanguine about the political and ethical immunity of empiricism from the descent into barbarism. Such faith in common-sense inoculation from fascism helped explain the charismatic fragility of the Nazi regime for another Marxist exile in England, Franz Borkenau: 'Prophecy is the contrary of common sense. If common sense prevailed, the regime would be useless and meaningless and cease to exist' (1939a: 22–3).

Crises can only be countered by 'will and cognition' through a controlled image of utopia. During the 1919 revolutionary crisis only 'a clear picture of the future … could have guided the will', Neurath argued, and prevented the worldwide calamities that followed (Cartwright et al., 1996: 256). Social theory often fixes on the recent past or the immediate present without giving the same attention to possible futures:

Perhaps we are now at the beginning of a scientific study of utopias. It would in any case serve our young people better than traditional economic theory and sociology, which, being restricted to the past and the accidental present, were in no way able to cope with the tremendous upheavals of war and revolution. (Neurath, 1973: 154)

Neurath's proposals for making happiness the measure of economy were often labelled pejoratively as 'utopian', an unrealistic fantasy construction. Neurath (1973: 150–5) saw his own conception of utopia as a kind of 'social engineering', an imagined future 'order of life' that had become possible in reality in the same way that engineers saw new possibilities in a different configuration of existing materials. Tomorrow's crises develop out of today's conditions; today's utopia is already ahead of the game (Nemeth and Stadler, 1996).

CRITIQUE AND DEVELOPMENT

Traditionally, social theory has imagined that it can transfer its terminology from one generation to the next. For Neurath the task of social theory is to take risks by creating a 'new folklore', inventing new terms for a new society. There is no need to limit sociological utopias to what is already known so long as any 'scientific utopia' freely recognises its discontinuities with empirical statements about social complexes. It may be more useful for a sociological utopia to speak about a world community, perhaps Comte's 'Humanity', than to endlessly re-describe whatever happens to exist in the present, such as a world system of rival nation-states, which may not last in any case.

Science grows out of 'comprehensive collective labour'. It is not the achievement of individuals but of generations. Social theory needed to protect itself from the muddle and prior claims of speculative philosophy. Some philosophers, even within the Vienna Circle, continued to talk about philosophy as 'the clarification of concepts'. A formal, neutral and exact language for knowledge became the dominant strand of Anglo-American analytical philosophy. A strict concern with philosophical logic permitted the abandonment of political and ethical valuation and the quiet retreat of intellectuals from public activism in a climate of conformism and 'academic McCarthyism' during the Cold War (Reisch, 2005).

Politics cannot legislate science. Whether an ultimate metaphysics of nation or race or God or democracy legitimates violent solutions to conditions of crisis is a purely empirical problem for sociology:

> The issues of war, unemployment, crisis and productive capacity ought to be investigated together, if one wanted to answer the question of how to put an end to the current social suffering. But this leads into comprehensive sociological and historical problems. (Neurath, 2004: 498)

While science produces empiricist hypotheses about social action it cannot resolve the struggle between competing values. Only practical social relations can decide between values:

> Perhaps struggle will decide which view about the best order of life shall be victorious; perhaps preference will be given to one order out of those in question, and the choice may be made with the help of an inadequate metaphysical theory or in some other way; tossing coins would be much more honest. (Neurath, 1973: 122)

Neurath refused to accept that empiricism resulted in a conservative relationship to every given reality, passively accepting as unchanging whatever exists, as Critical Theory would claim. While Neurath's emphasis on the unity of science would make him an unlikely ally of post-modern social theory of recent decades, his reflexive social theory, utopian science and fuzzy epistemology point beyond theoretical crisis today.

7

MODERNIST TURN: WALTER BENJAMIN AND SIEGFRIED KRACAUER

Long before such phrases became sociological clichés, in his classic 1929 study, *The Salaried Masses*, Siegfried Kracauer stated rather bluntly: 'Reality is a construction'. Similarly, for Walter Benjamin (2003: 396) history is also a 'construct' or a 'constellation'. Social theory involves not only the flow of thoughts but also their arrest in a construction or 'constellation' saturated with points of tension arranged in such a way as to produce a shock of critical recognition.

Kracauer and Benjamin defy easy assimilation into social theory. As public sociologists they jostled their way through the crowded public sphere of the Weimar Republic far beyond conventional sociology. There they worked outside of academic institutions and employed a diverse range of genres and formats: journalism, cultural criticism, sociology, history, essays, fiction, film, and book reviews. As Benjamin said of Kracauer's outsider status:

> This man is no longer playing along. Refusing to mask himself for the carnival that his fellow men are staging – he has even left the sociologist's doctoral cap at home – he elbows his way boorishly through the crowd, here and there lifting the mask of someone particularly jaunty. (1929: 109)

Their analyses of crisis and culture do not sit comfortably with the more familiar stock of sociological concepts, although they drew generously from the vocabulary of Marxism, German sociology, phenomenology, Freud, and literature. However, like other critical theorists their relationship to Marxism and academic sociology was always angular. They rejected the grand theoretical style built on abstract concepts, universal propositions and logical systems. Their writings could be poetic, elusive, and coded rather than transparent, definitive, and closed.

Benjamin and Kracauer were suspicious of how society represents itself as an unreliable guide as to how it is constituted in practice. They both emphasised the micro-logical detail of society's 'physiognomy'. A deeper understanding of the hidden depths of social processes may be gleaned from the inconspicuous surfaces of marginal objects. Social totality could be deciphered from the objective fragments of modernity (Frisby, 1985). Because they are produced 'unconsciously' such banal things as stadium sports, adverts, the street, shops, and film provide 'unmediated access to the fundamental substance of the state of things' (Kracauer, 1995: 75).

Since philosophy proved incapable of getting close to reality the task of theoretical reconstruction fell to social theory. For Kracauer (1929: 26) sociological examination of 'exemplary instances of reality' aimed to strike a 'legitimate counterblow' to the critical 'malnutrition' caused by German philosophy. However, observations remain random and arbitrary unless their sociological significance is disinterred by theoretical reflection: 'A hundred reports from a factory do not add up to the reality of the factory but remains for all eternity a hundred views of the factory' (1929: 32).

This chapter examines how Benjamin and Kracauer responded to the social and intellectual crises of their time. Never part of the Frankfurt inner circle, though on intimate terms with Adorno, Walter Benjamin and Siegfried Kracauer developed a material sociology which plumbed the depths of the social relations underlying cultural forms like urban architecture, entertainment, sports, film, and photography. Weimar Germany provided almost laboratory-like conditions for a critical sociology of modernity in crisis (Weitz, 2007). Through scrupulous, many-sided examination of ephemeral cultural objects they hoped that something of sociological significance might escape from the sealed tomb of reification. In so doing, they rejected the appeal of naive empiricism and straightforward observational description of 'reportage'. Instead, they developed a form of 'delicate empiricism which so intimately involves itself with the object that it becomes true theory' (Benjamin, 1999a: 520).

MATERIAL SOCIOLOGY

As the most 'sociological' of the critical theorists, Kracauer moved increasingly away from social philosophy without entirely relinquishing metaphysical suppositions. Kracauer (1995: 214) diagnosed the 'crisis of science', especially empirical sciences, including sociology, in a 'hatred of science' 'rampant' among the pre-1914 generation of academic youth who objected to the failure of the specialised sciences to provide them with a meaningful worldview. The more detached that science became the more perfectly it dominated the world. In response, metaphysics struggled in vain to fill the empty spaces of life. In the eternal flow of life in the life philosophy of Henri Bergson, Kracauer found expressed the historically specific constant agitation and flux of modernity.

To avoid both subjective short-circuiting of and objective resignation to alienation Kracauer and Benjamin adopted a 'cool' distance from formal social theory. Sociology seemed caught between maintaining value-free 'objectivity' at the cost of non-empirical 'conceptual formalism' and the relativism of 'subjectively' collecting meaningless facts on the basis of a pre-scientific valuation of reality.

This dilemma was resolved metaphysically in the philosophy of history by appeal to 'scientific-historical reflection'. Coherent meaning was imposed on diverse historical materials by a 'leap' of intuition from the perspective of the present.

Yet, Kracauer argued, the philosophy of history cannot escape the problem of relativism since any other historian could just as easily have made a different 'leap' of intuition. There are no metaphysical absolutes to ground a philosophy of history. Sociological materialism required, Kracauer argued, that 'a tunnel be built under the massive mountain of Hegel' leading from Marx to the humanists of the French enlightenment, Helvétius (1715–1771) and Holbach (1723–1789) – a tunnel that Kracauer tried to excavate in his lost monograph on 'The concept of the human being in Marx' (in Frisby, 1985: 126).

Weber

Max Weber refused to compromise science with metaphysics. As Kracauer (1995: 219) noted of Weber's lecture 'Science as a vocation', science cannot be consoled by metaphysical or theological compromises in the face of the 'disenchantment of the world'. Weber fought 'heroically' for disenchantment without illusions, which also meant giving up any claim to making the world meaningful again (1995: 136). All subjective values were excluded by Weber's construction of 'objective' ideal-types, which arbitrarily imposes conceptual limits on complex reality. As arbitrary constructions of reality, ideal-types are phantoms of objectivity. Weber is unable to protect 'objective' ideal-types from subjective judgements. In this way, Kracauer argued valuations take a 'secret revenge' for being sacrificed on the scaffold of objectivity.

Simmel

An alternative approach was provided by Georg Simmel. For traditional methodology analysis starts either from a general concept that absorbs particular examples or it begins from concrete particularities and gradually arrives at more general concepts. Refusing the false choices of methodology, Simmel occupied a middle ground, experimenting with general concepts and abstract forms while keeping the concrete content of particular objects in view. Everything is related to everything else in Simmel, without need for grand theory or metaphysics. This is summed up best for Kracauer (1995: 250) by Simmel's *Philosophy of Money* where 'every point in the totality is accessible from every other point; one phenomenon carries and supports another; there is nothing absolute that exists outside any links to the remaining phenomena and that has validity in and for itself.'

A model of 'extra-territoriality', Simmel wandered restlessly from relation to relation and sprawled out far and wide to make hidden connections visible and stimulate a growing sensitivity to the web of relations. Simmel mediates between the meaningless facts of empiricism and the unreal speculation of metaphysics to bring out the real significance of individual things. Individual facts are not methodically deduced from abstract concepts. Reality is grasped by observation, the core lesson that Kracauer derives from Simmel. In so doing, the trivially obvious – fashion, money, the face, space, and so on – is reconstructed from multiple perspectives as an autonomous complex of relations. Trivialities are no longer trivial but pregnant with connections and unnoticed possibilities. Even the simplest phenomenon is a symbol that provides access to many other relations and processes.

Yet, just as Weber could not overcome the dilemmas of objectivity, neither could Simmel surmount the dilemmas of relativism. Kracauer argued that Simmel tried to overcome relativism only by raising the life process itself into an absolute value: 'It was an act of desperation on the part of relativism, which, in its search for a solid foundation, ultimately came upon groundless and rootless life and thereby landed with itself – or perhaps did not land at all ...' (1995: 131–2).

Experiential materialism

Like Simmel, Kracauer wanted to get close to the reality of things in order to establish the unity of relationships. Unlike Simmel, Kracauer did not search for a hidden meaning in concrete reality or find aesthetic form in endless webs of social connections. Kracauer's solution to the 'crisis of science' was to maintain a distance from the abstract terms of academic debate and to recast it from the mid-1920s in phenomenological and Marxist terms as a kind of experiential materialism or 'critical realism' (Barnow, 1994). A dialectical stance of involved detachment required, as the phenomenologist Edmund Husserl had urged, a return to 'the things themselves' rather than inferring inner experiences from external signs.

A return to reality was no easy matter. For one thing, a self-consciously 'material sociology' that, starting from the object itself, puts last things first could be perceived as theoretically incompetent, as Adorno (1992: 58–76) seemed to conclude. More importantly, reality had become chaotic, inscrutable, ambiguous, and opaque, making its meaning, if it had any, difficult to decipher. Both naive empiricism and philosophical absolutes were ruled out. Since society was no longer bound together as a moral community filled with meaning, social theory was forced to renounce all comprehensive theoretical systems.

Kracauer and Benjamin distrusted the alternative metaphysical system of Lukacs' (1971) *History and Class Consciousness*, where the concrete is displaced by a formal conceptual construction. Instead of looking empirically at the experience of workers under capitalism, Lukacs simply deduced ideal forms of knowledge that workers would have, were reality not obscured by the commodity fetish. Reality would be brought into line with philosophy, not the other way round.

In contrast, for Kracauer and Benjamin the possibility of a just reality can be discovered only in the fragments, traces and ruins of everyday life, not in the conceptual apparatus of a total philosophy of history. Material sociology tries to stick close to banal objects. Drawing from Simmel and Weber, Kracauer (1995: 6) set out in his 1922 essay 'Sociology as science' an early programme for a phenomenology of a reality that lacked any unifying meaning such as religion had once provided. Against the 'empty spaces' of formal philosophy and pure empiricism, descriptive microanalysis of 'discrete events' and constructive social theory emerge together. Without a moral community to bind people together, Kracauer (1995: 174–5) claimed in his study of the detective novel (1922–25), 'the public' is constructed by the rule of Law, as points suspended in 'empty space', held in place by tensions between legality and illegality, higher and lower regions of life (sin), inside and outside spaces (danger), above and below (mystery), dominant and dominated groups (Koch, 2000: ch. 2; Frisby, 1985: 126–34). In this unreal reality, only the detective figure, an 'extra-territorial' point of tension between the police and the criminal, is able to 'construct a whole out of the blindly scattered elements of a disintegrated world' (1995: 175).

Through pleasurably abstract games of puzzle-solving the detective reveals that reality is constructed by nothing more than fortuitous coincidences without rhyme or reason. Kracauer and Benjamin similarly searched for clues about the traces of human experience inscribed by commodity society in everyday objects as sites of repressed meaning, dreaming, and memory (Reeh, 2004; Frisby, 2001). Commodities that were debased in some way, either out of date, used up, or culturally disdained, provided spatial images, or 'hieroglyphs', that could be analysed in terms of obscured social relations: 'Spatial images are the dreams of society. Wherever the hieroglyphics of any spatial image is deciphered, there the basis for social reality presents itself' (Kracauer, 1997: 60).

Kracauer (1995: 75) saw spatial images as society dreaming about itself in ways that are normally blocked by more self-conscious representations, although he recognised the danger of falling into a nostalgic reverie through an overly 'romantic' approach to collective dreaming: 'The position that an epoch occupies in the historical process can be determined more strikingly from an analysis of its inconspicuous surface-level expressions than from that epoch's judgments about itself'. Benjamin praised Kracauer as a sociological 'ragpicker', gathering and carting away for analysis the banal, fragmentary scraps of everyday life, the spent cultural rubbish littering the streets of large cities,

> grumblingly, stubbornly, somewhat the worse for drink, and not without now and again letting one or other of these faded calicoes – 'humanity', 'inner nature', 'enrichment' – flutter ironically in the dawn breeze. A ragpicker at daybreak – in the dawn of the day of revolution. (Benjamin, 1998: 114)

At the same time, illumination depends on theoretical interpretation of the superficial and the banal: 'The fundamental substance of an epoch and its unheeded impulses illuminate each other reciprocally' (Kracauer, 1995: 75).

URBAN DREAMING

Nowhere was collective dreaming in 'spatial images' stimulated more than in the spaces of urban modernity (Frisby, 2001; Gilloch, 1997; Reeh, 2004). Buried in urban fragments, Kracauer and Benjamin discovered fresh possibilities for sociological consciousness. Urban fragments contain sociological secrets about historical and contemporary crisis. Rapid spatial change stimulates a specifically urban consciousness. Unable to organise its contents in a stable order dictated by spatial continuity and narrative tradition, city life is marked instead by a fugitive semi-consciousness demanded by temporary, fortuitous encounters in the empty spaces of the ever-new. Moment by moment distractions fill the void, suppressing collective memory, tradition and experience.

Both adopted the extra-territorial perspective of the stranger when examining the surfaces of foreign cities like Paris (Jay, 1986: 152–97). For Kracauer, a trained architect, the value of cities rests in the spaces that it makes available for improvisations in popular life against centralised economic and political power (Reeh, 2004). In Paris, Kracauer (1995: 41–4) noted the spatial tension between the soon-to-be-demolished *faubourgs*, historical suburbs of impoverished humanity, and the fashionable boulevards of the centre. Populated by leisurely, absent-minded consumers in the midst of super-abundant goods and sensations, the centre of Paris was a site of 'sensory splendour' increasingly emptied of historical difference. Displaying the money price of luxurious goods in shop displays merely compounded the forced separation of the spectator from material things.

In the 1920s Benjamin composed what he called 'thought-images' (*Denkbilder*), experiential pictures of the topography of various cities that he visited, including Naples, Moscow, Weimar, Marseilles, and San Gimignano (Szondi, 1988). Such thought-images meditated on spatial relations of inside and outside, public and private, proximity and distance (Richter, 2007). With thought-images Benjamin wanted to avoid what might be called 'theory effect' where deductive theoretical abstractions and predetermined judgements prevent factual description from making contact with material things as experienced at a precise moment in time: 'all factuality is already theory' (Benjamin, 1994: 313). Again and again Benjamin attempted to treat insignificant, transient, lived features of the urban landscape – shops, street signs, parks, houses, light, monuments, postcards, crowds, cafés, zoos, and so on – as pregnant with sociological secrets that would be revealed in a flash by dream-like poetic description otherwise concealed by jaded theoretical concepts.

The flaneur

This procedure was realised with striking effect in Benjamin's (1996: 444–88) 'One-way street' (1928), a compendium of reflexive snapshots about contradictory conditions in Berlin and Paris. Modern cities required a modernist method of montage that juxtaposed inherent tensions of boredom and excitement, fear and fascination, tolerance and callousness, eroticism and indifference, snobbery and democracy. Paris acquired a central importance for Benjamin's attempts to recover something of the pre-history of modernity before commodity circulation became fully effective and routinised. Here the figure of the *flaneur*, represented by the poet Charles Baudelaire (1821–1867), observed and recorded in microscopic detail the fleeting and fugitive material of everyday life in nineteenth-century Paris. As a sociological figure, the *flaneur* strolled idly through crowded streets, shops, and cafés. As a social type the *flaneur* was facing decline, pushed out by the new, wide boulevards and department stores of reconstructed Paris, commercial busyness and labour process efficiencies, best captured for Benjamin (2003: 31) in the phrase of F.W. Taylor, theorist of 'scientific management' – 'Down with dawdling!'

As a proto-sociologist, the *flaneur* adopted a cool, detached persona as they wandered aimlessly through crowds, observing and documenting changing fashions, conduct, attitudes, and objects (Frisby, 1994). For Benjamin (2002: 40), by taking seriously the physiognomy of the crowd at home in the street – 'now a landscape, now a room' – the *flaneur* revealed the city as a 'phantasmagoria' that transcended the private/public boundary. Being at home in public space became the principle of the modern department store and later the shopping mall, where the practice of *flanerie* perhaps continues, albeit with little regard for sociological documentation. Economically precarious artists and intellectuals were compared by Benajmin to the *flaneur* to the extent that they came to observe the market in changing fashions, but, in practice, they actually came to sell their labour power as part of the expanding commodity society. Since the idling *flaneur* had no understanding of the world of production, they became experts on the market and prices (Benjamin, 1999b: 374).

Benjamin (1999c: 262–7) saw the resurrection of the critic-*flaneur* in rapidly changing 1920s Berlin. Ordinary Berliners inhabited the streets as much as their own houses, turning public space into a sphere of domestic intimacy, as when outdoor workers hang their coats on railings as if in their own private hallway, a newspaper stand functions as a private library, benches as a sofa, and so on. In Berlin, however, the observant critic-*flaneur* Franz Hessel (1929: 420–2) came under suspicion as a lingering 'trespasser'. Threatening and intimidating, crowds took him not as a 'philosopher out for a stroll' but as 'the werewolf at large in the social jungle' (Benjamin, 1999c: 265).

Just as Benjamin had done for the Paris of Baudelaire, Kracauer (2002) attempted, unsuccessfully according to Benjamin and Adorno (1999: 183–7), to produce a 'societal biography' of Paris as it passed through revolutionary crises of 1830, 1848 and 1870–71 by focussing on the popular composer Jacques Offenbach (1819–1880). Societal biography – Kracauer took Trotsky's (1975) autobiography as a model – discloses the 'social function' of the individual by approaching 'the breaking point of our societal construct and, from this advanced position, tackle the social forces that embody reality today' (Kracauer, 1995: 104). In contrast, conventional biographies of individualised personalities fail to embed them sociologically in structured relations of class.

As conceived by Kracauer (2002: 24), the flight from reality in Paris after 1848 described in *Jacques Offenbach and the Paris of His Time* possessed a contemporary relevance for the grotesque fantasy constructs of fascist dictatorship in crisis-ridden 1930s Europe. Both the pompous dictatorship of Louis Napoleon (1852–1870) and Offenbach's comedic operettas tried to combat boredom and social listlessness with collective hallucinations and absurd diversions. In the dreamworld of financial speculation, urban glamour, fashion, and entertainment, and state repression of all dissent, rudely interrupted by the crisis of 1848, society resembled the unreal world of the operetta, which it also made possible. Except that, Kracauer added, Offenbach's mockery and satire contained hidden promises about a changed reality through laughter, and that it went deeper than mere amusement under dictatorship and financial instability.

Arcadian ruins

In Berlin a contemporary obsession with the present and whatever is brand new eliminated the traces of the past from the urban landscape (Weitz, 2007: ch. 2). The prospect of exile prompted Benjamin (1999a: 595–637; 2002: 344–13) to reflect on a rapidly changing Berlin in 'Berlin chronicle' (1932) and 'Berlin Childhood around 1900' (1934–8). Similarly, Kracauer (1995: 337–42) reported that dark passageways in the city like the Linden Arcade were haunted by childhood nightmares. Banished into the 'furtive half-light' of the passageway, behind the visible facades of the bourgeois public sphere, were slightly shady and unfashionable cast-offs and curiosities from the commodity world – an anatomical museum, a paperback bookshop, a postcard shop, travel agencies, a lottery stall, and so on. These 'homeless images' were driven from the public sphere outside to 'the inner Siberia' of the arcade. By honouring the rapid obsolescence of commodities, homeless images took their revenge on the pretentiousness of bourgeois ideals. Redeveloped in a bland architectural style, the arcade became yet another empty, neutral space that 'may later spawn who knows what – perhaps fascism, or perhaps nothing at all. What would be the point of an arcade in a society that is itself only a passageway?' (1995: 342).

Benjamin (1999a) spent the last decade and a half of his life (1926–1940) trying to answer Kracauer's question about society as a passageway. In his collection of fragments known as *The Arcades Project* (1999b) he furnished a unique model of early to mid-nineteenth century Paris. This took the unusual form of a collection of notes and quotations arranged in thirty-six files, or 'convolutes', labelled *inter alia* as 'Fashion', 'Boredom', 'Exhibitions', 'Advertising', 'Prostitution', 'Gambling', 'Mirrors', 'Modes of lighting', 'Marx', 'Photography', 'Idleness', and so on. Influenced by surrealism, Benjamin juxtaposed the mass of fragments into a montage of 'dialectical images' that, he hoped, would produce insights of recognition and critique. Benjamin's principle was 'Don't tell, show', although he often resorted to discursive commentary to illuminate what he considered exemplary instances of reality.

Paris may have been the 'capital of modernity' but it was marked by struggle, upheaval and rebellion before the domination of society by capitalism had yet to be secured. Modernity had not led to progress in any straightforward way. Instead it but had been a catastrophe for entire classes forced to live in a permanent 'state of emergency' (Benjamin, 2003: 392). For the sociologist determined to dredge the bottom of modernity, something like the provisional nature of 'the destructive character' was required (1999c: 541–2). Often misunderstood, destructive theory simplifies the world by testing it to the limit, adopts a historical consciousness that takes nothing as permanent, clears a space without dictating what should occupy it, and finds a path through what is not yet known, echoing Norbert Elias' (1978: ch. 2) later image of the sociologist as 'a destroyer of myths'.

Positivism could only see the progress made by science and technology but failed to grasp the destructive energies unleashed by 'the bungled reception of

technology'. This 'bungling' of technology consisted of 'a series of energetic, constantly renewed efforts, all attempting to overcome the fact that technology serves
this society only by producing commodities' (Benjamin, 2002: 266). A particularly
graphic example of bungled technology was given by Benjamin (1999a: 563–8) in
a radio lecture on the River Tay railway bridge disaster of 1879 (Mehlman, 1993).
A storm destroyed a section of the bridge resulting in the deaths of two hundred
passengers. Railroad capital had leapt ahead with the iron construction of bridges
despite warnings from bridge builders that the material properties of iron construction were not well understood yet. In the century to come, technology would
repeatedly misfire to even greater destructive effect under the imperative of
impersonal accumulation and fragmented social relations.

DISTRACTION AND ABSTRACTION

Perhaps Kracauer's major contribution to substantive social theory concerns the
relationship between a mass culture of distraction and the structure of abstraction. Already in 1917 Kracauer attempted to radicalise Simmel's and Weber's
tragic sociology of culture (Frisby, 1985: 113). Modern science ensures a dramatic
increase in knowledge at the same time as disenchantment and abstraction reduce
meaning in and experience of the world. In this, science is at one with capitalism.
Both capitalism and science are orientated instrumentally to action; both depend
on an abstract intellect; both deal in logical categories of exchange that reduce
diversity to similarity, quality to quantity, and ends to means; and both display a
deep indifference to the intrinsic qualities of things.

Kracauer's perspicacious theory of distraction and abstraction culminated in
his brilliant sociological study of the new middle classes, *Die Angelstellen* (*The
Salaried Masses*, 1929[1998]). There Kracauer intimately dissected the sociological significance of Berlin as the ambivalent location where 'the decisive practical
and ideological clashes take place' (1929[1998]: 32). Unlike Adorno, Kracauer felt
self-consciously part of the insecure salaried class. Fundamentally misrecognising
its own proletarian status during the years of economic upswing, this class would
prove ideologically adrift in the storms and stresses of social, economic, and
political crises to come. Four years before Hitler assumed power Kracauer diagnosed the sociological eddies of this new stratum:

> The mass of salaried employees differ from the worker proletariat in that they are
> spiritually homeless. For the time being, they cannot find their way to their comrades,
> and the house of bourgeois ideas and feelings in which they used to live has col-
> lapsed, its foundations eroded by economic development. They are living at present
> without a doctrine to look up at or a goal they might ascertain. So they live in fear of
> looking up and asking their way to the destination. (1929[1998]: 88)

Such a refusal to face up to the predicament of proletarianisation and insecurity
led white-collar workers to sink deeper into mythical illusions and false solutions.

'Ideologically homeless' they become indifferent to knowledge and ethics and allowed themselves to be manipulated as an ambivalent mass by cultural forms cleansed of critical content. Disarmed by aesthetic ornaments and with nothing left to defend, they listlessly affirmed the apparent omnipotence of fascist power and violence (Mack, 2000).

Kracauer examined the large, opulent movie theatres and picture palaces of 1920s Berlin in terms of surface pleasure. In these spaces, thousands gathered to worship the 'cult of distraction'. Lights, acoustics, and visuals assault the senses: 'They raise distraction to the level of culture; they are aimed at the *masses*' (1995: 324). In the provinces the masses are made to feel culturally inferior by bourgeois guardians of culture and education. Things are different in dynamic Berlin, a city of four million people, where the masses make their own demands on culture (Boyd White and Frisby, 2012; Weitz, 2007). If the addiction to distraction is stronger in Berlin, that is because diversion compensates for intense but unfulfilling types of work.

> In a profound sense, Berlin audiences act truthfully when they increasingly shun art events (which, for good reason, remain caught in mere pretense), preferring instead the surface glamour of the stars, films, revues, and spectacular shows. Here, in pure externality, the audience encounters itself; its own reality is revealed in the fragmented sequence of splendid sense impressions. (Kracauer, 1995: 326)

Distraction is a social and economic reality, not a moral failing or a psychological state. It corresponds to social fragmentation, constant disturbance, and the historical contingency of the prevailing order, to which fascism would shortly apply violent mythological solutions.

Even within the picture palaces, Kracauer noticed that efforts were being made to bring distraction to heel by invoking the organic unity of theatrical coherence as the revenge of outdated high culture. Against such three-dimensional pretensions, the two-dimensional medium of film fought back. A 'homogenous cosmopolitan audience' for mass taste has already been set in process. Mass pleasure in urban distractions increasingly invaded the provinces against the self-pitying whining of cultural elites in retreat.

MASS ORNAMENT

In *The Mass Ornament* (1995), Kracauer's 1927 analysis of body culture – 'two words that belong together' – 'the masses' are organised with mathematical precision in geometrical lines by stadiums, parades, streets, cabaret shows, and cinema palaces. This new form of mass abstraction differs from meaningful organic communities of the past since 'community and personality perish when what is demanded is calculability' (1995: 78). Unlike a military parade, which serves as a means to a patriotic end, the mass ornament has no end other than itself. It empties the mass figuration of all erotic individuality by means of body discipline arranged in anonymous lines like the body formations; the then-famous dancing troupe the Tiller Girls.

Like the capitalist labour process the mass ornament is organised rationally from above as an end in itself. Mass figurations can only be made out from above, like aerial photographs of landscapes and cities, by spectators who have a purely abstract relationship to the spectacle. Despite what its supporters feel, the mythological cult of body culture cements an alliance with domination and blocks substantive rationality. As Kracauer argues:

> Physical training expropriates people's energy, while the production and mindless consumption of the ornamental patterns divert them from the imperative to change the reigning order. (1995: 85)

Yet the ideology of the mass ornament also fails to seduce in changed economic conditions. Following the stock market crash, in 'Girls and crisis' Kracauer (1931a: 565) noted how the mass ornament had turned 'ghostly', emptied of the vitality and optimism of the boom years: 'the happy dreams they are supposed to inspire have been revealed for several years now as foolish illusions.'

Yet because fear has become abstract it is not easily assuaged. Benjamin described how the inflationary crisis in Germany of late 1920s normalised insecurity for the panic-stricken bourgeoisie who could see little way out of the crisis. Routine feelings of trust, calm, and health were increasingly replaced by feelings of shame, humiliation, and disgrace as poverty and instability spread throughout society. In 'Murder trials and society', Kracauer (1931b: 740–1) diagnosed how the lack of routine, the contrived neutrality of the public sphere, and loss of substantive social bonds produced 'a deadening of the capacity to distinguish' where 'people are slipping toward atrocity without noticing their slide' (see also Lethen, 2002: 206–10).

Within a situation of general social decay only fantastical theories and grand illusions restored any sense of prestige. It also inflated social fear. Kracauer noted that when wide city streets empty, a menacing feeling of panic and dread arrives. Something ominous hangs in the air. Individuals feel exposed – that suddenly anything might happen, like a sudden attack by a Nazi gang on people at a café. Benjamin recognised that other Europeans found oppressive and 'incomprehensible' the fetish of violence and coldness in Germany, a mendacity apparent even in routine functions: 'Bus conductors, officials, workmen, salesman – they all feel themselves to be the representatives of a refractory material world whose menace they take pains to demonstrate through their own surliness' (1996: 454).

For Benjamin (2002: 122) the 'godless mythological cult' of the physical culminated in the fascist 'aestheticization of politics'. Capitalism's sadomasochistic relationship to technology produced a form of self-alienation which 'can experience its own annihilation as a supreme aesthetic pleasure'. Even war becomes a metaphysical abstraction, a 'fetish of doom', where technology is used to subordinate mysterious nature in the name of a mythical nation (Leslie, 2000). Unless a new relationship with technology and society is reached in time, Benjamin predicted that 'millions of human bodies will indeed inevitably be chopped to pieces and chewed up by iron and gas' (1999c: 320–1).

AMBIVALENT LEGITIMACY

Benjamin and Kracauer did not set out to denounce mass culture, as other critical theorists did. Low cultural forms reveal to society things that it routinely fails to register. In detective novels, for instance, everything seems normal on the surface but behind the social masks, trivial conversations and empty conventions of anonymous atoms, something evil is afoot. In the hotel lobby, where such novels are often set, spiritual homelessness is given pleasurable aesthetic form by the emotional distances established by empty surfaces and neutral space: 'Remnants of individuals slip into the nirvana of relaxation, faces disappear behind newspapers, and the artificial continuous light illuminates nothing but mannequins' (Kracauer, 1995: 183; Lethen, 2002). The hotel lobby resembles a 'negative church', an 'inverted image of the house of God', only where the latter unifies the community of believers the hotel lobby sanctifies the dissolution of all community.

Mass ornaments produce 'legitimate' aesthetic pleasure as one of the few cultural figurations that give concrete expression to abstract rationality. The masses are already subject to formal rationality in workplaces obscured from public view. If nothing else the mass ornament gives aesthetic shape to invisible aspects of obdurate reality. This contact with reality attains a higher degree of legitimacy than traditional types of art 'which cultivate outdated noble sentiments in obsolete forms' (Kracauer, 1995: 79). Since they acknowledge the facts of society, the masses are superior in this respect to the cultured middles classes, who 'disavow the phenomenon in order to continue seeking edification at art events that have remained untouched by the reality present in the stadium patterns' (1995: 85).

Kracauer rejected the formulae of romantic anti-capitalism that put its trust in an essential human nature untouched by rationality: 'they fail to grasp capitalism's core defect: it rationalizes not too much but rather too little' (Kracauer, 1995: 81). Romantic mythology protests against the reification of nature by scientific abstraction. True, capitalism is marked all the way down by abstraction but the answer to this cannot be a false concreteness unmediated by theoretical reflection. Abstract thought is a historical achievement of human culture that today has become 'ambivalent'. Indifferent to the empirical particularities of social life, capitalist rationality is capable only of an 'empty formalism', leaving human reason behind while inviting 'nature' to take its revenge.

Similarly, the mass ornament is ambivalent. On the one hand, it has moved towards 'illumination through reason' beyond myths about the organic integrity of unique individuality and ontological depth. But, on the other hand, the mass ornament is a 'mythological cult' clothed in abstractions that block true knowledge of its real condition. Unlike the meaningful world of earlier religious cults, the formal cult of the abstract mass is deprived of substantive content. Those who try to invest body culture with some higher meaning merely flee from the contemporary reality of mass distraction instead of confronting and passing through it. A decade later, in his study of pre-Nazi film, Kracauer (1947) forensically analysed how the body cult was artificially infused with higher meaning by film culture with catastrophic consequences.

'Spiritual homelessness'

Experience sundered from community was the price of material progress. Attached to no convictions in particular, except the absolute inter-changeability of all values, Kracauer called this stratam the 'spiritually homeless' (after Lukacs). Isolated individuals are at home everywhere and nowhere, equally close to and equally distant from every cultural or spiritual possibility: 'It is this metaphysical suffering from the lack of a higher meaning in the world, a suffering due to an existence in an empty space, which makes these people companions in misfortune' (Kracauer, 1995: 129). Alienation was 'short-circuited' by declarations of faith in something absolute like God or 'experience' but only in the artificial form of self-deception, certainty, and fanaticism, especially among cultured middle-class groups. Feelings of spiritual emptiness produced messianic movements demanding 'pure experiences' saturated with the apocalyptic visions of 'chiliastic dreamers' as well as calls for hierarchal reintegration by religious 'believers in form'.

In his famous essay on 'The work of art in the age of its reproducibility', Benjamin (2003: 251–83) drew a distinction between distraction and concentration. Mass spectators distracted by entertainment directly absorb the work of art as a tactile process. In contrast, the art lover concentrates attention on being absorbed by the great artwork as an object of 'devotion'. While the cultural tourist concentrates attentively on the visual details of a famous building, it is experienced casually by the tactile habits of urban masses caught up in a state of distraction. Habitual tasks are performed by casual 'apperception' rather than contemplative perception. Technologically reproducible art like film plays a crucial physiological role by constantly shifting what is experienced on screen:

> Reception in distraction – the sort of reception which is increasingly noticeable in all areas of art and is a symptom of profound changes in apperception – finds in film its true training ground. Film, by virtue of its shock effects, is predisposed to this form of reception. It makes cult value recede into the background, not only because it encourages an evaluating attitude in the audience but also because, at the movies, the evaluating attitude requires no attention. The audience is an examiner, but a distracted one. (Benjamin, 2003: 269)

Benjamin hoped that distraction would have a critical, evaluative edge to it. Before the age of reproduction, art needed to have a long life by expressing eternal sacred values, producing the special effect of distance that Benjamin called 'aura'. When art forms like film become disposable and quickly 'worn out' as victims of changes in fashion they lose any sacred or eternal value. Benjamin does not mourn the loss of aura or 'authenticity' but tries to uncover the critical element in commodified culture. By bringing cultural images closer to the viewer, photography and film turn audiences into critics, albeit distracted ones.

SOCIOLOGY OF PHOTOGRAPHY

Photography killed off 'aura' but not before it tried to save it, Benjamin (2002) argued in his short history of photography. With the technical luminosity of early photography, aura had one final flourish in the complementary match between the ascending bourgeoisie and new camera technology of the 1840s: 'in this early period subject and technique were as exactly congruent as they became incongruent in the period of decline that immediately followed' (2002: 517). At that time sitters had to be perfectly still for the camera, producing a self-controlled poise and 'air of permanence' that bourgeois subjects effortlessly evoked before 1850.

Symptomatic of the decline of photography was the 'bungling' of the technical possibilities as photographers aspired to the status of artist in an artificial effort to restore the prestige effect of aura. Photography was 'the first truly revolutionary means of reproduction'. Quantity and proximity would shatter the aura of the unique original, offering untold possibilities of political and cultural renewal. Premised on the egalitarian demands of the masses, the reproducible image would, Benjamin claimed, abolish outmoded concepts of 'creativity and genius, eternal value and mystery' associated with the conservative tradition of art (Benjamin, 2003: 252).

Photography captures spatial images as fragments divorced from the context that originally gave them meaning. By indexing the contingency of reality at a unique moment in time and space through close-ups or telescopic lens, photography also revealed the taken-for-granted backdrop to social life that usually goes unnoticed by distracted individuals and sinks into what Benjamin called, drawing on Freud, 'the optical unconscious'. By bringing such images into consciousness, photography might produce a shock of recognition in 'a tiny spark of contingency'.

Similarly, Kracauer compared the image of a young film diva on the cover of a magazine with a photograph of his grandmother at the same age sixty years ago. Everyone recognises the celebrity in the photograph but of the image of Grandmother, if that's who she is, only her old-fashioned clothes sparks recognition.

> When grandmother stood in front of the lens, she was present for one second in the spatial continuum that presented itself to the lens. But it was this aspect and not the grandmother that was eternalized. (Kracauer, 1995: 56)

Photography is related to time in the same way as fashion or an old hit song. As they age, fashion and photographs seem comical and ridiculous. The pure contingency of the elements in the photograph freeze the spatial configuration of a fleeting moment. Nothing remains in an old photograph of the identity of the person, which, given the gaps in memory, has to be taken on trust.

Photography, even then before the rise of digital technology, had become ubiquitous, dulling the responsiveness of memory to details. Everything is waiting to be photographed, ready to be absorbed into its spatial continuum, as the world puts on its 'photographic face'. The torrent of photographs threatens to destroy consciousness and foster indifference towards meaning. In the case of photography, distraction is ambivalent; it is both an illumination of reality and an obstacle to cognition:

Never before has an age been so informed about itself, if being informed means having an image of objects that resembles them in a photographic sense ... Never before has a period known so little about itself. In the hands of the ruling society, the invention of illustrated magazines is one of the most powerful means for organising a strike against understanding. (Kracauer, 1995: 58)

By eternalising the present, photography represents a flight from death only to succumb to it in reality. Yet historical contingency could potentially ignite social change. Once the organising principle for the original spatial continuum is lost from memory every configuration can be recognised as necessarily provisional and constructed. If the valid order of things is not yet known, habitual reality itself might be suspended and the inventory of nature put in the right order: 'The turn to photography is the go-for-broke game of history' (Kracauer, 1995: 61).

SOCIOLOGY OF FILM

Benjamin and Kracauer claimed that popular film both records the obtuse meanings of the routine, habitual, and familiar that tend not to enter directly into conscious awareness and, at the same time, reveals the fragility of human consciousness by devastating it with violent shocks, rapid motion, angles, and images of catastrophe (Hansen, 2012). Any serious film critic needs to go beyond a critique of film aesthetics to become also a 'social critic' in order to 'unveil the social images and ideologies hidden in mainstream films and through this unveiling to undermine the influence of the films themselves where necessary' (Kracauer, 1932a: 635). For instance, Kracauer (1930) took to task the lavishly praised and skilfully made film *The Blue Angel* for operating in an aesthetic and spiritual vacuum, substituting a 'lost inwardness' for the 'outer reality' of contemporary social crisis.

Kracauer argued that despite their often poor quality, the kind of films made in Weimar Germany possessed deep clues about widespread psychological and ideological currents. No matter how trivial or ridiculous they may appear, films represent suppressed longings, 'the daydreams of society' as Kracauer put it.

In order to investigate today's society, one must listen to the confessions of the products of its film industries. They are all blabbing a rude secret, without really wanting to. In the endless sequences of films, a limited number of typical themes recur again and again; they reveal how society wants to see itself. (Kracauer, 1995: 292)

Film demands distracted attention appropriate to a society that has erected disorder, disruption and chaos as its governing principle. Film reorganises disjointed nature in new, unfamiliar configurations but, crucially, maintains fragmentation as the principle of its technical construction. Here distraction is potentially productive in the same way that rationalised working conditions are productive; time during the working day is fully occupied but lacks any sort of fulfilment whatsoever (Kracauer, 1995: 325)

In his 1938 notebooks sketching out a planned book on film, Kracauer summed up the material depths that film plunges the audience into, stripping away the surface of the sovereign individual to reveal human mortality:

> Film brings the whole material world into play; reaching beyond theater and paint-ing, it for the first time sets that which exists in motion. It does not aim upward, toward intention, but pushes toward the bottom, to gather and carry along the dregs. It is interested in refuse, in what is just there – both in and outside the human being. The face counts for nothing in film unless it includes the *death's-head* beneath. 'Danse Macabre'. (in Hansen, 2012: 259)

In contrast to formal theories like semiotics or narrative analysis that limit film spectatorship to the disembodied viewing of visual codes, Kracauer and Benjamin examined the physiological, tactile effects of the medium. Film viewing puts the human sensorium to work in a dialectic of active and passive perception. As Heide Schlupmann put it, 'faced with the crisis of meaning and the social suffering which was intensifying to the point of destruction, [Kracauer] considered the active passivity of the cinema spectator to be the appropriate exertion of aesthetic capacity' (1987: 108).

Pleasure barracks to concentration camps

Kracauer shifted from an earlier emphasis on the phenomenology of cinema to more urgently excavating the ideological significance of film. Film's signifi-cance rests on the relationship of the whole, spatially organised experience of the cinema to the concrete nature of an alienated reality that has become 'sec-ond nature'. Kracauer (1929) likened the film theatre to a 'pleasure barracks', providing shelter for the 'spiritually homeless'. At home in the pleasure bar-racks, film's production of fantastical conflict resolution fed mass resentment and calcified emotional reflexes: 'The consequence was mental forlornness: they persisted in a kind of vacuum which added further to their psychological obduracy' (Kracauer, 1947: 11).

Film recursively mobilises a narrow range of motifs consistent with society's self-image. In Weimar Germany this meant sending realistic images of the crisis into an 'abyss of imageless oblivion' (Kracauer, 1929: 94). In his classic 1947 study, *From Caligari to Hitler*, Kracauer analysed German films of the 1920s as repeat-edly expressing the fascist impulse to submit to irrational authority: 'Since Germany thus carried out what had been anticipated by her cinema from its very beginning, conspicuous screen characters now came true in life itself' (1947: 272).

For Kracauer it became necessary to break the practical hold of film as part of a more general understanding of the crisis of German society (Hansen, 2012). Film 'psycho-technics' possess an affinity with mass consciousness in two inter-related ways. First, since films, like masses, are collective endeavours they tend to erase arbitrary or idiosyncratic motifs and images: 'Since any film production unit embodies a mixture of heterogeneous interests and inclinations, teamwork in this field tends to exclude arbitrary handling of screen material, suppressing individual peculiarities in favor of traits common to many people' (Kracauer, 1947: 5). Second, screen motifs do not simply distort or manipulate popular desires but attempt to respond to what they perceive is expected by or acceptable to anonymous mass audiences. Failure to do so hurts profitability.

Film operates obtusely through 'visible hieroglyphs' well below the level of consciousness or the level of narrative. Such 'hieroglyphs' are captured by the organisation and editing of camera shots. These enter into the film's visual apparatus precisely because their appearance is barely noticed. In this they plumb the secret depths of national mass consciousness at a particular historical moment. As Kracauer put it, 'visible hieroglyphs' permeate both narrative and the visual at the level of 'unseen dynamics of human relations' which are 'more or less characteristic of the inner life of the nation from which the films emerge' (1947: 7).

Far from appealing to an ahistorical, fixed national mentality, Kracauer had in mind how a national habitus permeated all social groups in pre-Nazi Germany (Mack, 2000). Psychological tendencies that start life as the derivative effects of external forces like war, economic collapse, or political disillusionment can assume an independent after-life and re-emerge later to lend a hidden structure to social and political change.

> Since the Germans opposed Hitler on the political plane, their strange preparedness for the Nazi creed must have originated in psychological dispositions stronger than any ideological scruples. The films of the pre-Hitler period shed no small light on the psychological situation. (Kracauer, 1947: 204)

Kracauer identified two kinds of film, one unconsciously predisposed towards fascism and one more consciously opposed to it. Even films by anti-fascists, like Fritz Lang's *Metropolis,* depict the masses as ornaments moulded by tyrannical individuals in ways not so different from Nazi films like Riefenstahl's *Triumph of the Will*:

> It is the complete triumph of the ornamental over the human. Absolute authority asserts itself by arranging people under its domination in pleasing designs. This can also be seen in the Nazi regime, which manifested strong ornamental inclinations in organizing masses. (Kracauer, 1947: 94)

Since commercial films are 'forced to answer to mass desires' even a radical expressionist film like *Das Cabinet des Dr. Caligari* was ultimately conformist in nature (Roberts, 2004). *Caligari* resembled the double aspect of class relations in the Weimar Republic. On one hand, traditional authority was in crisis but, on the other, people were not prepared to take decisive action to remove it. Hence the film registered mass ambivalence and prefigured the possibility of a Nazi solution 'in which Caligari's authority triumphs with a hallucination in which the same authority is overthrown' (Kracauer, 1947: 67). Respecting the ambivalence of the mass ornament even Nazi wartime propaganda films rarely depicted violence and suffering in order to keep its own nihilism concealed from German audiences (Kracauer, 1947: 302–6).

Kracauer identified recurring motifs that could only retrospectively be understood as national dispositions. Films are not a copy of reality but sociological documents. Film's dynamic reproduction of images meets the receptive audience half-way by expressing their everyday perceptions, allowing the film public to operate as distracted but critical experts on what is placed in front of their eyes. Kracauer readily admitted that a margin exists for 'cultural initiative' on the part of the film industry. Neither did he have a fatalistic view of the historical process. He did not project 'essential' psychological dispositions onto the German nation, but focussed on the ambivalent nature of the mass ornament. In his sociology of the new middles class he found only the faintest trace of submission to authority depicted in German cinema. During the economic crisis of the early 1930s, working women were 'no longer so easily enchanted' by the 'distraction industry' (Kracauer, 1932b: 216).

Hollywood fascism

It may be tempting to reduce complex sociological processes that produced fascism to 'crazy' beliefs or 'cognitive-moral' pathologies. The crisis that gave rise to fascism in Europe was not an aberration for Kracauer, peculiar to a certain kind of authoritarian national mentality that only Germans possessed. In a time out of joint, the social atmosphere is pervaded by insecurity and fear that, at any moment, the inevitable disaster may strike. The more that personal risk is experienced as an arbitrary effect of a shattered world lacking any discernible pattern or social meaning, the more that the individual feels unable to mediate external shocks.

For Kracauer psychological disintegration was a widespread phenomenon that extended from Weimar art cinema to Hollywood thrillers. What began as wartime anti-Nazi messages in American film – 'Gestapo tortures, shining parades that alternated with silent agonies, life under the oppressive atmosphere of Nazi-conquered Europe' – settled into familiar, everyday life, where the next-door neighbour might be a sadistic maniac, sinister conspiracies abound and, at any moment, violence and murder can break out (Kracauer, 2012: 41). Such threats of 'compulsive, sadistic urges' extends the reach of barbarism into the banal spaces of the city street, the small town, and the living room. Even inanimate objects in the physical environment, hotel rooms, streets, stairs, shops, bars, and so on, are filled to the brim with dark foreboding.

Vicarious participation in sadistic cruelty is left unresolved by Hollywood's happy endings, since these have 'become even more meaningless than usual':

> The feeling of uneasiness stirred up in the audience at the spectacle of an everyday world full of totalitarian horrors is left unrelieved. The sickness of the psyche is, essentially, taken for granted, and the impression remains that nothing can be done to cure it. (Kracauer, 2012: 44)

This is far from inevitable. Film can tackle crisis by refusing sentimental solutions that only circumvent rather than confront the problem. Kracauer's favoured example is *Rome, Open City* (Rossellini, 1945), a film that does not shrink from depicting fascist tortures, cruelty, and depravity but, instead of the vicarious emptiness of Hollywood, also shows human integrity and resistance 'rendered with a profound compassion for the tortured, the killed, the despondent' (Kracauer, 2012: 102).

CRITIQUE AND DEVELOPMENT

Benjamin's social theory had a political-pedagogical purpose – to turn readers into active producers and collaborators. By discovering 'in the analysis of the smallest individual moment the crystal of the total event' Benjamin (1999a: 461) aimed to break from mechanical theories of historical progress in crude versions of Marxism and positivism. His educative idea of 'dialectical images' aimed to construct unstable points of tensions between past, present, and future in order to reposition socially situated readers as active, critical producers (Leslie, 2000, 2006a.) Any possibility for the utopian dream of free human association was lodged for Benjamin and Kracauer in the traces of banal objects.

Like the new middle classes, abstract reason is ambivalent; it illuminates nature and demythologises organic unities but remains mired within the formal, self-serving needs of the accumulation process. Here the 'body culture' of stadium sports, gymnastics, and dance troupes speaks of a shallow, distracted reality, a 'rational and empty form' of abstraction. Kracauer names this the 'mass ornament' because, like the capitalist production process, it organises masses instrumentally with little, if any, critical ideological content, as reasonless formations to be manipulated as ends in themselves. Positivism placed too much faith in the progress of science and technology without considering how they were shaped by the social relations of capitalism (Benjamin, 2002: 266). The repeatedly 'bungled reception of technology' consisted in the need for all forms of technology to serve society only by producing commodities. Beyond a certain level of development, technology acquired a 'destructive energy' culminating in total warfare and human annihilation and a flattening of cultural possibilites, as with the contemporary replacement of the 35mm film print by new digtal formats.

More recently the shared interest of Benjamin and Kracauer in the social and technical relations of culture and class has come to be over-laid with a postmodern concern with the classless consumption of culture. Here the isolated academic figure as a *flaneur*-observer or ragpicker-collector comments on the subtlety of cultural consumption of fictional narratives. For some 'post-Marxist' and feminist theorists fascinated by Benjamin the standpoint of the individual *flaneur* observing public space voyeuristically smacks of masculinity in crisis (Wilson, 1991: ch. 4). Women were often pictured as the passive objects of culture – as dancers, models, celebrities, prostitutes – not its subjects, unless as consumers of degraded cultural objects, expressed in Kracauer's patronising title 'The little shop girls go to the movies' (Petro, 1989: 57–68). Such critique tends to neglect how Benjamin and Kracauer saw women as actively occupying public zones of consumption and production in urban modernity as salaried workers and prostitutes, which is to say as commodities of a special kind, potentially disruptive of social and political domination (Leslie, 2006a).

In contrast, Adorno distrusted Kracauer's and Benjamin's micro-logical method of working from the 'exemplary instances' of concrete reality since, in a society structured by the circulation of commodities, appearances are always deceptive. While developing a 'penetrating theoretical defense' of qualitative analysis, Adorno claimed that Kracauer's sociological empiricism was too 'ambivalent':

> On the one hand, he sympathises with it, in the sense that he has reservations about social theory; on the other, judging by the criterion of his conception of experience, he has emphatic reservations about a method that pinpoints and quantifies. (Adorno, 1992: 67)

Moreover, Adorno registered Kracauer's increasingly affirmative stance towards popular cultural forms and, later, with American society itself. However, the idea of an 'epistemological break' between an earlier revolutionary Kracauer concerned with 'material dialectics' and a later conformist Kracauer concerned with formal theory ignores an underlying concern with critique in different (and difficult) institutional and national contexts. Even in his later 'conformist' work Kracauer advocated a dialectic combination of Marx and Freud: 'Freud probes deeper than Marx into the forces conspiring against the rule of reason. Marx, intent on widening that rule, could not well make use of discouraging profundities. When you want to travel far your luggage had better be light' (Kracauer, 1960: 290).

Social theory begins with the material 'physiognomy' of substantive and superficial surfaces. With Simmel as an important precursor (Frisby, 1992: ch. 3), the *flaneur*-sociologist belongs to a series of 'extra-territorial' figures that include detectives in a crime novel, refuse collectors, immigrants in a foreign land, and strangers to the big city, in the search for clues and traces of collective experience and meaning. Kracauer and Benjamin warned against a 'premature' rejection of theoretical abstraction 'in favour of that false mythological concreteness whose aim is organism and form' (Kracauer, 1995: 81). Myth creates a rigid boundary between reason and nature. It attributes magical powers to nature, and naturalises social relations. By de-naturalising social relations, social theory assists the process of demythologising the fantasy images of social groups. As 'delicate empiricists' Benjamin and Kracauer advanced the role of social theory as a 'destroyer of myths'.

8

CRITICAL TURN:
THE FRANKFURT SCHOOL

'Critical theory' is the term given to the approach developed by a group of radical intellectuals at the Institute for Social Research housed in the German city of Frankfurt; hence they are also known as 'the Frankfurt School'. Rejecting 'traditional philosophy', the critical theorists were not ready to abandon philosophy to social theory or science. For them philosophical argument and cultural critique could potentially keep the door of freedom wedged open in the face of the worst catastrophe afflicting humanity: fascist atrocity. Initially attracted to Marx's critique of political economy, they increasingly looked to the industrial organisation of mass culture and media for an explanation for the non-revolutionary character of the working class in Europe and America.

In the process they shifted their emphasis from a Marxist analysis of the class relations of production to a social philosophical critique of ideology. It is difficult to settle on a single picture of critical theory. Different theorists passed through different phases, more or less political or economic, more or less sociological or psychological, more or less materialist or idealist. Of course, the idea of 'critique' was present in Marx, who famously ridiculed the unreality of 'critical criticism' in the 1840s, but it was also present in Kant's three 'critiques' of theory, morality and aesthetics. Social philosophy only became critical theory in 1937 after a period where it had been called 'materialism', indicating a shift from the language of classical Marxism.

Founded in 1923, the Institute began life under the Austro-Marxist Carl Grünberg as director, who conceived it as a centre of classical Marxism (Jay, 1973; Wiggerhaus, 1994). Stimulated by the proximity of crisis and revolution in 1920s' Europe, a number of outstanding problems in Marxist political economy were tackled, especially ones related to the transformation of modes of production. In this phase major studies were undertaken by Karl Wittfogel on the so-called 'Asiatic mode of production' in China, Henryk Grossmann (1992) on the logic of the capitalist breakdown, Franz Borkenau (1987) on the intellectual roots of the bourgeois revolution, and Friedrich Pollock on the problems of a planned economy in the Soviet Union.

By then Max Horkheimer (1895–1973) had begun to transform the Institute into what we now know as 'the Frankfurt School' of social theory (Abromeit, 2011). Among the leading figures associated with the Institute in this phase were Theodor Adorno (1903–1969), Herbert Marcuse (1898–1979), Walter Benjamin (1892–1940), Siegfried Kracauer (1889–1966), Leo Löwenthal (1900–1993), Alfred Sohn-Rethel (1899–1990) and Eric Fromm (1900–1980). With any revolutionary change ruled out by the 1930s that might launch human happiness as society's purpose, critical theory became permanently scarred by pessimism and sadness (Rose, 1978). The idea of critical theory was continued into the twenty-first century on a more hopeful basis by Jürgen Habermas and Axel Honneth.

Over the decades critical theory engaged social theory in different ways, with different accents and for different purposes. A central concern was the changing relationship of crisis to social theory. After initial sympathy for the Russian revolution and political activism, most critical theorists became fierce opponents of Soviet communism or 'state capitalism' as Pollock called it. In the 1930s critical theory identified widespread material poverty as the main obstacle to human happiness. But from the 1940s mass consumerism, not mass poverty, was identified as the main barrier to freedom and happiness. In the 1930s Horkheimer (1972: 45) argued that the transition to a 'better reality' was the core 'theme of contemporary theory and practice'. Later any hope of transition was postponed indefinitely and any relationship to political praxis abandoned. In the 1930s, ideals were seen as a spur to action in social struggles, although social theory could not be founded on arbitrary ideals. Later on, the youthful ideals of the struggles of the 1960s would be rejected by critical theory as misguided and dangerously provocative of powerful enemies. Ideals like freedom and happiness served 'critical theory', not political practice.

These concerns were rooted in the sociology of Weber and Simmel, Freud's psychoanalysis, German philosophy, as well as Marxism. Critical theory further developed this legacy through critique and theoretical renovation in changing fields and contexts. One key influence was the collection of essays by the Hegelian Marxist Georg Lukacs' *History and Class Consciousness* (1923[1971]). There Lukacs reconstructed philosophical foundations for an active subject in history, the revolutionary working class, or at least the revolutionary party. Theory was not to be generated by passive contemplation of an external object but actively, through praxis. With the social theorist actively engaged in a structured but changing world, theory becomes a constitutive part of that world as a prelude to changing it. Because of the strategic structural position of the proletariat in the relations of production the spell of false consciousness cast by ideology and reification could potentially be broken. Crucially, for critical theory, Lukacs introduced the concept of reification into social theory (Rose, 1978; Vandenberghe, 2009). This shifted the focus away from economics and science to problems of culture and consciousness, the traditional ground of German philosophy.

This chapter describes how critical theory emerged in the 1930s as social theory in a philosophical idiom. In their earlier dismissal of Comte, Marx and Engels were followed into the twentieth century by Horkheimer and others, who wanted to combat what they saw as the pernicious influence of positivism or 'scientism' and its supposed intellectual affinity with fascism. They objected to almost every aspect of positivism, not least what they saw as its uncritical attitude to scientific progress. Such claims were developed further by Adorno, Marcuse and Habermas in disputes about positivism in sociology from the 1940s to the 1960s, helping to ensure that the critique of 'positivism' was repeated as a matter of routine down to the present.

This tendentious judgement irrevocably tarnished the credibility of positivism in social theory. Before that another line of critical theory was prematurely closed down by Horkheimer, that of Franz Borkenau's analysis of ideology and science as a solution to contemporary and historical crisis, a development that would have complemented the increasing interest of critical theory in the critique of ideology. At that stage, however, Horkheimer was still concerned for 'social philosophy' to adhere to the language and themes of classical Marxism (Abromeit, 2011).

SOCIAL PHILOSOPHY

Under Max Horkheimer's leadership, the Institute in the 1930s evolved from classical Marxism into critical theory. With the labour movement destroyed by the Nazi state and the Soviet Union under the brutal dictatorship of Stalin, the prospects for revolution were worse than zero. Briefly stabilised by the hegemonic authority of the Bolshevik revolution, Marxism itself was plunged into crisis and fragmented into rival theoretical currents and apostasies, ranging from sophisticated versions of utopian and Hegelian Marxism to crude mechanical Stalinism.

Horkheimer, a philosopher by training, responded to the crisis of Marxism with a programme to preserve its emancipatory spirit in theory at the moment of its defeat in reality, harbouring the distant hope that the future might redeem the doomed present (Wiggerhaus, 1994). Resistance to reality was placed firmly on the theoretical plane, with little relationship to 'the earthly plane' of political practice. It was hoped that if the language of classical Marxism was used sparingly it would be allowed a surreptitious passage beyond the present danger.

From his inaugural lecture in 1930, Horkheimer (1993) envisaged critical social theory in a philosophical idiom. He initially called this 'social philosophy', a circumlocution that even then avoided too direct an association with the language of classical Marxism. By social philosophy Horkheimer meant 'the philosophical interpretation of the vicissitudes of human fate', not in the traditional philosophical sense of theory about theory but a philosophical interpretation of 'the entire material and intellectual culture of humanity' (1993: 1).

Horkheimer's 'social philosophy' was rooted in the German philosophical tradition going back to Hegel and Kant. Where Kant began from a critical analysis of the isolated individual subject, Hegel began from a universal philosophy of history dealing with the fate of entire societies as expressed in the formation of the state. Philosophy 'transfigures' reality by operating above the immense human suffering of actual individuals at the level of universal reason. Progress occurs through self-consciousness, not social structures. For Hegel's philosophy a hidden 'cunning' makes human beings realise history's goals behind their backs, although Hegel did recognise that real conflicts of interest drive actual historical developments.

Hegel's ideal sense of the whole, Horkheimer contended, no longer corresponded to the 'medley of arbitrariness' of the emerging society of individuals. Modernity is premised on particularity not universality, fragments not totality. Social philosophy in the shape of neo-Kantianism began to address the new individualism by emphasising aggregate forms of life gathered together in states, nations and classes. The only serious rival to social philosophy in the 1930s appeared to be Martin Heidegger's 'melancholy philosophy' of finite existence and death as a fundamental human experience.

No rigid boundary exists between sociology and social philosophy. Social philosophy does not stand aloof from empirical sociology but judges its epistemological and normative value. Horkheimer singled out 'the Pareto School' of positivism for reducing class, nation, and humanity to mere worldviews whose truth or validity can never be judged. Likewise positivism offers no grounds to evaluate the very different social theories of Comte, Marx, and Weber.

Philosophy does not specialise in 'the really decisive problems' of human existence, nor does it create theories disconnected from 'long, boring' empirical studies, which would only culminate in 'a chaos of countless enclaves of specialists'. Instead Horkheimer proposed a dialectical development of philosophical theory and sociology:

> Chaotic specialization will not be overcome by way of bad syntheses of specialized research results, just as unbiased empirical research will not come about by attempting to reduce its theoretical element to nothing. Rather, this situation can be overcome to the extent that philosophy – as a theoretical undertaking oriented to the general, the 'essential' – is capable of giving particular studies animating impulses, and at the same time remains open enough to let itself be influenced and changed by these concrete studies. (1993: 9)

Horkheimer envisaged that the Institute would bring together philosophers, sociologists, economists, historians, and psychologists in continuous collaboration. Nonetheless the problems for investigation would be determined by contemporary philosophy. Social science's role would be to supplement and refine 'the contemporary version of the oldest and most important set of philosophical problems' (1993: 11).

For Horkheimer the central philosophical problem concerned the relationship between social classes, psychology, and culture. This conception of social philosophy was, for Adorno, insufficiently philosophical and sounded too much like interdisciplinary empirical social theory. From Adorno's perspective Horkheimer risked becoming both 'a theoretical positivist and a practical materialist' (in

Rabinbach, 1997: 172). Where Horkheimer insisted on starting from a conception of 'the whole' and the facts of 'substantial relations', Adorno discriminated between the 'positivist conception of facts and our concept of substantial relations'.

Positivism was useful in so far as it brought to an end any pretensions that philosophy entertained of becoming a science. Science accepts its findings as binding while philosophy provisionally deciphers 'riddles': 'Plainly put: the idea of science [*Wissenschaft*] is research; that of philosophy is interpretation' (Adorno, 2000a: 31). Interpretation here is not that of the endless hermeneutic search for 'meaning'. For Adorno the reified world has no intrinsic meaning for theory to reveal (Benzer, 2011). Nor does it involve the Kantian problem of getting behind the phenomenal world to interpret 'a world-in-itself'. Philosophy was envisaged by Adorno as a materialist form of interpretation. Following Walter Benjamin, in 1931 Adorno (2000a: 32) saw the task of philosophy as interpreting and illuminating the traces of unintended reality by the construction of 'figures or images', which science analyses by more exact methods.

For Adorno (2000a: 44) both logical positivism and the philosophy of Heidegger, although hostile to each other, were united by a common opposition to philosophical speculation. If positivism was not possessed by 'humanistic tendencies' it would probably try to do away with theory altogether, Adorno ruminated, and replace it with the classification of facts, pure and simple. Facts are what are left over from theory, Adorno argued, while theory, paradoxically, attempts to discover something that cannot be thought. Theory, concepts and facts are not timeless or static truths but the deposits of historical processes (Adorno, 1974: 127). Observation of reality is always mediated by concepts, and concepts are always socially constituted. By naively enforcing the fact of the division of scientific labour as the criterion of its own truth, positivism is trapped in a circularity of its own making. Positivism's fixation on given reality neglects the historical constitution of both facts and science (Adorno, 2000a: 30).

MATERIALISM AND CRISIS

In the 1930s the main rival to Horkheimer's social philosophy was positivism. Positivism merely examines the particulars, individuals and facts of analytical science, a necessary stage of investigation that Horkheimer was not prepared to dispute. Social philosophy opposes both 'unprovable' traditional metaphysical ideas about essences, totalities, objective spirit, unities of meaning, 'national character' as well as the 'unprovable' metaphysical preconditions of positivism.

Initially Horkheimer sought the cooperation of Neurath and other social theorists in Europe but came increasingly to view logical empiricism as a dangerous rival in the struggle for hegemony over critical social theory. A long campaign to destroy 'positivism' was set in motion. This 'anti-positivist' reflex continues to haunt social theory.

Horkheimer's 'physicalist materialism'

Until then Neurath had good reason to assume that he shared much in common with Horkheimer on most general questions about science, metaphysics, and social theory. First, in his 1932 'Notes on science and the crisis' Horkheimer, like Neurath, criticised non-rational metaphysics (Horkheimer, 1972). Metaphysics rejuvenated itself briefly with a new anti-science mysticism concerned with vital 'life' forces, mysterious 'existence', and arbitrary 'intuition'. Indeed, scientific rationality is mistakenly blamed for the crisis by the metaphysical way of thinking. Metaphysics limited science to instrumental matters of industrial technique and hindered a theoretical critique of society as a whole and the place of human valuations within it. As the independent sociologist and Frankfurt associate Siegfried Kracauer (1995: 81) put it in 1927, far from being over-rational, capitalism is not rational enough.

Second, Horkheimer, like Neurath, agreed that the crisis in science was inseparable from the general crisis. The crisis destroys human and material resources and prevents science from realising its potential to improve social conditions. Yet science neglected the social crisis and 'introduced a confusion of its own by hypostatizing isolated, abstractly conceived man and thereby belittling the importance of a theoretical comprehension of social processes' (Horkheimer, 1972: 7). Science therefore confronts a double contradiction: first, it is critical about its object but lacks critical reflection about itself; second, it seeks comprehensive knowledge but lacks knowledge about its relationship to the social order. Science identified its own self-imposed limits with the limits to human knowledge. Horkheimer separated corroboration of theory from its wider human significance: 'The test of the truth of a judgement is something different from the test of its importance for human life' (1972: 3).

Third, like Neurath, Horkheimer refused to countenance any rigidly 'positivist' separation of theory and practice. Social theory served the existing social order ideologically by making it seem permanent, despite the increasing and more intense succession of crises, war, and upheaval:

> The ideological dimension [of science] usually comes to light less in false judgements than in its lack of clarity, its perplexity, its obscure language, its manner of posing problems, its methods, the direction of its research, and, above all, in what it closes its eyes to. (Horkheimer, 1972: 8)

Theory became petrified by timeless categories and mechanical methods. During the struggle for bourgeois emancipation from feudal rule, 'positivism' played a progressive role by countering the obscurities of scholasticism. But by the mid-nineteenth century it placed rigid limits on science that restricted it to description, classification, and generalisation (though these self-imposed limitations were overcome at this very time in the social sciences by Karl Marx).

Fourth, what Horkheimer termed 'materialism' resembled what Neurath understood by 'physicalism'. What Horkheimer (1972: 25) in the early 1930s called 'physicalist materialism' referred to 'the fundamental historic role of economic relations', though it meant something more general for Neurath. For Horkheimer, timeless philosophical categories have been superseded by concepts derived from specific socio-historical processes. As grasped by Marx and Engels the present cannot simply be projected unchanged into the future: 'contemporary materialism does not build up supratemporal concepts and abstract from the differences introduced by time' (1972: 25). 'Physicalist materialism' for Horkheimer, like Neurath, has no ultimate foundations. It is created in a specific time and place, it is imperfect and never complete, and it aims at improving human happiness. Because of the approximate and provisional state of knowledge there can be 'no general formula' for dealing with the play of objective and subjective factors in social theory (1972: 29).

Materialism is misconstrued as the philosophical antinomy of idealism or spiritualism. Even self-professed adherents of materialism start from a metaphysical opposition to idealism. To say that 'everything real is material' is, like physicalism, to make a minimal general claim with limited implications for particular analyses. For the materialist, 'judgements which embrace all reality are always questionable, because [they are] far removed from the kind of activity which generated them' (Horkheimer, 1972: 20).

Metaphysics make the opposite claim. Particulars are merely specific examples of eternal universal knowledge. Metaphysics seeks to provide foundations for theory and practice by discovering 'the ultimate ground of things' in 'being', 'totality', 'life', 'essence', 'reality', 'consciousness' or whatever (Horkheimer, 1972: 18). Idealism addresses eternal riddles and converses with philosophers across the ages. Concepts like time and space become frozen and absolute. History is refused the 'dignity' of theory. In terms of Kant's epistemology, empirical *phenomena* are essentially unknowable 'in themselves' in contrast to the supra-sensible *noumena* of concepts. Universal categories justify their claims by transcending concrete relations in time and space. Ruling groups are able to justify their particular interests in universal and absolute categories like 'justice' or 'freedom'. Similarly, individuals try to justify their actions as 'moral', reasonable, and right, not in terms of concrete feelings of anger, joy, or compassion.

Fifth, for both Horkheimer and Neurath knowledge is always historical, which means that it is also inherently changeable along with social conditions. The failure of Comte and Spencer's system in Horkheimer's (1972: 49) view was not that they attempted to characterise entire stages of development but that, as sociologists, they failed to demonstrate 'how their individual theories and concept formations and, in general, every step they take are grounded in the problematic of their own time'. As we have seen, however, the grounding of social theory in the problematic of the age, however inadequate, was precisely what Comte (and Neurath) attempted.

THE CRITICAL DEFENCE OF METAPHYSICS

After the relatively measured critique of positivism of the early 1930s, Horkheimer (1972: 132–187) launched a full-blown polemic with his 1937 article 'The latest attack on metaphysics'. Positivism and metaphysics represent torn halves of the same page. On the positivist half, exoteric science eliminates the traces of unreal metaphysics, while for the metaphysical half, science is disdained as mere technique, inferior to higher esoteric knowledge. Metaphysics allows insignificant individuals to feel that in their inner life they are the special agent of their own existence even when obdurate reality shows otherwise: 'In private life this philosophical belittling of science acts as an opiate; in society, as a fraud' (Horkheimer, 1972: 138).

Pure positivism

Horkheimer acknowledged that there are no pure representatives of what he meant by 'positivism' in the history of philosophy. Not even Comte and Spencer qualify since their philosophies of science were mixed with commitment to particular worldviews. Horkheimer resorted to a composite ideal metaphysical model and ignored any differences or tensions within 'positivism'. Construed in this rather arbitrary way, Horkheimer asserted that 'the special metaphysical theses of positivism' include the fragmentation of social wholes into isolated elements, the reconstruction of isolated data into social aggregates, unchanging natural laws, and the construction of a 'definitive' theoretical system (Horkheimer, 1972: 40):

> The ideal it pursues is knowledge in the form of a mathematically formulated universal science deducible from the smallest number of axioms, a system which assures the calculation of the probable occurrence of all events. (1972: 138)

As the latest branch of positivism, logical empiricism continued to root theory in the facts of sense perception. It differed only in its self-conscious translation of direct sense perception to statements about observations. Idiosyncratic subjective differences are eliminated by studying whole populations, not individuals and the collective dialogue of science. From this Horkheimer asserted that positivism settles theoretical differences with a 'crucial experiment' rather than argument and struggle, a view that Neurath decisively rejected. Horkheimer simply ignored statements by Neurath that contradicted his claim that for positivism nothing in knowledge ever changes *notwithstanding* some of its assertions' (1972: 148, emphasis added) or the legend that empiricism is modelled on mathematics.

If positivism was insufficiently historical about its own assumptions and preconditions it was also insufficiently 'immanent' in so far as it did not derive its findings from the inner logic of things themselves. Limited to the surface appearance of phenomena, Comte derived 'laws' from constant relations of succession or similarity, not from the 'inner nature' of things or from their final and efficient causes. Where metaphysics exaggerates and absolutises theory, positivism belittles knowledge to a collection of external observations. In so doing, positivism makes the metaphysical assumption that observed object and the observing subject are fundamentally separate.

By allowing for an unknowable realm completely closed off from human knowledge, positivism betrayed Kant's demand – dare to know. Its ascetic stricture against the non-rational disarms positivism from being able to challenge superstitious beliefs, which is left unhindered to dominate non-rational values. In this way, Horkheimer identified critical theory with reason whereas positivism, trapped in 'a median position in society', between the two major classes, is 'opposed to thought, whether it tend forward with reason, or backward with metaphysics' (Horkheimer, 1972: 186). Positivism is thoughtless, critical theory thoughtful. 'Dialectics' as metaphysical assertion appears to require no 'materialist' corroboration.

Horkheimer's *coup de grâce* was to elide logical empiricism and fascism. He made plain his intent (and fundamental misunderstanding of Neurath's project) in a letter to Adorno:

> Basically the whole thing is only a miserable rearguard action by the formalistic epistemology of Liberalism, which, also in this area segues into open fawning in the service of fascism. (in Wheatland, 2009: 117)

While Horkheimer recognised the long-established anti-totalitarian credentials of positivism, it 'may not seem obvious at first' but positivism was now bound to the fascist state and its impoverished middle-class supporters:

> This principle is particularly significant in a world whose magnificent exterior radiates complete unity and order while panic and distress prevail beneath. Autocrats, cruel governors, and sadistic prison wardens have always wished for visitors with this positivist mentality. (1972: 151)

Positivism represented a regression from trusting in human perception to superficial expediencies and false neutrality. Science was placed beyond critique just as interests and power were placed outside of science.

Any attempt to strengthen the epistemological autonomy of science was an aid to 'universal injustice'. Whereas the earlier rationalism of Leibniz allowed for agency and decisions, placing it closer to the materialist conception of history, for Horkheimer the subject is eliminated completely by empiricism, again ignoring the considerable scope allowed by Neurath for subjective decisions and judgements in specific conditions.

Philosophical privileges

Shocked by this crude caricature Neurath penned a measured reply, which Horkheimer refused to publish, defying the usual scholarly convention of critique followed by response. In the face of metaphysical and emotional provocations Neurath attempted to strike a dispassionate tone, such that Horkheimer's hyperbole 'carry no argumentative force to the empiricist' (2011: 26). Against Horkheimer's distorted ideal-type model, Neurath retorted clearly enough: 'Empiricists have often emphasized in plain words that any theory can be traced back to the subjective interests of groups of humans' (2011: 21).

Only later would positivism be routinely decried as totalitarian and technocratic. This association had not yet hardened into a shibboleth. At the same time as accusing Neurath of objective complicity with fascism, Horkheimer (1972: 147) contradictorily linked the Unity of Science movement to liberalism, with its view of a consensual world of harmony, where 'one can come to an understanding with everybody on every subject', that was then passing away under authoritarian regimes. Positivism thus supports both, or either, fascism and liberalism as the 'dialectic' demands.

As Neurath (2011:19) noted in his reply, no support was given for this or any other assertions like it. Indeed, empiricism was charged by Horkheimer, on the one hand, of passively accepting the facts of what is given and refusing to make prognoses while, on the other hand, of actively making predictions and calculating probabilities for 'all events' yet to come. In conditions of rapid change and tumultuous upheaval 'foresight' is only acquired by social theory with great difficulty. As Neurath argued: 'How can the as yet unaltered way of thinking foresee what the future altered way of thinking is like and predict how one is going to evaluate the contemporary situation retrospectively?' (2011: 16).

Horkheimer's deeper motive was to preserve social theory in a philosophical idiom. For Horkheimer, positivism does 'not belong to a science that *deserves the respect* of philosophical thought' (1972: 184, emphasis added). Where Neurath aimed to eliminate metaphysics completely, Horkheimer wished to transcend the division between metaphysics and science. Positivism, it was alleged, failed to recognise the changed historical conditions of twentieth-century crisis as different in kind from seventeenth-century crisis when the struggle of science against metaphysics represented something revolutionary. Critical theory relativises absolute distinctions in philosophy, such as those between appearance and reality or subject and object, by making all concepts historical. Theory is pragmatic, never autonomous or all-embracing. Even the absolute distinction between science and philosophy needs to be relativised. Otherwise the limited practice of science would be cut off from the general insights of philosophy, Horkheimer (1972: 34) maintained.

Such a continuing and privileged role for philosophy was rejected by Neurath. Critical theory and metaphysical intuition are closer to each other than Horkheimer's 'materialism' suggests. In staying on the ground of metaphysical critique Horkheimer 'has to shrink back from subjecting those "correct" theses to scientific test, because then he would enter the domain of science, which he wants to criticise after all' (2011: 22). For Horkheimer (1972: 162) the only valid test of theory was to be on the 'right side' in social struggles, which simultaneously confirms 'sound common sense' and the correct theory of the world. The 'right' social theory comes from decisions that arise from social struggles yet at the same time provides 'the key' for understanding the same struggles (1972: 159).

Horkheimer wanted to preserve a privileged status for dialectics and materialism couched in gilded language with little need of a substantive social theory. Adorno, 'the metaphysician who distrusted metaphysics', praised Horkheimer, 'the materialist who distrusted positivism', for having 'liquidated the entire positivistic heritage of Marxism' (in Rabinbach, 1997: 173). It is the special, elusive language of Horkheimer's meta-theory that enables everything in its sights to be critiqued with little concern for empirical statements.

Neurath objected to any extra-scientific critique of science that refused to specify testable propositions in an intelligible language. For instance, vague talk by Horkheimer about 'a self-modifying moment', 'subjective interests in the unfolding of society as a whole', 'the inexpressible' and so on would need to be translated into physicalist language of testable statements to advance human knowledge beyond profound-sounding phrases.

It is not that Horkheimer was incapable of empirically controlled language, as Neurath noted of his empirical study of 'Authority and the family' (1972: 47–128). Scientific language needs to control, in so far as it may, for unintended associations or ideological commitments so that the barriers of scientific discourse might be reduced if not removed. Outside of science, however, all sorts of terms are used routinely to elicit emotional support and ideological agreement on political and cultural matters.

FRANZ BORKENAU – WORLD-PICTURES AND CRISIS

In a striking parallel with the process sociology of Norbert Elias of that other Frankfurt School, Franz Borkenau (1900–1957) filtered the language of critical theory through the problematic framed by Weber and Nietzsche (Szakolczai, 2000). Borkenau had been brought to the Institute by Grünberg and contributed reviews of Alfred Schütz, Erich Fromm, and Marx and Engels' *The German Ideology* (1845–6) to the first volume of the Frankfurt house journal *Zeitschrift für Sozialforschung*. His own, admittedly limited, study of Pareto's social theory was reviewed favourably for the Institute by the sociologist T.H. Marshall, who thought it 'a more important work than its size might suggest … packed with suggestive ideas, any one of which repays careful consideration and might lead to extensive sociological speculation' (1936: 406–1).

In his earliest work at the Institute, Borkenau (1987) examined the crisis of 'world-pictures' in the transformation of the feudal world. World-pictures (*Weltbildes*) refer to axiomatic beliefs presupposed by particular forms of knowledge and values. This phrase was taken up by Martin Heidegger's 1938 lecture on science, 'The art of the world picture'. For Heidegger (1977: 129) the important point was that the modern world had itself become a picture which constantly re-presents 'that which is', above all, people looking at themselves in ways that were simply not possible in any previous age.

Crisis and the civilising process

Borkenau began from the crisis of the feudal world. The dissolution of social and intellectual order raised fundamental questions about taken-for-granted assumptions of the old world-picture. Under crisis conditions pessimism predominates, the future is a source of dread, and power is reassembled through violent contest. As Borkenau later put it, civilisations 'almost always arise out of barbaric ages whose chaotic disintegration and paranoiac savagery make the reshaping and reestablishment of tradition an overwhelming necessity' (1981: 55). In the seventeenth century the critical role is played by the class of the 'middling sort', erroneously termed 'gentry' by Borkenau, though this hardly affects the central argument. Within this contradictory position the pressure points between the old order and the new order are felt most acutely.

From the early seventeenth century new systems of philosophy emerged that established the conditions for natural and social science. Metaphysics and epistemology on one side, and physics and social theory on the other, were not yet rigidly separated. Borkenau described this new 'mathematical-mechanistic world-picture' as closely related to the rise of pre-industrial 'manufacture' in this period. At this stage, science was not yet integrated into the labour process. Yet, somehow, manufacture presented an abstract picture for science to follow in its development.

Borkenau set this within the language of classical Marxism of class struggle related to the emerging capitalist mode of production. The new mechanistic image of nature shattered traditional forms of natural law that assumed a harmonious cosmic order. Increasingly, middle terms like 'contract' were introduced between social doctrine and the picture of nature. Social relations were no longer experienced as 'natural' but imposed by external forces.

In a situation of crisis and anxiety it fell to 'theory' to establish the essential good of the world in the face of its evil 'empirical' appearance. In response, epistemology imitated metaphysics. On the one hand, if it is claimed that there is an eternal order in nature there must also be an eternal order of human reason. On the other hand, if it is claimed that the world is split in two parts – a realm of necessity and a realm of contingency – then there must also be two forms of knowledge, eternal *rationality* and changeable *opinion*: 'The theory of knowledge, apparently a presupposition, proves to be an outcome of the socially conditioned view of the world order' (Borkenau, 1987: 114). The grounds for human knowledge of the external world became more uncertain and open to question.

As the static social order gave way to a more dynamic one, a more active picture of nature emerged, finding its starkest image in the astronomy of Copernicus. The optimistic cosmos of the earlier theology of Aquinas no longer holds, replaced by the pessimistic corrupt humanity of Calvin and Pascal. Order is restored in theory, if not in reality, by the geometrical method (Descartes) and concentrated state power (Hobbes).

Calvin

Borkenau placed Calvin at the pressure point of the collapsing natural social order. Without God-given social and natural order there can only be the devil-inspired evil of naturally sinful individuals. Borkenau generally accepted Weber's thesis about religion and capitalism. Inner-worldly asceticism was an adaptation to the disruption of the traditional economy by monetary capital, making possible the capitalist-rational labour process. For Borkenau it was less the positive doctrine of predestination that proved crucial, as Weber assumed, than the pessimistic Calvinist image of the meaningless depravity of humanity without God.

> In the final analysis inner-worldly asceticism is irrationally founded. But precisely thus is Calvinism spared the problem of bringing the meaninglessness of capitalistic existence and the war of all against all into accord with some ideal of the good and the beautiful. Instead, it accepts this as fact. (Borkenau, 1987: 116–7)

Catholic sects such as the Jesuits and Jansenists also felt the pressure of a crumbling social order. In contrast to Calvinist pessimism, however, Catholicism needed to infer God's goodness. The result was an elite Catholic space of moral life for the 'virtuosos of asceticism' cut off from earthly temptation. In this sphere, Catholic optimism became inverted, abandoning the rest of humanity to worldly corruption in the daily struggle to meet earthly needs.

Descartes

Descartes attempted to solve the profound social and existential crisis by transforming human contingency into natural necessity. By adopting an inner contemplative attitude – 'I think therefore I am' – the outer world is made to submit to inner reason. Cartesian philosophy solves the historical crisis by ensuring that the outer world corresponds to the ontological security provided by pure thought. The reduction of the world to pure reason resulted in an optimistic picture of inevitable processes. Descartes reduced existential and social crises to a geometrical world-picture of mathematical precision and logical deduction. Appearances become self-evident in the new Cartesian world-picture: 'the infinite striving of the bourgeois as being human essence pure and simple' (Borkenau, 1987: 123). Any limit to human striving in the emerging capitalist social order was perceived as an 'error' of will and a failure of rationality.

Hobbes

Hobbes stands between rationalism and empiricism. Social theory begins from assumptions about individual human nature, not reason, and arrives at absolute state power by logical deduction, not empirical demonstration. As 'the first consistent bourgeois theorist of the state', albeit a thoroughly 'conservative' one, Hobbes was concerned above all to justify absolutist formal-juridical state power, not its concrete content (Borkenau, 1987: 125). As a convinced mechanistic materialist, Hobbes, unlike Descartes, had no optimistic illusions in perfectible human nature. People are essentially wicked and strive for power to satisfy material comfort and egoistic pleasure. Society is pictured as imploding under atomised competition to the death – a war of all against all. Civil war is the normal condition of society unless absolute power is invested in the state. Once the state monopolises the means of violence the price of rebellion becomes overwhelming. Yet the state cannot possibly be stronger than the combined force of individuals in society. Therefore the state faces contradictory pressures to legitimate itself by winning the allegiance of its subjects while dominating them through concentrated violence.

Pascal

With Pascal the mechanistic world-picture becomes self-evident. Against the rationalist systems of Descartes and Hobbes, Pascal remained in close contact with practical life. Existential and social crises cannot be solved by pure thought. Rationalism turns into a relationship of necessity what, for Pascal, are essentially moral judgements. From Hobbes' mechanistic pessimism Pascal accepted that 'might is right' but his critique of 'divertissement' went beyond this to argue that worldly pursuits and pleasures have no meaning in themselves. Never-ending but pointless striving finds its limit in the material fact of death as 'the meaning-destructive central truth of life' (Borkenau, 1987: 126).

Pascal's contradictory world-picture of infinite striving and finite existence produced what Borkenau called a 'negative dialectic', a term taken up by Adorno in a different context. People need to want to be saved from alienation in conditions that cannot be saved. In the absence of physical evidence of God, individuals are helpless 'thinking reeds' who must exercise a force of will to become great, a theme later transvalued by Nietzsche with explosive effect. For Pascal, such a fate can be stoically accepted only if alienation is first made intelligible by theory. Like nature, positive signs must be found to confirm the 'hidden God' in logical calculations of probability and the practical habits of the faithful (see Goldmann, 1964).

Grossmann's critique

Objections to Borkenau's account of the mechanistic world-picture concentrated on the idea that theory could derive in any direct way from the production process (Postone, 1993: 177). Even if the mechanical world-picture proved useful in social struggles during the crisis, ideological functions do not explain the foundations of theory. In fact Borkenau did not propose a unilinear causal relationship rising from the manufacturer's workshop to a world-picture, but something closer to what Bourdieu (1984: 230) termed 'a logic of homology' between two relatively autonomous fields. 'Manufacture' and world-picture bisect each other. As such they are doubly determined by the interests of classes and by the specific logic of fields, producing significant differences between Calvin, Hobbes, Descartes, and Pascal.

The most ferocious response was a review by Henryk Grossmann (1987), prominent Marxist scholar at the Institute, soon after Borkenau's book-length version *The Transition from the Feudal to the Bourgeois World-Picture* was published by the Institute in 1934 (Borkenau, 1976). After failing to interest Walter Benjamin to critically review Borkenau's book, Horkheimer persuaded Grossmann (Kuhn, 2009: 247). Grossmann (2006, 2009) produced a series of studies 'refuting' Borkenau's 'uncritical' acceptance of Weber's thesis of Protestant capitalism and presented a more historically accurate account of the division of labour and science (Kuhn, 2006).

Grossmann carried out his critique in such a devastating fashion that Borkenau's study is barely known to Anglophone social theory, while Grossmann's own contribution is beginning to be recognised alongside the path-breaking Marxist history of physics by Boris Hessen (Freudenthal and McLaughlin, 2009). He concentrated his fire mainly on Borkenau's Weberian account of the role of small producers ('striving little men'), the role of manufacture in the rise of capitalism, and the neglect of the mechanistic Catholic rationality of Leonardo da Vinci.

As well as challenging Borkenau on the historical evidence Grossmann also objected to his mode of argument. Borkenau rejected a descriptive history of events for a structural analysis of the shift in the world-picture from natural law to mechanistic principles. This was not so dissimilar to the simplifying abstractions that Marx adopted in *Capital*, a procedure endorsed by Grossmann in his major study of the logic of capitalist crisis:

> The real world of concrete, empirically given appearances is that which is to be investigated. But in itself this is much too complicated to be known directly. We gain an approach to it only by stages. To this end we make various simplifying assumptions that enable us to gain an understanding of the inner structure of the object under investigation. … It is clear that thanks to these fictitious assumptions, we achieve a certain distance from empirical reality, even while the latter remains the target of our explanations. (Grossmann, 1992: 30)

Grossmann noted that Marx's initial simplifying hypotheses were too often taken for final results rather than provisional findings. A subsequent process was necessary to take into account the empirical detail that was disregarded at the start. In this way theory 'draws nearer to the complicated appearances of the concrete world and becomes consistent with it' (Grossmann, 1992: 31).

Nonetheless, Grossmann (1987: 158) saw in Borkenau's structural method a general disdain for the facts in an 'empty formula of incipient monetary capitalism as a general explanation'. Borkenau conceded that his main concern was with changes in theory and world-pictures rather than a detailed historical sociology of manufacture and technology. Borkenau had only been persuaded after the fact by Horkheimer to put greater emphasis on manufacture and its relationship to mechanistic science, the focus of Grossmann's demolition job. At this stage fidelity to the shade of Karl Marx was still important to critical theory.

Pareto and totalitarianism

It is less sociological speculation than an original analysis of authoritarian solutions to crisis that marks out Borkenau's significance for social theory (Jones, 1992, 1999). Borkenau appropriated Pareto's biological theory of the reproduction of elites to develop a distinctive sociology of state dictatorships, fascist and communist, as different expressions of the same form of total rule. For Pareto modern society was locked in to an eternal cycle of crisis and violence, continuing a pattern of pessimistic social theory that Borkenau traced through Hegel, Nietzsche and the historian A.J. Toynbee, and which could also be soon appended to his erstwhile colleagues in Frankfurt. Instead of 'logical' class interests both Soviet and fascist regimes appealed to 'non-logical' impersonal ideals. In these social orders rationalism is relegated to technical matters while irrational beliefs predominate in social life.

In the face of an opaque social order, non-rational totalitarian 'ideals' offered the one remaining faith that would make social life intelligible and transparent, all the while unfolding a terrible logic of self-destruction: 'the acceptance of authority instead of rational consideration, the eulogy of activity in the place of thought, the unconsidered acceptance of a few metaphysical principles taken for granted and the rejection of any "problems" not solved by these official axioms' (Borkenau, 1936: 211).

Crisis hastened the transition from liberal market capitalism to state dictatorship, appearing to resolve the conflict between private and public interests. As the political logic of competition displaced the market logic of competition, crisis was extended and deepened:

> Crises become greater, not less, but state intervention remains necessary, as less intervention would not mean minor crises but still more terrible effects of crises. The point is soon reached where the mass of the population of important communities is faced with the danger of losing its very existence. The state is the arbitrator. And in general distress and downfall, it must decide who shall go under and who survive. The more the state becomes an economic arbitrator, the more politics become economically important. And the more economic life is shattered, the more the state becomes important for the very life of every one of its citizens, who fight a desperate battle for domination over it in order to preserve their existence and make the other perish. (Borkenau, 1936: 202–3)

Pareto gave forceful expression to social and personal pessimism following the collapse of a liberal social order, even more resolutely ominous than Nietzsche's bleak vista of 'eternal recurrence'. At least Nietzsche hoped against hope that a superman would appear to save the day. So despondent was Pareto with state-sponsored corruption in Italy, all he could do was to embrace an ideology of violent overcoming that left an ambiguous legacy for social theory.

No 'synthesis' will ever emerge for Pareto to dialectically resolve the eternal contradictions of crisis. Pareto elected for a metaphysics that endlessly repeats the same underlying essence in different guises for different cycles of crisis. Perhaps unwittingly, Pareto paralleled Hegel's idea of historical recurrence of the same forms of social life in different civilizations, only without allowing for Hegel's emphasis on difference: 'Difference in sameness and sameness in difference is the essential point of Hegel's dialectics' (Borkenau, 1936: 158). Hegelian difference, or 'non-identity', would become the central motif in Adorno's meta-critique of social theory.

An exclusive stress on either pole of similarity or difference resulted in a one-sided social theory, Borkenau argued. Committed to building a philosophical system, Pareto's underlying belief in repetition had little to do with empirical theory. This was 'social philosophy' in the grand pessimistic style rather than sociology controlled by social research. Pareto showed little interest in putting his pessimistic philosophy to the stringent test of empirical analysis. Borkenau accepted that because struggles between groups in society are a permanent feature no social theory is ever likely to be entirely free from political and social values, but without empirical controls, social theory more readily succumbs to political desires that require unremittingly tragic world-pictures: 'Pareto's "Sociology" is simply a political manifesto in scientific guise, expressing not only one among the leading tendencies of our time, but probably the overriding one' (Borkenau, 1936: 169).

Although Pareto lacked reflexivity and relied on unobservable metaphysical axioms, Borkenau found some value in his theory of 'residues' and 'derivations' for opposing abstract rationalism, and in the theory of elites for dispelling illusions about social egalitarianism. Residues referred to the same sentiment of domination and submission repeated over and over through different social forms. This had the merit for Borkenau of introducing some kind of psychological dimension into social theory. Derivations referred to the idea that underlying sentiments of domination always come packaged with some logical or 'ideological' justification. While ideological 'derivations' provide a mask for self-deception Pareto failed to allow for any genuine difference of worldview between social groups. More successful for Borkenau was Pareto's theory of elites, which he developed more systematically than predecessors like Carlyle and Nietzsche, though again insufficiently conditioned by empirical details.

Pareto provided Borkenau with a sounding board to develop his own theory of totalitarian states, which he soon broadened by close analysis of the ruling regimes in Spain, Germany, Austria, and the Soviet Union in a rapid flood of books of varying quality, ranging from his classic *The Spanish Cockpit* (1937), *The Communist International* (1938b), *Austria and After* (1938a), and *The New German Empire* (1939a) to the cruder *The Totalitarian Enemy* (1940). Following his developing analysis of 'totalitarianism' and despite serious reservations about free-market democracies Borkenau became a trenchant Cold War anti-communist.

CRITIQUE AND DEVELOPMENT

Social theory needs to be renovated by each generation to overcome the 'misuse' of concepts by the previous one, particularly when dialogue and assimilation are blocked by field struggles over relatively small differences. This chapter dealt with how two promising currents in social theory, Neurath and Borkenau, were broken on the wheel of critical theory. Only now is the potential of such theories being seriously re-examined to illuminate current concerns with science, values, state, and crisis.

Until his early death Borkenau harboured an ambitious project prompted thirty years earlier when he (1938c, 1939b) reviewed his friend Norbert Elias' then almost universally ignored but now classic study *The Civilising Process* soon after the first two volumes appeared. His posthumously published *End and Beginning* (1981) was an attempt to extend the long-term perspective of Elias' civilising process to the fifth century and the fall of the Roman Empire, tracing modern individualism to the migration of Celtic, Viking, and Germanic groups, while allowing a more central role to religion in the civilising process than Elias, focussing on the civilising missionary role of Anglo-Irish religious orders in Germanic lands (Szakolczai, 2000).

Retreating from his earlier aim to unify science and philosophy as dictated by historical materialism, Horkheimer now erected a predetermined mixture of science, formal logic, irrationalism, and barbarism largely of his own making. In the process he casually denounced those, like Neurath, who were attempting to put empirical social theory on a new cognitive and political footing. Philosophy, Horkheimer claimed, needed protection from science. By sowing romantic illusions metaphysics had performed a useful function for a type of individuality that had almost ceased to exist under technological capitalism. Positivism wanted to cruelly rob alienated individuals of this last refuge by reducing 'truth' to sense data or abandoning it altogether.

Horkheimer and Neurath expressed very different conceptions of science. For Horkheimer, science is essentially static and reifying in contrast to 'dialectical logic', which expresses movement and process. For Neurath, science has no 'essence' as such. It is a practical achievement, accomplished by a permanent process of self-criticism. Neurath's concern for prediction looked forward to a utopia of unified science that had expelled metaphysics. Horkheimer, in contrast, looked back to a period when science and metaphysics were like energetic children, peddling illusions for sure but with the saving grace of working at a human level (Barck, 2011).

Two decades before critical theory discovered the 'negative dialectic' of reason turning into unreason, Neurath's colleague in the Vienna Circle, Philipp Frank, had already outlined the process of what he called 'pseudo-rationalism': 'It destroys the old system of concepts, but while it is constructing a new system, it is also already laying the foundation for new misuse. For there is no theory without auxiliary concepts and every such concept is necessarily misused in the course of time' (1949: 78). Frank drew support from Nietzsche, the philosopher furthest removed from scientific apologia, who argued that the metaphysical reification of 'things in themselves' is an 'idle hypothesis'. All concepts must be seen as relational without collapsing into false dichotomies like appearance and essence, autonomy and determinism, change and permanence, contradiction and non-contradiction, among other philosophically 'interesting' puzzles.

9

NEGATIVE TURN: HORKHEIMER, ADORNO AND HABERMAS

Critical theory was formed in the shadow of catastrophe. Filtered by the critique of positivism, the experience of fascism haunted critical theory. Written under enforced conditions of US exile in the mid-1940s *Dialectic of Enlightenment* (1972) was Horkheimer and Adorno's attempt to theorise the catastrophe in Europe. Fascism was no aberration but the terrible symptom of new forms of domination introduced by capitalist modernity. To begin with, critical theory located fascism within the crisis of capitalism. As late as 1939, before the full horror of the Nazi genocide to come, Horkheimer was in no doubt that fascism could not be understood in isolation from the political economy of capitalism: 'whoever is not willing to talk about capitalism should also keep quiet about fascism' (Horkheimer, 1989: 78). However, by 1949 Adorno could mark the shift away from the crisis of capitalism to the critique of ideology when he identified the complicity of culture with absolute atrocity in his notorious comment, '*To write poetry after Auschwitz is barbaric*' (1967: 34).

'Fascism is the truth of modern society, which this theory has grasped from the beginning', argued Horkheimer (1989: 78). This could be taken in a number of ways. First, that fascism was predicated on the economic theory of the transition from market capitalism to bureaucratic state capitalism. As the economy surrenders to political control, fascism, or something like it, is the logical result and endgame of political economy. With the economy centrally organised and planned there seemed to be less likelihood that it would break down under the weight of its own contradictions as Marxist logic predicted.

Second, fascism fulfils a psychological need as autonomous subjects submit to the demands of a strong leader, thus displacing individual responsibility and anxiety to a higher level. However, Adorno rejected any direct causal relationship between psychology and fascism: 'Psychological dispositions do not actually cause fascism; rather, fascism defines a psychological area which can be successfully exploited by the forces which promote it for entirely non-psychological reasons of self-interest' (1991: 130).

Third, and most pervasive, fascism is the logical unfolding of a metaphysical process of positivist unreason specific to modern life. If, as Horkheimer assumed, people are not brought to reason by means of reason but by pain and suffering, then fascism is, paradoxically, the source and end point of rationality. Here the truth of fascism expresses the philosophical teleology of Weber's impersonal instrumental rationality. By drawing on the idea of reification implicit in Marx and made explicit by Lukacs, critical theory transformed Weber's theory of rationalisation and disenchantment into a total critique of capitalism. Only where Lukacs identified the source of reification in the specific nature of a society premised on the commodity form, critical theory located it in the earliest forms of rational thought.

The chapter examines how the critique of positivism was related to the primal domination of nature, including human nature, in ancient mythology through to the horror of the concentration camps. Critical theory returned again and again over the next three decades to attack 'positivism' as the symptom of a sickly society. Positivism and culture were fused in Adorno's much-disputed concept of 'the culture industry'. Horkheimer and Adorno's 'reductive' approach to the culture industry is ritualistically condemned for failing to acknowledge the inherent pleasures and multiple readings of texts. Instead of cultural subversion and subjective autonomy, Horkheimer and Adorno emphasised a pernicious strain of conformism, cruelty and dependency. The chapter highlights Horkheimer's 'social theory of rackets', abandoned by critical theory yet potentially the basis of a substantive theory of social power, violence, and dependency. Finally, Habermas' elaboration of an intersubjective communicative theory of society initially provided a more nuanced idea of subsystems and social integration in the logic of crisis, later supplanted by Habermas' concern with normative political philosophy and discursive ethics.

CRITICAL THEORY IN A REIFIED WORLD

For Adorno (1967: 34) the world after the Holocaust resembled an 'open-air prison'. A totalising process of reification had taken hold of society: 'All phenomena rigidify, become insignias of the absolute rule of that which is.' The 'absolute rule of that which is' had, of course, been the main accusation levelled against positivism. Reified social theory was the intellectual counterpart of a reified 'culture industry'. 'Absolute reification' threatened to obliterate critical culture by turning it into yet another harmless discourse of 'idle chatter'. The only hope, a slim one, was for critical theory to break out of what Adorno called 'self-satisfied contemplation'.

Exactly how, Adorno does not say. His own approach was to form elliptical and elusive arguments in order to strike a blow against stale, reified concepts. In this way Adorno hoped to stimulate active thinking about freedom to complement the positivist demand for a more exact empirical sociology (Benzer, 2011). Yet critical theory shifted from 'interdisciplinary materialism' to ideology critique to philosophical anthropology and a philosophy of consciousness. Here the traditional philosophical distinction between essence and appearance enabled critical theory to discover a deeper structure of ideological domination behind the apparent freedom of capitalist society. Unless the deep structure of reification is recognised and addressed, society is doomed to continually reproduce the conditions for fascism or something like it in 'the authoritarian personality' or 'one-dimensional man'. Ever the same, critical theory adopted general criteria to explain the function of ideological repetition for a self-reproducing system, the kind of universal explanation that Horkheimer (1972) had previously rejected as 'traditional theory'.

Dialectic of enlightenment

In Horkheimer and Adorno's (1972) *Dialectic of Enlightenment* the 'dialectic' of the title pointed to the tension between culture and barbarism. In no small measure this was due to their reception of Walter Benjamin's (2003: 389–400) final work, 'On the concept of history', composed before he took his life fleeing fascism. In eighteen pithy theses Benjamin dissected the many layers of crisis: political, technological, theoretical, and methodological. While recoiling at Benjamin's 'undisguised' Marxist terminology, Adorno saw it as close to his own conception of history as permanent catastrophe, domination, destruction of nature, and manipulation of culture.

Horkheimer originally planned an interdisciplinary study of ideology centred on a sociological examination of class, bureaucracy and political economy, 'filled to bursting point with historical and economic detail, or else it will look like speculation' (in Wiggerhaus, 1994: 316). In any event, the crisis was explained less in terms of the specific dynamics of capitalism than in speculative terms of fallen human nature's primal need to dominate nature. As such, twentieth-century crisis was not caused primarily by a retreat into the mythology of nation and race but by the Enlightenment's own fear of truth. Knowledge was advanced to dominate not liberate nature, including human nature – Weber's disenchantment of the world taken to extremes.

This was demonstrated not by sociological analysis but by the splendid just-so stories of philosophical anthropology and theological speculation about the origins of domination that somehow continues to determine culture today. Philosophical anthropology rests on the supposedly eternal dilemma for human beings caught between happiness and barbarism. Either submit to inner and outer nature (happiness) or dominate nature through repression and self-mutilation (barbarism). In its recurring crises Western humanity always chose the latter course:

> At the turning points of Western civilization, from the transition to Olympian religion up to the Renaissance, Reformation, and bourgeois atheism, whenever new nations and classes more firmly repressed myth, the fear of uncomprehended, threatening nature, the consequence of its very materialization and objectification, were reduced to animistic superstition, and the subjugation of nature was made the absolute purpose of life within and without. (Horkheimer and Adorno, 1972: 31)

In Horkheimer's hands, Weber's disenchantment of the world from a geographically and historically specific set of conditions pertaining to modernity in northern Europe now transcended capitalist rationality to encompass a cyclical persistence of mythical ideas over thousands of years and across the unspecified terrain of 'Western civilisation'.

Myth and positivism

Written in philosophical fragments, *Dialectic of Enlightenment* (Horkheimer and Adorno, 1972) traced the crisis of civilisation back to its original source in Homer's myth of Odysseus. 'Enlightenment' was not limited to the philosophy of the seventeenth and eighteenth centuries as conventionally understood but stretched across three thousand years of reason and mythology. A fragmentary style of presentation was necessary because of the collusion of scientific and everyday concepts in the still-unfolding crisis of civilisation. An eternally recurring philosophical paradox presents itself: social freedom needs enlightened thinking but enlightened thinking repeatedly becomes self-destructive.

It seems that there are two enlightenments: one promoting imperious and self-destructive 'subjective reason', positivism above all; and another, 'objective reason', promoting freedom and truth about nature, including human nature, critical theory above all. Enlightenment, in the sense of progressive thought, aimed at human liberation from fear and superstition yet it led, paradoxically, to the complete collapse of freedom: 'Enlightenment is totalitarian' (1972: 6). Rationality has become not, as Durkheim supposed, a free expression of social solidarity 'but of the inscrutable unity of society and domination' (1972: 21).

Myth was not banished by reason but reanimated as scientific concepts that functioned as magical charms to ward off demonic spirits of the unknowable. By bracketing out what is not yet known, positivism already knew in advance what it needed through the logical techniques of scientific closure. Positivism fears whatever is outside itself. Radically divorced from art, science nevertheless secretes its own detached aesthetic system of abstract symbols. It can only ever approach 'the given' as abstract spatio-temporal facts, 'grasped' as frozen moments outside the developmental process of their social, historical and human significance.

Because positivism inevitably reproduces what already exists it inevitably succumbs to mythology: 'mythology had the essence of the *status quo*: cycle, fate, and domination of the world reflected as the truth and deprived of hope' (1972: 27). Positivism perpetuates social injustice, its unacknowledged starting point, by surrendering all protection for individuals from the 'threatening collectivity' of social norms. Positivist logic in the lecture theatre ratifies reification in the workplace. In Homer's ancient myth Odysseus enjoys the song of the Sirens by being bound to the mast while the oarsmen have their ears plugged to save them being distracted from their labour. Similarly, modern bosses are bound to an abstract relationship to the source of wealth and a contemplative relationship to art, while the human qualities of workers are reduced to the impersonal functions of the factory, the movie theatre, or the nation. Eventually, every theory succumbs to 'the destructive criticism that it is only a belief' (Horkheimer and

Adorno, 1972: 11). Every event and object is approached comparatively, reinforcing the mythical form of repetition that abstract rationality was meant to escape and control:

> With the extension of the bourgeois commodity economy, the dark horizon of myth is illuminated by the sun of calculating reason, beneath whose cold rays the seed of the new barbarism grows to fruition. (1972: 32)

In a fragment titled 'Why it is better not to know all the answers' Horkheimer and Adorno (1972: 210), asserted that reason, which presupposes dialogue and free exchange, is blocked as soon as science exercises unilateral power to demand agreement: 'For positivism, which represents the court of judgement of enlightened reason, to digress into intelligible worlds is no longer merely forbidden, but meaningless prattle' (1972: 25).

Dialectic of Enlightenment continued the critique of positivism laid down by Horkheimer in the 1930s and supplemented Herbert Marcuse' (1941) study of the rise of social theory, *Reason and Revolution*, and set the tone for further attacks on positivism over the next three decades. Positive philosophy, Marcuse claimed, represented a reaction against Hegel's 'negative philosophy'. For Marcuse, Hegel rejected all that was irrational and false in bourgeois society whereas Comte reified the 'progress' made by state and society as operating under the same 'objective necessity' as nature, comprehended only through the universal application of the scientific method. In so doing, Comte substituted tolerant, provisional, and relative knowledge for the absolute claims of Hegel's philosophy, a diametrically opposite claim to the standard cliché that positivism is intolerant, certain and dogmatic.

Because it renounced transcendental philosophical critique, positivism became a core plank of what Marcuse (1968: ch. 3) called 'affirmative culture'. Positivism resigned itself to whatever existed as fact and refused to make any negative critique of given reality. Philosophy, on the other hand, pushes beyond empirical limitations to critique society from the transcendental standpoint of reason and freedom. Positivism is unable to provide a guide for action until it first perfects the scientific theory of society. On the other hand, as Marcuse (1941: 359) concedes, this is belied by Comte's vision of the 'real universal' of a post-national human society beyond anything conceived by Hegel's fixation on the state. Even here Marcuse charges Comte's universal humanism as the bad conscience of positivism's authoritarian polity and meaningless unified science.

METHOD AND THEORY

In the debates over positivism in the 1960s, critical theory insisted again on the fundamental distinction between social theory and natural science. Critical theory is concerned above all with the capacity for human society to think about its ultimate ends. According to Adorno positivism denies that a transcendental theory is either possible or necessary:

The core of the critique of positivism is that it shuts itself off from both the experience of the blindly dominating totality and the driving desire that it should ultimately become something else. (Adorno et al., 1976: 14)

When the critique of positivism was debated within German sociology in 1961 it was not at all clear that the disputants, from Popper to Habermas, were referring to the same thing, such was the diversity of how 'positivism' was conceived (Adorno et al., 1976). Long-time critic of the Vienna Circle, Karl Popper (Adorno et al., 1976) identified positivism with the method of induction, in contrast to his own method of deduction from the situational 'logic' of subjective agents. Knowledge starts from practical and theoretical problems, Popper argued, not isolated observations (unless they reveal a general problem).

Despite radically different philosophies and politics, Adorno and Popper found themselves in awkward agreement in their hostility to positivism. Popper's description of 'totally mistaken' positivism beginning from 'value-free' observations and proceeding by induction to theoretical generalisations generally corresponded with that of critical theory. Under the influence of positivism, Popper claimed, sociology became an observational 'pseudo-science' that subordinated 'purely theoretical sociology' to a descriptive sub-discipline of anthropology (Adorno, et al., 1976: 91–2).

Beyond that, however, their assumptions proved incompatible, leading to a largely abstract debate about sociology and scientific methods. At the end of the debate Adorno accepted Popper's label of critical theory as 'pre-Marxist' since in non-revolutionary conditions, theory cannot rouse people to action. Marxism can only dogmatically assert revolution as a proposition (Adorno et al., 1976: 128–9). Popper (Adorno et al., 1976: 129) for his part claimed to be 'pre-Hegel', a classical liberal who modestly and optimistically proposed piecemeal change rather than succumb to the disappointed utopian despair and theoretical hubris of Adorno.

Against Popper's deductive method, Adorno argued that method cannot be separated from its object. Ignoring Neurath's boat, Adorno (Adorno et al., 1976: 9) responded to an imagined 'positivist' accusation 'that dialectics lacks a foundation upon which everything can be grounded'. In contrast to 'positivism' dialectics possesses no guarantee of truth, is not a closed circle of knowledge, and has no tradition of thought it can appeal to, only 'experience':

Knowledge comes to us through a network of prejudices, opinions, innervations, self-corrections, presuppositions and exaggerations, in short through the dense, firmly-founded but by no means uniformly transparent medium of experience. (Adorno, 1974: 80).

Dialectics for Adorno signifies the mediation of individual experience by the objective social totality and, contrariwise, social totality is nothing other than the interdependent effect of individuals on each other and on the totality. This totality of lengthy social networks cannot be fixed by a collection of observations or deductions but only by immanent critique.

PHILOSOPHY AND SOCIOLOGY

Adorno (2000b: 22) wanted to dialectically overcome the false polarisation between sociology as a positive empirical science and philosophy as a critical theory of experience. This required a theory of what Adorno called the 'non-identity' of essence and appearance in order to force into view the obscured essence of social relations. Here Adorno uses two senses of 'essence': first, in the logic of social relations and, second, in pre-empirical, self-contained concepts like society, class, capitalism, and alienation. Such concepts always 'imply a pre-existing context of propositions and judgements, an over-arching theoretical construct, which cannot be abstracted from individual concepts or entities in isolation' (2000b: 25).

Alongside common sense, philosophical speculation introduces 'subjective caprice' into social theory: caprice, because it lacks empirical restraints, and subjective, because theoretical concepts are arbitrarily conflated with things in themselves (Adorno et al., 1976: 5). On the other hand, ascetic positivism rules out *ex cathedra* speculative predictions, thus eliminating common sense (Adorno, 1974: 124). Positivism's claim to objectivity is contradicted by the subjective reason of protocol statements which depend on the practical activity of individual observations.

Positivism cannot attain the 'non-factual' reality of the totality because it is fixated on general categories and discrete observations. The result is over-general social theory that, like 'hotel gravy', is 'poured indiscriminately over any dish' (Adorno, 2000b: 29). Karl Mannheim, for instance, is criticised by Adorno for accepting the positivist fallacy of general categories illustrated by convenient examples in his formal sociology of knowledge (Adorno, 1967: 43–6). Critical theory, in contrast, plays with exaggeration and rejects any literal reflection of reality. Adorno explores the absolute limits of reason while positivism is limited to the self-confirming truth that everything is relative. If all knowledge is relative and interchangeable in this way (as current talk about 'transferable skills' assumes), it becomes a purely functional mechanism for 'academic technicians' lacking any individual capacity for self-critique. Self-validating technocratic clichés require no further thinking.

Theoretical concepts do not and cannot correspond to reality in any direct way. A reflexive, fragile distance must be maintained between facts and theory: 'Distance is not a safety zone but a field of tension' (Adorno, 1974: 127). Adorno detected a contradiction between formal logic and empirical data. Formal social theory, as constructed by Simmel, is not necessarily mistaken except in so far as it reifies arbitrary concepts. The problem is how to allow the material to speak while accounting conceptually for its deceptive appearance. Adorno gave priority to contradictory experience of a contradictory reality not only theoretically but also in empirical studies like *The Authoritarian Personality* (1980), in his cultural criticism and in his philosophy of music.

Here the sober practical judgements of common sense constitute for Adorno 'a moment of critical thinking', let down only by the social consensus of its general character: 'For opinion in its generality, accepted directly as that of society as it is, necessarily has agreement as its concrete content' (1974: 72). Where Adorno diagnosed consensual 'healthy common sense' as sickly, Habermas would later medicate consensus for a more positive role in social theory.

CULTURE INDUSTRY

Social theory textbooks tend to isolate the chapter on the culture industry from this philosophical context and treat it as a substantive (and wrong-headed) theory of mass culture. Adorno's highly original quasi-Marxist allegory attempted to make Homer's ancient poem relevant to contemporary concerns about renunciation, sacrifice and self-mortification in mass culture. By combining 'culture' and 'industry' in a single category Adorno aimed to outrage the defenders of an outdated conservative tradition of culture premised on beliefs about personal sensitivity and innate genius. Culture is an industry that not only classifies and disciplines consumers but also appeases their needs, which are manufactured in the first place (Horkheimer and Adorno, 1972: 123). Culture is transferred from the objective reason of individual judgement to the subjective reason of the industrial organisation of technology.

Clearly, the rise of the culture industry was a relatively recent empirical development, connected to the transition from liberal individualism to bureaucratic society, rather than something inscribed in culture since Odysseus three thousand years ago. Yet this myth is where Adorno locates the origins of the schism between 'high culture' and 'low culture' in the original division between art and work. Bound to the mast Odysseus can only contemplate the beauty of the Sirens' song without any sensuous happiness while aesthetic thought is cut off completely from the purely physical function of the ship's proletarian rowers.

With his high modernist sensibility, Adorno (2002) argued that it is no use complaining about the loss of an organic 'high' culture created by master artists. Against his reputation as a cultural mandarin, Adorno refused to indulge illusions about high art as the pure expression of freedom. This merely justified art as a 'false universality' which not only excluded the mass of people but was premised on the continuation of social suffering. The *division* itself between high and low culture corresponded to the truth of the matter (Horkheimer and Adorno, 1972: 136). Serious art demands concentrated attention, while mass culture serves a need for distraction without much mental effort. The culture industry subsumes this division by minor variations in cultural formats combined with endless repetition of cultural contents.

Neither is 'high culture' more technically skilful. Today's specialists have as much or more technical skill as traditional master artists. An unrivalled technical method consciously creates mass cultural effects. With its repertoire of pre-programmed effects, the culture industry finally deciphered the mystery of Kant's conceptual a-priori. Specialised experts calculate in advance the reception by consumers of consciously constructed effects in hit songs, film blockbusters, short stories, jokes, and so on. Nothing is left to chance for imagination, spontaneity, or reflection. Reaction is automatic, geared to the simple reproduction of consumer consciousness.

Technical virtuosity covers over the jaded ideological formulae of cultural products. The standardisation of mass production drastically reduced the difference between an unjust everyday life and cultural technologies like film, radio, magazines, and television: 'A technological rationale is the rationale of domination itself' (Horkheimer and Adorno, 1972: 121). When technical discipline is breached by a virtuoso, as in the films of Orson Welles, 'they almost attain the subtlety of the devices of an avant-garde work as against those of truth' (1972: 129). Adorno (1974: 50) repudiated 'the false riches' in the high production values of the culture industry for 'ascetic barbarism', not unlike the trash punk aesthetic of the 1970s.

Great artists from Mozart to Schönberg expressed the truth of art negatively by confronting the conventions of style, rupturing the false unity of form and content, and risking non-recognition in its radical dissent from the flow of cultural tradition. However, art gives up its autonomy as soon as money enters the equation. When money is around, nothing is inherently valuable in its own right. Art only acquires value if it can be used for something else, that is, if it takes the form of what Bourdieu called 'cultural capital'. Attempts to lower economic and educational barriers to high culture without an equalisation of social conditions debase both art and the masses:

> The abolition of educational privilege by the device of clearance sales does not open for the masses the spheres from which they were formerly excluded, but, given existing social conditions, contributes directly to the decay of education and the progress of barbaric meaninglessness. (Horkheimer and Adorno, 1972: 160)

The cheapening of cultural goods makes them less, not more, capable of being assimilated, even when given away as rewards and gifts, such as free entry to art galleries, sweetly coated by the ubiquitous advertising culture. Only groups that might gain an advantage in social competition will seize the chance to blindly accumulate 'culture'.

A democratic leveller, mass culture always falls short because it has to speak the everyday language of consumers and fails to test itself against refractory material. It mass-produces magnificent spectacles. A cheap cinema ticket gives access to a film that cost millions to make. This satisfies the 'pretence of choice', an illusion then being swept away by 'a society of huge Fascist rackets' which rules by direct orders and open bullying. It flatters the 'misplaced love of the common people for the wrong which is done them' while despising the pretensions of the connoisseur and the knowledge of the expert (Horkheimer and Adorno, 1972: 134). Even the film star is merely an interchangeable copy of the democratic multitude, selected by blind chance from the anonymous many by the calculations of the few, a theme developed later in Adorno's (1994) analysis of fate and luck in newspaper astrology columns.

Technically slick, 'pre-digested' film merely reinforced the everyday habit of repetitive, distracted attention (Adorno, 1991: 154). Because it was consciously organised to produce involuntary responses, Adorno called fascist propaganda 'applied psycho-technics', 'reminiscent of the calculated effect conspicuous in most presentations of today's mass culture – such as in movies and broadcasts' (Adorno,

1994: 223). Where Benjamin detected unconscious revolutionary desires in the laughter of a cinema audience, Adorno found it 'anything but good and revolutionary; instead it is full of the worst bourgeois sadism' (Adorno et. al., 1977: 123).

IDEOLOGY AND AMBIGUITY

The culture industry trades on ambiguity. Adorno identified a tension between the rising average intellect of the masses and the uniform banality of culture. The fusion of culture and entertainment intellectualises amusement at the same time as it degrades the intellect (Horkheimer and Adorno, 1972: 143). People know they are being misled but go along with it anyway and even take pleasure in it. In the administered society, dissent is incorporated into the dominant style in the end as in the beginning. Ideology is careful not to commit itself to anything too concrete that can be measured. Ambiguity and monotony are the latest means of domination, though where ambiguity fits with the calculating rationality of means and ends is unclear.

Paradoxically, the ruling ideology offers few concrete promises or explanations of the crisis. It cannot appeal to ultimate ends by promising the good life, which everyone would see through during the crisis. Instead, ideology becomes 'photological', sliding between factual duplication and deceitful monotony: 'Ideology is split into the photograph of stubborn life and the naked lie about its meaning – which is not expressed but suggested and yet drummed in' (1972: 147). The photological world displaces meaning and right with repetition of the facts of the matter.

Whatever keeps repeating itself, whether economic crisis, biology or cultural formulae, must be both inevitable and right. Propaganda succeeds less through the persuasiveness of its message than through the fact that 'the howling of sirens announcing panic' seems to be broadcast everywhere by new media like radio:

> The metaphysical charisma of the Fuhrer invented by the sociology of religion has finally turned out to be no more than the omnipotence of his speeches on the radio, which are a demoniacal parody of the omnipresence of the divine spirit. The giant fact that the speech penetrates everywhere replaces its content ... (1972: 159)

The whole point of propaganda and advertising is to manipulate people by overpowering them with 'a pure representation of social power' (1972: 163).

Social reproduction itself is the main thing. Making fundamental change to social relations has become unthinkable. This gets confirmed day in and day out with unrelenting monotony by the same old stereotypes and clichés of the culture industry. Language is ground down by the wheels of publicity. Words are detached from their experiential rootedness in everyday life and emptied as carriers of substantive meaning. People are conditioned to respond in prescribed ways to the latest corporate phraseology – 'quality', 'going forward', 'incentivising', 'performance indicators' – as language is used in increasingly ambiguous and euphemistic ways.

Names become trademarks – 'McDonald's' – not a symbol of family history. Words become reified things, as when positivism demands ruthless clarity for its terms (in contrast again, Neurath allowed for a fairly loose conceptual language).

All that can be done is to join in and stay up to date, or face social death. From childhood people are corralled by a system of voluntary institutions, churches, clubs, professional bodies, and so on. These provide the most sensitive barometer of social conformism. Here it is easier to determine who fits in and, more importantly, who doesn't. In the professions, prescribed types of conduct are as vital to social survival as expert knowledge. Individuals feel that their position has become more precarious with the advance of technology. More people fall under the control of the administrators of the welfare state. As Horkheimer and Adorno put it seventy years ago, 'Under liberalism the poor were thought to be lazy; now they are automatically objects of suspicion' (1972: 150).

PSEUDO-INDIVIDUALITY

At least the welfare state cast 'a conciliatory shadow' over the culture industry, though only in the same way that the workplace is more efficient when management create a pleasant workplace atmosphere, and the militant is challenged by an uncomprehending supervisor about any expressions of dissent. Every recalcitrant emotion is disavowed. Social integration enforces relations of dependency. Dependency imposes masochism on the self, infinitely adaptable and flexible, with no inner core to prevent assimilation to outside orders: 'The capacity to find refuge, to survive one's own ruin, by which tragedy is defeated, is found in the new generation: they can do any work because the work process does not let them become attached to any' (Horkheimer and Adorno, 1972: 154).

Against the collective identity, or sameness, of (empirical) mass culture, critical theory advanced a (normative) theory of the non-identity, or difference, of critical individual egoism. Horkheimer and Adorno's account of enlightenment and morality reported a counter-tradition of demythologisation where libertines struggle against totalitarianism (de Sade) and reason is defined as thinking alone without others in the interests of self-preservation (Kant). A 'secret utopia' is present in Kantian 'reason' when individuals independently discover their common interest, which positivism would level down to mere instrumental functions (Horkheimer and Adorno, 1972: 84). Individuals thinking alone find their own way to 'objective reason' independent of the functional coercion of 'subjective reason' as an instrumental means to secure self-interest. Reason reflects private thought. Happiness is identified with cruel primal instincts of individuals rather than, say, the Scottish Enlightenment's stress on the happiness from social sympathies and moral sentiments of being together.

Society suffers from the pathologies of over-integration. It celebrates the self-destruction of individuality, what Durkheim (1952: 225) called 'altruistic suicide'. 'Pseudo-individuality' measures stylistic difference in fractions of a millimetre just like the intricate mechanism of a Yale lock. People no longer live lives but adopt 'lifestyles':

> The most intimate reactions of human beings have been so thoroughly reified that the idea of anything specific to themselves now persists only as an utterly abstract notion: personality scarcely signifies anything more than shining white teeth and freedom from body odor and emotions. (Horkheimer and Adorno, 1972: 167)

For instance, Adorno (1974: 59) saw the mania for health and fitness and the steady disposition as the 'sickness of the normal', an expression of the repressed pain that the administered society requires to fit in.

Even in the liberal age, individuality was always contradictory. Freedom to choose an ideology was always already an ideology. Harsh conditions of market competition forced a split between individual freedom and social function. Individuation, the effort to be different, came at the expense of individuality, simply being different. Liberal individuation – 'the effort to be different' – was finally replaced by the pseudo-individuality of the culture industry – 'the effort to imitate'.

Adorno (Horkheimer and Adorno, 1972: 132–3) briefly explained how avant-garde artists and critical intellectuals (like himself) survived the flattening onslaught of the culture industry in Germany. The late arrival of democracy in Germany after 1918 meant that it only superficially permeated social relations. Under the shelter of state patronage, avant-garde self-critique was largely protected from marketisation. Many cultural institutions, including education, universities, art museums, serious theatre, and large orchestras, were largely untouched by 'the market mechanism'. Successful commercial publishers enhanced their reputations by supporting non-marketable authors, although even then the pressure for deviant artists to fit in or face exclusion was always present.

Capitalism's irrationality, or its rationality of means over ends, demands an irrational psychological economy. Life seems to be dependent on accidental forces. It easier to go with the flow, however half-heartedly, than to object and resist 'as an attempt to strengthen and somehow justify painful conditions which seem to be more tolerable if an affirmative attitude is taken towards them' (Adorno, 1994: 155). Under capitalism the anomic personality is faced with boundless possibilities for concrete pleasure and happiness but is forced to submit neurotically to abstract demands for refinement and self-denial. Constantly swinging between extreme busyness and mindless monotony, relatively free from material want or doubt, the bourgeois ego keeps itself in check. Dialectically speaking, egoism has a good and a bad side. On the good side, egoism demands unconditional happiness denied by abstract rationality. On the bad side, egoism, as recognised by de Sade and Nietzsche, needs to find expression for cruelty in a higher form of existence, which self-restraint disallows.

THEORY OF RACKETS

Unlimited brutal egoism found its most distorted expression in fascist rackets and atrocities. Not that the culture industry hides social suffering. On the contrary, it tells it like it is. With a 'pathos of composure' it justifies social suffering as necessary and unavoidable. More discerning consumers of the culture industry demand hard-edged products, from music and films to box sets and digital games today. Cultural prestige requires uncompromising representations, just as the line manager disqualifies human solidarity unless it helps to meet output targets. If cynical regret – 'I'm doing all I can to help' – fails to soothe dissent, then a merciless attitude – 'Stop complaining or else' – will do just as well.

Tragedy now lies not in the hopeless resistance of its classical form but in the punishment that must be meted out to pointless discontent. The culture industry teaches the meaning of tragedy today as one of avoidable punishment:

> The masses, demoralized by their life under the pressure of the system, and who show sign of civilization only in modes of behaviour which have been forced on them and through which fury and recalcitrance show everywhere, are to be kept in order by the sight of an inexorable life and exemplary behaviour. (Horkheimer and Adorno, 1972: 152)

A vicarious pleasure in social suffering is produced by the culture industry. Even the great novels of Weimar Germany – Adorno mentions Alfred Döblin's *Berlin Alexanderplatz* (1929) and Hans Fallada's *Little Man, What Now?* (1932) – share with the products of the culture industry a contempt for the desperate situation of ordinary people.

Horkheimer and Adorno had planned to develop a general 'theory of the rackets' as the latest form of social power (Horkheimer, 1985; Stirk, 1992: ch. 6). 'Rackets' are monopolised by armed status groups, of which gangsterism is only a special case. Ruling cliques monopolise social positions through threats, intimidation, extortion, and violence, arbitrarily selecting victims and demanding personal loyalty. The racket has put its seal on all historical forms of social domination, from the racket of the clergy, the court, landowners, race, men, adults, family, police, crime, and so on. Most generally, the racket usurps and protects social privilege and violently repulses all challengers.

Horkheimer (1985) developed his theory of rackets from the anthropological claim that early human groups jealously maintained hierarchical privileges, from strongest to weakest, by physical force. As societies adopted tools and symbols, social position replaced physical force, with privileges now preserved by more regulated social processes. Rackets, as Simmel understood, have a close affinity to secrets and to dynamic relations of inside and outside. From whispers in the council of clan chiefs to the agreements between industry and the military in clubs and boardrooms, secrets of the powerful must be protected, not least because of the suspected brutality of the enemy.

When organised force becomes powerful enough a more stable rule of conduct, including rackets, is enshrined in the form of the legal code. Horkheimer (1985) gave the example of the academic racket. With the university dissertation the adept demonstrates thoughts, feelings and ways of speaking that take the irrevocable form of the academic racket. Qualifications are their own incentive but are never binding on the racket itself. Sanctioned by the state, which legislates on behalf of all, academic titles merely bestow on the adept membership of a particular racket and therefore of the system overall.

Adorno (2003: 102) developed a class theory of the rackets. As political oligarchy displaces economic competition, formal sociological classes are replaced by the power struggles of cliques, gangs, and groups: 'The theory that learns how to identify the different gangs within the classes today is a parody of the formal sociology that denies the existence of class in order to make these gangs permanent' (2003: 102). For Horkheimer (1985) the racket of dominant groups in securing the strongest against the weakest survives in the brutalising rackets of the poor as a vicious protest against defencelessness.

No longer confined to the criminal underworld, political rackets, backed by force, now appropriate or 'privatise' socially necessary functions. Public power became the private power of ruling oligarchies, blurring state and non-state forms of power. This was particularly evident in the case of the Nazi usurpation of state power, although Horkheimer thought it a more general trend. In *Dialectic of Enlightenment* (Horkheimer and Adorno, 1972) this led him to underestimate the specific nature of Nazi terror against Jews, claiming that the anti-Semitic racket could just as readily be exchanged for some other persecution racket. Sadistic Nazi projection fell mainly upon the Jews since they came to embody all the contradictory attributes of fascist legend:

> Jews were blamed simultaneously for capitalistic and revolutionary, relativistic and dogmatic, tolerant and intolerant 'mindedness'. Such contradictory accusations do not in fact reflect upon the Jews but rather upon the state of mankind in the present historical period. The Jews are but the bearers of society's inconsistencies. (Adorno, 1994: 208).

Since the claims made about the terrorised minority were so outrageous that no one could possibly believe them, they succeeded as a construction of absolute abstract difference (Adorno, 1974: 108). Only a huge lie, monotonously repeated, induced the mass fear and mass sadism needed for totalitarian rackets.

Psycho-dynamics of the rackets

Racketeering is a conspiracy against the human spirit, Horkheimer (1985) argued. The racket feels no pity for any life that is outside itself and only recognises the law of self-preservation. Initiation into the racket demands absolutely binding guarantees of loyalty and reliability. Without reservation the individual must surrender any independent existence and destroy all bridges to the past. For Adorno the hierarchical structures of administered capitalism mesh completely with the desires of the sado-masochistic personality: 'Hitler's famous formula, *Verantwortung nach oben, Autorität nach unten*, (responsibility towards above, authority towards below) nicely rationalizes this character's ambivalence' (1991: 123). A century earlier Marx noted how social dependency was related to authoritarian cruelty:

> Those who are most cowardly, who are least capable of resistance themselves, become unyielding as soon as they *can exert absolute parental authority*. The abuse of *that authority* also serves as a *cruel substitute* for all the submissiveness and dependency people in bourgeois society acquiesce in, willingly or unwillingly. (1846: 53–4)

In conditions of total administration the authority figures of the bourgeois family are supplanted by impersonal authority. In crisis conditions, the state, controlled by cliques, becomes both the impersonal instrument of terror and protector against terror. Protection rackets are among the oldest rackets.

Open critique of the rackets provokes resentment and violent rage as the neurotic personality suffers narcissistic loss and collapses more fully into the death-drive: 'The unconscious psychological desire for self-annihilation faithfully reproduces the structure of a political movement which ultimately transforms its followers into victims' (Adorno, 1994: 230). Sadistic cruelty is not the 'binary opposite' of masochistic submission to the racket. For Freud, 'The sadism of the superego and the masochism of the ego supplement each other and unite to produce the same effects' (1984: 425). Hence, the masochistic drive to irrational self-destruction through the totalitarian racket was combined with the sadistic impulse to annihilate groups that seem to personify rational critique of irrational values.

Ambivalence and rackets

Freud's hostility to pleasure and reason, however, has an ambivalent affinity to a repressive society. Psychoanalysis and the culture industry perform similar functions for the rackets: 'a technique by which one particular racket among others binds suffering and helpless people irrevocably to itself, in order to command and exploit them' (Adorno, 1974: 64). By suspending the gap between dramaturgical roles and psychodynamic depths, ambivalence performs an insidious function for the fascist racket.

> Just as little as people believe in the depth of their hearts that the Jews are the devil, do they completely believe in their leader. They do not really identify themselves with him but act this identification, perform their own enthusiasm, and thus participate in their leader's performance. (Adorno, 1991: 133)

Narcissistic identification with the Fuhrer required that the leader-celebrity possess the ambivalent characteristics of a 'great little man'; part superman, part everyman. Hitler posed as 'a composite of King Kong and the suburban barber … the superman must still resemble his follower's own ego and appear as his "enlargement" … a person who suggests both omnipotence and the idea that he is just one of the folks' (Adorno, 1991: 122).

Such radical ambivalence makes fascist crowds merciless in obeying the leader's veiled permission to abandon social inhibitions on paranoiac projection and violent gratification. Inured by the culture industry, the masses respond to constructed sentimentality with a bad conscience:

> The sentimentality of the common people is by no means primitive, unreflecting emotion. On the contrary, it is pretense, a fictitious, shabby imitation of real feeling, often self-conscious and slightly contemptuous of itself. This fictitiousness is the life element of the fascist propaganda performances … in which the expression of emotions is sanctioned by an agency of social control. (Adorno, 1991: 225)

The virulent social pathology of the rackets demands a 'leap into the abyss' as people shut themselves off from the objective logic of spiralling violence that will later visit unforeseen suffering on their heads (Adorno, 1974: 104–8).

Anti-Semitic rackets turn from the propaganda ritual to the bloodshedding ritual. In both cases the ritualistic nature of propaganda and mass murder transfers responsibility from individuals to an external power. Weakness is transformed into strength, irrationality into rationality. Here the psychology of fascist rackets takes on a life of its own. It lurked almost wherever it was looked for: in Adorno's (1980) fascist personality test, the F-Scale, or in the structure of popular film (Kracauer, 1947). For Adorno (1974: 55), catastrophe appeared to be a permanent condition as the cycle of violence and counter-violence became institutionalised and the rackets organised with administrative efficiency.

The theory of rackets was the provenance for what Adorno (1974) called a 'melancholy science' in *Minima Moralia*, his excoriating reflection about a 'damaged life'. Here the obscured reality of capitalist reification was related to the obscured strategies of conspiratorial rackets. With the social ubiquity of rackets, relationships become instrumental opportunities to get ahead by the affable 'arts and dodges' of ingratiation, adaptation and self-promotion. In a tough-guy world cynicism is a universal code. When everyone is in the know about what's what, no one can afford to be honest even as fidelity to the truth is routinely proclaimed. The mediation of direct domination by formal conventions of politeness and tact give way to casual informality and the indifference of direct domination: 'Matter-of-factness between people, doing away with all ideological ornamentation between them, has already become an ideology for treating people as things' (1974: 42).

HABERMAS: COMMUNICATION IN A RATIONAL WORLD

Like Horkheimer and Adorno, in his early work Jurgen Habermas (1973, 1989) placed critical theory in a broadly Marxist vein. Marx transformed Hegel's world history as a never-ending crisis of spirit into the objective tendencies of economic crises, Habermas (1973: 218) argued, in the process replacing the philosophical 'resolution' of crisis with its socio-historical constitution. Historically produced, alienated labour can only be resolved practically, not ideally, by the subjects themselves. While Marx's theory of crisis was economic, the resolution of crisis required a critique of ideological misrecognition, including science and philosophy, which obscures historical processes with quasi-natural fixed concepts. In so doing, Marx illegitimately universalised the class struggle of his day into a world-historical crisis structure (Habermas, 1973: 249).

Although critical of 'positivism' and 'scientism', Habermas (1984: 386) took a different tack from Adorno. He wanted to return to the earlier promise of Horkheimer's 'interdisciplinary materialism' before the critical theory of society was 'interrupted' by the philosophy of consciousness. Critical theory was caught in a philosophical bind of its own making. If reification and instrumental reason were as total as Horkheimer and Adorno assumed, then emancipation and reconciliation will never occur: '*Dialectic of Enlightenment* holds out scarcely any prospect for an escape from the myth of purposive rationality that has turned into objective violence' (Habermas, 1987: 114). Critique was possible only from 'the ironically distanced perspective of an objective reason that had fallen irreparably into ruin' (Habermas, 1984: 377).

To rescue rational social theory from the sweeping critique of instrumental reason meant abandoning 'German' social theory centred on the problem of reification, from the idealist philosophy of Kant and Hegel, through Marx and Weber, to Lukacs and high critical theory. Habermas proposed to free Weber's theory of rationalisation from the dead end of the philosophy of consciousness by supplementing it with the sociology of communications in George Herbert Mead, the sociology of social solidarity in Emile Durkheim, and the philosophical pragmatism of Peirce, James, and Dewey. An ambitious formal synthesis of philosophy and sociology was attempted in Habermas' (1984) theory of communicative action. Critical rationality cannot be grounded in either contradictory experience (Adorno) or deductive argument (Popper). It must find its ground, counter-factually, in unfettered communication between autonomous speakers reaching consensus 'implied' by the 'public sphere': 'Critique lays claim to no more than what is implied in everyday discourse, but also to no less' (Habermas, 1983: 107).

Self-defeating theory

As far as Habermas is concerned, there is little sense in critical theory that science, morality, and art are differentiated subsystems subject to their own laws of expert judgement and validity claims. Habermas (1987: 111) objects not to the critique of positivism as such but to the fact that positivism is identified with science and the 'totalized reproach that the sciences themselves have been absorbed by instrumental reason'. On the one hand, positivism was criticised using the categories of traditional philosophy – truth, dialectics, freedom, reason, and so on – but, on the other hand, philosophy was criticised as ideological from the perspective of social theory.

In making this double-edged critique too much was surrendered by critical theory of the rational heritage of the Enlightenment for Habermas' liking. Instead of a positive role for rationality Adorno offered a negative critique of reason. Theoretical critique of suspect ideas is a necessary first step of enlightenment. But a second step is necessary for reflexive social theory – a suspicion of ideology critique itself for failing to produce any further truth content. Critical theory increasingly found Marxist theory, the original ideology critique, increasingly untenable but nonetheless attempted to preserve it as an ideal.

For Habermas, this underlies Horkheimer's appeal to the 'black' nihilism of Nietzsche and de Sade. A total suspicion of all ideology rejected not merely what is untrue and irrational in bourgeois culture but also what is rational and poten- tially true. Instead of the validity claims of substantive rationality Nietzsche proposed a poetic critique in the aesthetic evaluations of language and images. Artistic judgement renders morality (good and evil) and science (true and false) meaningless. But once this happens, Habermas (1987: 125) argues, there is no rational criteria by which to evaluate the validity of any claim except that given by the most powerful groups, and no way to contest claims established by the fiat of power.

Legitimation crisis

Instead of an inexorable system of total reification Habermas allowed for instabil- ity and crisis of more or less autonomous sub-systems. Starting from three 'sub-systems' – economic, political, and socio-cultural – Habermas (1976) sche- matically deduced the main 'crisis tendencies' specific to 'late capitalism'. First, economic crisis tendencies are generated by the falling rate of profit which state intervention proves unable to meliorate. Second, political crisis tendencies have a dual form. On one side, a 'rationality crisis' occurs when the logic of an over- burdened administrative system cannot be aligned with the logic of the economic system, inducing a crisis of governmental management. On the other side, follow- ing Weber, a 'legitimation crisis' occurs when the political-administrative system no longer receives popular consent as it implements measures that politicise but cannot cure economic crisis. Increasing levels of state intervention demystify the blind play of market forces, thereby constantly raising (unrealisable) expectations about the efficacy of political decision making.

Third, socio-cultural crisis tendencies threaten to turn the crisis of *system* inte- gration into a crisis of *social* integration as a result of a 'motivation crisis' (Habermas, 1976: 95). Following Freud, Durkheim, and Mead, the socio-cultural system produces meaningful motivations for action, 'shaped through the int- ernalization of symbolically represented structures of expectation'. Traditional motivational ideologies are eroded by the general process of rationalisation. Unitary belief systems based on religion fragment, while bourgeois individualism is undermined by social complexity. Within late capitalism motivation takes the dual form of 'privatism'. First, 'civic privatism' corresponds to the structure of a depoliticised public sphere where individuals take a passive interest in the fiscal and welfare outputs of the political system without engaging in much or any pub- lic participation (1976: 75). Second, 'familial-vocational privatism' occurs when individual lives are centred on family and career, and interested in domestic con- sumption and leisure and in the competitive structures of educational and occupational systems.

Together legitimation crisis and motivation crisis produce 'social identity cri- ses'. Identity crises disrupt the political quiescence of privatism on which the political-administrative system counts. Legitimation and motivation crises threaten to turn system-specific crises of politics and economics into a general crisis of social integration. For instance, rising levels of educational achievement raises individual aspirations that cannot be accommodated in all or most cases by the occupational structure. Such a motivation crisis underpinned student rebellion in the late 1960s across Western societies. As fewer people exchange their labour power in the market – welfare recipients, students, criminals, disabled, unemployed, military – the socialisation effect of employment is weakened. Even the seemingly inviolable public authority of 'scientism', which promotes 'a positivistic common consciousness that sustains the public realm', is challenged as dogmatic, anti-democratic, and elitist (Habermas, 1976: 84).

A crisis of social integration can be avoided long-term only if the class structure is transformed or the need for legitimation of the political system is replaced by socialisation through a flourishing public sphere (Habermas, 1976: 93). However, neoliberalism promoted the rackets of state-sponsored marketisation and financialisation, a deepening of individual privatism, and the further atrophying of the media-dominated public sphere. With the lengthening crisis of neoliberal political economy and political representation, a substantive social theory of legitimation crisis potentially complements a contemporary social theory of the rackets. Instead, Habermas developed an elaborate ideal model of consensus through communication.

Communicative theory

Habermas (1984) famously elaborated his theory of communicative action to try to surmount the self-defeating logic of critical theory. In contrast, he sought to ground social theory in the foundations of 'the lifeworld', a term derived from the phenomenological philosophy of Husserl. Following David Lockwood (1992: Appendix), Habermas split the social world in two parts: 'system integration' (Parsons) and 'social integration' (Durkheim). Systems like politics and economics are integrated impersonally by functions, such as voting and representation or supply and demand. Social integration is achieved by shared meanings and norms communicated between people 'inter-subjectively' in the lifeworld.

Rather than an all-encompassing technocratic system, individuals engage inter-subjectively in normatively regulated communication. While Habermas famously argued that the lifeworld is 'colonised' by the system, replacing his earlier sub-Marxist focus on crisis, even instrumental systems like science and administration depend on inter-subjective dialogue and action. Social systems coordinate labour power, technologies and strategies of the forces of production in order to adapt outer nature to society (1987: 9). Here the 'purposive-rational action' of technical efficiency depends on the 'communicative rational action' of democratic dialogue. Communication is rational only when not 'distorted' by coercion, and disagreements are argued out openly, ending with consensual understanding.

Discourse depends on an implicit grasp of 'universal pragmatics' and 'speech acts' where ordinary speech is always performed as socially competent action. Even though language is always particular and novel communication depends on invariant presuppositions, every utterance implicitly claims to be true, intelligible, appropriate, and sincere. In an 'ideal speech situation' the power to speak is symmetrical and equal in terms of turn-taking and the right to dissent. What is implicit in common discourse and what the ideal model of the public sphere provides are valid claims in the pursuit of a 'genuine life'. In this way Habermas' ideal model leapt over the structures of reification that connected critical theory back to Lukacs and Marx.

Habermas later put more emphasis on the counter-factual ideals of political philosophy, discourse ethics and legal theory in defence of rationality against what he saw as post-modern irrationalism. Here social integration comes to depend on the checks and balances of the law rather than the lifeworld. Normative ideals are already embedded in the sociological fact of the public sphere, which the law merely summarises and transmits to the political system as its legitimation mechanism (1996: 328). In turn, the lifeworld is no longer 'colonised' by the system but held at a distance by a public sphere crowded with mass media and public relations.

Only in an exceptional crisis, not the endemic structural crisis of legitimation, might the social movements of the lifeworld rebalance the relationship. Democracy is now more or less permanently subordinate to administration. All that communicative action can now achieve is to act as a lightning rod to warn elites about emerging de-legitimisation processes by influencing the political system from the outside. This much-diminished public sphere forgets that the specifically bourgeois public sphere that Habermas (1989) originally adopted as his ideal model abstractly promoted 'the general will' above any specific class, gender, and national particularity (Fraser and Nash, 2013; Negt and Kluge, 1993). This became especially apparent in the civilising role that Habermas (2012) more recently identifies the European Union as playing, in contrast to de-civilised racketeering elsewhere. In this way, Habermas completed his journey from Marx's critical theory of society to Kant's idealist cosmopolitan order (Anderson, 2009).

CRITIQUE AND DEVELOPMENT

At the start of *Negative Dialectics*, Adorno (1973: 3) commented on Marx's judgement that the revolution would abolish philosophy at the same time as realising its ideals: 'Philosophy, which once seemed obsolete, lives on because the moment to realize it was missed.' In the shadow of the failed revolution, appeals were made for a return to an 'authentic' nature or existence against the reified 'second nature' of abstraction, distraction and function. Fascist rackets attempted to resolve the crisis by destroying what they saw as the 'inauthentic' circulation of cosmopolitan finance capital and socialist internationalism, both personified as 'Jewish' (Postone, 1980). Bodies, technology, production, and the nation were 'renaturalised' as concrete forms of life superior to the artificial 'parasitical' nature of finance capital, abstract reason, bourgeois legality, and citizenship.

Weber's theory of rationalisation and disenchantment was transformed by critical theory into a total critique of capitalism. But instead of something specific to capitalism, reification proved to be trans-historical, stretching back to Greek mythology. Since critique was limited to a problem of mythical reason little or no sense was given of the sociological conditions that might make demythologisation possible. Great store was placed in the role of myth in Western literary-theological-philosophical civilisation, none at all on the specialised sciences themselves, and little on the diversity of Enlightenment thought, whose bad side is equated with 'positivism' as critical theory understood it.

With the masses ambivalently assimilated to the culture industry, all that remained possible in conditions of crisis was detached critique and negative dialectics instead of reconstructed substantive social theory. Horkheimer and Adorno could only hope that things would get better: 'Hope for better circumstances – if it is not a mere illusion – is not so much based on the assurance that these circumstances would be guaranteed, durable, and final, but on the lack of respect for all that is so firmly rooted in the general suffering' (1972: 225).

For Marx what ideology expresses needs to be explained, rather than the source explained by ideology. Critical theory added cultural and psychological dimensions, sometimes at the expense of traditional Marxist themes of class and capitalism. As Habermas and others argue, to be effective ideology critique needed to show how arbitrary social power distorts the validity of social theory. Yet there is no 'pure' ground of validity (in nature or individual consciousness) for social theory to occupy.

Critique is always tangled up with theory, theory with argument, argument with reason, and reason with validity conditions. Although never enough to ensure that the better theory succeeds, theoretical argumentation must proceed *as if* it might. Despite problems with the theory of rackets, not least its inflated sense of impersonal freedom in market society, with some revision it might potentially contribute to a substantive social theory of power and dependency relations. Whatever kind of social change is possible must bear a relationship to an empirical theory of the conditions that need changed.

10

QUOTIDIAN TURN: HENRI LEFEBVRE

Henri Lefebvre (1901–1991) bequeathed a rich, if largely ignored, sociological legacy in his sustained effort to theorise imperceptible, long-term changes in the banal forms of everyday life, or the quotidian (ordinary, daily, common), from the 1930s down to the late twentieth century. While some consider his 1947 *Critique of Everyday Life* (1991b) 'an enduring classic of modern social thought' and 'the defining element in Lefebvre's social theory', it has largely been neglected in English language social theory (Gardiner, 2000: 73; Butler, 2012: 107). The empirical grounding of his social theory was eclipsed by the reception in English-language 'human geography' of Lefebvre's (1991a) endlessly resourceful, though highly abstract theory of space, *The Production of Space*. This optic tends to eclipse the way that Lefebvre's theory of everyday life runs like a red thread through his analyses of modernity, technology, time and space, politics and the state, processes of difference, the city and the rural, and the worldwide (Elden, 2004: 120; Lefebvre, 2009).

In an earlier book, *The Sociology of Marx*, Lefebvre (1968a: 22) argued that while there is a sociology *in* Marx, he cannot be pigeonholed *as* a sociologist. Lefebvre rejected two possible ways of constructing Marxism as sociology. First, a theoretical system could be deduced from fundamental philosophical categories like materialism. Alternatively, dialectics might provide sociology with a universal method for analysing society. The problem in both cases is that scholarly knowledge is divorced from worldly practice, with the result that form is separated from content, systems from processes, structure from agency. With its concern for the 'facts' empirical sociology neglects the play of contradictory forces in the social totality. Instead of theoretical closure of philosophical systems such as existentialism and structuralism Lefebvre insisted on the open, creative possibilities of human struggle and heightened 'moments of presence' (Shields, 1999).

This also meant clarifying the relationship between politics and social theory. Just as Marx was not a superior economist, neither was he specifically a 'political theorist'. In contrast to Hegel, for Marx people are not essentially 'political animals' but social beings (Lefebvre, 1968a: 123). In the words of the poet Arthur Rimbaud (1854–1891), the point is to 'change life' not merely to change governments (Lefebvre, 1969: 90; 1991a: 59; Kolakowski and Lefebvre, 1974: 248). Political change is 'conjunctural' whereas social revolution heralds a profound 'structural' transformation (Lefebvre, 1976: 95). Lefebvre emphasised that, beyond any narrow concern with economics, alienation in everyday life is the central problem of Marxist theory. If the philosophical concept of alienation is integrated into sociology, then 'it becomes scientific and allows the sociology of everyday life to become a science as well as a critique' (Lefebvre, 1991b: 36).

This chapter first introduces Lefebvre's approach to social theory. Lefebvre's social theory rested on a distinctive approach that he hoped would demonstrate that Marxism is a creative, living theory of possibility rather than a stale dogma. The rest of the chapter concentrates on his fifty-year long critique of everyday life, oriented around Marx's problematic of alienation. This leads into a consideration of modernity, crisis and those intense moments when everyday life is transcended for a time. Lefebvre resisted the pessimism of much critical sociology that everyday life is a closed book, that alienation is self-sustaining, and that conditions of crisis are necessarily catastrophic for society. Lefebvre does not simply paint a bleak picture of social suffering and 'inauthenticity' in the manner of the 'sincere' clichés of existentialism and critical theory. Life may be re-enchanted in ways that social theory has not yet recognised. Social change does not obey a prescriptive model but requires a sociological wager on the future.

LEFEBVRE'S SOCIOLOGY

With the crisis of French society in the 1930s Lefebvre shifted from the artistic and philosophical rebellions of surrealism and existentialism to Marxism (Burkhard, 2000; Merrifield, 2006). One problem with symbolic rebellions of art and philosophy is that they often rely on a 'transcendental contempt for the real, for work for example' (Lefebvre, 1991b: 29). Lefebvre was immersed in contemporary philosophical currents, especially Heidegger and Husserl, and by the discovery of Marx's early writings on philosophy (Elden, 2004). After the 1939–1945 war, philosophy, Marxist and non-Marxist, found itself in crisis, caught between analytical vacuity and ideological dogma:

> On one side, the non-Marxist side, the symptoms are obscurity, jargon, technicality, illusory profundity. On the Marxist side they are false clarity, pedagogy which takes itself as a measure of thought, desiccated dogmatism and skeletal schematization, propagandist exploitation of ideological themes. (Lefebvre, 2002: 84)

Lefebvre (1946: 6–13) was especially critical of the 'humanist' rejection by existentialist philosophy of the mundane, banal and trivial as 'inauthentic' compared to the metaphysical mysteries and 'comfortable indeterminacy' of personal anguish, the tragedy of choice, and social nihilism, encapsulated in the famous phrase of the existential philosopher Jean-Paul Sartre (1905–1980): 'Hell is other people'.

On the other hand, Lefebvre was deeply critical of the intellectual fashion for 'structuralism' as a pure form of 'scientific' knowledge opposed to 'ideology'. In its willingness to move away from a dialectical theory of praxis and onto the non-Marxist ground of a systematic theory of formal knowledge, structuralism was symptomatic of a deep-seated crisis in Marxist theory. Lefebvre argued that the retreat into the formal structures of knowledge evaded the problems and failures of post-war Marxism to accommodate technocratic demands for epistemological foundations. An influential strand of Marxist structuralism was developed by Louis Althusser (1918–1990) and his followers. Althusser (2008) argued that 'science' should be purified of any lingering 'ideology', such as the dialectical method and the concept of alienation, viewed by Althusser as 'unscientific' hangovers of philosophical idealism. The fact that Marxist theory was forced to submit to abstract criteria merely demonstrated to Lefebvre the depth of the crisis of a theory that had lost contact with all-too-human processes of social life.

Lefebvre's critical sociology aimed to change theory and life. Too often, social theory merely contemplates the world – 'Why change the real rather than merely noting it down?' (Lefebvre, 2002: 186) – and looks down on everyday life from the perspective of more elevated experiences like science, literature, culture, and philosophy: 'People who gather flowers and nothing but flowers tend to look upon the soil as something dirty' (Lefebvre, 1991b: 87). Marxism is often accused of inverting these priorities by becoming mired in the dirty business of the economy or technology and treating everything else – art, ideology, politics and so on – as mere reflections of class interests. For Lefebvre, this leaves human praxis out of account. Humans produce the alienating structures that dominate them but they also make social change possible. As Marx famously asserted, people make history but not in conditions that they choose freely. Praxis relies on two temporal coordinates: it depends on the past (as determination) and it faces into the future (as possibility) (Lefebvre, 1968a: 55). 'Determination' by the past need not, therefore, mean 'determinism' by monolithic structures.

Sociological analysis begins, then, neither from some transcendental ideal nor by fetishising the empirical details of social structures but by inserting these into a theoretical critique of a whole way of life, including its creative possibilities (Lefebvre, 1968b: 162). Since understanding depends on a reciprocal relationship between two interlocutors, sociologists should avoid imposing their specialist language on the subjects being studied and undertake 'the sociologist's catharsis' through a detour back to their own everyday reality (Lefebvre, 2002: 103). Yet the sociologist should in no way renounce the specialised language of science since it is the symbolic lubricant connecting diverse social groups. Without contact between practical language and scientific language, concepts become 'jargon', an arbitrary language with no purpose other than its own obscurity. Sociology must begin from some position within a totality that cannot be grasped all at once. Lefebvre (2002: 143) cites Picasso's method: 'First of all I find something, then I start to search for it'.

Totality was conceived by Lefebvre as an unfinished process of becoming, not a frozen social structure. Distinct levels of the social whole alternately complement and contradict each other. As such, totality cannot be confined by the specialised categories of sociology, economics, psychology, or history. Simply because totality is fragmented, knowledge should not be broken up into discrete social sciences. Particular branches of sociology – sociology of the family, the city and the countryside, classes, nations, states, knowledge, and so on – should reveal their relationship to totality: 'the indispensable presuppositions in the social sciences remain the unity of knowledge and the total character of reality' (Lefebvre, 1968a: 23–4).

Study of the social process as a whole and the social whole as a process requires what Lefebvre (1953: 117; 1991a: 66) called a 'regressive-progressive' method. This passes through three stages of description-dating-explanation. Lefebvre (1980: 50) insisted that dialectical theory must always have a triadic structure beyond the static dualisms of structuralism, such as inside and outside, male and female, symbol and reality, structure and action, and so on. Such opposed pairs of fixed concepts merely refer back to each other in a vicious circle, now one thing, now the other, now the macro-level, now the micro-level, and so on ad infinitum. A third concept must be introduced to mediate between two concepts, now no longer static, as when the opposition between empiricism and speculation is mediated by 'theory'.

Theory starts from a *description* of present-day conditions, where sociologists begin from observations of the present constructed from fieldwork and survey data, not as pure facts but as research material disciplined by experience and general theory. Second, at the *analytico-regressive* stage, observational descriptions are compared with the past, with precise *dates* making the comparisons specific, to show how survivals from the past function as preconditions of the present. Finally, at the *historico-genetic* stage a 'genetic classification' of structures accounts for movement in the process of development. An attempt is made to return 'progressively' to the present, now put in a different light, to *explain* the overall process of development 'genetically', with all its arbitrariness, contingency, reasons, and causes.

One difficulty with Lefebvre's approach is that the regressive stage and the progressive stage may become confused in the research process or in the presentation of the analysis. To control the different stages of analysis it is therefore necessary to begin logically from a theoretical concept, a 'concrete abstraction' that both derives from and illuminates social relations and processes, as Marx had done with the concept of value in *Capital* (1976). Lefebvre variously begins from concrete abstractions like modernity, everyday life, 'the production of space', 'the urban revolution', to arrive at distinct analyses of the contradictory processes of alienation and de-alienation in changed conditions.

This processual method of concept-description-explanation, Lefebvre argued, dissolves fixed oppositions and static categories. As structures, forms and systems, survivals from the past continue to exert an active influence on the present. Sociology examines structural survivals in the present as a 'sociology of forms'. 'Form' refers to the inner structure of social relations, its rules, rituals, conventions, categories, apperception and sequences, repeated in many different instances and situations across time and place. Central to social forms, however, are also processes that undermine or reverse the automatic reproduction of structures. Attempts were made by Lefebvre (1969, 1976) to understand how capitalism survived the revolution of May 1968 and, despite itself, continue to reproduce the social relations of production.

CRITIQUE OF EVERYDAY LIFE

Social survivals are reproduced in and by everyday life. For fifty years Lefebvre regularly revisited the problem of everyday life in a series of studies, from an initial critique of 1933, the four volumes of *Critique of Everyday Life* (original dates 1947, 1961, 1981, 1992), *Introduction to Modernity* (originally 1962), *Everyday Life in the Modern World* (originally 1968), *The Production of Space* (originally 1974), *The Urban Revolution* (originally 1970), *The Survival of Capitalism* (originally 1973), and *The Explosion* (on the May 1968 revolt; originally 1968). This series of studies charted changes in Lefebvre's theory of everyday life, from the rise of fascism and the crisis of the 1930s, the optimism of the Liberation, the emergence of technocracy and consumer society in the 1960s, the ideology of information technology in the 1970s, to the fully mediatised everyday of the 1980s (Burkhard, 2000; Elden, 2004: 115). Throughout, Lefebvre reflexively reviewed and criticised his own earlier analyses.

While Lefebvre produced a number of studies of major literary and philosophical figures – Pascal, Descartes, Hegel, Diderot, Nietzsche – his 'critique of everyday life' aimed to combat arid 'philosophism'. From Heidegger's philosophy he seems to have assimilated Lukacs' concept of 'everydayness' as an inferior realm of reality compared to Marx's idea of the 'total man' [sic] beyond alienation (Lefebvre, 1968b: 148–65; 1991b: 64–8; 2005: 18–20; Goldmann, 1977). Lefebvre took a more ambiguous view of everyday life than Lukacs and Heidegger: it is the site of alienation but it is also where alienation might be overcome.

By concentrating on the problem of the quotidian, Lefebvre argued, the crisis of Marxist theory might be contained: 'We will therefore go so far as to argue that critique of everyday life – radical critique aimed at attaining the radical metamorphosis of everyday life – is alone in taking up the authentic Marxist project again and in continuing it: to supersede philosophy and to fulfil it' (Lefebvre, 2002: 23). Everyday life is a creative process whereby people produce themselves as humans along with their conditions of life, as well as the possibilities for changing their situation.

> There are determined biological, historical, economic, sociological *conditions* (which are taken over and modified by their own creative praxis), which constitute the 'real' in its accepted sense. There are *processes*, which contain the evolution and forward movement of the real. These conditions and processes point towards *possibilities*. (Lefebvre, 2002: 110–11)

Not only would the critique of everyday life rejuvenate Marxist theory but Lefebvre's conception of Marxism was fundamentally defined by the description, analysis, and explanation of everyday life (Lefebvre, 1991b: 148). By the 1930s official Marxism had been codified into a closed book that neglected the wider problem of everyday life. At the same time, radical non-Marxist theory took the modern world to task but evaded the problem of capitalism until it was imposed by the pandemonium of crisis: 'capitalism isn't a country in which you spend three weeks so that you can come back with a book' (Lefebvre and Guterman, 1933: 77).

Simply because the familiar is familiar does not mean that it is readily understood (Lefebvre, 1991b: 15). On the other hand, Lefebvre argues, the sociology of everyday life too often results in a trivial analysis of trivia. 'Ordinariness' cannot be analysed in an 'ordinary' way (Lefebvre, 1962: 100). Lefebvre's student Georges Perec (1999: 126) closed his sociological novel *Things* with a misappropriated envoi from Marx to the effect that the method of inquiry is as much part of the truth as the final conclusion. As Marx put it in one of his earliest articles:

> Truth includes not only the result but also the path to it. The investigation of truth must itself be true; true investigation is developed truth, the dispersed elements of which are brought together in the result. And should not the manner of investigation alter according to the object? If the object is a matter for laughter, the manner has to seem serious, if the object is disagreeable, it has to be modest. (1842: 113)

If the present is to be understood as a historical process long in the making, then the correct procedure seems to be to work from the present back to the past and to retrace our steps back to the present. This procedure accounts for historical processes without being entirely subordinated to them: 'The sociologist has first to observe, and analyse, in order to explain. He [sic] uses history as an ancillary, subordinate science in the study of social processes as a whole' (Lefebvre, 1953: 116).

MODERNITY AND EVERYDAY LIFE

Historically, people have always constructed daily routines and habits but they have not always had an 'everyday life'. Prior to modernity diverse social forms, structures, and functions – eating, drinking, sleeping, working, travelling, and so on – were experienced as part of a whole 'style of life'. Everyday life only became possible once divisions were established between work, home, and leisure, politics and economics, public and private and, later, between modernity and modernism. In modernity, things, from cars to coins to coffee-grinders, become separated out, named and integrated as functional objects within systems. For instance, food is organised as a system of interdependent functional parts, fridges, freezers, microwave ovens, supermarkets, advertising, transport, industrial farms, and so on. The everyday does not itself form a 'system' but integrates and connects systems like food with other systems, say the leisure system or the educational system.

Everyday life is, first, a residual zone, whatever is left over once all distinct, specialised functions are subtracted; second, it forms the common ground that connects isolated systems together; and third, it expresses 'the totality of the real' in partial and incomplete social relations like friendship, love, play, communication, comradeship, and so on (Lefebvre, 1991b: 97): 'The everyday can therefore be defined as a set of functions which connect and join together systems that might appear to be distinct' (Lefebvre, 1987: 9). Everyday life mediates between culture and nature. So-called 'higher' activities of art, science and philosophy impose structured forms on the spontaneous ambiguity of the lived everyday: 'And yet it is the spontaneity nobody can do without. And yet, compared with nature it is already more ordered and more beautiful, and more economical with its means and its ends' (Lefebvre, 2002: 357).

Modernity contains within itself a wide range of variation at the leading edges of cultural, technological, scientific, and intellectual development. In the 1840s, Marx identified modernity with a form of political power invested in raising the state above everyday life (Lefebvre, 1995: 170). It is also to be found in the beginning of a sociology of the everyday in Charles Baudelaire's poetic notion of 'modernity' as residing in whatever is fashionable, ephemeral, and fleeting. What Marx saw as abstract and unnatural, Baudelaire saw as concrete and social. With the failure of the 1848 Revolution, modernity became a parody of revolution for Baudelaire while for Marx it became the site of revolutionary praxis.

Well before Marx, theorists of civil society like Adam Ferguson (1723–1816) had located the roots of the state in the spontaneous order of institutionalised social relations. However, Hegel (1770–1831) severed the umbilical cord and elevated the state above civil society as a mystified 'world spirit'. Social relations, including contradictions that produce antagonisms and struggles between classes, account for the state as a 'concrete abstraction', not the other way around (Lefebvre, 2009: 109). Indeed, the state became a concentrated but contradictory 'centre' for economic growth and the reproduction of the social relations of production on which it depends. Increasingly, a worldwide process (*mondialisation*) enmeshes states, markets, urbanism, and the everyday, and 'pulverises' social space in the multiple tensions between functional homogenisation and concrete differentials of space (2009). As the micro-manager of everyday life within its own boundaries, the function of the state changed: 'Previously, what was not prohibited was permitted. Today, everything that is not permitted is prohibited' (Lefebvre, 2005: 126).

A 'silent catastrophe' befell modernity in the early twentieth century with the collapse of the core reference systems of European civilisation. In science, Einstein's theory of relativity undermined the old geometric systems of Euclid and Newton. In painting, Cezanne and Cubism overthrew illusory perspectives of three-dimensional space. In music, classical tonality was dissolved by atonality. This silent catastrophe foreshadowed the 'noisy catastrophe' of the technological warfare of 1914.

When all that remains of the dominant codes of modernity are 'relics: a word, images, metaphors', then reality has proven itself more radical than critical social theory:

> Around 1910 a certain space was shattered. It was the space of common sense, of knowledge (*savoir*), of social practice, of political power, a space hitherto enshrined in everyday discourse, just as in abstract thought, as the environment of and channel for communications; the space, too, of classical perspective and geometry, developed from the Renaissance onwards on the basis of the Greek tradition (Euclid, logic) and bodied forth in Western art and philosophy, as in the form of the city and town. Such were the shocks and onslaughts suffered by this space that today it retains a feeble pedagogical reality, and then only with great difficulty, within a conservative educational system. (Lefebvre, 1991b: 25)

Nonetheless, the crisis of modernity cannot be resolved by a romantic rejection of technics in order to return to an imaginary pre-technological past (Lefebvre, 1995: 279). In practice, everyday life continues to observe the old, familiar representations of space, time, and sound, and finds itself left behind by specialised culture. In this way, everyday life became radically separated from the leading edge of culture and science, opening up a yawning gap between modernity, as self-reflexive, critical knowledge, and modernism, the triumphalist self-images of the age (Lefebvre, 1995: 1–2). Modernity as an optimistic ideology of the ever-new became marginalised while modernism trumpets 'the ideology of the end of ideology' as technological practice marches on, promoting a retro-culture of the ever-same.

From the 1950s to the 1970s, everyday life formed the precondition for the emergence of what Lefebvre (1971) called 'the bureaucratic society of controlled consumption'. In this society, older forms of scarcity are replaced by a rationally planned abundance and programmed obsolescence, and spontaneous self-regulation is replaced by 'voluntary programmed self-regulation' (Lefebvre, 1971: 72). Later, Lefebvre (2005: 28) claimed that his model of programmed consumption uncritically accepted at face value the bureaucratic ideology of organised social integration when counter-processes of social fragmentation were already far advanced. Tensions of everyday life, already expressed by the cultural models of the middle classes, 'exploded' into the open in May 1968 (Lefebvre, 1969). What had been implicit in everyday life suddenly became explicit.

BODILY RHYTHMS

Modernity installs a new conception of time. All human societies are founded on repetition through cycles of biology, night and day, seasons, life and death, hunger and satisfaction, activity and rest. In the repetition of everyday life, however, cyclical time is dominated by 'linear time', the time of accumulation, 'rationality', work, and consumption. Cyclical time is also divided up by the quantification of time in clocks, timetables, and calendars. In everyday life, routine processes hammer rhythms into new shapes: 'The everyday is simultaneously the site of, the theatre for and what is at stake in a conflict between the great indestructible rhythms and the processes imposed by the socio-economic organisation of production, consumption, circulation and habitat' (Lefebvre, 2004a: 73).

Circadian rhythms are disrupted by the extension of repetitious activities into periods traditionally reserved for rest and piety, weekend and late night shift-working, 'overtime', shopping and leisure time (Lefebvre gives the example of 'Saturday Night Fever' at the end of the working week) (2004a: 74). Bodily rhythms – sleeping, eating, resting, defecating, and so on – are retrained for and by the social routines of modernity. Cultural products of everyday life like sport, novels, and films represent 'a liberation from worry and necessity' that may be scrutinised for evidence of a growing consciousness of alienation and the prospects of de-alienation, though they more often merely confirm alienation and passivity (Lefebvre, 1991b: 33).

Daily life is repeated *every* single day. Everyday life is filled with monotony yet, at the same time, it changes imperceptibly thanks to planned obsolescence and unplanned interaction. Everyday life mediates between the 'stagnation' of cyclical time and the 'progress' of linear time: 'Some people cry out against the acceleration of time, others cry out against stagnation. They're both right' (Lefebvre, 1987: 10). Women, the working class, and young people are forced by the structures of planned consumption to adopt the role of passive spectators. However, because everyday life turns what is relative to social relations into something absolutely essential and predictable, it doesn't take much to expose its constructed basis. Falling sick or in love, sleepless nights, unemployment, and numerous other unplanned disruptions to bodily rhythms produce a changed relationship to 'everydayness'.

Lefebvre (1991a: 40) located bodies in social space according to three conceptual coordinates – 'perceived-conceived-lived' relations of social practice. Social practices presuppose, first, the use of the body, hands, limbs, and sensory organs, as *practical perceptions* of the spaces of daily routines and familiar routes. Second, the body is an abstraction, *conceived* by specialists in scientific representations, anatomy, medicine, physiology, therapists, fitness instructors, and so on. Third, the body as *lived experience* is found in cultural spaces of representations. Cultural symbols, norms and morality operate on the body to produce an involuntary discipline, an instinctive 'body without organs'. Just as representations of space as specialised knowledge dominate other relations of social space, so the body is also subject to the symbolic domination of expert knowledge.

Lived bodies in everyday space may be dominated but they also incite creative resistance to abstract control. Lived rhythms of the body engaged in social practices cannot be wholly reduced to abstract analytical conceptions (Lefebvre, 1991a: 205–6). Crises, festivals and revolutions alter the ratio of the senses since they disrupt the rhythm of routine; custom, attitudes, conduct, work, and everyday life more generally: 'Disruptions and crises always have their origins in and effects on rhythms: those of institutions, of growth, of the population, of exchanges, of work, therefore those which make or express the complexity of present societies' (Lefebvre, 2004a: 45). Festivals like the Paris Commune of 1871 or the events of May 1968 were constitutive acts that practically and momentarily united the passion and ordinariness of the world on a higher plane, demonstrating the possibility of de-alienation in everyday life (McDonough, 2009: 172–6).

THEORY OF MOMENTS

Such disruptions belong to what Lefebvre (1989; 2002) called the 'sociology of moments'. By the term 'moments' Lefebvre specified a relatively autonomous aspect of heightened social reality. Lefebvre's theory of moments is sometimes presented as the opposite of alienation, understood as an *absence* of human connection while moments signify a fully human *presence* (Merrifield, 2006: 21–38; Shields, 1999). In keeping with Lefebvre's triadic method, however, the relationship between presence and absence is not that of a binary pair of fixed concepts – absence – presence or alienation–transcendence – but is a relation-ship mediated by a third term, 'the other'. Presence is not absence but neither is it its absolute opposite, just as moments are not the absolute opposite of aliena-tion. Neither absence nor alienation are pure concepts. As re-presentations they are made present once again.

All concepts are relativised by a third one: other, representation, contradiction, action, love, knowledge, creation, and so on. Any rigid separation into reified concepts brings processes to a pathological standstill: 'Pathology comes from the cessation of movement, from fixity in absence and emptiness, from the feeling of never escaping it, a state of nothingness' (Lefebvre, 1980: 56). Where social theory separates concepts into opposing pairs it transfixes them into something that they are not: substantial entities in their own right. In a similar way, substantiality is grafted on to the self-images of the age, its politics, ideology, technology, culture.

In previous societies, segregated moments of play, games, home, and work were not rigidly divided as they are by modernity. Distinct 'moments' are *separated* out from the more equivocal ambiguity of everyday life as discrete but connected activities: the game, justice, art, poetry, leisure, and so on. Civilisation imposes order on diffuse contents dredged from human and non-human nature. Moments socialise nature and naturalise sociality. Since each moment is unique but also generic the theory of moments overcomes the old antinomies between nature and non-nature, individual and society, plurality and totality, structure and action, discovery and invention, fact and value.

Sociology studies social forms, relations, and the groups that constitute them. A 'moment' is defined by its *form* independent of particular content (Lefebvre, 1989: 171). Presence is only made manifest in a form, yet form, taken by itself, is empty, hence it is also an absence. Forms are repeated on each occasion yet at the same time re-invented. In everyday speech, a moment is not the same as an 'instant', which is ephemeral, forgettable, and transitory. In Hegelian philosophy a 'moment' is a vital stage in the dialectical movement of alienation. From this, the moment is defined by Lefebvre as a privileged 'higher form of repetition, renewal and reappearance, and of the recognition of certain determinable relations with otherness (or the other) and with the self' (2002: 344). It becomes an *absolute* moment in itself of limited *duration*, which creates an intense consciousness that the moment will not last no matter how much we may want it to. A moment is a mediating term, neither continuous with the time of everyday life nor the pure discontinuity of a sudden irruption or revolution.

FORMS OF THE MOMENT

Everyday life combines a plurality of separate moments. Lefebvre (2002: 352) distinguishes conjuncture, structure, moment, and situation. A *situation* is created by a decision to wager on the moment. The moment gives *structure* to the form – 'ritual, ceremony and necessary succession' – of the changed situation. This form is only made possible by a *conjuncture* of circumstances encountered in everyday life. The structured form of moments adds something vital that intensifies everyday life, its performance, communication, and enjoyment. Without this, everyday life would lack richness and diversity. The pleasure of moments overcomes stale binaries of lightness and heaviness, and levity and seriousness. Moments make 'festivals' of everyday monotony by imposing new social forms on the spontaneous ambiguity of the everyday.

Play makes the players, while players are consumed by the game. Appetite comes only with eating. As an 'impossible possibility', a wager is placed with stakes borrowed from everyday life that are not part of the game itself. This is the moment of decision that Weber had in mind when he described science as vocation: 'Whoever wants knowledge sacrifices everything which is not knowledge in pursuit of knowledge: everything becomes an object of knowledge and a means of knowing the object it is pursuing' (Lefebvre, 2002: 347). When cultural theory describes the moment as representation it loses hold of it as an act (Lefebvre, 1980: 55). Sociological recognition of the arbitrary nature of moments can result in a reluctance to wager and engage in practical critique and so hesitate indefinitely from deciding to act. Social theory must form a judgement about the appropriate level of engagement. In so doing, it 'reserves for itself possibilities, choices, options, disengagement and commitment' (Lefebvre, 1989: 176).

As a distinct 'moment' of everyday life, play is radically transformed by formalised 'rules of the game'. To become a player in modern games – chess, cards, sport, love, sociality – is to be 'in the moment', an intensified, self-contained point of alienation (absence) from the routine concerns of social life. In the 'moment of rest' the struggle to overcome activity and to 'take it easy' in modernity requires specific bodily techniques and specific places set aside for leisure at certain times. To be in 'the moment of poetry' is to not be somewhere else. And so on. The 'moment of justice', for instance, is defined by the specific form of the trial, evidence, and judgement: 'It is easy to notice the similarity between the inner ceremony of the virtuous mind, and the highly externalised formalism of justice as an institution' (Lefebvre, 2002: 355). In the moment of formal justice everything is subordinated to the passion for justice, which becomes separated from the moral judgements of everyday life. There, judgements are made ritualistically by self-appointed judges, appealing to some non-existent higher principle, even though the evidential basis for the final verdict is arbitrary, weak or wholly unreliable.

MOMENTS OF ESCAPE

All levels of society maintain imaginary escape routes from everyday life. Only they never leave. Young people are initiated into the myth of autonomous adulthood, yet adults are already integrated, child-like, into institutional structures and functional organisations where responsibility is transferred to a socially appointed superior. Even the cultural transgressions of the middle classes merely confirm the social integration of the group in familiar routines and habits acquired from reading the right newspaper, conversing about the latest gritty drama, or choice of schools or neighbourhood. Social relations are mystified by myths but, on the other hand, myth colludes with truth and expresses something of reality:

> For bourgeois culture, like every ideology, has real content; it expresses and reflects something of the truth. The mystification lies in the presentation, use and fragmentation of that content; culture, taken as a whole, lives parasitically on this real content, which it has ceased to renew. (Lefebvre and Guterman, 1933: 74)

By starting from everyday conditions sociology avoids constructing communication as an ideal model, 'a communication of angelic and disembodied minds', where perfect speech situations are bought at the price of the ambiguous depths, passions, and shifting levels of life as it is lived (Lefebvre, 2002: 343). Moments are not forgotten but enter into collective and individual *memory* as a specific re-cognition of the *content* of everyday life, of which it remains part, while constructing something *original* that takes on the force of necessity.

Only passion formed in and by the risks of 'the moment' makes possible what was previously impossible about everyday life. Heedless passion leads into the 'madness' of a specific alienation, of the obsessive lover, the reckless gambler, the blind devotion to theory, that can never totally succeed on its own terms and is fated to return, chastened, to the banality of everyday life. The tragic contradiction of everyday life consists in the effort to transcend it in moments whose inevitable failure prepares the way for a return to the mundane and trivial. Until, that is, a fresh decision is taken to wager again and break out of repetition: 'The fact of making a decision changes what was a distant possibility into an imminent possibility' (Lefebvre, 2002: 351).

In this, Lefebvre's decisionist theory of moments shares something with the wager of Pascal and Nietzsche. A wager always implies the risk of failure as well as creating 'situations' that would not otherwise exist in the same way: 'To obtain the gifts of chance and chance encounters, risks must be taken – the risks of failure, poverty, vain pursuit, the risk that the moment of presence will end, leaving behind it wounds and nostalgia' (Lefebvre, 1980: 54). There is no escaping a wager on the 'tragic festival' of the moment since, without the tragic passion it engenders, all that would be left would be the prosaic, desolate stubbornness of everyday monotony.

THE RIGHT TO DIFFERENCE

A theory of moments allows for 'the right to difference'. Difference was implicit under the technocratic demand for uniformity and centralism, in which Marxist economism colluded. Demands for the right to difference broke into the open in the 1960s with the rise of diverse social movements, of women, nations, race, ethnicity and sexuality. Lefebvre (2005: 111) distinguishes between 'particularism' and 'differences'. Particularism appeals to absolute natural essences – skin colour, genitalia, age, origin – giving rise to racism, sexism, homophobia, and integral nationalism. Difference, on the other hand, is constructed as a group perception relative to and reciprocal with other perceptions. The right to difference develops out of struggles over particularism. These stand in constant, ambiguous tension with each other.

Difference was understood by the ideologues of the New Right as sub-Nietzschean inequalities of innate superiority and inferiority types, bolstered by the claims of sociobiology. For 'hypercritics' on the Left, all claims to rights of difference are dismissed as the traditional illusions of the middle class in formal rights rather than the need for genuine equality, as when the working class is priced out of city centres by the urban middle class. In terms of urban space, maximal difference shatters the homogenising power of abstract centrality. Neoliberal ideology promotes an anti-bureaucratic ideology of decentralisation and minimal difference, subordinating once-dominant institutions like public planning to private interests. Fragmentation can further homogeneity rather than lead to a difference of equals as cultural theory too often assumes (Goonewardena et al., 2008; Stanek, 2011).

Like Gramsci, Lefebvre takes a conjunctural approach to democratic struggles over difference against the essentialist foreclosure of particularism based on nationalism or ethnicity. Conjunctural analysis of the crisis of society 'based on the ideological predominance of these composite, heterogeneous classes, under the hegemony of capital' connects the struggles for difference to struggles over political and economic domination (Lefebvre, 2005: 121). Sociologists – Lefebvre is thinking of Bourdieu here – substitute 'distinction' for difference, with the result that classes are identified with a cultural 'classification' system, eliminating contradictions and ambiguities in social relations of difference. Lefebvre objects that Bourdieu's 'scientific sociology' lacks a critique of the process, neglects difference and history, and abolishes 'the values attached to the art works themselves and not the groups, values that are detached and killed by this sociological description. In defining these values exclusively by their social relation conceived as a factor of distinction, positive knowledge abolishes them' (2005: 116). Positivist 'sociologism', like Bourdieu's, reduces social reality to one dimension – class – a 'static essentialism' and, unlike Adorno, fails to allow for the critical possibilities of aesthetics.

Social relations of production are bound to the production of social relations. An economistic ideology of production, centred on the workplace, encouraged the working class, still a relatively homogenous group, to seek to 'positively' reproduce the relations of production, albeit on a more just basis, rather than 'negatively' abolish them, the goal that Marx allocated to the dispossessed proletariat (Lefebvre, 1976: 99). Now the old alienation within production is overlaid with the new alienation of consumption, producing a general crisis of misrecognition:

> It is the transition from a culture based on the curbing of desires, thriftiness and the necessity of eking out goods in short supply to a new culture resulting from production and consumption at their highest ebb, but against a background of general crisis. (Lefebvre, 1971: 55–6)

Unlike Bourdieu, Lefebvre (1976: 38–40) constructs a theoretical concept of the working class 'constituting itself' as an 'autonomous social class' that will 'realise its concept' when it overcomes the 'productivist ideology' produced by a particular historical conjuncture through the 'self-management' of social need.

Here Lefebvre distinguishes between 'the local working class', integrated into modernity by an ideology of economic growth and everyday life, and 'the worldwide proletariat'. Separated from the means of production, the process of proletarianisation creates a vast but disparate group of the world's dispossessed:

> The vast proletarianisation of the world contrasts with the working class bloc, which stays solid. It includes youth, and intellectuals whom learning fails to link with the means of production; it includes black and immigrant workers. It is an enormous process, corresponding with the utmost precision to the initial Marxist notion of a class separated from the means of production, charged with negativity, and capable under certain conditions of a struggle to the death to change everything. (Lefebvre, 1976: 97)

In what sense is the working class now a class 'in itself', let alone a revolutionary class 'for itself', as Marx argued, if it is defined by an absolute notion of economic and political dispossession?

Instead of an historical and processual conception of class, Lefebvre's self-constituting 'class in itself' adopts the substantialist conception of class that Bourdieu's relational conception of class aimed to overcome. Rather than seeing class in terms of the fixed concept of a 'solid bloc', Bourdieu treated it as a relationship of power in social space, not as a substantial 'bloc', reproduced over time but also subject to conflict and desubordination. This relational conception of class departs from Lefebvre's substantialist concept of 'class in itself'.

IN EVERY DREAM HOME A HEARTACHE

If everyday life is dressed in ambiguity, then alienation is a relative, not an absolute, condition. It is experienced at a discrete level below higher levels such as politics and the State, high technology and high culture, and prepares a space for a critique of superior cultural forms and ideologies. As an intermediate level it mediates in concrete ways the movements of need and desire, pleasure and pain, satisfaction and privation, fulfilment and tedium, work and non-work, seriousness and trivia. As such, everyday life is a system of representations, not merely a system of needs (Lefebvre, 2002: 61).

Here an internally stratified middle class predominates over everyday life. They populate the welfare state as professionals, functionaries, and clients, embodying the required virtues of competence, commitment, and integrity, and flood the field of consumption as people of good sense, sound judgement and fine taste. Everyday life is premised on middle-class consumption patterns, 'not a style of life but a lifestyle. The term "style" refers to an aesthetic or ethical bearing in which the middle classes are precisely lacking' (Lefebvre, 2005: 160). Middle-class consumers and producers prescribe and describe everyday lifestyles, from food to fashion, to furnishings and parenting. On the other hand, Lefebvre recognises that the women's movement emerged from the middle class and that some urban centres were revived by middle-class gentrifiers.

At his most 'structuralist' Lefebvre described everyday life as a 'social text' that needs to be deciphered. On a city street everybody is simultaneously reader and read, decoder and code, signifier and sign:

> Do faces express anything? A little, but not much. Clothes and body language signify. So the spectacle of the street stimulates our desire to see things and forms our way of seeing them. How many women there are who have unknowingly become part of subtle systems of signs, entering them from within, and using them to classify other women with one simple glance at their shoes, their stockings, their hair, their hands and fingernails, their jewellery and their general appearance! (Lefebvre, 2002: 311).

Women are compelled to negotiate the ambiguities of everyday mythology, to be both weak and strong, mundane and divine, immanent and transcendent. Lefebvre deciphered the women's magazine *Elle* as a glorious parade of myths, constantly moving from dream to reality and back again. Such switching invokes the greatest myth of all: 'the omnipotence of technology', represented in the magazine by lotions, furniture, 'healthy eating' formulae, and so on.

> Put your trust in technology, that is, in the products of modern technology, which are involved in all of our everyday chores – all those demeaning, tiresome chores, like going to the office, taking the metro, sweeping floors, doing pieces of writing – and all those boring everyday things will be imbued with morning freshness if you put your trust in modern technology. (Lefebvre, 1962: 102)

Reconciliation with the impossibility of escaping from the everyday is secured by the dream-myth of happiness promised by consumer society. How might we live if only we could win the lottery?

If everyday life is indeed mystified by the inverted 'topsy-turvy' world of commodity fetishism, as Marx argued, then public discourse will also tend to be mystified. As Lefebvre put it, anticipating George Orwell's 'Newspeak' by more than a decade, and with continuing relevance:

> Who can be surprised if at this point armament is called disarmament, if preparation for war is called peace, if rescuing banks is called the march to socialism, and so on and so forth? All reality is enveloped in its opposite, and expresses itself as it. (Lefebvre and Guterman, 1933: 82)

With the crisis of the 1930s, cultivated eloquence in everyday life was supplanted by a cult of well-meaning 'sincerity' and a hard-headed attitude towards the 'facts'. For all his catastrophic fantasies who could doubt that Adolf Hitler was 'sincere'?

WORLDWIDE CRISIS

Until the 1970s a technocratic ideology of endless economic growth ruled out any future crisis and justified blind faith in 'productivism', production for production's sake, and its philosophical and sociological counterparts, structuralism and functionalism (Lefebvre, 1976: 113). Against this, theories of social and political 'peripheries' – youth, sexuality, women, prisons, psychiatry – exercised a radical critique of centralised power. In focussing on radical peripheries, however, the problem of power centres was neglected. The emerging crisis was a crisis of centres and the centrality of authority that produce peripheries in the first place, 'a crisis in the reproduction of the relations of production, and especially of the centres and centrality' (1976: 117).

Lefebvre called this a 'space of catastrophe' because the process of *mondialisation* threatens to commit the 'terricide' of planetary destruction. Influenced by the neglected Marxist theorist, Kostas Axelos (1924–2010), *mondialisation* refers to the dynamic and contradictory process of making the planet 'worldly', that is, by conceiving social relations on a world scale, in contrast to the more familiar concept of 'globalisation', which tends to suggest a one-way process of domination of the local, regional, and national by the global level of geopolitical and economic power. This *mondialisation* process both 'settles' and 'unsettles' social space in the serious human game of 'playing' with planet earth. A 'stratified morphology' arranges and embeds social space into hierarchical levels, ascending from a room, building, neighbourhood, city, region, state, or continent to the planetary level. As states seek to suppress resistance to the logic of morphological embedding, simultaneously settling and unsettling social space, geopolitical crises, antagonisms, and violence result.

States impose dominant space over dominated ones and homogenise world-wide space to compensate for or contain its fragmentation by market relations (Lefebvre, 2009: 234). As the state becomes worldly it also begins the process of withering away but in a chaotic, life-threatening fashion, 'torn apart by what overwhelms it from the inside and from the outside' (2009: 278). As the state balances between risks to its existence – from other states, its population and, above all, multinational capital – it tries to arrest the process of its decline as a power centre. The state refuses to wither away without resistance by renewing and consolidating its stock of coercive and invasive capabilities to meet new threats from worldwide terrorism, urbanisation, social movements, technologies and everyday life.

With the onset of crisis, discontent over the state form is expressed in a relatively undifferentiated way. 'Bureaucracy' is castigated as brutal and inefficient, and official institutions are distrusted (Lefebvre, 2005: 99). Everything that is distant from the everyday and the local reeks of corruption and indifference, leading to localism, scepticism, and nihilism, and a distrust of theory. Yet trust in immediacy and proximity misrecognises the local level as the site where social relations are reproduced. They are reproduced by far wider movements in society – the market, everyday life, the city – as well as on a world scale with the planetary realisation, distribution, and consumption of socially produced surplus value and other world-making activities: art, culture, science, military organisation, and so on (Lefebvre, 1976: 96). All this benefits neo-liberalism, a counter-movement that Lefebvre (2003: 78) identified at the earliest stages of the crisis as maximising incentives for private businesses, facilitated and overseen by the state.

Centres of institutional authority weigh heavily on everyday life by isolating decision-making power from routine habits, common sense, and discourses of triviality. Everyday life is suspended only when decision-making power is reclaimed by ordinary speech and spontaneous public action, as in May 1968 (Lefebvre, 1969). The revolutionary events of 1968 were not triggered by a classic economic crisis of the traditional Marxist model but by the alienating separation of everyday life and institutional centres. Lefebvre considered that exposure to critical sociology distinguished the youth rebellions against alienation in different national contexts: 'what has distinguished the French student movement from, for example, the American is that it hasn't tried to create micro-societies or marginal societies, but has attacked society itself in its entirety and in its totality' (Kolakowski and Lefebvre, 1974: 258). Everyday life itself was suspended by a series of 'absences' produced by strikes – no mail, no fuel, no transport, no banks, and so on. In the context of such absences, social practice began to actively overcome the separation of private life, work, leisure, politics, and public discourse.

CRISIS AS PRACTICAL CRITIQUE

Crisis is now 'total and permanent' (Lefebvre, 2004b: 2). It is total to the extent that crisis is not confined to the economy but extends to all established values and norms, and it is permanent to the extent that crisis constitutes the normal way of life in the modern world, as in the symptomatic announcement of the end of everything that came before yesterday. Another symptom of intractable crisis was that cities like New York, Chicago, and Los Angeles were becoming ungovernable and uninhabitable in the 1970s, forcing either the relocation of power centres (bourgeois flight) or the recolonisation of the urban centre at huge cost (gentrification). Hence the triumphalist ideology of one period (1950–1970) gave way to the apocalyptic ideology and foreboding of the next (1970–1990), followed by even briefer triumphalism ('end of history', humanitarian interventionism, financial bubbles) and the neo-apocalyptic ideology of the past few decades ('war on terror', institutional, economic, and ecological crisis).

Modern societies live under permanent crisis – threats, risk, ruin, decay, upheaval, displacement. Crisis is not pathological but the normal condition. All that can be done is to respond to crisis through permanent invention of temporary solutions: 'Invent or perish!' If there is any hope it is that the negative destruction of institutions and values might play an unforeseen creative role. By the 1980s 'crisis' no longer referred to a temporary phase of instability bracketed by two stable periods:

> Neither the thesis of a crisis of economy and society; nor that of a crisis of the bourgeoisie and the working class; nor that of the middle classes as relatively stable supports of established institutions; nor the very widespread thesis of a critical period for institutions, values and culture – none of these accounts for the situation, does justice to its gravity or the extent of the problematic. (Lefebvre, 2005: 37)

A continuum of perspectives on the crisis ranges from 'no crisis' to 'total crisis'. In the former case, a new international division of labour and technological development (the information and communications revolution) has merely redistributed wealth, production and power worldwide. For the catastrophic perspective, crisis threatens everything: culture, politics, values, and society. A more optimistic version of catastrophe theory insists that a social movement will emerge to prevent total disaster. None of these adequately explains crisis and the as-yet-unknown turns it will take (Lefebvre, 2004b: 11). Everyday life in crisis is 'a site of ambiguity, gambles and wagers' as it fluctuates unevenly between decline in one area and sudden revival in another (Lefebvre, 2005: 39).

One expression of the crisis of modernity is the fetish of living in the permanent present, constantly extolling the arrival of the 'new' and the 'end' of the old – the end of class, the end of ideology, the end of Marxism, the end of reality, the end of modernity, and so on, and, at the same time, celebrating 'the new', post-modern philosophy, architecture and art, the New Right and the New Left, even 'new' food (*nouvelle cuisine*). The ideology of 'the new' became a fetish that, in many cases, referred simply to cyclical changes in fashion – political, intellectual, cultural, architectural – that revived the old, retro-style, rather than generating anything particularly new, as in the latest announcement of apocalyptical crisis or playful 'post-modernity'.

This scenario of unremitting crisis is far from the bureaucratic programme of controlled consumption Lefebvre identified a decade earlier. Once the moment had been missed for the realisation of philosophy in the revolutionary events of May 1968, Lefebvre advanced the radical claim that crisis continued the work of social transformation as a 'practical critique' and dissolution of the established order: 'The theory of permanent crisis replaces that of permanent revolution' (Lefebvre, 2005: 39). There is now no point in dwelling on the crisis of Marxism as the critical theory of crisis. Against the practical critique of reality imposed by conditions of crisis, critical theory dissolved into 'hypercriticism'. It became more shrill and indifferent to the transformations and possibilities of the 'bad' side of crisis as a negative critique of reality, pregnant with hidden possibilities.

CRITIQUE AND DEVELOPMENT

Like Gramsci, Lefebvre began to move social theory away from the blanket denigration of everyday life by critical theory as a negative, pre-theoretical and inferior domain of uniform alienation, whatever is left over by more 'authentic' or exceptional moments of revolution, culture, art, and science. Lefebvre established some of the ways in which everyday life is a site for moments of desire and praxis, as well as a site of monotony and repetition. Lefebvre's critique of everyday life aimed to control the ambiguity that exists between concrete abstractions and fictitious reality. Everyday life becomes tragic the more it denies the reality of tragedy as its own negative: death, violence, wars, crime, aggression, crises, decline, ruins (Lefebvre, 2005: 166). Knowledge of the tragic, Lefebvre hoped, would transform the possibilities of everyday life from falling into nihilism and melancholy under the weight of crisis. It is precisely this gap between everyday life and images that more recent post-modern social theory has contested.

Analysing 'the explosion' of 1968, Lefebvre (1969: 41) claimed that although social reality had changed considerably over the past century, 'the appearance and surface of society have changed much more, as have the resulting illusions'. As Lefebvre put it, the 'prose of the world' had come to dominate the 'poetry of existence'. Moments of intense pleasure are swapped for a steady flow of mere satisfaction. Everyday life is invaded by the world of 'publicity', blurring the gap between representation and reality. Made-to-order spectacles of mass media momentarily rupture the fabric of everyday monotony with images of violence, death, disaster, and celebrities, cementing the gap between the ordinary and the extra-ordinary. Everyday life was rebranded as 'popular culture'.

Instead of celebrating or denouncing everyday life and adopting the heroic myth of (male) transcendence as ideal models, social theory is arguably better served by Lefebvre's (1968b) reflexive inquiry into changing empirical patterns

QUOTIDIAN TURN: HENRI LEFEBVRE

guided by meta-theoretical principles. Lefebvre recognised that the time of daily life cannot rest on a rigid distinction between progressive linear time and routine cyclical time, since the everyday is itself a product of history and is experienced through the memory and identity of groups and individuals. Neither should time (dynamic) be privileged over space (static), as in recent ideas of the fluid, rootless post-modern subject. Everyday life is too ambivalent for critical social theory to be satisfied with a rigid demarcation between the mundane and the spectacular.

In a debate with Leszek Kolakowski, leading historian of both Marxism and positivism, Lefebvre repeated the objections of critical theory to positivism as eliminating critique, tragedy and struggle from social theory. As Kolakowski pointed out, however, this ignores the critique by positivism since David Hume against unfounded myths and prejudices (Kolakowski and Lefebvre, 1974: 222–6). In turn, Kolakowski dismissed the obscurity of Lefebvre's concept of 'meta-philosophy' as mere reflection about philosophy when 'what philosophers do is quite simply to articulate the daily experiences of a certain community in a slightly complicated language' (Kolakowski and Lefebvre, 1974: 203).

Towards the end of his life Lefebvre (1990) returned again to the problem of how to change everyday life, a theme that had pursued him for sixty years, in radically different circumstances. Out of the crisis a new sense of democratic rights embedded in social practice might emerge, bypassing the inertia of both critical theory and positivism:

> Thus, neither absolute negativism and its corollaries: pessimism, nihilism and despair, nor positivism: realism that blocks the horizon. Neither stagnation nor catastrophe. (Lefebvre, 1990: 254)

Citizenship could be transferred from the legal-juridical control of the state to the tacit agreement and habits of mutual recognition in everyday life. In this way, Lefebvre hoped that the state might wither away, the old abandoned project of Marx, without unnecessary brutality, suffering, and violence.

11

CORPOREAL TURN: MAURICE MERLEAU-PONTY

Phenomenology attempts to form a meeting point for extremes – the theoretical extremes of subjectivism and objectivism. In this way, phenomenology hopes to relativise the theoretical conceit of absolute certainty: the cursed conceit of being absolutely right that afflicts many theorists. It takes as its point of departure the ordinary sense of 'phenomenal' as referring to something amazing, wondrous and astonishing (Ferguson, 2006). Phenomenology attempts to make the ordinary extraordinary, the routine unusual, the familiar strange, the natural artificial. In doing so, gives definite shape to barely expressible, dimly perceived aspects of everyday life. As protection against one-sided certainty, phenomenology relativises the social world by grounding it variously in fundamental or essential phenomena: consciousness, experience, the body, flesh, intersubjectivity, common sense, interaction, tacit knowledge, or language.

Phenomenology has had a wide influence on social theory. Ordinary experience is made the starting point. However, experience is difficult to grasp because it is caught up in the flow of life. Experience is always an interpretation of something appearing to a unified stream of consciousness. Experiences cannot be grasped empirically but only through ideal or 'exemplary constructions', such as the triangle in geometry, that are selected intuitively from an infinite variety of possibilities. In everyday life the 'natural attitude', a practical sense of the world, is held in common. A world of other people is inhabited naturally. If the social world is based on 'first-order' categories that cover over fundamental experience, then sociology must be a 'second-order' discipline since it overlays its own specialised categories on top of the generic categories of common sense. Phenomenology therefore reduces the diversity of the social world in such a way that 'self-evident' common sense that constitutes the social world might be examined and controlled.

Phenomenology covers a wide and disparate field of philosophy, social theory, and sociology. This book is mainly concerned with the relevance of phenomenology to social theory and crisis, beginning with the phenemonology of Edmund Husserl, and how this was developed in the theories of Alfred Schütz, ethnomethodology, Berger and Luckman and, in this chapter, Maurice Merleau-Ponty. A brief outline is given of the context for Merleau-Ponty's radical phenomenology by Husserl's delineation of the crisis of European theory in the 1930s. Merleau-Ponty attempted to negotiate the extremes of subjectivity and objectivity by shifting the focus of phenomenology from consciousness to the body. He was less concerned than Husserl with establishing the essence of human existence with absolute certainty than with opening up the ambiguous nature of what he calls the 'interworld'. In this way phenomenology potentially complements theoretically the empirical analyses of sociology. For a time Merleau-Ponty also entertained the possibility that phenomenology might alleviate the crisis of Marxism, a prospect that Merleau-Ponty abandoned in the 1950s. Finally, brief consideration is given to attempts to found phenomenology as a critical theory.

PHENOMENOLOGY AND CRISIS

Phenomenology acquired its modern sense of going beyond the dualist separation of subject and object when the philosopher Edmund Husserl (1859–1938) prioritised experience over logical categories. In his unfinished study *The Crisis of European Sciences*, Husserl (1970) put the crisis of humanity in the 1930s in historical context. As experience became increasingly divorced from scientific reason European modernity entered into a profound 'crisis'. The crisis consisted in the loss of philosophy's role in critically analysing the human foundations of science, a loss of meaning that gave rise to anti-intellectualism, scepticism, and hostility to 'rigorous science'. Husserl objected to the devaluation of philosophy as the deepest, most careful form of knowledge about the human condition by the purely empirical and contingent validity of 'positivist' science. To grasp the crisis meant going beyond the self-imposed limits of phenomenological reflection on consciousness separated, or 'bracketed', from the 'natural attitude' of common sense.

All theory derives from a 'theoretical attitude' in contrast to the pre-theoretical 'natural attitude'. In Europe the theoretical attitude, *theoria*, originated with ancient Greek philosophy. *Theoria* represented a break from the practical consciousness of everyday life. A theoretical attitude of detached contemplation and wonder appeared only when the seriousness of life could be suspended to allow playful curiosity and idle speculation, unaffected by social interests and involvements (Husserl, 1970: 285).

Phenomenology refuses to endorse the unexamined life. Instead, it seeks certainty and clarity about fundamental experience. Nothing already 'given' by everyday life can be taken at face value if any certainty is to be established about the foundations of human existence. It is in this sense that Husserl urged phenomenology to return 'to the things themselves' before they became covered over by the noise of living.

Theoretical detachment always presupposes practical, pre-theoretical engagement in the 'lifeworld' (*Lebenswelt*). Husserl's concept of the lifeworld refers variously to the 'world of immediate experience' and to the inter-subjective cultural world, with the cultural lifeworld forming the precondition for the experiential lifeworld. This is complicated further since the theoretical attitude of science enters into the cultural lifeworld rather than simply being premised upon it as its external, pre-given horizon. Because people 'live together' in the world 'inter-subjectively' they reciprocally correct and modify their collective understanding and collectively validate what has already been experienced and what might possibly be experienced in the 'open horizon' of the future (Husserl, 1970: 164).

Living together with other people forms the 'world-horizon' of a common civilisation. This presupposes a shared ability to communicate with each other and pass on the cultural inheritance through language, even if its origins are long forgotten. Culture takes on an objective form when it becomes independent of the immediate context of interaction. An ancient science like geometry, for instance, generates new meanings that 'reactivate' the validity of the original meaning of geometry, as when Galileo and Descartes perpetuated the living tradition of science even while undermining its original foundations. Where for the Greeks geometry remained attached to human practice, Galileo could treat it as a purely mathematical abstraction (forgetting its human origins), while Descartes could effect an absolute separation between physical reality and the rational mind capable of abstraction.

> What was a passive meaning-pattern has now become one constructed through active production ... Through this activity, now, further activities become possible – self-evident constructions of new judgements on the basis of those already valid for us. (Husserl, 1970: 364).

This has relevance for social theory conceived as a collective, living tradition of reactivation and not as a discontinuous set of statements about the present that invalidates all earlier constructions. As theory is revised it works logically with the sediment of the fundamental concepts of earlier constructions. If social theory fails to recall its pre-theoretical premises, then it becomes emptied of the meaning that initiated it, producing the kind of crisis that Husserl identified for science.

Abstract theoretical amnesia about concrete pre-theoretical origins lies at the root of the crisis of modernity for Husserl. Textbooks present ready-made concepts and summaries without identifying the source of the crisis in theory as rooted in the crisis of everyday life. Social theory therefore must be traced to the pre-theoretical lifeworld. Its historical horizon is the historical present: 'the present and the whole of historical time implied in it is that of a historically coherent and unified civilisation, coherent through its generative bond and constant communalisation in cultivating what has already been cultivated before, whether in cooperative work or reciprocal interaction' (Husserl, 1970: 374). This horizon gives the theoretical attitude primacy for Husserl since all claims staked on empirical facts acquire meaning only by presupposing a historical tradition.

MERLEAU-PONTY

In Europe phenomenology was taken in a radical direction by Maurice Merleau-Ponty (1908–1961). Merleau-Ponty had been one of the first to study the full unpublished manuscript of Husserl's *Crisis of European Sciences*. By accounting for experience on the basis of the 'lifeworld' Husserl established 'the method of a phenomenological positivism which bases the possible on the real' (Merleau-Ponty, 2002: xix). Merleau-Ponty went further and located experience in the sense-making body and inter-subjective social relations, not in an external relationship of consciousness to reality.

Unlike the existential philosophy of Jean-Paul Sartre, for Merleau-Ponty the world does not consist of 'pure being' but is a relational unity formed inter-subjectively, 'when I either take up my past experiences in those of the present, or other people's in my own' (2002: xx). Rather than conceiving subject and object as separate domains Merleau-Ponty focussed on the body, and later the flesh, as the ambiguous meeting point of an 'interworld' between the perceiving subject and the intended object. For Merleau-Ponty, this had also been the method prastised by Hegel, Marx, Nietzsche, and Freud (2002: viii). From this perspective the phenomenological reduction has particular methodological value:

> It is because we are through and through compounded of relationships with the world that for us the only way to become aware of the fact is to suspend the resultant activity, to refuse it our complicity … to put it 'out of play'. Not because we reject the certainties of common sense and a natural attitude to things … but, because, being the presupposed basis of any thought, they are taken for granted, and go unnoticed, and because to arouse them and bring them into view, we have to suspend for a moment our recognition of them. (Merleau-Ponty, 2002: xiv–xv)

From the French reception of Hegel's dialectic Merleau-Ponty understood the social world as a relational whole rather than the free play of individual atoms that have a purely external relation to each other. This relational ambiguity of inside and outside, whole and part, subject and object makes the body central to phenomenology.

As with Marx's 'sensuous-practical activity', Merleau-Ponty conceived the body as a *subject* rather than an object (2002: 90–1). Objects, like a chair or a table, may be present to me in a certain aspect right now but they will not always appear in front of me showing only this aspect. My body is present in the sense that it cannot disappear from the field of perception. It is present to me as an invariant perspective. It is neither consciousness nor a physical thing but a body unified in process: 'Thus experience of one's body runs counter to the reflective procedure which detaches subject and object from each other, and which gives us only the thought about the body, or the body as an idea, and not the experience of the body or the body in reality' (2002: 231). This gives it an ambiguous quality. So while I can observe objects with my body, get different perspectives on them, move round them, pick them up and so on, none of this is possible for the body itself. I cannot walk round my body or pick it up in order to observe it. Hence, the body is a subject not an object. At the same time, the body is a thoroughly ambiguous subject, marked in its dispositions and gestures by cultural differences that produce varied emotions and feelings in the social world as it is lived.

Neither empiricism nor rationalism is adequate to the phenomenological understanding of the body. Empiricism fails to recognise how cultural experience gives significance to the phenomenon selected for study, while rationalist 'intellectualism' fails to allow contingency into theory, which always seems to know where it is going in advance. Neither perspective grasps the act of learning as an intentional process oriented towards what is not yet known.

What is needed is a 'chiasmic' theory. Chiasmus comes from the Greek *chi* to refer to the ambiguous criss-crossing or intertwining of two terms, an 'inter-world', as with the meeting of subjective experience and objective existence in a single point, the body. While the two aspects can only be understood through the third term, they do not become fully fused in a dialectic synthesis but each aspect retains a degree of autonomy. In chiasmic theory, structure (world) and agency (intentions) are always intertwined in the socio-historical process. Later Merleau-Ponty (1968) would develop the concepts of chiasmus to explicate his idea of 'the flesh' as the surface where many points meet: body and world, touch and being touched, the visible and the invisible, perception and motion. In another sense, chiasmic theory could also form the point for bringing philosophy and social science together while allowing them their separate styles of argument (Crossley, 2004).

Merleau-Ponty's metaphysics of the body is sometimes criticised for neglecting the problem of structural power. However, Merleau-Ponty (1974: 113–16) accepted the force of structures acting in the social world (Schmidt, 1985). The notion of structure overcomes the subject–object dualism because it is both outside human beings, as nature and social systems, and within human beings, as symbolic functions (1974: 120). For Merleau-Ponty, unlike Durkheim, social facts are neither things nor representations, but structures of relations. Like Saussure's 'diacritical' structuralism, where signs function through their differences, society was conceived by Merleau-Ponty as a dense 'structure of structures' – economic, linguistic, cultural, political, familial, and so on.

Merleau-Ponty (1973a: 23) was one of the first to grasp the possibilities of Ferdinand de Saussure's (1857–1913) structural linguistics for founding a theory of historical meaning and for introducing a 'linguistics of speech'. Signs cannot mean anything on their own but only take on meaning in relation to other signs as part of a general system. Saussure (1983) excluded living speech (*la parole*) from his linguistic system in favour of language as a static structural model (*la langue*). Saussure's 'structuralism' was criticised for reducing social, cultural and psychological (diachronic) processes to static, closed (synchronic) systems of difference.

Merleau-Ponty accepted the structuralist argument that language, understood as a cultural institution formed by conventional relations between signs and signifiers, constrains the possibilities for speech (1973a: 13). Merleau-Ponty's main emphasis, however, was not on language as a rule-bound system but on the creative, expressive possibilities of concrete speech, something that Saussure excluded as contingent and therefore non-scientific. Languages are learned piece by piece, not as an overarching system. Every concrete act of speech does not passively reproduce the whole language system but hands to speaking subjects the means for 'going beyond signs toward their meaning' (Merleau-Ponty, 1974: 78). While Claude Lévi-Strauss (1966) dedicated his major work of structural anthropology, *The Savage Mind*, to the memory of Merleau-Ponty, social theory inspired by Saussure's method, principally the anthropology of Lévi-Strauss, the psychoanalysis of Jacques Lacan and the philosophy of Louis Althusser, who later condemned the world-making inter-subjectivity of Merleau-Ponty's phenomenology as a humanist myth.

Phenomenology attempted to unite the extremes of subjectivism and objectivism with the twin notions of the world and rationality. Rationality is not detached from a world external to it, as in rationalist systems. Rationality discloses experiences where 'perspectives blend, perceptions confirm each other, [and] meaning emerges':

> Rationality is not a *problem*. There is behind it no unknown quantity which has to be determined by deduction, or, beginning with it, demonstrated inductively. We witness every minute the miracle of related experience, and yet nobody knows better than we do how this miracle is worked, for we are ourselves this network of relationships. (Merleau-Ponty, 2002: xxii–xxiii)

If humans are essentially rational beings, as Husserl claimed, then the quality of being human can only be truly realised within rational human communities. As Merleau-Ponty's social theory would have it, 'we are what we do to others' (2000: 109). If human societies need to take care of what we do to others, then a self-consciously *social* theory of human development is needed as a means of guidance and orientation for the realisation of human potential, what Greek philosophy called *entelechy*.

If lived perception anchors bodies to the world, then it may well conflict with the objective knowledge of science. For instance, with our bodies we perceive a situation where the earth does not appear to revolve while the sun appears to move from east to west over the course of the day. Since Copernicus astronomy has demonstrated the opposite: that the earth orbits around the sun. Objective knowledge of science helps explain some of the intellectual disdain for the naive perception of ordinary life. Practical knowledge cannot be trusted. What this conceit forgets is that the lived world of perception provides the ground for the objective world of cognition.

> Reflection can never make me stop seeing the sun two hundred yards away on a misty day, or seeing it 'rise' or 'set', or thinking with the cultural apparatus with which my education, my previous efforts, my personal history, have provided me. (Merleau-Ponty, 2002: 71)

The abstract 'I think' of theory cannot escape from the concrete 'I perceive' of the body. Science derives its meaning from experience here in the lived world, not from some point in outer space (Descombes, 1980: 61). Merleau-Ponty

(2007: 112) attempted to return the static conceptions of science to the dynamic perceptions of the body as the human basis of any increase in objective knowledge. Science, in turn, promises an increase in human freedom.

BODY, THINGS AND WORLD

Drawing on the late Husserl, Merleau-Ponty overcame the dualism between subject and object, mysteriously reproduced by pure internal consciousness and pure external nature. Consciousness does not exist in itself but exists only if it is projected towards something beyond. In this sense consciousness is always 'intentional' and purposeful. Theory does not simply reflect a given reality but brings it into play as something to be wondered about and astonished by (Ferguson, 2006). Merleau-Ponty (1973b: 200) rejected how Sartre split the world into consciousness and things. If the dichotomy between subject and object is assumed, as with Sartre, then every individual consciousness, as the privileged subject that creates meaning, is made responsible for the whole of history, moment to moment (Merleau-Ponty 1973b: 200). This is an intolerable position, not to say an impractical one, conjured up by the word-play of philosophers.

By contrast, for Merleau-Ponty meaning is possible because embodied human relationships are mediated by an 'interworld' consisting of history, knowledge, culture and symbols. Bodily perception is a process that gradually gets covered over by the sedimentation of later knowledge. Phenomenology tries to dig through this sedimentation to arrive at how the world is 'grasped' through the body. The world is structured by spontaneity in the present and by 'sedimentations' from the past. In any living institution the past does not merely survive but, as in art, is intentionally taken in new directions 'as the invitation to a sequel, the necessity of a future' (Merleau-Ponty, 1970: 41). Sedimentation is not a finished, inert mass buried in the depths of consciousness but is continually replenished by the spontaneous demands of the phenomenal body to demarcate what appears to be significant in novel situations (Merleau-Ponty, 2002: 150).

Just as social theory today routinely rejects the classic mind–body dualism of Descartes as untenable, since it reduces the body effectively to an epiphenomenon of the thinking 'mind', neither should the body be reduced to a reified object, external and distinct from the lifeworld that encompasses it. Bodies are not the 'first-order' objects of 'second-order' cognition or reflection: 'In so far as it sees and touches the world, my body can therefore be neither seen nor touched' (Merleau-Ponty, 2002: 105). It is the absolute ground, not the cause, for changing relations in the perceptual field of the presence and disappearance of external objects. Subjects do not usually think first about moving their arms and legs and then carry out individual moves. Bodies carry out actions without premeditation to meet the demands placed on them by the situational context.

Philosophy traditionally leapt over the problem of knowledge of other people from a standpoint of speaking from everywhere and, therefore, from nowhere in particular. However, subjects are not in the lifeworld in the same way that objects are contained in a box. Neither is the world constituted anew each time by individual consciousnesses. Subject and lifeworld are a mutually constitutive process. The lifeworld makes subjects possible as subjects project themselves into the lifeworld:

> The world is inseparable from the subject, but from a subject which is nothing but a project of the world, and the subject is inseparable from the world, but from a world which it projects itself. (Merleau-Ponty, 2002: 499)

All experience is perceived from the standpoint of the body in the world. When theoretical reflection wants to transcend embodied perception, it forgets that knowledge is founded on perception and that it is simply impossible to stop living in the inherited world of perception.

Bodies conform to a 'logic of the world' that makes possible 'things of inter-sensory significance' (Merleau-Ponty, 2002: 380). Merleau-Ponty identifies the body as a 'third term' that operates as the background assumption behind things and the world. Embodied movement is simultaneously movement and consciousness of movement. This is what Merleau-Ponty calls 'motor intentionality' (2002: 127). With motor intentionality Merleau-Ponty argues that there can be no bodily movement in itself, somehow operating 'automatically' without any contact with consciousness (2002: 142). Perception and movement constitute a unified bodily system that varies flexibly. When we wave at a friend we see suddenly across the street our intention is not, first, to send an ideal representation of a wave to our body that instructs the arms to perform a physical act.

Motor intentionality is the primary form of praxis, although this is obscured by the traditional theory–action dualism.

> It is not easy to reveal pure motor intentionality: it is concealed behind the objective world which it helps to build up. The history of apraxia would show how the description of Praxis is almost always contaminated and finally made impossible by the notion of representation. (Merleau-Ponty, 2002: 159)

'Apraxia' refers to the condition where motor intentionality is impaired in patients even though the object in its context is understood. In such cases, the dualism between representation and body fails to grasp the inherently practical nature of consciousness. The body is perceived only when motor intentionality pushes it out from the background to grasp something in the world. Even then the body is peripheral compared to the thing in the world being reached for. Merleau-Ponty stressed that the world is not merely an external object but is always 'grasped':

> That is why, in their first attempts at grasping, children look, not at their hand, but at the object: the various parts of the body are known to us through their functional value only, and their coordination is not learnt. (2002: 172)

Things in the world present themselves to us in their everyday familiarity as sensible objects. Sensible objects are always ambiguously incomplete to our perceptions of the lived world. Yet they are sufficiently present for us to 'grasp' them through the practical functioning of motor intentionality. In the famous example of the cube, its six equal sides cannot be perceived all at once and so some sides will always be 'invisible' to perception, and their hidden reality assumed (2002: 237).

Perception gives the thing significance for us but does not coincide with it since the universal schema of the body transcends the localised moment of perception: 'A thing is, therefore, not actually *given* in perception, it is internally taken up by us, reconstituted and experienced by us in so far as it is bound up with a world, the basic structures of which we carry with us, and of which it is merely one of many possible concrete forms' (2002: 381). It is able to do so because the body is trained by habit-forming practices not merely by innate mechanical reflexes. These habits are ingrained by structured movements of social worlds, in games, sports, language, dancing, swimming, ironing, and other motorised conventions. Habits are acquired by the motor grasping of a motor significance.

Habit is neither a cognitive representation nor an involuntary action but a feel for the social world. Through habitual practice, the body understands not 'the mind'. It constitutes an 'expressive space', an anchor in and medium for the world. A habit for dancing, for instance, is formed by practically rehearsing the formula of movement by building on previously acquired movements like walking, running, swaying, and so on. As in art, the thing expressed by the body cannot be separated from its medium of expression:

> A novel, poem, picture or musical work are individuals, that is, being in which the expression is indistinguishable from the thing expressed, their meaning, accessible only through direct contact, being radiated with no change of their temporal and spatial situation. It is in this sense that our body is comparable to a work of art. (Merleau-Ponty, 2002: 175)

Every habit is both motor and perceptual. In texting, we know which keys to press on the phone pad with barely a glance and, at the same time, move our arms and fingers without self-conscious instruction. In movement, our body is spontaneously just there. We do not have to discover where our fingers, hands or arms are at any particular time. In this sense, it is the pre-given 'phenomenal body' that moves, not the 'objective body', which can only exist as someone else's perspective.

An ambiguous, three-way relationship exists between our bodies, sense of selfhood, and external things. Such embodied ambiguity is navigated by learned predispositions that make the social world familiar to us. Our body is not a mere instrument or means but is the most visible expression in the world of our intentions. Bodies do not occupy space in the manner of inert things but only as a system of possible movements or 'motor projects'. Spatial distance is not plotted according to objective points in space, as in geometry, but in relations coordinated from the central perspective of the active body. It is not a 'spatiality of position' but a 'spatiality of situation' (2002: 115).

BETWEEN SOCIOLOGY AND PHILOSOPHY

For Merleau-Ponty (1974: 95) there is no rigid dividing line between sociology and philosophy. Any schism between them relies on ideal-types that the respective disciplines construct for themselves. Such segregation of two complementary forms of fundamental knowledge, Merleau-Ponty argues, threatens human culture with a state of 'permanent crisis'. In reality, scientific practice and philosophical reflection are interdependent. Sociologists philosophise each time empirical facts are interpreted, and philosophers sociologise every time they think about something in the world. All learning, philosophical or sociological, is subject to a process of 'imaginary variation' that throws our embodied experience of social relationships in and out of focus. Imaginary variation invites an understanding of other possible experiences and relationships beyond immediate perception.

Husserl's early philosophy acquired the appearance of absolute autonomy because it concentrated on trying to get to an imagined ideal essence of actual things like language as the key to certainty. Sartre also argued that empirical study was largely irrelevant to the essence of emotion and imagination. On the contrary, theory does not constitute inter-subjective communication by a pure act of cognition but is constituted by it. Later Husserl responded positively to the anthropology of Levy-Bruhl, realising that human groups in the distant past did not exist through collective representations, as Durkheim might have it, but lived in an enlarged, inter-subjective social-natural world (Moran and Steinacher, 2008). According to Merleau-Ponty this encounter forced Husserl to 'admit that the philosopher could not possibly have immediate access to the universal by reflection alone' (1974: 104).

'Imaginative variation' is therefore no longer sufficient to account for the variety of human experience revealed by sociological facts. Merleau-Ponty quoted Husserl's famous letter to Levy-Bruhl: 'It is a task of the highest importance, which may be actually achieved, to feel our way into a humanity whose life is enclosed in a vital, social tradition and to understand it in this unified social life' (1974: 274).

Philosophy can no longer claim access to the universal truth of civilisations by a purely imaginary variation of personal experiences. Sociological facts, Merleau-Ponty argued, must be allowed to live to allow the philosopher to enter into the lived experience of community. Pure abstract theory has been discredited by modernity's consciousness of itself as history. In contrast, sociology is concerned with a wide and diverse historical range of empirical social processes and cultural formations. Even so, sociology always selects some things for investigation as more 'essential' than other things. In this way, sociology more methodically perceives and re-lives, through ideal models, what is first experienced in everyday life.

Sociology tends to present the social world as something external to individuals and which determines all facets of existence. By the same token, by supplanting pure theory, sociology cannot set itself up as an absolute authority outside of the time and space of the culture that makes sociology possible. Recognition of historical and cultural relativism does not lead to the 'superficial' idea that any claim to truth is an impossible illusion. This is so only if truth is identified with an absolute ideal of validity outside of any determinate point of view in time and space.

Philosophy cannot have the first word, as the early Husserl had hoped with the idea of pre-empirical essences, so, Merleau-Ponty argued, it ought to have the last word, once the empirical social sciences have done their work. Philosophy theorises the inter-subjective 'symbolic consciousness' of a community while sociology engages in objective analyses of its institutional structures. Merleau-Ponty claimed that Husserl later abandoned the ideal essence of language constructed by detached theory for the more open-ended functioning of a living language community. Phenomenological theory no longer constructs a priori essences to establish non-empirical preconditions that make things possible, but instead develops in reflexive contact with the social world as it is presently constituted. Philosophy's role now is to make manifest the rationality that is latent within the contingencies of the social world, while sociology is conceived by Merleau-Ponty as limited to tracing objective relations of cause and effect.

As he became disillusioned with Marxist politics Merleau-Ponty took inspiration from the 'heroic liberalism' of Max Weber's approach to social theory without dogmatism. He began from Weber's recognition of the political limits of sociological understanding. As classical liberalism became disenchanted with the impossible ideal of social harmony on its own terms, it began to recognise and confront its adversaries as legitimate interlocutors and 'heroically' tried to reconcile and provide intellectual space for contrary social forces, including outlawed forms of Marxism. Weber's liberalism allowed for considerable ambiguity 'because he admits that truth always leaves a margin of doubt, that it does not exhaust the reality of the past and still less that of the present, and that history is the natural seat of violence' (1973b: 9).

Weber gave up any claim to finished 'categorical knowledge', since all knowledge must be revised at some point. Theory and practice approach historical reality from opposite directions as two poles of the same world. Theory is provisional, open, and conditional, while practice depends on decisions that are absolute, partial, and irreversible. Weber's ideal-types do not get inside the minds of great personalities or reflect all the objective facts. Instead they get beyond the subject–object dualism by constructing an analytical horizon for the meaning of social action. Merleau-Ponty acknowledged that Weber related 'the Protestant ethic' to 'the capitalist spirit' by starting from provisional definitions (rationalisation as a social principle) constructed selectively from known facts (Benjamin Franklin's sayings such as 'time is money') that makes legible still other facts – disenchantment as an unintended consequence – a conclusion that was not contained in the original concept of rationalisation.

In this way Weber's 'fecund scheme' surged beyond a provisional definition of rationalisation to establish a system-wide social intention – spirit, ethic – in what Merleau-Ponty (1973b: 14) called 'the dialectic of a whole'. Rationalisation was not always systematic but had to become so. Not only does capitalism produce rational subjects, it was founded by them. Only later did these human choices, the religious calling, become a 'situation' imposing its own logic. In the elective affinities between Calvinism and capitalism Weber revealed 'the very advent of meaning' in the process of rationalisation becoming a self-producing system. Such ambiguities, carefully handled, 'allow us to read in a religious fact the first draft of an economic system' or, conversely, in an economic fact the first draft of a new social system (1973b: 18–19).

From Weber's open-ended method Merleau-Ponty concluded that since complete truth is a chimera no situation is entirely without hope. History is never exhausted by the historian's categories. Advances in theory are made by addressing errors and doubling back on itself in order to come to terms with deviations, accidents, chances, and all manner of unexpected human contingencies. As Weber argued, the idea that any closed system of theoretical concepts could contain within itself all social and historical variation and from which all eventualities could be deduced 'will be nonsense in itself' (1973b: 24). It is possible to understand the meaning of other cultures, past and present, from a different point of view. Since we are already living in culture a conscious standpoint can be adopted in order to judge, situate, and organise the relative significance of those events that our concepts abstract from the whole situation. However, Merleau-Ponty argued that Weber failed to realise that his pure ideal-types were also subject to the historical process of scientific rationalisation. Relativism was insufficiently relativised, a paradox that 'Weberian Marxists' like Lukacs and Merleau-Ponty himself attempted to overcome.

PHENOMENOLOGY AND MARXISM

Merleau-Ponty attempted to throw a bridge between phenomenology and Marxism. It didn't last. He refused to reduce Marxism to a 'scientism', an intellectual style that tends to resurface in non-revolutionary periods. Historical materialism aspired to project the human significance of 'ways of existing and co-existing, on human relationships' (Merleau-Ponty, 2002: 199). It not only examines the official, formal institutions of society, economy, and politics but also

> its latent content, or the relations between human persons as they are actually established in concrete living … in more general terms the living subject, man as creativity, as a person trying to endow his life with form, loving, hating, creating or not creating works of art, having or not having children. Historical materialism is not a causality exclusive to economics. (Merleau-Ponty, 2002: 199)

Marx's laws of capitalism are not universal but are limited to a historically specific structure. In reference to its Hegelian framework, Merleau-Ponty compared Marx's *Capital* to 'a concrete *Phenomenology of Mind*' (Hegel, 2003). By this he meant that the economy and, by extension everyday life, is bound up with social relations:

> The point of connection between these two problem areas lies in the Hegelian idea that every system of production and property implies a system of relations between men [sic] such that their social relations become imprinted upon their relations to nature, and these in turn imprint upon *their* social relations. (Merleau-Ponty, 2000: 101)

Just as the meaning of a painting cannot be separated from the painting's material existence, its texture, frame, colours, lines, and so on, neither can ideology be reduced to the economy since both form part of a unified structural whole.

Objective class positions do not exhaust the possibilities for consciousness. Class is not simply pre-given by representations but comes into being in the process of experiencing a common social horizon. Poverty or the depths of crisis do not necessarily radicalise people. Indeed this experience often produces demoralisation, while the experience of prosperity can contribute to a more radical social horizon: 'It is because the easing of living conditions makes a fresh structure of social space possible: the horizon is not restricted to the most immediate concerns' (Merleau-Ponty, 2002: 518).

In any case, the opposition between objective social position and subjective consciousness perpetuates the abstract dualism of Descartes. Theoretical dualism is an inadequate way of posing the problem of social action since the social world cannot be divided up precisely into one part that is determined and another part that is autonomous and does the determining. These are merely two different ways of neglecting the phenomenon itself of being in the world: 'What makes me a proletarian is not the economic system or society considered as systems of impersonal forces, but these institutions as I carry them within me and experience them; nor is it an intellectual operation devoid of motive, but my way of being in the world within this institutional framework' (Merleau-Ponty, 2002: 515). Being in the world (not the economy alone) determines consciousness (not the mind alone). We are neither wholly determined by the situation nor absolutely free to choose.

REVOLUTION GROWN HEAVY

In *Adventures of the Dialectic* Merleau-Ponty subjected Marxist theory and practice to critical examination in the light of the monstrous regime that emerged in its name in the Soviet Union. As a historically bound theory, Marxism lacked what it claims to have: a total view of universal history (Merleau-Ponty, 1973b: 51). Merleau-Ponty did not become a virulent anti-Communist as many other disillusioned Marxists did in the Cold War period but discovered a living dialectic in Max Weber's notion of a 'political calling'. No Marxist himself but deeply versed in Marxist currents, Weber was suspicious of the vainglorious motives of revolutionary commitment and ardour. While 'lack of distance' is 'the professional disease of academic and intellectual circles', in politics revolutionary 'braggarts' noisily announce their purity of heart and get carried away by romantic phrases about historical destiny, without taking responsibility for the consequences of their actions.

Of the revolutionary generation, only Lenin and Trotsky grasped the revolutionary 'calling' at the most personal core of their being. For them, like their political opponent Weber, history is not a philosophical formula but a living process. In this sense, for Merleau-Ponty dialectical social theory could only be advanced by what he called 'Weberian Marxism':

> If history does not have a direction, like a river, but has a meaning, if it teaches us, not a truth, but errors to avoid, if its practice is not deduced from a dogmatic philosophy of history, then it is not superficial to base a politics on the analysis of the political man [sic]. (1973b: 28)

Like Weber, for Merleau-Ponty (1964: 179) political commitment is a matter of 'faith', not pure theory, since political action has to deal with the world as it exists. Dialectical theory is an adventure because it must pass through error after error (Merleau-Ponty, 1973b: 204). In times of crisis, everything depends on what opposing forces think of each other. There is never a purely economic causality since actions are undertaken that have acquired an intra-social significance.

Only those political or economic factors that are effective are lived and taken up by human subjects. 'Permanent equivocation' weighs heavily on the historical process (Merleau-Ponty, 2002: 199). As the dialectic is transposed from idealism to materialism it grows 'heavy', slowed down by the inertia of institutions, not unlike Gramsci's civil society, as the sedimentation of human inter-subjectivity (Merleau-Ponty, 1973b: 33). Every institution is a symbolic system that, like the structure of language, provides the medium of inter-subjectivity. Intense moments in history are freighted with terrible risks, unforeseen consequences, and contingencies of the changing situation. Since good intentions alone are no guarantee of the right policy it is necessary to coolly appraise the ambiguities. As the situation in the Soviet Union deteriorated, Merleau-Ponty argued that it was more important than ever to maintain a 'habit of discussion, criticism, research, and the apparatus of social and political culture' (2000: xxiii).

Revolutions see themselves as producing a new synthesis that rights the old wrongs but in reality they reproduce the old antinomy of rulers and ruled. Merleau-Ponty argued that revolutions are 'relatively progressive' but will fall short of the absolute ideal of progress intended by the revolutionaries themselves (1973b: 222). Here 'the essence' of revolution appears in the open tension of the fall of the old ruling class before a new class has been able to assume power. Once new leaders take power the revolution as an open process is closed down and the negative power of living resistance is arrested by the positive power of regime loyalty.

By announcing that history is now at an end the new regime aims to bring the dialectical process to a halt (1973b: 206). Intellectuals armed with a philosophy of history know what the masses need to do; the masses, limited to practical sense, need intellectual leadership to go beyond limited day-to-day struggles. As the wave of uprisings known as the Arab Spring shows, beginning in Tunisia in 2010 and spreading across the Middle East and North Africa, the process of revolution expresses real tensions and crises while the post-revolutionary institution demands stability and order: 'Revolutions are true as movements and false as regimes' (1973b: 207).

Merleau-Ponty reserved the sharpest critique for his former friend Jean-Paul Sartre's justification of the Community Party as the necessary instrument to bring the masses out of their normal condition of unreason and into a special relationship to revolutionary reason (even though the post-war Communist Party was in practice far from a revolutionary party). Sartre was rebuked by his former friend for espousing the 'ultrabolshevik' myth of pure, spontaneous action in denial of the historical ballast of institutional density (Merleau-Ponty, 1973b: 124). On becoming a Marxist, Sartre simply transposed the radical freedom of 'pure consciousness' of his existentialist philosophy into political analysis and failed to grasp the ambiguous interworld praxis of corporeal inter-subjectivity. Later Sartre (2004) would answer Merleau-Ponty's problem of the historical inertia of institutions as a drag on political agency with his own Merleau-Pontian concept of the 'practico-inert' and the idea of the 'series' as passive group unity (in contrast to the active unity achieved by 'groups').

For Merleau-Ponty, Marxism posed the problem of revolution as abstract alternatives: either it is a spontaneous mass process or it is led by professional revolutionaries. In the former case, the revolution fails to occur, while in the latter case it is made in the name of the masses and ends in terror. Violence could only be justified if the proletariat proved in practice Marx's hypothesis that it truly represented universal humanity (Merleau-Ponty, 2000: 106).

The dilemma of revolution was most sharply expressed, Merleau-Ponty believed, by the case of the Russian Marxist Leon Trotsky (1879–1940). Trotsky began from a theory of mass spontaneity outside the Party, then conformed to Party discipline, engaged in an internal critique of the broken relationship between the Party and the working class, and, once defeated and exiled from the Soviet Union, returned again to appeal for spontaneous struggle against the ruling bureaucracy. Merleau-Ponty's alternative to this dilemma was to renew the critique of society, rather than continue to critique the old critique (Marxism), from the point of view of the social relations of lived inter-subjectivity, shaped by common human experiences, institutions and traditions.

PHENOMENOLOGY AS A THIRD WAY

Adventures of the Dialectic represented Merleau-Ponty's abandonment of Marxism (Elliott, 1987). It provoked a predictable backlash from orthodox Marxists, including Henri Lefebvre and Georg Lukacs (Garaudy et al., 1956). Still engaged at that time in hack Party diatribes, Lefebvre charged Merleau-Ponty with theoretical 'eclecticism' and incomprehensible ambiguity that cloaked an otherwise superficial analysis which only serves to justify the present situation (Howard, 1977: 208). Such critique disregarded Merleau-Ponty's emphasis on the wholeness or totality of human experience against an eclectic, ill-fitting collection of parts (Silverman, 1997). Later Merleau-Ponty would shelve Marx and address the problem of historical ambiguity in terms borrowed from Husserl and Heidegger, less as a relational whole than as the contingency of social significations (Poster, 1977: 159).

Later famous for heralding 'the post-modern condition', Jean-Francois Lyotard (1991: 105) in his first book, *Phenomenology* (1954), argued that phenomenological description can only take place on the basis of the empirical findings of sociology, which itself is only possible on 'a prior objectivation of the social'. At that time, Lyotard was attracted to a non-dogmatic form of Marxism and argued that something could be learned from phenomenology's effort to overcome the subject–object dualism that Marxism so often oscillated between. From the major study of phenomenology (1986) by the Vietnamese Marxist Tran Duc Thao (1917–1993),

Lyotard argued that phenomenology's stress on intentional analysis, as consciousness of something, led to a neglect of the material reality of the world (1991: 135). Husserl's attempt to create intentional analysis justified itself by recourse to a speculative philosophy of history. Where phenomenology imposed an ambiguity on history, that ambiguity was phenomenology's own creation as it tried to find an objective 'third way' out of the crisis without the wager of structural change.

More positively, Husserl and Merleau-Ponty attempted to overcome the dualism between subjectivism and objectivism (Gane, 1998). By subordinating meaning to perception, Merleau-Ponty bridges between extremes of 'simple subjectivism' and 'brutal objectivism' without forcibly unifying them:

> Clearly the immediate understanding that we have of a withdrawn young girl on the sidelines of the dance floor or the playground bears no guarantee of truth. This sort of spontaneous and 'evident' understanding results, in reality, from complex sedimentations of our individual history and of the history of our culture; in other words, we must first do a sociology or a psychology of the observer in order to understand his [sic] understanding. (Lyotard, 1991: 99)

On the other hand, Lyotard (1991: 135) argues that there is a sense in which the objective world already contains the subjective. Treating the social world as a recalcitrant object, as with Durkheim's social facts, is only the reverse of reducing it to a sum of the personal attitudes of individuals at any single point in time, as with opinion polls and attitude surveys.

While Lyotard rejects both approaches, he retained the distinction between phenomenology and sociology. Following Merleau-Ponty, he claims that there can be no 'phenomenological sociology', merely a philosophy and a sociology that deal with the same problems – world, people, and mind. Sociology objectivates its object while philosophy attempts to understand it, neglecting the entire hermeneutic tradition in sociology, from Weber onwards. Lyotard argues that phenomenology promised a descriptive philosophy of the concrete, grounded by sociological data. In turn, phenomenology frames the problematic of sociology, guides its research and analysis, as an explanatory science of the genesis and functions of institutions (1991: 75).

Alongside Merleau-Ponty's failed attempt to reconcile phenomenology and Marxism, Tran Duc Thao (1986) tried to integrate philosophy and politics more closely. If bodily perception is not fixed by ideology as formalistic Marxist theory assumes, then it becomes possible for phenomenology to conceive of a radically changed human praxis. An adequate theory of the phenomena of the social world needs to take into account the fact that perception cannot but be shaped by capitalist institutions like money, division of labour, wage labour, and the mode of production. In the capitalist universe external objects become private possessions. As such, they reinforce a privatised psychology of consciousness. It is therefore necessary, Thao argues, to go beyond a phenomenology of lived experience to a phenomenology of lived material reality.

So long as theory is divorced from the production of objects, Thao claims, philosophy is unable to grasp the dialectical relationship between the sensible and the intelligible. Material reality is conceived as an object of consciousness rather than consciousness being directly dependent on objective material reality. Thao locates inter-subjective relations within the long historical development of human production as cooperative, reciprocal relations mediated by a complex system of symbols, an analysis taken up by Derrida (1973) in his critique of Husserl, though without the 'grand narrative' of dialectical materialism (Herrick, 2005). In this respect, Derrida is closer to Merleau-Ponty, who maintained a distinction between philosophy and politics and refused to allow economic production the same latitude for perception as Thao demanded.

CRITIQUE AND DEVELOPMENT

Phenomenology makes ordinary practices, especially body comportment, the privileged point of entry and ground for other experiences and structures. Here a tacit assumption is made by pure phenomenology that 'bracketing' out common sense does not interfere with objective knowledge and clarity of science as a self-knowing procedure. As the sociology of science has shown, science itself depends on tacit bodily knowledge. Husserl viewed the crisis of the 1930s in terms of a problem of abstract rationalism rather than one of political ideologies and economic crisis. Unlike Sartre, Merleau-Ponty tended to maintain a gap between his radical political philosophy and his phenomenology of body perception.

Philosophers like Jacques Derrida maintained that phenomenology has no need of the facts of lived experience and must be kept strictly separate from social science, for which it functions as an a-priori framework (Dews, 2007: 20–1). Merleau-Ponty viewed phenomenology as providing a reflexive awareness of the limits of sociological knowledge, embedded as it is in wider relations of institutional, political, economic, and historical power. French Marxists close to Merleau-Ponty attempted to give phenomenology a more radical critical edge to it while holding on to the aspiration for theoretical rigour. Tran Duc Thao and the early Lyotard attempted to work between phenomenology and Marxism.

Despite some similarities between Husserl's analysis of science and the European crisis and *Dialectic of the Enlightenment*, Adorno (2013) denied that a critical phenomenology was possible. He objected to any epistemology, such as Husserl's, that begins from consciousness or subjectivity and tries to erect everything else on top of an essence that has merely been produced by an effort of pure thought. Phenomenology engages in a trade-off between empiricism and rationalism that denies the concrete social basis of philosophy. Adorno contrasted his 'immanent' method of metacritique to Husserl's 'transcendental' theory in order to expose, working from phenomenology's own premises, how it protects itself from the social world by consciousness and experience at a point when these were being diminished by instrumental domination:

metacritique presents it with its promissory note and forces from it the external insight, gained from society, that equivalence is not truth and that a fair trade-off is not justice. The real life process of society is not something sociologically smuggled into philosophy through associates. It is rather the core of the contents of logic itself. (Adorno, 2013: 26)

Objective reality, Adorno argued, is reduced by Husserl to subjective consciousness rather than mediated dialectically. If, according to Adorno's dialectical method, everything is mediated, then Husserl's phenomenological 'reduction' of everything to an original unmediated state, consciousness, lacks reality.

Free of any particular content or critical judgement, Husserl's retreat from the world remains passively complicit with it. Husserl's critique of rationalism was limited by the divorce of the abstract 'theoretical attitude' from worldly interests (Habermas, 1986). Later, however, under the influence of the anthropologist Levy-Bruhl, Husserl attempted to correct this deficiency in the face of the worsening crisis of European civilisation, and recognised the need for philosophy to be informed by empirical social science.

Trying to establish a critical phenomenological sociology, John O'Neill (1972) memorably compared sociology to a 'skin trade', involved in the necessarily 'dirty work' of acquiring the status and paraphernalia of a science and a profession. This presents a dilemma for young sociologists attracted by the critical relevance of sociology to questions of power, class, gender, race, war, poverty, and the body. In response to this demand, O'Neill (1975) argued for a 'wild sociology', one that dwells upon commonplaces, conventions, prejudices, places, love and the predicaments of ordinary life without descending into condescension or exoticism. When the 'bad times' return, sociology again and again finds itself compelled to negotiate with the 'ills of society'.

In various ways, phenomenology has subsequently formed the framework for critical sociology. Some of the uses that feminism has made of phenomenological traditions are considered in the following chapter. In terms of a phenomenology of class, a powerful empirical account of working-class experience was elaborated recently by Simon Charlesworth (2000). Charlesworth paradoxically attempted to return from complex phenomenological theory to the pre-theoretical experiences of working-class existence: 'that invisible realm of imperceptibles, the past living in the gestural, purely practical sense of this community as it is sedimented in the comportment of these people as they make a clearing for what matters in the way they make experience available to each other' (2000: 75).

While the setting is specific, the impoverished de-industrialised town of Rotherham in England, the study has a much wider significance for all places where the working class finds itself dispossessed, with only a marginal function, if any, for capital accumulation. Bodies and voices express the invisible suffering felt by social degradation and the immense personal struggles to cope with meaningless hurt. Charlesworth shows how class as a relation of force is inscribed onto the flesh of damned bodies at subterranean depths of social experience.

Phenomenological 'critique' does not have a timeless and universal relevance. As Charlesworth so powerfully shows, theory must submit to the common-sense relevance of everyday life if it is to be reflexively grounded in the context of a durable tradition of membership that Merleau-Ponty referred to as an 'institution': 'Human institutions are the ground of our common and individual achievements, enriching us and impoverishing us with a legacy which was never quite intended for us and is yet never totally rejected by us, even when we refuse it' (O'Neill, 1972: 233). Institutions, such as social theory, live when they are subject to dialogical dispute, judgement, argument, persuasion, evidence, and criticism. Otherwise, they are moribund.

12

PRAGMATIC TURN:
SOCIAL THEORY IN THE US

Do not block the way of inquiry.

Charles S. Peirce

As discontent with established sociology grew in the 1960s, a wide range of sociological perspectives presented themselves under the label 'sociology of everyday life'. Increased attention was given by social theory to local contingencies, language, and the body. Much of this drew on the philosophical traditions of phenomenology, pragmatism and, latterly, what came to be known as 'post-structuralism'. Many, though not all, social theorists accept that sociology is obliged to provide philosophical justifications for its theoretical and methodological statements. New grounds for the development of social theory were laid by developments in twentieth-century philosophy in Europe and America, even though the translation from textual abstractions to substantive social analysis was and is far from straightforward.

This chapter traces the translation of phenomenology from Europe to the US. There it met the American philosophical tradition known as 'pragmatism'. In the US, the sociologically inclined followers of Alfred Schütz (1899–1959) took Husserl's phenomenology in a different direction from the encounter that it had with Marxism in France. Schütz's sociological phenomenology became the 'social construction of reality', in the words of Berger and Luckmann (1967). One important strand of this was what Harold Garfinkel (1967) called 'ethnomethodology'. While Garfinkel had little interest in developing a formal theoretical system or debating philosophical subtleties, his approach gave rise to increasingly specialised studies of conversations. Other approaches returned to the pre-linguistic phenomenological focus on practical 'tacit knowledge'.

Phenomenology occupied some of the same theoretical space as pragmatism. Durkheim criticised pragmatism as a threat to rational science, neglecting the pragmatists' commitment to a self-critical scientific community as the basis of radical democracy. One of the few pre-1960s sociologists whose reputation survived the political and cultural changes was the radical Weberian C. Wright Mills (1964) whose first major study was on sociology and pragmatism (Eldridge, 1983; Scott and Nilsen, 2013). Also influenced by pragmatist philosophy, as well as German theory, was G.H. Mead, whose social psychology focussed on social participation in language. Mead allowed for a degree of collective creativity, a claim developed more recently by the pragmatic social theory of Hans Joas (1993, 1996). Joas contends that classical sociology was conceived by its founders not as grounded on traditional philosophical problems, but as forming a new philosophical project in its own right (1996: 69). Mead is often problematically grouped as a 'symbolic interactionist', along with the sociology of Erving Goffman. Goffman is well known for his major theoretical study of frame analysis and his use of theatre as a metaphor for social interaction.

Recent developments in social theory and feminist theory show that phenomenology and pragmatism remain fertile theoretical traditions when brought into contact with other approaches. Phenomenology and pragmatism, along with other influences, significantly shaped the development of feminist theory. Feminists made the body and the concrete standpoint of women in specific situational contexts more central to the present concerns of social theory. In different ways, the feminist theories of Judith Butler, Iris Marion Young, and Dorothy Smith, among others, renewed phenomenology through a radical commitment to social justice and political change.

PHENOMENOLOGICAL SOCIOLOGY

Phenomenology was transposed into sociology in the US by a sustained encounter with Max Weber alongside national theoretical influences. To make Husserl's transcendental philosophy relevant to US sociology, Schütz drew not only from the interpretative sociology of Weber and Max Scheler but also from the functionalist sociology of Talcott Parsons, then dominant in the US. However, Husserl's emphasis on European crisis was replaced in the US by an emphasis on the consensual grounds for inter-subjective understanding. Instead of 'bracketing' everyday life to discover the essence of consciousness in the manner of Husserl, Schütz made 'the natural attitude' of everyday life the central object for interpretative sociology.

Sociology takes the already formed social world as its point of departure. Against the traditional emphasis on individual consciousness, this is not too far removed from Husserl's late reworking of the lifeworld. It is necessary, Schütz thought, to prevent common sense from forming the unexamined presuppositions of social theory. Schütz adapted the objectively given lifeworld of Husserl to a more subjective sense that the lifeworld is constituted or constructed by consensual social action (Ferguson, 2006: 96). Weber's great merit for Schütz (1967: 5) lay in releasing sociology from 'metaphysical speculation' and restricting it to 'the simple and accurate description of life in society'.

Weber reduced social action to individual intentions by means of essences distilled in 'ideal-types' as 'the central problem of all the social sciences' (Schütz, 1967: 226). Both everyday life and science are organised by 'types' as simplified categories of reality. Processes of 'typification' provide both a means of interpretation and a means of orientation for individuals in the social world by submitting each unique encounter to a tried-and-tested schema of perception. In relation to postal workers or police officers, for instance, a typical objective-meaning context is inferred that transcends the specific individuals who happen to perform these functions. When measured against the unintended meaning of typifications, the closer individuals come to the ideal-type the more anonymous and objective they appear (Schütz, 1967: 37). Natanson (1986: 21) glosses Schütz's conception of 'anonymity' as referring 'primarily (but not exclusively) to the typified structures of the "objective" aspect of the social world, that is, to the social world viewed as an interlocking complex of meanings which enable any actor to manage his [sic] affairs in the world of working and to find his [sic] way to other provinces of meaning' (1986: 21).

Weber's limited interest in theoretical and methodological problems meant that his ideal-types were not as basic as they needed to be from the point of view of phenomenological sociology (although see Weber, 2012: 124–37). Specifically, Weber failed to register the complex system of perspectives in the social world, from the meaning that my own experience has for me and the meaning that the experience of others, immediately present or mediately absent predecessors or contemporaries, might have for me. Schütz (1967: 39) argued that Weber's model of meaningful action conflated action still in process (*actio*) with the already completed act (*actum*). Action is bound to subjects while an act is objective.

Schütz developed Weber's ideal of meaningful social action by addressing the issue of how people become subjectively meaningful to each other. His notion of 'motivational relevance' was concerned to examine how a deeper level of lived experiences lends meaning to action by selecting a discrete 'intended' experience from all other possible experiences taking place before, after, and at the present moment. Intended meaning is for Schütz 'the fundamental and basic principle of knowledge' (1967: 43). Instead of putting ourselves in the (inaccessible) mind of others, Schütz (1967: 121) claimed that we can only really infer meaning from our own point of view by putting the sign in a context that has a significance for us.

For Schütz, the phenomenological meaning of signs therefore takes precedence over the realist ontology of objects in establishing reality (Schütz, 1967: 252). Everyday life is an inter-subjective 'lifeworld' comprehended through an accumulated 'stock of knowledge' that people pass on to each other, add to and revise as part of the living tradition of common sense. Knowledge of other people is inferred through the intermediary of the other's body. It is 'appresented', that is, the experience is referred to past experiences to make sense of unknown features of the situation and arrange them for perception.

SOCIAL CONSTRUCTION OF REIFIED REALITY

Influenced by Schütz, Berger and Luckmann (1967) drew on G.H. Mead alongside the classical sociology of Marx, Simmel, Weber and Durkheim. For them the attitudes and moods of common-sense experience results in an objectively coherent and subjectively meaningful everyday reality: 'It is a world that originates in [ordinary] thoughts and actions, and is maintained as real by these' (1967: 33). This sense of the 'real' takes on an objective force. From Schütz, they argue that typifications and local interactions in everyday life produce social structures. Everyday life is structured, as Simmel argued, around relations of social distance from a central axis of the 'here' of my body and the 'now' of the present. Language emerges from everyday life but also transcends it altogether and becomes an objective social fact imposed on everyday life (1967: 54).

How does coercive objectivity emerge from meaningful subjectivity? By the type of knowledge that is habitually constructed in social interaction. Consciousness of reality is, as Berger and Luckmann said, 'socially constructed', a now over used term but one that in the 1960s signalled a move away from reified ideas of social systems of functionalist sociology. However, following Lukacs, the socially constructed reality is also a reified reality. Individuals are dominated by processes of 'objectivation' that naturalise socially constructed institutions (1967: 78). In the ordinary course of life, 'objectivation' processes construct reality as an independent, discrete, and brute external social fact. Objective reality is stabilised by the routines, roles, and habits of institutionalisation.

Unlike Lukacs, however, Berger and Luckmann (1967: 106–7) view reification as an inescapably 'typical' aspect of the human condition where the 'original apprehension of the social world is highly reified'. Reification is for them a problem of subjective 'apprehension' rather than a structural effect of capitalist relations as Marx and Lukacs had claimed. It is only with modernity, they argue, that a relative *de-reification* of consciousness occurs as traditional institutions experience crises, the segregation of social groups breaks down, and the experience of marginality provides an alternative standpoint of reality.

ETHNOMETHODOLOGY

Instead of the phenomenal properties of experience, Harold Garfinkel's (1967) ethnomethodology shifted the analysis of everyday life to the structuring of practices through unnoticed rules and procedures. *Ethno* refers to a social group, *method* to practical routines, and *ology* to a study of their logic (Rawls, 2000: 546). If society coheres, then it cannot simply be because numerous individuals happen to share the same ideas. Rather, some common method or procedure must guide practical relations in such a way that order (usually) is the result.

In this way, Durkheim's problem of specifying the concrete conditions for objective social facts was addressed by focussing less on individual states of consciousness than on the organised practices of local situations in everyday life. Sociologists can only understand how such routines work by having a deep familiarity with the situation and by becoming competent participants, acquiring what Garfinkel (2002: 124) calls 'unique adequacy'. Unique adequacy presents few obstacles for understanding the implicit methods of everyday life, but is more difficult to achieve with specialised institutions such as the professions or criminality.

With 'ethnomethodology' Garfinkel did not insist on any particular research method or tool. Using various research instruments, belief is suspended in order to observe the practical methods or rules by which people routinely interpret, come to know, make sense of, and produce everyday life. Such 'rules' are not exhaustive, formal or well-defined but tacitly buried deep into the assumptions of social interaction. They depend on ad-hoc improvisations and contingencies to secure a degree of 'interpretative realism'. Everyday realism is secured practically through 'reflexive accounts'. People need to know at the outset the settings in which they operate so that they are able to produce a recognisable account of its particular, located features.

> They treat as the most passing matter of fact that members' accounts, of every sort, in all their logical modes, with all of their uses, and for every method for their assembly are constituent features of the settings they make observable. Members know, require, count on, and make use of this reflexivity to produce, accomplish, recognize, or demonstrate rational-adequacy-for-all-practical-purposes of their procedures and findings. (Garfinkel, 1967: 8)

Reflexive accounting practices make the routine activities of everyday life recognisable as familiar, commonplace activities. Every repetition of common sense is misrecognised as 'another first time'.

Everyday life is an unending practical, artful achievement (Garfinkel, 1967: 32). Garfinkel did not develop a 'cognitive sociology', as is sometimes assumed (Cicourel 1973), where reality is ordered by mental concepts, but returned sociology to the phenomenological project of unsettling empirical accounts that defamiliarise the familiar. Subjective imagination is inseparable from the interpersonal accounts that accomplish factual and immediate objectivity. In other words, an accomplished accountability is skilfully produced even though the rules are known only vaguely, tacitly, and unaccountably (Garfinkel, 1967: 10). Rules are made to work by the 'et cetera principle', a shortcut for 'burying monsters' when routine expectations are confounded: 'practices of etc., let it pass, pretense of agreeing, the use of sanctioned vagueness, the waiting for something later to happen which promises to clarify what has gone before, the avoidance of monsters even when they occur and the borrowing of exceptions' (Garfinkel, in Heritage, 1984: 125–6).

Rules embedded in social practices cannot be grasped by a formal theory but only by ongoing, open-ended exploration. Garfinkel temporarily dispelled familiar routines and made the social world strange by causing some kind of unaccountable disruption that would 'produce and sustain bewilderment, consternation, and confusion; to produce the socially structured affects of anxiety, shame, guilt and indignation; and to produce disorganized interaction should tell us something about how the structures of everyday activities are ordinarily and routinely produced and maintained' (1967: 38). Garfinkel's pedagogical use of the famous 'breaching experiments' counter-intuitively opened up to students the intelligible social order of daily life. For instance, when young students were asked to deliberately behave like lodgers in the family home, routine assumptions about domestic life were disrupted and forced into the open (1967: 47).

In this way, Garfinkel attempted to move beyond micro–macro dichotomies and to demonstrate empirically that social order was inseparable from local inter-action as a matter of practices and not primarily as individual interpretations or conceptual representations (Heritage, 1984). In everyday life, people are neither passive 'judgemental dopes' nor are they constantly self-reflexive about everyday experience. Garfinkel reacted against the tendency in formal social theory to view the social order as an inevitable outcome of interaction, diminishing the flexibility and improvisations of situated common sense as inconsequential epiphenomena (1967: 68). Common sense acts as a rule of thumb that allows people to navigate different and novel situations. So even when the social world is disrupted or made strange in some way, Garfinkel's subjects worked to 'normalise' the situation by drawing on trusted common-sense assumptions to explain away any discrepancy, while in other cases, such as the breaching experiments, social relations faced complete breakdown under a strong sense of incomprehension, anger, and shame at an inexplicable violation of social bonds.

Garfinkel (1967: 78) adapted Mannheim's 'documentary method of interpre-tation' to uncover the underlying pattern of social order given the wide diversity of local practices. Each observation of interaction stands in as 'the document' of the presumed underlying pattern. Everyday life, like formal theory, justifies prac-tices by the documentary method of common sense that retrospectively mobilises a conceptual order to brush over the contingent details of situations. In both theory and common sense the phenomenon itself gets lost under the demands for conceptual order. Any discrepancies result in the underlying documentary pattern being given the benefit of the doubt over any appearances to the contrary.

SPEECH RULES

Garfinkel's 'cognitive revolution' depended on a non-representational theory of language use. The meaning of words is not fixed to the object to which it refers but is indexical to the context of its use. Indexicality is constitutive of practical reason. This means that the concrete utterance is part of the context rather than some ideal point outside it. Speakers embed their utterances to its context by using indexical, or *deictic*, terms like 'this', 'that', 'you', 'them', 'they', 'us', 'near', 'far', 'soon', 'late', and so on. Relying on unstated assumptions about shared background knowledge, *deixis* makes the process of communication more economical and precise (Garfinkel, 1967: 153). *Deixis*, from the Greek for 'pointing', anchors meaning to the context of time and place. One example of this is where the definite article allows media texts to assume an in-group 'we' when daily banal talk about '*the* weather' assumes that the hearer will also take for granted the naturalised national context for the weather of '*our* national homeland' (Billig, 1995). It is not only that there is an agreement between speaker and audience about the meaning of terms like 'country', 'nation', 'America', but that it also depends on a tacit method of common-sense procedures for arriving at situational understanding (or incomprehension).

Buoyed by 'the linguistic turn' in social science, ethnomethodology provided the original basis for 'conversational analysis', which became an established scientific method in various fields (Silverman, 1998). Its premises were originally established by Garfinkel's collaborator Harvey Sacks (1995) as the analysis of context-dependent social competencies in verbal interaction. For conversations to succeed there must be an underlying method that structures competence and mutual obligations which all participants must observe. Even the most banal conversation shines a light on how social order is produced just as much, or even more so, than analysis of large-scale institutional structures. As formal descriptions of methodical interactions in specific contexts, conversation was thought to provide a laboratory for the 'natural' observation of how elementary social order is produced. Analysis of ordinary conversations in their 'natural' situation reveals that they are structured by routinely ordered temporal sequences such as taking turns to speak, recognising cues, answering questions, interruptions, hesitations, and so on.

Sacks had a naive belief in the purity of observational description in science, which his collaborator Emmanuel Schegloff (b. 1937) attempted to secure by producing an account of the method used to produce an account of the observation, a problem that Neurath also tried to resolve using observational protocols. A key issue here is that accounting for accounts leads potentially into an infinite regress, as Michael Lynch argues: 'If reproducible methods depend on reproducible accounts of those methods, what accounts for the reproducibility of those accounts' (1993: 214). Methods accounts are a constitutive part of, and are only made possible by, what is being observed. An excessive technical focus on sequences of turn-taking within conversations may also drain analysis of its context. Clearly, as conversational analysis professionalised its instruments and aspired to context-free universal methods and empiricism it retreated from the interpretative project of ethnomethodology. Formalisation heralded a shift from the programmatic aims of ethnomethodology of accounts that almost anyone could recognise, despite Garfinkel's sometimes obtuse language, without any need for a formal theory and technical method of analysis.

TACIT KNOWLEDGE

Michael Polanyi's (1958) notion of 'tacit knowledge', a practical knowledge of how to do things that are difficult to fully communicate fully with words, has had a wide influence on areas like the sociology of science. Tacit knowledge is distinguished from 'explicit knowledge', though the two are clearly interrelated. This shares some family resemblances with the situated reflexivity of Garfinkel. Polanyi (1958) gave the famous example of being able to ride a bicycle without being able to give an explicit account of the rules for bike-riding.

In the sociology of science, explicitly codified knowledge was once assumed to be universal and foundational. Now there is a greater understanding that science transmits knowledge not only through explicit instruction but also interpersonally through tactile bodily example. Science is made to work through routine verbal and physical interactions rather than only by elaborate scientific schemas.

Harry Collins (2010) argues that rather than explicit knowledge being dependent on tacit knowledge the reverse actually seems more plausible, logically and empirically. Three forms of tacit knowledge are outlined by Collins. First, the weakest form of tacit knowledge Collins calls 'relational' in that it arises from a failure to communicate, perhaps for reasons of secrecy or forgetfulness; but this knowledge could in principle be made explicit at some point. Second, a medium form of tacit knowledge Collins describes as 'somatic', knowledge inscribed in the body, as in Polanyi's famous example of riding a bike without being able to describe the rules precisely. Third, the strongest form of tacit knowledge Collins calls 'collective' because it is deeply embedded in social relations, such as acquiring a first language or simply knowing the culturally specific social distance that needs to be observed when passing a stranger in the street or queuing for a bus.

Tacit knowledge is a long-term process for embedding social competencies in bodies until they become 'second nature'. Richard Sennett (2008) argues that the development of higher skills also depends on the translation of explicit knowledge into tacit knowledge and back again. As skills become more refined and exacting a constant interplay occurs between tacit knowledge anchored by the body and explicit knowledge as the critic of error. For higher skills to be embedded in the individual or the collective a slow accretion through the repetition of patient, disciplined practice is needed. Yet, Sennett argues, modern managerialism, frustrated at weak supervisory control over autonomous professions, insists on constant change, audits, targets, and staff performance systems as failing attempts to submit expert and craft tacit knowledge to explicit managerial knowledge and, therefore, external control. In the process, the steady concentration and disciplined practices needed to develop sophisticated, creative problem-solving capacities are continually disrupted and deflected.

PRAGMATISM

Perhaps only the American philosophy of pragmatism can rival the influence on social theory of the German philosophy of Kant and Hegel. Its influence ranges from the social psychology of George Herbert Mead, the symbolic interactionism of Herbert Blumer, the dramaturgy of Erving Goffman, the radical sociology of

C. Wright Mills, through to the more recent 'pragmatic turn' partly under the influence of the neo-pragmatism of Richard Rorty (1982) and the social theory of Richard J. Bernstein (1971, 2010). Although it is still roughly treated by more analytical approaches, in Europe, pragmatism has shaped the various social theories of Jurgen Habermas (1986), Luc Boltanski (2011), Hans Joas (1993, 1996), Axel Honneth (2008) and Patrick Baert (2005).

While pragmatism has different strands its main feature is that it rejects any absolute idea of truth in favour of more realistic concerns with plausible explanations that make sense of practice in concrete situations. Pragmatism aimed to put an end to the abstract dualisms of philosophical rationalism: body and mind, subject and object, structure and agency. Far from being a theory of expediency, as is often supposed, pragmatism had an ethical and political significance.

Charles Sanders Peirce (1839–1914) is credited with founding pragmatism as a modern philosophical tendency (Rochberg-Halton, 1986). For Peirce science provided a model for pragmatism in the need to demonstrate the practical relevance, clarity, and plausibility of theoretical concepts. Peirce also developed a semiotic theory that emphasised the constant reinterpretation of reality through changing sequences of signs. Theory therefore cannot take some ideal point as its datum but must begin from where it is and allow erroneous theories to be corrected by a self-critical community of scientists.

Despite disagreements, Peirce's ideas were popularised by William James (1842–1910) with his 1907 book *Pragmatism: A New Name for Some Old Ways of Thinking* (1975). For James experience does not arrive in discrete chunks but is present only as a continuous flow that cognition creatively organises. Pragmatism, in James' view, is distinguished above all by its focus on 'the concrete way of seeing' (2002: 216). In James' version of epistemological realism, statements must be considered true when they correspond with individual beliefs acquired over time (Kloppenberg, 1996). James assumed that reality exists independently of ordinary social experience but was not troubled to try to justify his realism, leading critics like Durkheim to claim that pragmatism reduced reality to whatever was thought about it.

Pragmatism supports an active, not a passive, theory of knowledge. The radical pragmatist philosopher John Dewey (1859–1952) was critical of what he famously called 'the spectator theory of knowledge' (Dewey, 1929: 23). For Dewey a personal commitment to scientific theory and values has personal, ethical, and political implications. Science, so often viewed as the enemy of ethics today, promotes democratic and independent critical inquiry guided by ethical concerns for truth. For Dewey's conception of radical democracy, ends and means are always interdependent (Bernstein, 2010). Trotsky was famously criticised by Dewey (1973) for being prepared to use any means necessary to achieve the end goal of socialist democracy deduced from so-called laws of development. No end can be an absolute ideal in itself just as no means can be entirely instrumental. Yet that does not result for Dewey in a cynical justification of abandoning all firm principles. If means and ends are interrelated, then the means will always have a direct relationship to the end.

DURKHEIM'S CRITIQUE

In 1913–14 Durkheim (1983) gave a lecture course on the then-fashionable philosophy of pragmatism. Positively, Durkheim recognised that by making human values incarnate in the world, pragmatism gives meaning to action. Like sociology, pragmatism understands that knowledge is relative to changing human conditions. However, while the pragmatists were right to challenge dogmatic forms of rationalism and empiricism, Durkheim saw the pragmatism of James in particular as a form of 'irrationalism'. Durkheim conceived pragmatism both as a 'radical empiricism' and a 'logical utilitarianism' where all ideals and values, from truth to God, are reduced to mere objects of experience. Durkheim attributed to James' theory of 'logical utilitarianism' the sole principle of expediency where only 'the useful is true' (Durkheim, 1983: 72).

Durkheim read pragmatism as a rigid form of 'relativism'. It encourages an intellectual free-for-all where anything goes since no one can dispute the truth and utility of anybody else in a different situation. Durkheim was concerned about what has been termed 'intellectual anomie' where truth is subjected to insufficient levels of regulation (Allcock, in Durkheim, 1983: xxxvii). Reality is reduced to individual sensibilities by pragmatism where for Durkheim truth and reality are produced collectively as independent social facts. Action and thought cannot be conflated, as pragmatism assumes. For instance, for a performing musician or footballer thought is dependent on embodied practice. Mistakes will be made if they start to think too self-consciously about what they are doing (1983: 73). On the other hand, the conscientious intellectual puts disembodied thought before practice and often prevaricates rather than take decisive action (1983: 80).

Pragmatism, therefore, lacked a sociological theory of collective representation to establish whether truth claims conform to reality. Truth is a norm for theory in the same way that morality is a norm for conduct (1983: 98). From Durkheim's Kantian perspective, collective representations do not somehow reflect objects but impose reality on them (1983: 173). In science, individual intellects serve an impersonal scientific synthesis and are also tempered by it. In society, representations prove acceptable to individuals because they respond to things in reality, although they are not a mere 'copy' of reality. Ideas have value in so far as they do not simply reflect reality or adapt to situations but contribute to the construction of a future reality. Social action cannot wait indefinitely until scientific theory has solved all problems, as even Comte understood.

Durkheim was worried that pragmatism would have a corrupting effect on rationalism and, therefore, on French culture as a whole. Its empiricism, he claimed, was wholly abstract and lacked empirical anchors. According to Mauss, Durkheim was more sympathetic to Dewey than James (Fournier, 2013: 649). Yet Durkheim has also been accused of misrepresenting pragmatism, by Dewey in particular (Joas, 1993: 59). As Hans Joas (1993: 71) notes, far from being a form of 'logical utilitarianism' pragmatism is deeply critical of the Cartesian mind–body split that underpins utilitarianism. Indeed, by separating thought and action, and individual and society, in his model of 'homo duplex', Durkheim sailed pretty close to the Cartesian dualism himself. It is important to note, however, that Durkheim's lectures were as much a defence of his own theory of the truth content of collective representations as they were a balanced survey of pragmatism itself (Meštrović, 1988). He did not deny the need for theory to be oriented to practice but objected to what he saw as a misplaced attack on truth and representation.

G.H. MEAD AND SOCIAL PSYCHOLOGY

Although he drew out the implications of pragmatism for a particular kind of social theory, George Herbert Mead (1863–1931) began to identify himself as a pragmatist only relatively late in his career (Joas, 1985). Like James and Dewey, for Mead the radical democracy engendered by science and rationality is the key to the process of social reform. Although Mead was steeped in the critique of rationalism in German philosophy, he was committed to the natural sciences as a source of reason and freedom, and distanced his theory of truth from James' attempt to reduce it to immediate usefulness.

Unlike the German philosopher Wilhelm Dilthey (1833–1911), Mead viewed personality not as something inherent to individuals but as shaped profoundly by social interaction. While Mead (1964: 292) dissented from Comte's dismissal of psychology, he recognised that Comte rightly made the individual dependent on society as the starting point of a human science that advances 'from the study of society to the individual rather than from the individual to society'.

Mead's is a theory of the social formation of the self through symbols. Individuals learn actively in the process of surviving in a specific environment. Symbols allow individuals to begin to see the world through the eyes of others and how they might perceive and respond to communication. Some symbols are more significant for individuals than others. Like his contemporary Charles Horton Cooley (1864–1929), Mead allowed a role for the imagination to interpret social interaction. For Mead, however, Cooley's idea of 'the looking glass self' relied on an overly subjective form of imagination and needed also to include the objective side of the imagination. Individuals do not interact just as they please but in an organised social environment (Mead, 1964: 244).

Only through symbols can things take on meaning and discipline social action. Meaning is not something fixed in the consciousness of individual. A social process of communication occurs in every gesture as a 'significant symbol' and a response that was anticipated by the initial gesture, verbal or physical. Only if the response is imagined as appropriate to the original gesture can the communication process be understood as properly social in character. Social psychology needs to account for both inner experience and outer expression starting from observable activity: 'the act, then, and not the tract, is the fundamental datum' (Mead, 1964: 122).

Mead's theory of the social self is developmental. Children, he asserts, develop from one kind of activity, 'play', to another, 'games'. At the play stage, children play out all the roles of an imagined interaction of gesture and response. At the game stage, children are conscious that others have roles in orderly, rule-bound social interaction. An organised social group provides an individual with a 'unity of self' that Mead terms 'the generalised other': 'in the case of such a social group as a ball team, the team is the generalised other in so far as it enters – as an organized process or social activity – into the experience of any one of the individual members of it' (Mead, 1934: 154).

Not unlike Freud's internally divided model of the psyche or Durkheim's 'homo duplex', Mead famously split the self into two parts: the 'I' and the 'me'. Because the self takes the form of unified social process these are two phases of the same development. The 'I' represents the immediate, uncertain and creative response while the 'me', represents self-conscious control, responsibility and reflexivity (Mead, 1964: 238). A greater sense of individuality is made possible in modern societies. Here the 'I' predominates over the 'me' in contrast to earlier societies where the controlled 'me', prevailed over the creative 'I'. Mead's evolution of the self therefore rests on a questionable assumption when so much social theory, from Elias to Foucault to Beck and Giddens, plots the reverse process where creative individuality of the 'I' is subordinated to the reflexive discipline and self-restraint of the 'me'.

With the accent specifically on human creativity, Mead has been more recently charged with an anthropocentric theory of social learning. Humans communicate by symbols that isolate and recombine elements as a self-conscious thought process rather than the practical trial and error that Mead attributed to animals. Animals may cluck, bark, or howl but, Mead (1934: 139) assumed that, such instinctive communication is directed to others not to the self. Approaches that restrict selfhood to humans and exclude animals have been challenged more recently by the emerging field of animal sociology, which often holds Mead responsible for the animal–human rift in sociology (Wilkie and McKinnon, 2013).

Although Mead is often classified as a 'symbolic interactionist' the term was only later put into circulation by Herbert Blumer (1986). As independent individuals interact, meaning emerges from the independent interpretations that each attaches to symbols. For instance, as a symbol a tree means different things to a botanist, lumberjack or poet (Blumer, 1986: 69). While symbolic interactionism takes inspiration from Mead it does so selectively. It reduces action to interaction; it grounds perception and meaning in verbal consensus about definitions rather than inter-subjective praxis and it neglects longer-term historical processes (Joas, 1985: 7).

PRAGMATIC TURN

C. Wright Mills admired the pragmatists because they attempted to relate theory to practice. Mills' (1964) dissertation analyses how the leading Pragmatists were able to take responsibility as public intellectuals for the body politic. He was influenced by Mead at an early stage, although Mead was surprisingly absent from his dissertation on sociology and pragmatism, an omission that Mills retrospectively deemed 'intellectually unwarranted'. While he deals mainly with the theoretical relevance of Peirce, James, and Dewey for sociology, Mead contributed the biographical perspective to the other two elements of history and social structure in Mill's (2000) famous Erinity of the 'sociological imagination'.

Mills showed how pragmatism responded to the changed social structure and new publics that emerged in America after the Civil War. Seeing the fields of science, logic, and philosophy as distinct from the need for public certainty and practical solutions, Peirce was marginal to the popularisation of pragmatism. Yet, Mills (1964: 207) argued, the piety of a self-critical community of scientists provided Peirce with a critical detachment 'against any contamination of theory by practice', contrary to Durkheim's sweeping claims about 'logical utilitarianism'. Peirce defended what he called 'critical common-sensism' against the uncritical Scottish common-sense philosophy that he saw as justifying the self-interested ethics of Protestant bourgeois individualism (1964: 203).

In contrast to Peirce's reticence about public engagement, James threw himself into proselytising for pragmatism. From his relativist perspective James was able to accommodate the needs of different publics. After all, even the most refined theoretical systems cannot agree with each other. Mills saw James as a 'modern liberal' typical of the realism of a class of intellectuals and professionals always ready to adapt positively to reality, in contrast to the defiance needed to remake the world represented by the 'old middle class' of Weber's Puritan ideal-type (1964: 242). Yet, James' individualism also inoculated him against state-sponsored imperialism and militarism, which naturally endeared him to Mills' later opposition to 'Yankee imperialism'.

By far the longest and most detailed account Mills gives is that of John Dewey. Dewey (2012) identified a new public in education with the expansion of the school system and the professionalisation of teaching. Dewey's theory offered the prospect of autonomous, self-constituting publics modelled on small-scale rural communities of small farmers and tradesmen. In the 1920s this world was already being swept away by the rise of big corporations, bureaucracy and urbanisation. Dewey rather nostalgically hoped that the education of publics would revive civic action and democratic participation, and clung on to an outdated idea of 'the social' as *Gemeinschaft* of local face-to-face interdependencies as a protest against the growing 'alienation' of corporate capitalism. As Mills commented, 'It is not accidental that his stress upon it occurs in a cultural context which is beginning to deny in fact an individualistically organized society, yet a society in which individualism and independence are a dominant ideology' (1964: 443).

Like Mills, Bernstein (1971: 199) invokes pragmatism to propose a self-critical community of socially oriented inquiry as an antidote to the scholasticism of what Bernstein (2010: 26) calls the 'analytical ideology' found in the latest 'respectable' philosophical journals. With the political struggles of the 1960s in the US, Dewey's arguments for radical democracy and autonomy found a new resonance (Bernstein, 1976). Bernstein experienced 'deja vu all over again' when he found the themes of the much-derided pragmatists resurfacing in new guises, finding echoes of Peirce in the analytical philosophy of Wilfrid Sellars; Dewey's democracy in the political philosophy of Hannah Arendt; or Dewey's concept of experience in Hans-Georg Gadamer's hermeneutics.

Habermas more openly embraces pragmatism as a radical theory of modernity, though he remains entangled in the rigid Kantian separation of theoretical knowledge and practical knowledge. Even the modish appeal of post-modernism's promise to kick away all theoretical foundations and certainties rehearsed certain pragmatic themes in a new, more self-consciously dramatic style. Pragmatism's project of making radical democracy, collective self-critique, and pluralism a reality in everyday life, Bernstein concedes, underestimated the power of the forces moving in the opposite direction in periods of crisis.

Against the abstract rationalism of much social theory, caught up in the sterile structure-agency bind, Hans Joas (1996) recently developed a social theory of creative action based on pragmatism, as well as Simmel and Nietzsche. Drawing on the four major representatives of pragmatism, Peirce, James, Dewey, and Mead, Joas locates creativity, not in the pathos of the individual genius, but within the emergent situations and demands of everyday life (Joas, 1996: 4–5). First, Peirce attempted to restore the idea of creativity as part of the logic of science, and to address how something new might emerge in nature. Second, James struggled to establish a place for free will against natural and religious constraints as crucial to human survival. Third, Dewey's artistic theory of human experience explored the meaningfulness of action itself. Finally, Mead's theory rejected any idea of the self as a substantialist, pre-given entity for an image of selfhood as an emergent property of individual action.

One problem for social theory today is that it typically operates with two categories of action: rational action and normative action. This, Joas (1996) argues, badly needs supplementing by a third type, creative action, in order to avoid impoverished accounts of human agency. Action is orientated creatively to the situation in which it occurs rather than to some distant ideal. However, Joas contends, social theory has failed to integrate creativity as concretely situated practice rather than as an abstractly conceived category of rational action. This is now felt as a pressing need as social and technological change opens up possibilities for a widespread culture of creativity that potentially enables individuals to imaginatively pursue their own projects.

What is needed is to specify creative practice as situated, and embodied. First, action is not orientated to some distant teleological goal but intentionality occurs in concrete situations. Second, with echoes of Merleau-Ponty, the body is more than an instrumental means; body control is relaxed as soon as we are removed from a public situation. Third, intentionality is premised on the situated interaction of social bodies. Not unlike Dewey, for Joas a substantive theory of situated creativity potentially deepens democratic political action currently weakened by one-sided instrumental power games.

FRAME THEORY

A major figure usually filed under 'symbolic interaction' is Erving Goffman (1922–1982), even though he point-blank refused to join that club. Neither did he see himself particularly as a 'theorist' since he aimed to produce empirically rich studies (Burns, 1999). Goffman was concerned with 'social interaction' as the following of rules and rituals that all human cultures are endowed with but that specific societies shape in particular ways. Interactions are dramatic social encounters. In *The Presentation of Self in Everyday Life*, Goffman (1959) drew his famous dramaturgical analogy with the theatre. Interactions become performances which individuals prepare 'backstage' for so that they can better manage impressions when they are 'frontstage' before an audience. In public interactions individuals put on a personal 'front' of demeanour, clothes, posture, and so on. Stretching the analogy to credulity, many critics have argued that the role-playing dramaturgy soon becomes threadbare where it neglects the structuring of social life by large-scale institutions and systems.

Goffman's (1986) most ambitious attempt to isolate a social theory in his studies was the obtuse and unwieldy *Frame Analysis*. Here Goffman drew from phenomenology and pragmatism to construct a social psychology of how perception frames and discriminates between things in everyday life. A picture frame focusses attention on the image inside from everything else outside it, as Georg Simmel (1994) explained. Goffman aimed to uncover how things are routinely taken to be real as attention becomes focussed through what W.I. Thomas (2002) famously called the 'definition of the situation'. Selfhood is not some hidden essence of personality 'but a changeable formula for managing oneself [in different situations]' (Goffman, 1986: 573). Following Gregory Bateson (1972), situations are perceived through 'primary frameworks'. These are formed by accumulated understandings from previous situations that stamp the current situation as manageable and recognisable.

If individuals find it funny when others fail to live up to the primary framework, then this suggests to Goffman (1986: 39) that everybody and everything are, all the time, being actively evaluated by the operation of the frame of reference. Ordinarily, a correspondence or 'isomorphism' is assumed between perception and what is being perceived (1986: 26). However, primary social frameworks can be disturbed by 'natural' frameworks as in the loss of control over the body, like eye twitching. 'Gaffes', 'astounding' phenomena, fortuitous events, and seemingly impossible feats may also call into question the primary framework. A degree of flexibility allows frames to be switched, or 'keyed', in a different mode, as when fighting and aggression become the model for play in ways that everybody understands as non-violent, or further 're-keyed', as when a play is adapted for a film. A change of 'key' registers for everyone a change in what is going on (Goffman, 1986: 47).

Such frames operate at a remove from the primary frames. In cases where serious or literal meanings are suspended as in make-believe, competitive games, ceremonies, role-playing, and role-switching, frames are keyed and re-keyed until each layer reaches the edge of an isomorphic reality at 'the rim of the frame' (1986: 82). Such switching of frames also opens up layers of 'fabrication' that falsify, mislead, and deceive others kept outside the frame. For instance, innocent victims are 'framed' to shoulder the blame by the conscious construction of a falsified frame, albeit one seasoned with plausibility. To complicate matters further, Goffman expanded at length on the multiple ways that keys become fabrications and vice versa, as in acts of legitimated duplicity like state surveillance, layer upon layer, until the basis of primary frames in mutual trust is jeopardised by an atmosphere of mutual suspicion.

Although Goffman's approach has been widely criticised on a number of grounds, frame analysis has also been taken up by a disparate range of areas, often without Goffman's ascending levels of complex elaboration. In media studies, frame analysis is often reduced to a matter of how stories define public issues and political issues. In the study of protest movements the study of frames has proliferated to show how problems, demands, and action are constructed by movement leaders and the degree to which they correspond or 'align' with those populations that they wish to mobilise (Benford and Snow, 2000).

Frames organise narratives in specific ways to 'define problems, diagnose causes, make moral judgments, and suggest remedies', as in the case of the ideological justification for the 'war on terror' (Kuypers, 2009: 8). In *Frames of War*, Judith Butler (2009) used framing in a more abstract way to uncover the epistemological codes through which the lives of others are apprehended or denied. Frames constitute subjects by establishing normative schemes that 'recognise' some people as fully human, deserving of our empathy, but find others more difficult to comprehend. Butler refines the frame of 'recognition' with two further terms. First, 'apprehension' is a way of knowing that falls short of recognition and, second, intelligibility is a general historical schema that establishes what is knowable. For a life to be recognised it has to meet certain conceptions of what life is (intelligibility). Yet historical schemas of life and death vary considerably. For instance, there is extensive scope for dispute over the status of the fetus as a recognisably human life, or whether death is defined by the brain or heart failure or medical and legal certificates (Boltanski, 2013).

Such disputes do not mean that life and death are decided purely by discourse, something Butler (2009: 7) considers an 'absurd' conclusion, but that 'there is no life and no death without a relation to some frame'. While frames determine the value of what can be recognised, they threaten to escape and circulate beyond its intended context, as when prisoner poetry from Guantanamo Bay or torture photographs from Abu Ghraib prison in Iraq were put into circulation and reproduced in many different contexts: 'What is taken for granted in one instance becomes thematized critically or even incredulously in another' (2009: 10). Outrage and shock induced by the broken frame exposes what could not be apprehended before – our inability to see what we see – in this case, the framing of the 'war on terror' in such ways that we 'mourn for some lives but respond with coldness to the loss of others' (2009: 36).

CORPOREAL FEMINISM

What has been called 'corporeal feminism' (Grosz, 2004) brought concerns with the material effects of gendered bodies to the centre of social theory. A wide range of feminist theory examines the matter of bodies, drawing on phenomenology and post-structuralism, ranging from Merleau-Ponty to Foucault, with a sprinkling of psychoanalysis (Howson, 2005). In her *Bodies That Matter*, Judith Butler (1993) locates the materiality of the body within discourses that impose regulatory norms of heterosexuality. Bodies are not simply anatomy or biology but are the subjects of discursive power. Not only gender but sex too is socially constructed. Any return to the physical matter of bodies must also be a return to discourses that impinge on matter. Gender is enacted through the 'performativity' of discourses that confer a binding power on the action performed. Performativity captures something of how power is constituted in a way that is neglected by Goffman's dramaturgy.

As well as the bodies that matter there are the bodies that don't, marginalised by heterosexual norms. If sexuality is a social construct, then once-derogatory terms like 'queer' can be reappropriated as a positive denominator and bring into view other forms of sexuality, challenging normative heterosexuality. Butler's 'queer theory' has generated considerable debate within feminist social theory. Materiality tends to be reduced to discourses, as in Butler's (1990) example of drag performances as a material practice determined by a 'heterosexual matrix' of normative discourse. This leads into the criticism raised against much post-structuralism that substantive embodied practices are reduced to the effects of textual practices (Hughes and Witz, 2004: 201).

Iris Marion Young (2005) further develops the phenomenological approach to the experience of the lived body in everyday life to take account of how it is affected by gender. In terms of ordinary purposeful orientation of the body, Young claims that women are denied the autonomy and creativity that define what it is to be human, and which men enjoy automatically (2005: 31). She famously described the different ways that boys and girls use their bodies while throwing a ball. While boys put their whole body into throwing, girls limit their movement to the arms. This example indicates that women do not exercise their full embodied subjectivity. When women sit, walk, stand, run, or carry books, bodily comportment and motility is restricted. Relative to men, women's spatial and lateral potential is reduced by what Young calls an 'inhibited intentionality' where body subjectivity is subordinate to objectivity. In existential language borrowed from Simone de Beauvoir, immanence fails to be realised as transcendence. From early on girls tend to see their own bodies as objects that inhibit them from extending into the world, a defensive process of internalisation reinforced throughout the lives of women by the everyday male gaze.

Young recognises that the instrumental task of learning a new sport (which she selected to compare female and male physicality) neglected the many other body tasks that women perform routinely. Moreover, Young relegates the social context of body comportment and tends to locate the 'problem' in the consciousness of individual women. Women are concerned about how their bodies are seen by others where social judgements function as a constant mirror, watching others watching herself (Berger, 1972; Weiss, 1999). In a reflexive note, Young (1998) accepted some of the limitations of her original analysis and recognised significant social and cultural changes twenty years later, although women's bodies are still objectified. It should also be remembered that pioneers in social theory do not have the benefit of decades of subsequent critique and later developments.

Feminists like Young have pointed to a further lacuna in theories of everyday life – the assumption that public space is the action zone of modernity. In important respects, as feminists argue, the home more than the street establishes the zero-point of everyday life. For instance, Rita Felski (2000) challenges the view that women's daily life, centred on the routines of home-making, is antithetical to the transcendental experience of 'authentic modernity', which is to say, street-centred, fleeting, temporary, and transient. She argues that everyday life brings together experience (habits), time (repetition), and space (street and home) in ways that produce security, predictability, and control that make other experiences possible. Women are thought by 'malestream' social theory to be trapped in cyclical rhythms of the everyday for essentially biological reasons, social reproduction in the home, and consumer fashions.

STANDPOINT THEORY

In the *Everyday World as Problematic*, Dorothy Smith (1987) advanced a sociology *for* women known as 'standpoint theory'. Standpoint because feminist theory addresses everyday life from the perspective of women in society. The standpoint referred to is not that of a pre-existing ideological project that sets out to universalise the experience of oppression and disadvantage. Standpoint theory aims to preserve the active presence of women as knowledgeable and creative subjects of sociological theory. Smith argues that this is less a 'theory', if by that is meant formal explanations, than a 'method of thinking' about how to write sociologically in order to make the social relations of women visible as subjects. Smith (1987: 106) recognises that the real subject – women – exists outside texts, but also that sociological texts have an indexical relationship in the self-recognition of women readers. Traditionally excluded by a male-centred, or androcentric, 'ruling apparatus' of cultural production, women are in an ideal position to complete the meaning of sociological texts produced by other women from their particular perspective in social space.

Lacking a 'public language', feminist standpoint theory grounded itself in women's experience outside of institutional knowledge. This had some parallels with Lukacs' (1971) Marxist standpoint theory that privileged proletarian knowledge from the vantage point of the ideal position of the exploited class within the relations of production. But whereas Lukacs premised proletarian self-knowledge on their strategic or privileged position within the production process, feminists like Sandra Harding (1986: 91) argued that women understand power relations better than their male masters because of their marginal situation in everyday life. Feminist social theory therefore rejects 'malestream' scientific empiricism. It concentrates upon the 'context of justification', that is, testing hypotheses and explaining evidence, rather than the 'context of discovery', that is, how research problems are derived from and defined by lived practices and unequal power to define reality (1986: 25).

If women's 'experience' cannot be reduced to that of a single subject position, then the concept 'woman', like 'proletariat' or 'black', must be a political one rather than a unified theoretical concept that reflects an existing reality. Recognition of this led Smith (2005) to refuse to identify 'women' in terms of a socially determined position in society in favour of creating a theoretical 'subject position' as an aid to researching women's everyday lives. What Smith calls 'institutional ethnography' discovers how the social in its widest sense organises women's lives and experiences. The aim is to locate personal experience of actual women in wider relations of power – the 'ruling relations': 'that extraordinary yet ordinary complex of relations that are textually mediated, that connect and organize our everyday lives – the corporations, government bureaucracies, academic and professional discourses, mass media, and the complex of relations that interconnect them' (2005: 10).

Ruling forms of consciousness and organisation emerged in the late nineteenth century from the administrative controls of large-scale bureaucratic corporations that were constituted beyond particular people and places. Knowledge is not the result of the intended consciousness of individuals but of the pre-verbal, impersonal regulation of discourse, as described by Foucault. The extension of the ruling relations into every nook and cranny of everyday life created contradictory situations for women, particularly middle-class women, Smith (2005: 19) claims. On one side, the trans-local power of the ruling relations displaced the domestic sphere as a site of middle-class gender relations, while on the other side, middle-class women entered higher education, mainly to study the humanities and social sciences.

Sociology is therefore part of a middle-class and male ruling apparatus that discounted the existing knowledge of women, the working class, and racial minorities (Smith, 1990). Its subject matter and evidence too often relies on and gives succour to the ideological constructions of the relations of ruling – crime, mental illness, violence, riots, neighbourhoods, education, work, and so on. And its procedure turns the subjects of sociological texts into objects of analysis. Feminist standpoint theory suggests two unequal ways of knowing: institutional and experiential. As a dominated subject position, the concrete, embodied experience of women is forced to adapt to the abstract worldview of dominant institutions.

This subordination of women's concrete experience to the ruling relations produces what Smith (1987) calls a 'bifurcation of consciousness'. Smith's own dual world experience – as an academic and as a single parent – shaped her critical standpoint to the male-centred assumptions of institutional sociology. Her academic subjectivity relied upon the disembodied relations of administration by texts divorced from the particular relationships of motherhood and home. On one side, pragmatic relations of practical consciousness, and on the other side, the codified relations of theoretical consciousness. This reproduces the traditional split in philosophy between body and mind of the Cartesian subject that feminist sociology aims to transcend.

A distinction is made by Smith (1987) between norms and social relations in order to get beyond directly observed behaviour of following norms and examine how wider social relations constrain and condition local practices. For instance, the very language used to describe local interaction in everyday life is also formed by social relations not immediately present at the scene of the action (1987: 176).

To examine everyday life as 'problematic' ought not, therefore, restrict sociological analysis to local situations only. A phenomenological exploration of the lifeworld needs to be situated within a wider analysis of institutional structures coupled with an engaged moral and political critique. Difficulties of generalising from localised studies are overcome if they are understood less as unique 'case' studies than points of entry into wider social processes. At the most general level, abstract social relations, for instance the social division of labour, condition the most local, particular experiences.

An alternative to standpoint theory is 'post-modern feminism'. Post-modernism makes a virtue out of the fragmentation of knowledge, narrative construction, and historically relative, specific, and contingent contexts (Hekman, 1990). Here the lived experience privileged by standpoint theory possesses no inherent capacity to disrupt the ruling relations, a category that merely establishes another a-priori grand narrative to flatten local and particular subjectivities. Post-modern feminism questions the possibility of arriving at objective and universally valid feminist knowledge given the diversity of women's experience. If, as feminist standpoint theory assumes, authentic knowledge is available to oppressed groups on the grounds of marginalised experience, then some women are more powerless than others, on the grounds of class, race, sexuality, able-bodied, age, and colonialism. Women's self-knowledge will always be overlaid by the multiple sources of marginalisation circulating in public discourses.

CRITIQUE AND DEVELOPMENT

Some critics accuse phenomenology of being too abstractly theoretical, focussed on texts and indifferent to the material practices and structural power. For others, theory is eclipsed by an empiricism where ethnography or conversational analysis unlocks pre-theoretical accounts. Ideas about a pre-theoretical research field of material bodies or ordinary speech are not credible. Far from being a literal account of conversations, standardised orthographic representations of transcription are laden with theoretical assumptions about legibility (Atkinson, 1988). Conversations are not merely instances of empirical contingency but sequences, say of questions and answers, that conform to logical conventions. Accounts allow for a degree of improvisation and flexibility to bring order to the situation.

In contrast, post-modern feminism aims to undermine any appeal to a stable, knowable 'reality' as an anti-democratic attack on local, small-scale narratives of 'difference'. Here the crisis of modern social theory is welcomed as opening up other, hitherto-submerged narratives to creatively subvert male-dominated theory. One response has been the development of intersectional theory to address overlapping 'intersections' of domination and subjectivity as they emerged from 'critical race theory', especially critical legal theory and black feminist critiques of the assumptions of the experiences of white middle-class women as the basis for the standpoint of all women (Hill Collins, 1990). Gender, race, class, national identity, disability, and sexuality combine in numerous ways to produce multiple identities that operate to secure relations of domination and inferiority in different contexts (Yuval-Davis, 2011). While this approach promises a concrete analysis of mutually constitutive identities rather than reduction to an abstract ontological category of 'woman' or 'race' it also courts the risk of further theoretical and political fragmentation that re-describe rather than explain micro-differences of history and identity.

Yet the crisis of theoretical fragmentation is not the same thing as the crisis of social fragmentation. If everything is contingent, fragmented and localised, then how might a general explanation of gender inequality be constructed and a moral and political appeal for equality be formulated without some shared frame of reference about what might constitute explanatory adequacy (Holmwood, 1995)? Standpoint feminism is further concerned that if all knowledge is relative, particular, and contingent, then structured patterns of patriarchal authority that reproduce male power may well disappear from view. From the recognition of fragmentation and plurality of difference, not least by government agencies, it became possible for post-modern feminism to segue into a depoliticised 'post-feminism' in cultural theory and journalistic adaptations to neoliberal capitalism, individualised suffering, and the entitlements of victimhood (McRobbie, 2009).

This raises more general issues about social theory that ascribes an ideal standpoint to oppressed groups, which they too would recognise if only their interests could be separated from their actual position of domination, which has the effect of obscuring from them the ideal standpoint discovered by critical theory. Any position of relative powerlessness will have effects on how the dominated view their predicament, which will typically fall short of the scope and language of social theory. Social dispossession may also mean cognitive dispossession of adequate knowledge of dispossession (Bourdieu, 2001).

Generally, 'critique' means deconstructing the contradictory assumptions of social theory by demonstrating both its internal incoherence (logic) and its external blindspots (evidence). This demands expert knowledge of both social theory and social power beyond the situational descriptions of dominated groups. Marxist standpoint theory grants epistemological privilege to the proletariat but then explains the absence of class consciousness by ideology and cultural domination. Similarly, feminist standpoint theory also faces the difficulty that women as subjects may not recognise themselves in feminist explanations of their predicament (McRobbie, 2011). Mutual incomprehension presents a major difficulty for Smith's (1990) concern with 'primary narratives' that relate theory in terms explicable to subjects, in order to get beyond expert knowledge and validate women's lived experience.

The issues raised in contemporary feminist theory point to the recurring tension in social theory between science and critique. Ethnomethodology, for instance, refrains from judging the veracity or desirability of situated accounts but seeks to uncover how accounts are constructed. Pragmatism's interweaving of creativity and situation seemed to critical theory to provide grounds that it supported a conservative conformism to pre-given conditions. Pragmatism was seen as a servile, boot-licking theory, or as Mead (in Joas, 1985: 36) put it, condemned as 'the worship of success ... the contemptuous swagger of a glib and restless upstart in the company of the mighty', an efficiency engineer introduced to speed up the production of theories.

Pragmatism is mistakenly and repeatedly claimed to reduce (and justify) social action to the types of instrumental action that ideologically characterises 'the American way of life'. This prevented critical theory from seeing the parallels between pragmatism and praxis as theories of social action (Bernstein, 1971). Recent social theory has been at pains to spell out that, on the contrary, pragmatism advanced a sophisticated critique of the practical, can-do attitude of American culture (Joas 1996; Bernstein, 2010). Like praxis, pragmatism stresses the practical, experiential, and situated requirements of knowledge. Pragmatism and phenomenology threw down a challenge to all theories that claim to transcend human agency.

Although some may deny it, sociology, Alasdair MacIntyre (1981) argues, presupposes a moral philosophy. At the heart of Goffman's analysis is the idea that competent surface performances are their own measure of value: 'Goffman's world is empty of objective standards of achievement' (1981: 115). MacIntyre refers to this as 'emotivism', where all evaluative judgements – moral, political, or intellectual – are simply the expression of an attitude or feeling designed to have an effect on others, specifically to elicit agreement for action without the need for rational justification. Being well regarded because of a competent display of the self is the sole goal in Goffman's dramaturgical world without any objective criteria to award merit.

Not that Goffman is necessarily in the wrong or particularly cynical about social relations. It may well be the case that all there is to be honoured in the social world is the surface presentation of impression management. So while Goffman provides 'a perceptive account of forms of behaviour within a particular society which itself incorporates a moral philosophy in its characteristic modes of action and practice' he also reveals 'what human nature must be and therefore always has been' (Macintyre, 1981: 116–17). If social theory is emptied of historical, moral or comparative context, then the charge of uncritical conformism may well stick. Yet it is clear that, far from being uncritical apologists, phenomenology and pragmatism have generated some of the resources required for a critical theory of society today.

13

CULTURAL TURN: SOCIAL THEORY IN FRANCE AND BRITAIN

Under the double jeopardy of post-modern culture and neoliberal political economy, much social theory in the decades since the 1970s viewed the social world as increasingly emaciated and broken. In this perspective individuals appear to be increasingly closed off from each other in little privatised universes. As public culture atrophies, political cynicism becomes all-pervasive. This picture has been especially noticeable as the role of language and culture acquired greater significance in social theory than structured social relations and historical processes. Part of the context for this 'turn to culture' is widespread concern about the cultural and political effects of fragmentation, fluidity, speed, superficiality, identity, and contingency.

This chapter considers social theories that are concerned with cultural and political change. Its main focus is on developments in Britain and France. In both countries the influence of Marxism in social theory began to recede by the 1980s. This was hastened by new social theories and the rise of cultural studies as part of the process of leaving behind Marxism in crisis. In a period when 'post' was affixed to all out-of-date formations, 'post-Marxist' theory disposed of unfashionable theories of class and economic relations. Some, like Anthony Giddens, were never Marxists. Indeed, Giddens (1982; 1985) had been a particularly astute critic of Marxist theory in his two-volume *A Contemporary Critique of Historical Materialism*. Others began a long withdrawal from Marxism through concerns with cultural and political problems of autonomy, language, media, street cultures, and everyday life.

First, developments in French social theory are outlined. Here the influence of Henri Lefebvre's studies of everyday life continued to be felt in what was known as 'Situationism', in the work of Michel de Certeau, and in the hyperbolic critique of media culture by Jean Baudrillard. Currently, Cornélius Castoriadis' (1922–1997) philosophy of 'the social imaginary' is increasingly being recognised in the English-speaking world as an important contribution to social theory. As part of the splintering of Marxist theory in France, Castoriadis attempted to pose an alternative social theory to post-modernism and post-structuralism at a high level of abstraction and generality.

Following this, consideration is given to social theory in Britain. Although not an original theorist, Stuart Hall attempted to produce a theoretical synthesis indebted to the 'culturalism' of Gramsci and the structuralism of Althusser in order to understand the particular nature of the crisis in British society and politics. At a more abstract level, Anthony Giddens' idea of 'structuration' similarly tried to synthesise the poles of structure and agency. Finally, the Russian theorist Valentin Vološinov's (1973) dialogical theory of language is introduced. Dating from the 1920s, Vološinov proposed a phenomenology of the 'concrete utterance' that would enable social theory to grasp changes and tensions in social relations.

SITUATIONS AND SPECTACLES

Henri Lefebvre's erstwhile collaborators, the anti-art movement the Situationist International (1957–1972), longed to shatter the taken-for-granted assumptions of everyday life. For leading Situationist Guy Debord (1983), in his famous 1960s pamphlet, *Society of the Spectacle*, society now presents itself as an immense accumulation of 'spectacles', paraphrasing Marx's comment about society as an immense accumulation of commodities. Almost everything has become a representation. Debord located the spectacle in social relations:

> The spectacle is not a collection of images, but a social relation among people, mediated by images … it is the heart of the unrealism of the real society … reality rises up within the spectacle, and the spectacle is real. (1983: 4, 6, 8)

Later one of Lefebvre's other former collaborators, Jean Baudrillard, would claim that social relations were not so much mediated by images as obliterated by them. At that time, however, society still remained divided by the spectacle in terms similar to how Marx described the division and superiority of the state over civil society: 'In the spectacle, one part of the world *represents itself* to the world and is superior to it' (Debord, 1983: 29).

Developing Lefebvre's notion of 'moments' as forms of life, everyday life became for the Situationists the locale for 'situations': cultural-political interventions, outrages, provocations, confrontations, disruptions. Both sought to transform the hierarchies of social practice that place culture and politics above everyday life through an aesthetic and political critique and, vice versa, to critique art and politics by everyday life; and to critique the real by the possible and, vice versa, the possible by the real (Lefebvre, 2002: 19; Roberts, 2006; Ross, 1997). Lefebvre warmed to the 'lived utopianism' of the Situationists as a youthful avant-garde group testing out the art of the possible from a shared theoretical perspective, even if isolated artistic actions could never by themselves transform everyday life. In the end, Debord parted from Lefebvre for supposedly plagiarising the idea of the Paris Commune as a festival, although not before they had learned something from each other in their 'moment' of friendship and collaboration (McDonough, 2009: 168–79; Ross, 1997).

Shortly before the events of May 1968 the Situationist Raoul Vaneigem (1994), in a work translated as *The Revolution of Everyday Life*, developed Lefebvre's critique of everyday life as the sum of constraints. Bare survival is the result of a life preoccupied by consumption and working to consume. Survival in everyday life requires that passion, creativity, and spontaneity be renounced. Inauthentic survival through impersonal roles and stereotypes is counterposed by Vaneigem to 'authentic' lives, festivity, and genuine experience. Vaneigem imagined this poetically as a problem of 'lived immediacy', where a self-conscious individual might achieve a 'reversal of perspective' and slough off social conditioning: 'To reverse perspective is to stop seeing things through the eyes of the community, of ideology, of the family, of other people. To grasp hold of oneself as of something solid, to take oneself as starting point and centre' (1994: 188). Such appeals to an 'authenic' individuality ran the risk of recuperation by the solipsistic ideology of neoliberal consumerism.

TACTICS AND STRATEGIES

A more positive assessment of everyday life was provided by Michel de Certeau's (1984) *The Practice of Everyday Life*. De Certeau was at pains to theorise microforms of resistance to cultural domination in order to challenge what he viewed as the crude verities of critical theory's analysis of 'mass culture' (Rigby, 1991). Instead of deducing cultural practices from the totality of commodification, de Certeau was more concerned with routine ways of doing things at the micro-level. Practices have their own 'logic' that subverts dominant cultural narratives as social bodies wander through the subterranean depths of the everyday and make themselves known to each other.

Consumption is mediated by inversions that can only be understood in the context of specific *uses* and *ruses*: 'ruses, fragmentation (the result of circumstances), its poaching, its clandestine nature, its tireless but quiet activity, in short by its quasi-invisibility, since it shows itself not in its own products … but in an art of using those imposed on it' (de Certeau, 1984: 31). Cultural products – books, films, sports, and so on – are appropriated selectively for whatever might be found useful in them from the tactical position of the reader or viewer. The point is that cultural objects are never simply swallowed whole, 'literally', as intended by cultural producers (de Certeau, 1984: 171). There is an active process of mediation and interpretation through concrete uses that cannot be gainsaid in advance by social theory or the culture industry itself.

For de Certeau radical social theory should legitimise popular uses of cultural objects and texts rather than denigrate and denounce them in advance as insensible, alienated and passive objects. To do this it needs to distinguish between *the place of strategy* and *the time of tactics*. A strategy involves the visible calculations of institutional control over physical and theoretical resources and places, as in economic competition, output targets, political conflict, group rivalry, or research 'objects'. A tactic, on the other hand, has no specific place but operates within restricted time-frames. Tactics involve taking opportunities and seizing chances as they arise. Everyday life is an 'art of war' caught between two forms of struggle, depending on whether groups wager on place or on time. Tactics are always mobile, decision-making episodes. Everyday practices are typically tactical in nature rather than strategic – talking, walking, shopping, eating, cooking, reading, wit, jokes, ruses, trickery, and so on – little moments of resistance practised by the weakly positioned.

SIMULACRUM

Lefebvre's former student Jean Baudrillard (1996) analysed consumption, displays, media, and advertising as a linguistic system of codes that went far beyond all previous critiques of everyday life and ideology. A kind of delirium is produced by the system of signs that refers to other signs rather than an object that exists independently of the sign. While this meets the social need for difference, Baudrillard claims, it is a need that can never be satisfied. This culminated in the *Mirror of Production*, a critique of a critique (Marx's) of political economy. The system of economic exchange was now definitively supplanted for Baudrillard (1975) by a system of symbolic exchange. Only death, as the final symbolic act, can defy the mutual self-referentiality of all signs with each other, although even this distinction is placed in doubt by 'hyper-reality' as representations become their own reality (Baudrillard, 1993). Disneyland, for instance, makes a fake display of its artificiality to restore belief that the world outside is 'real'. However, in a hyper-real world of endless simulations Disneyland is as 'real' as America itself (Baudrillard, 1994a: 12–14).

With increasingly hyperbolic pronouncements, Baudrillard adopted a heroic critique of the slavish banality of everyday life, 'the desert of the real', left behind by the overloaded anomie of hyper-reality (1994a: 1). Announcing 'the end' of the real, the distinction between social theory and fiction became blurred. Many of the objections to Baudrillard's style of critique – that it was factually wrong, illogical, or an unoriginal update of the 1960s media theory of Marshall McLuhan (2001) – were met with a blank refusal by Baudrillard to play the game of theoretical adequacy or to demonstrate the validity of truth claims as pointless (Rojek and Turner, 1993).

For a while his more extravagant declarations caused outrage, for instance in claims that the Gulf War never happened since television viewers only experienced media simulations of it, when in fact he was making a fairly banal claim about the media saturation of everyday life. Baudrillard later explained away his own claims about the end of 'real' events of war and revolution, even modernity itself, in light of the supposed restarting of history with the unforeseen overthrow of the Stalinist regimes and a renewed cycle of war and terror (Baudrillard, 1994b).

As Lefebvre (2005: 137) noted, Baudrillard extrapolated general claims from a reality increasingly erased by the endless effects of signs as their own cause to the point of absurdity. Two decades earlier, Lefebvre already recognised that reality was becoming saturated with symbols and images to be consumed: 'Consuming of displays of consuming, consuming of signs and signs of consuming' (1971: 108). But where Lefebvre maintained an attachment to Marxist social theory, Baudrillard (1975) became increasingly critical of the naturalistic anthropology of Marxism that counterposed abstract, alienated exchange value to an underlying 'humanist' truth, the 'original referent' of the use value of concrete things, that somehow eluded the code of exchange.

Baudrillard's increasingly allusive wordplay did not allow space for Lefebvre's discrete moments of lived intensity that occasionally puncture the endless play of signs. Unlike Baudrillard, Lefebvre (2002: 77) kept open the gap between representations and reality. The circuit of communications could never become a totally self-enclosed universe:

> It would be a closed circuit, a circuit from hell, a perfect circuit in which the absence of communication and communication pushed to the point of paroxysm would meet and their identities would merge. But it will never come full circle. There will always be something new and unforeseen, if only in terms of sheer horror. (Lefebvre, 2002: 77)

Discourse upon and about discourse may have created subjects without essence and an absence that goes unrecognised except by way of inchoate resentments. Against the 'crazy illusion' of the totality of simulacra, Lefebvre proposed 'a guerrilla war of signs' by naming presence wherever it is to be found: 'The variety of presences is infinite, but the word has a universal and univocal import: intensification of experience, a force that is persuasive without being brutal (whether in the form of irruption, impregnation, choice, etc.)' (1980: 56). Since reality was already mediated into oblivion, Baudrillard was left stranded with no way back from the sign. Not that he cared to return.

SOCIAL IMAGINARY

Two Marxist philosophers associated with the French non-Communist political grouping 'Socialism or Barbarism', Cornélius Castoriadis and Claude Lefort, saw in Merleau-Ponty's phenomenology theoretical resources that might attenuate the crisis of Marxism (Poster, 1977: 202; Memos, 2013). Phenomenology formed the ground for a critique of modern science and 'objectivity' as part of the political struggle for human autonomy. Along with Merleau-Ponty, the theorists of 'Socialism or Barbarism' were highly critical of the bureaucratic regime in the Soviet Union. Familiar with Max Weber's sociology, Castoriadis identified the ruling bureaucracy in Stalinist Russia as a new bureaucratic exploiting class that dominated the working class as a passive object. Castoriadis anti-bureaucratic demand for creative autonomy evolved into an artistic critique of domination in all its forms.

Increasingly, Marx became the original source for later practices committed in his name by authoritarian states. By reducing social relations to a closed economic system, Marx, it was claimed, excluded the unpredictable creativity of social struggles. Abstract theory crowded out concrete praxis. In becoming a closed theoretical system, Marxism forgot what Merleau-Ponty (and Marx himself) had understood: that human beings make their own history. By oscillating between a causal explanation of the laws of history and attributing to history a meaningful goal Marxism filled in all the gaps of what society must become. This goes back to Marx, who, in *Capital*, conceived capitalism as a closed system unaffected by human struggles, class, and culture. 'Theory' should not be isolated in this way from the creative 'activity of elucidation' (Castoriadis, 1984: 84). As Hans Joas (1989: 1188) argues, theory itself is part of the historical process that it aims to explain. For Castoriadis history is made by deciding to act despite the unforeseen consequences for a future that cannot yet be known.

Just as Castoriadis had decreed what Marxism was, so he also decreed the end of it (Memos, 2013). Marx was reduced to a closed theory that ruled out more open-ended interpretations and evaluations of theory. In its place, Castoriadis appealed for a metaphysics of autonomy bereft of substantive social content. A theory of social transformation is excluded since what is required is purely an effort of the creative imagination: '*because we will it* and because we know that others will it as well' (Castoriadis, 1987: 373). History is not an impersonal process as traditional social theory understood but is willed into existence. Autonomy is its own precondition.

Becoming less directly political and more abstract theoretically, Castoriadis' (1987) lengthy disengagement from Marxism crystallised in *The Imaginary Institution of Society*. There Castoriadis gave vent to a libertarian conception of the autonomous subjects of society. By 'imaginary' Castoriadis refers to the specific collective forms and symbols by which society orientates itself. Society is not an undifferentiated chaos of inter-subjectivity but institutes *ex nihilo* an imaginary coherence that goes beyond the multiplicity of local relations. For example, nations are conceived as 'imagined communities' (Anderson, 1991).

For Castoriadis, the imaginary is an original human self-creation, *autopoiesis*. Something self-made cannot be accounted for causally by finding its source in something else. An effort of creative imagination is needed to produce the real world of institutions. A unity of social action, meaning, and significations bursts through the sedimentation of institutional domination as what Castoriadis calls 'magma'. Institutions are 'instituted' historically and socially when discrete things are separated out and brought into a relationship. Institutionalisation is imaginary because meaning brings coherance to a specific set of human relations, through what Castoriadis calls an 'identitary' or 'ensemblist logic' (1987: 177). Society is imagined as determined by distinct elements in relationship to each other. In his critique of structuralism, Castoriadis argues that the arbitrary relation of a sign to a meaning is only stabilised by the institutionalisation of a sign system.

Society is conceived as a 'self-institution' in so far as it creates itself. Later it fails to recognise itself as self-instituted. Institutions are alienated from society when they no longer appear as what they are – social creations. Yet institutions do not stop instituting. They re-form continually. Here the originary logic (*legein*) of social representation is joined by a technology (*teukhein*) of social doing. While the former discriminates between what counts, the latter actively constructs what works. Embodied and weighed down by the interplay of logic and technology, the institution of society mediates and reproduces social objects, activities and individuals (Castoriadis, 1987: 373). Once instituted this logic reassembles the relations of other institutions. Marx similarly pointed out how capitalism cast 'a general illumination which bathes all the other colours and modifies their particularity. It is a specific ether which determines the specific gravity of every being which has materialized within it' (1973: 107).

If instituting the institutions seems to be a variation on the critical Weberian schema of instrumental rationality, Castoriadis allows for a process of de-alienation that more pessimistic Weberian theory would entertain only as a distant miracle. De-alienation is possible on account of a changed relationship between society and its institutions. This motivation to found institutions anew parallels the power of the unconscious in individual psyches.

Revising Freudian theory, Castoriadis argues that consciousness never exhausts the original unity of the unconscious. Socialisation is not a self-conscious intentional act but develops through an uneven relationship between individual imagination and social representations of institutions. The original pre-social state of undifferentiated, pleasurable unity between subject and object in the world of the young child cannot be represented by mental categories but remains an unconscious state of primordial bliss. This immediate unity is broken as the child becomes separated from the world of the mother. In later life a return to the undivided stage is unconsciously craved. Individuals only become autonomous through a changed relationship between psychological drives and external reality.

At this abstract level of philosophical speculation there is precious little empirical explication of the process of self-instituting. A generalised theory of creative will is advanced at the expense of concrete relations of domination, specifically class, race, gender, nation, and sexuality. If domination rests on ideological misrecognition, then there must be some level of social reality that the social imaginary is distorting (Thompson, 1984: 38). Yet since the 1970s, Castoriadis (1997: 262) argued, the space for autonomy is narrowing under a 'crisis of social imaginary significations'.

Jurgen Habermas (1987) makes a number of interrelated criticisms of Castoriadis' case for the radical creativity of the imaginary, not least because it undermines his own pragmatic appeal to the consensual function of communicative action (Elliott, 2002). First, the relation between individual and society is posed as a dualism where the 'psyche and society stand in a kind of metaphysical opposition to one another' (Habermas, 1987: 333). Second, society is personified as 'a poetic demiurge that releases ever new world-types from itself' (1987: 333). World-making praxis floats above concrete worlds. Third, Castoriadis fails to distinguish between meaning and validity. Whatever is meaningfully instituted *ex nihilo* is for Castariodis at the same time true.

Inter-subjective communication, in Habermas' view, imposes a need to make validity claims about the truth of utterances, therefore allowing learning and knowledge to accumulate. This is not possible for the social imaginary since 'there is no accumulation of knowledge that could affect the previous interpretation of the world and burst a given totality of meaning' (Habermas, 1987: 331). Castoriadis argues that autonomy is what society itself is demanding and that, anyway, autonomy is, after all, what it is to be human. Here, institutionalised social relations are conflated with their imaginary possibilities. As Thompson (1984: 39) notes, an empirical question about social tendencies is answered with an ontological fiat. What humans essentially are (creative and autonomous) so they will become.

CULTURAL STUDIES

What was to become 'Cultural Studies' began to emerge in Britain in the mid-1950s. Cultural Studies sprang from the democratic sentiment of cultural theorists and historians in post-war Britain that ordinary life ought to be studied as seriously as art and 'high culture' (Hall, 1980a). Culture was no longer restricted to ideas and objects like books and paintings but extended to social practices and relationships that constitute 'a whole way of life' (Williams, 1965). With its emphasis on the distinctive 'way of life' of the working-class, Cultural Studies initially developed under the influence of Marxism. Working-class culture, and later youth subcultures, it was claimed, represented a collective form of resistance to and recuperation by ideological domination.

This was captured in the title of one of the most important collection of essays: *Resistance Through Rituals* (Hall and Jefferson, 1976). Yet street-level resistance was complicit in certain ways with a more general crisis of culture. Any image of rebellious youth as a 'break' with the dominant culture 'misrecognised the crisis *within* the dominant culture as a conspiracy *against* the dominant culture' (Hall and Jefferson, 1976: 65, emphasis added). Any 'break' in the culture, such as that represented by the 1960s 'counter-culture' or mods, was merely a symbolic inversion of the new forms of consumer capitalism. Hedonistic rejection of society's materialism was only made possible by continuing access to the new circuits of consumption that alternative values and lifestyles rejected.

Cultural Studies came to be defined by what Stuart Hall (1932–2014) called the 'two paradigms'. One paradigm, 'culturalism', reworked Marx's concerns with class as defined by practical-sensuous relations and disavowed any mechanical relationship between the economic base and the ideological superstructure. The other paradigm, 'structuralism', reworked Marx's concept of ideology by analysing the internal relationship of categories and discursive frameworks. A major difference between them is that while culturalism identifies 'experience' as the authentic ground of culture, structuralism contends that experience is only made possible by the unconscious operation of ideological categories that structure lived reality (Hall, 1980a: 69). Culturalism accentuates the active, self-conscious processes of cultural differentiation while structuralism treats human agents as mere bearers or personifications of the logical unfolding of ideological categories that goes on 'behind their backs'.

Cultural Studies, Hall argued, needed to go beyond the stale dichotomies of pure theory versus empirical description or structure versus agency. By operating at higher levels of abstraction, structuralism had the advantage, as far as Hall was concerned, of illuminating the underlying relations of a unified structure, what Hall called 'the complexity of the real'. Culture was conceived by Hall as a unified structure, relatively autonomous from other structures, yet without fragmenting into an infinite number of absolutely autonomous cultures.

While Hall considered the high level of theoretical abstraction an advance over the descriptive humanism of culturalism, structuralism lacked culturalism's insistence on agency, struggle and political engagement. Drawing on semiotics, Hall (1980b) distinguished between the ideological 'encoding' of signs by the producers of texts and the active 'decoding' by consumers in divergent or oppositional readings. From this it was possible to read youth subcultures like punk as a subversive style created out of an ordered chaos of signs, images and texts plundered from the dross of consumer culture (Hebdige, 1979).

HEGEMONY: A VERY BRITISH CRISIS

As the post-war ideological consensus broke down in the late 1960s, Gramsci's idea of a crisis of hegemony took on particular salience for Marxist-influenced Cultural Studies. While Foucault's radical approach to discursive 'difference' marked a positive development in the concrete analysis of cultural formations, only Gramsci's framework of hegemony, Hall (1980a: 71) claimed, pointed beyond the phoney dualism of experience versus structure, culture versus ideology, theory versus empiricism, absolute autonomy versus absolute determinism, and onto the terrain of 'a properly materialist theory of culture'. In *Policing the Crisis*, Hall and his colleagues (Hall et al., 1978: viii) analysed media and political fears of 'mugging', a petty form of street robbery that was represented as a general threat of black youth to public safety and social order. Media representations of mugging provided an 'index of the disintegration of the social order, as a sign that the "British way of life" is coming apart at the seams' (1978: viii).

Policing the Crisis remains a brilliant dissection of how discourses about relatively minor acts – street crime – construct a new 'common sense' that presages profound shifts in the form of more repressive state rule (Rojek, 2003). 'Mugging', as a condensate of race, crime, and youth, articulated the crisis of hegemony by providing a convenient framework for authoritarian state power – a 'law and order society' – to counter the loss of ideological authority of Britain's dominant groups facing economic decline, popular militancy, and the end of empire. This wider structuring of crisis cannot be understood if a culturalist focus on the immediate 'scene of the crime' is taken as the exclusive focus for analysis – as it later became for studies of isolated youth subcultures, their fashions, leisure activities, rituals, and 'anti-social behaviour' – as fascinating in itself. Instead of a critique of policing and state coercion, the more recent appeal of everyday exotica for cultural sociology and criminology observes illegitimate miscreants on behalf of the legitimate authority of policing agencies.

In the wake of successive election victories in the 1980s for Margaret Thatcher's Conservatives in the UK, Hall identified a new form of ideological rule – 'authoritarian populism' – that emerged from the earlier drift into a 'law and order society'. If politics is essentially a struggle over representations then Thatcherism, Hall argues, was able to 'ground neo-liberal policies directly in an appeal to "the people"; to root them in the essentialist categories of commonsense experience and practical moralism – and thus to construct, not simply awaken, classes, groups and interests into a particular definition of "the people"' (1988: 71).

By generating popular consent for an authoritarian state and neoliberal economy in response to Britain's 'organic crisis', Thatcherism appeared more Gramscian than left-liberal Gramscians themselves. Authoritarian populism combined traditional Tory themes of family, standards, nation, authority, anti-welfare, and the strong state with the neoliberal themes of deregulated markets, self-interest, competition, individualism, and anti-bureaucracy. Such contradictory themes generated popular consent because, Hall argued, they corresponded to 'the contradictory elements of common sense, popular life and consciousness' (2011: 713).

The crisis from the mid-1970s to the late 1980s was not only talked about in these terms but, more significantly, it was experienced or 'lived in' as the taken-for-granted, world-defining themes of 'reactionary common sense'. This prepared the ground for the more advanced forms of neoliberalism that defines the terms of more recent current crisis. While the term 'neoliberalism' conceals a multitude of different practices and justifications, Hall accepts that it is a necessary concept because it lends the crisis a more defined shape for political intervention. Thatcher seized upon the crisis of the 1970s to make neoliberalism palatable to British tastes conditioned by collective institutions like the welfare state and mass trade unionism. Familiar liberal principles were re-coded to enable popular acceptance of the language of neoliberalism, ideas that 'have long been inscribed in social practices and institutions and sedimented into the "habitus" of everyday life, common sense and popular consciousness – "traces without an inventory"' (Hall, 2011: 711).

Neoliberalism therefore appears to be hegemonic despite widespread support for the welfare state. In this it is unclear if there has been one long 'organic' crisis or numerous short-lived 'conjunctural' crises since the 1970s. All governments since Thatcher deepened the neoliberal project. From New Labour (1997–2010) to the Tory-led coalition (2010–2015) UK governments the priority of wealth 'creation' over welfare 'redistribution' hardened into a new common sense. While Hall's theoretical synthesis shuffles between different levels of abstraction, the analysis of hegemony rarely goes beyond generalisations about 'common sense' or examples of particular episodes or 'conjunctures'. As Gramsci (1971: 177) argued, conjunctural analyses are limited to the flotsam and jetsam of short-lived political events and the to-ing and fro-ing of political leaders and personalities.

The Marxist theories of Gramsci and Althusser proved a staging post in the development of Cultural Studies, not a final destination. An uneasy tension between Marxism and Culture Studies was exacerbated by their relative neglect of race and gender and by an increasing emphasis on the absolute autonomy and complexity of cultural agency. Culture came to be seen by Hall (1996: 271) as 'de-centred', always escaping any effort to relate it to other structures like politics or economics. Yet culture is marked by traces of the institutional context of social power and resistance. Such ambiguities and tensions, Hall lamented, left Cultural Studies, particularly the 'post-modern' version in the US, exposed to processes of professionalisation, institutionalisation and formalisation emptied of political relevance and radical critique.

What Hall (1996: 273) called 'theoretical fluency' inflated the language of Cultural Studies – otherness, marginality, exclusion, domination, class, gender, race, identity, and so on – in endless theorisations, conceptual elaborations and textual productions. Textual theoretisation and 'intertextuality' allowed relations of power to disappear except as the effect of academic discourses. A commitment to political struggle was abandoned in the move away from earlier aspirations for a 'properly materialist theory of culture' towards a populist toleration of cultural difference. Depoliticisation enabled Cultural Studies to embrace 'popular culture' as inherently meaningful in its own terms through the textual analysis of, say, celebrities as if they were separate from unequal social relations, political economy and institutional power (Rojek, 2012). If ideology cannot be consistent about itself, then theories of ideology still need to aspire to internal consistency premised on an analysis of long-term 'organic' processes.

'RACE' IN CRISIS

Not all aspects of the crisis have been depoliticised by sociological analysis. Particularly significant has been the way that 'identity' – for instance, of gender, sexuality, 'race', religion, or nation – became a marker of political claim-making. In cases like 'queer' or 'black' identity, what was a negative, pejorative label of social inferiority was reclaimed as a defiant political badge of honour. For the social theorist Paul Gilroy (2000), the transformations under way in the twenty-first century mean that such defensive identities as 'race' need to be given up in preference for participation in what he rather unfashionably terms 'planetary humanism'. What escapes the excessive valorisation of cultural difference, group particularity, and exclusive identity is the 'crushingly obvious, almost banal human sameness' (2000: 29).

All the bio-political premises on which 'race' was staked historically, what Gilroy (2000) calls 'raciology', are now in crisis. Raciology is 'the lore that brings the virtual realities of "race" to dismal and destructive life', not least through the idea of absolute differences of biology and culture. The crisis represents a chance to overcome 'race':

> It is a crisis because the idea of 'race' has lost much of its common-sense credibility, because the elaborate cultural and ideological work that goes in to producing and reproducing it is more visible than ever before, because it has been stripped of its moral and intellectual integrity, and because there is a chance to prevent its rehabilitation. (2000: 28–9)

Far from denouncing technoscience in the manner of critical theory, post-modernism or religion, Gilroy uses developments in genetic engineering to cast doubt on the biological certainties that once underpinned the claims of raciology. Recent developments in biotechnology, especially genetic technology, have confounded many of the assumptions about 'race'. Genetic materials reveal the essential unity of the human species behind the immediate appearance of difference. In response, racism moved out of the shadow of biology and sheltered under the idea of culturally homogenous groups threatened by alien in-comers, a process of regressive culturalism that Martin Barker (1981) presciently identified in the early 1980s as 'the new racism'.

Against triumphant raciology non-racial humanism recognises the tragically weak bodies of human beings, as expressed for Gilroy by poetic figures from Friedrich Nietzsche, the philosopher, to Donny Hathaway, the soul singer. As Blaise Pascal put it in the seventeenth century: 'A human being is only a reed, the weakest in nature, but he is a thinking reed' (1995: 72). In other words, humans may be physically weak but they are capable of knowing as much. Sensing this weakness, abstract individualism takes flight from the frailties of embodiment. In contrast, recognising bodily weakness, pain, humiliation, and caring, Gilroy argues, makes human solidarity possible.

While images of blackness now proliferate in the consumer world of corporate multiculturalism, Gilroy is concerned that exceptionally glamorous bodies remain deeply racialised ones, operating within the hierarchical cultural codes of blackness as predatory, brutal, idle, excessive, and hyper-sexualised. As black political struggles for elementary rights are forgotten or sentimentalised, athletes and entertainers benefit from the limited prestige of blackness as objects of visceral pleasure. Commodification has a corrosive and trivialising effect on political culture as a lived tradition and collective memory. As Barker and Gilroy recognise, it is not only liberal post-modernists who know how to manipulate cultural tropes. Today's racist and neo-fascist movements have learned how to play with the cultural codes established by the horrors of the Holocaust and racial slavery.

ANTHONY GIDDENS AND MUTUAL KNOWLEDGE

Like Hall and Gilroy, Anthony Giddens aimed to develop a politically engaged social theory. Social theory, Giddens (1982: 72) once argued, involves 'firing critical salvos into reality'. By the 1990s this had morphed into the 'Third Way' favoured by New Labour (Giddens, 1998). For Giddens social theory must address the major public issues of the age. To do so effectively it needs to overcome its typical disdain for common sense as mere inertia or habit based on lazy, self-satisfied ideas about the social world. Social theory cannot simply be applied to the social world as a neutral corrective to the falsehoods of common sense.

Common sense cannot be understood in a common-sense way. Giddens analytically distinguishes what he calls tacit or 'mutual knowledge' from generic common sense:

By mutual knowledge I refer to knowledge of convention which actors must possess in common in order to make sense of what both they and other actors do in
the course of their day-to-day social lives. Meanings are produced and reproduced via the practical application and continued reformulation in practice of
'what everyone knows' ... Mutual knowledge refers to the methods used by lay
actors to generate the practices which are constitutive of the tissue of social life.
(1987b: 65–66)

Knowledge is not mutual in the sense that separate individual agents possess an
understanding of each other as individuals. It is mutual in the sense that individuals observe social conventions and rules in practical, sense-making activity.

Mutual knowledge is about what agents do routinely and practically. As such, it
is constitutive of the fabric of social life. Any theory of social action presupposes
access to the mutual knowledge already presupposed by social agents themselves.
Mutual knowledge according to Giddens is largely tacit and non-discursive.
It doesn't have to be spelled out in an explicit way but is exhibited in the practical
and routine capacity to 'go on' by working with the 'rules' of social life. What people
already know about the ordinary social world must at some level be constitutive
of that world.

People embody a 'practical consciousness' that cannot be entirely denoted by
the language used to describe action or meanings. This sense of practical consciousness places a definite limit on accounts of social worlds in terms of their
discursive construction as a semiotic system. Individuals who are perfectly competent users of language nevertheless find it difficult to give a discursive account
of the rules, strategies and tactics of routine language use. Practical consciousness
mediates between what is conscious and what is unconscious to the social agent
engaged in practical activity.

Socially learned practices allow action to be interpreted appropriately. Here the
emphasis is less on isolating words as discourse theory might and more on identifying what needs to be carried out in practice. Meaning is shifted from text to
context, from the word to practice, and from interpretation to observation. As
Wittgenstein argued, people tend to be knowledgeable and skilful users of ordinary language in everyday life where the vague lexical definitions of isolated
words acquire a precise meaning 'bound' to concrete time and space.

Social theory participates in mutual knowledge, otherwise it could never gain
access to the social world, in which it is embedded in any case. While the propositional statements of common sense are corrigible, can be true or false, and are
subject to critical examination, mutual knowledge as practical know-how (rules)
cannot be corrigible against the ideals of scholastic rationalism (Giddens, 1984:
336). Hence the banality of much social theory is only apparent according to
Giddens. Merely confirming the mutual knowledge of everyday life makes so
much social science seem banal and obvious in contrast to the discoveries by
natural science of unknown and hidden processes.

Even supposing that it is possible for social theory to know what common sense
knows, and that is far from straightforward, this raises a further problem: how
does social theory justify its existence as a specialised activity and contribute

something over and above what social agents already know? Giddens proposes three functions for critical social theory. First, it must undertake ethnographic description of ordinary social worlds. Second, social theory imposes a novel discursive form that disembeds mutual knowledge from the naturalised background universe of non-discursive practices. Third, social theory highlights the unintended consequences of action that often elude practical consciousness.

Critique is directed at common-sense beliefs while ethnographic description reconstructs mutual knowledge as a social process. If the subjects of social science already know what they are doing, then social theory can illuminate the tacit, non-discursive aspects of mutual knowledge by giving it a more defined, discursive form. Yet it is still necessary, Giddens further argued, for social science to go beyond an interpretation of the local situation where mutual knowledge operates to examine the unintended consequences of purposive action and the impersonal 'systems' or conventions that exist beyond the time and space of any particular localised interaction.

Mutual knowledge is implicit, grounded in practices, not a general set of explicit rules which are later applied to social worlds. Implicit rules become routine or second nature following repeated practice, although they were learned initially under explicit instruction – as in the automatic nature of literacy or numeracy skills – while other rules are strategic and involve skilful judgements, acquired through past exposure to a qualitatively diverse series of conditions. It is unclear if this is because long-forgotten meanings or rules, now understood implicitly, cannot find expression in any formal way or that they have always been beyond words.

DOUBLE HERMENEUTIC

Social theory is tied to the common sense of ordinary social worlds by what Giddens calls 'the double hermeneutic'. In this he critically follows the philosopher Peter Winch (1990) who claimed that sociology was essentially a philosophical enterprise because it was compelled to reflect critically on the meaning of common sense in a manner not dissimilar from Wittgenstein and ordinary language philosophy. However, Giddens departs from Winch's rigid separation of social theory and the social world to the extent that social science concepts are reciprocally absorbed into everyday life. Specialised concepts and theories are developed to make sense of social worlds to which agents themselves already apply their own concepts and theories.

Social theory needs to know something of what social agents know. Mutual knowledge also owes something to previous social theory. In some cases, it plays a constitutive role as theoretical ideas and concepts become absorbed into the routines of social worlds. Critical social theory, and social science more generally, need to adopt a reflexive understanding of the transformative consequences of the double hermeneutic for its own practices.

Positivist theory becomes untenable, Giddens claims, once it is grasped that social analysis is subject to a double hermeneutic, whereby social science affects the social world which it is, at the same time, trying to understand:

> a double hermeneutic, since the concepts and theories developed therein apply to a world constituted of the activities of conceptualizing and theorizing agents. The social scientist does not have to interpret the meanings of the social world to actors within it. To the contrary, the technical concepts of social science are, and must be, parasitical upon lay concepts. (Giddens, 1987b: 70).

Hence the 'impact' of social science is not technical in the same way as the findings of natural science, since it helps to constitute the social world and becomes part and parcel of the familiar routines that social theory is compelled to return once again to try to describe and explain (Giddens, 1984).

From the intractable position of the double hermeneutic the point is not to replace the false beliefs of people with the true findings of science but to develop a self-reflexive, critical theory. Where categories are already contested in everyday practices, say in the difference between a 'terrorist' and a 'freedom fighter', the sociologist is advised to find different categories that will allow a critical distance from emotionally- and ideologically-charged disputes.

In this way, Giddens is able to navigate dialectically between 'naturalistic' social science, which identifies what goes on behind the backs of social agents beyond their comprehension, and more interpretative approaches, which often fail to notice that ultimate consequences escape the mundane routines and intentions of localised social worlds. The double hermeneutic restores the relationship between the local intentions of purposive action and unintended global consequences. Social theory may share much of its interest in mundane social worlds and common sense with influential strands of 'sociological' philosophy, like Wittgenstein, ordinary language philosophy and phenomenology, but Giddens argues, social theory, unlike philosophy, acquires its purpose only in its usefulness for guiding programmes of empirical research.

If the double hermeneutic that Giddens proposes – that social theory knows what social agents know and gives non-discursive conventions discursive form – then does this demand the impossible from social theory? If common sense is inherently practical, fluid, unconscious, and vague can social theory perform intellectual alchemy by transforming this into something theoretical, self-conscious, stable, and precise? Theoretical descriptions of common sense cannot at the same time belong to the social worlds constituted by common sense. If common sense lacks definite discursive form, how is social action, purposively guided by explicit intentions, possible?

STRUCTURATION

With the idea of mutual knowledge Giddens enables the subjective constitution of the social world favoured by interpretative social theory to overrule 'naturalistic' social theory. Naturalism takes the structures of the social world as given, external social facts that limit the possibilities for social agency. Structure, for Giddens, cannot be conceived as an objective social fact external to and a constraint on subjective action. Rather than seeing structure and action as polar opposites, subjective action 'instantiates' institutions as abstract structures. This hermeneutical approach makes common sense a more active force in the constitution of society.

Giddens begins from a division between structure and agency. Structure refers to the rules and resources of social systems and structuration is the process by which agents reproduce social systems. Structures are double-sided in that they both constrain action and make action possible. Giddens calls this the 'duality of structure' and hopes in this way to overcome the traditional dichotomy of structure and action and the related schism between structuralism and hermeneutics in social theory, since neither structure nor action can exist independently of each other.

Social systems do not 'have' structures but exhibit structural *properties*, taking institutional form as 'time-space presence, only in its instantiations in such practices and as memory traces orienting the conduct of knowledge human agents' (Giddens, 1984: 17). Structural properties are 'both medium and outcome of the practices they recursively organize' (1984: 25). As such, structures do not exist apart from knowledgeable human agents, even if the wider consequences were not originally intended. Giddens adapts the distinction made by David Lockwood (1992: appendix) between 'system integration' and 'social integration'. Systems are integrated when agents are physically absent in space and time, while society is integrated only when agents are co-present, face-to-face in shared space and time.

In the duality of structure, priority is accorded to knowledgeable individual agents over impersonal social structures since, ultimately, the only active entities in social relations are human individuals using their power resources to make things happen (Giddens, 1984: 181). Control over resources confers power on agents but, at the same time, control of resources depends on practically understood rules about how to carry on with life. Agents become increasingly 'self-reflexive' about how to 'go on' (Giddens, 1990). Modernity is thereby constituted by increasingly self-conscious, constantly self-aware, and purposive social agents. This is why unintended consequences, such as natural disasters, produce in people not directly affected a certain heightening of ontological tension and anxiety.

A RUNAWAY WORLD

Late modernity is experienced as a 'juggernaut', a runaway world that humans feel that they are unable to control (Giddens, 1990: 139). In this giddy world, repetition is essential for human orientation and provides an emotive and cognitive anchor, what Giddens (1991: 35–69) calls 'ontological security'. A sense of trust and reliability is given by the confidence that people can have in the predictability of their surroundings and a continuous sense of self-identity. People pursue personal identity projects of 'self-fulfilment' and 'self-expression' in various projects like exercise, dieting, consuming, faith, and so on. Where critical theory may view this in terms of narcissistic self-absorption or middle-class pretension, Giddens more generously treats it as knowledgeable agents calling on expert knowledge to invest an impersonal social world with meaning.

In terms of personal relationships, trust is generated through intimate self-disclosure. At the same time disclosure makes people vulnerable to the risk of exposure and humiliation. Risk is balanced against trust, and safety with danger through expert systems. For instance, in taking the 'risk' of driving a car, drivers rely on their implicit trust in the road-building system, the fuel system, car manufacture and repair system, the traffic system – even navigation systems (Giddens, 1990: 28).

Needless to say, such ambitions for social theory have come in for sustained critique. Giddens' endorsement of a 'Third Way' in politics in the 1990s is seen by his critics as the sorry decline of a major social theorist who came to embrace a softer version of neoliberal capitalism (Giddens, 2000). Structuration theory was criticised for making structures a side-effect of what people do in everyday life rather than an independent analytical construct (Mouzelis, 1995). Many critics accept the dualism of structure and agency as essential constructs, and much of the debate seems to be about finding the right conceptual mechanism for reconciling the duality or maintaining the dualism as an analytical device, even though it is recognised that no such distinction exists in lived reality (King, 2004).

By defining structure in terms of language-governed rules and resources, Giddens excludes the specific role played by non-discursive social relations (Archer, 1995: 106). Language is only one medium in the process of structural reproduction. Constraints are also imposed by the relations of capitalist production and exchange where it may well be the case that the individual can exercise no agency in the sense of choosing between multiple actions (Thompson, 1984: 169). Here the main issue is that, in the end, Giddens privileges individual knowledge over impersonal structures, rather than allowing for the analytical autonomy of structure with its own coercive logic that stands in a relation of tension with the projects of individual human agents. For others, this debate about analytical distinctions removed from substantive issues indicates the continuing power of abstract philosophical rationalism to define the terms of sociological theory (Kilminster, 1998).

BACK IN THE USSR: SOCIOLOGICAL UTTERANCES

An arguably more successful sociology of language focussing on the 'concrete utterance' had been developed in the 1920s by the Russian theorist Valentin Vološinov (1895–1936). Like Giddens, Vološinov (1973: 48) attempted to mediate between the dominant ways of thinking about language as structure, on one hand, and language as agency, on the other hand. These extremes he called 'individualistic subjectivism' and 'abstract objectivism'. Individualistic subjectivism takes language to be a creative and unique process of individualised speech acts, which theory turns into an abstract construct purely for the sake of analysis. It relies on a theory of expression as a unique, creative impulse that travels from the inner life of individuals to outer reality by way of an external sign. Sociologically, the rigid dualism of inner and outer life is untenable since there can be no 'inner' experience unless it is embodied in socially derived signs: 'It is not experience that organizes expression but the other way round – *expression organizes experience*' (Vološinov, 1973: 85). Experience only acquires conscious form in the material of signs produced by groups in the process of social intercourse.

In contrast, abstract objectivism takes language to be a ready-made, fixed system whereby mutual understanding of a language community is guaranteed by the 'normative identity' of linguistic forms that stand over and above individuals. Where individualistic subjectivism relies on interpretation of unique speech acts, abstract objectivism analyses the inner logic of the relationship of one sign to another sign within a closed system. Linguistic conventions (*langue*) not speech (*langage*) form the point of departure, most influentially in the rationalist linguistic theory of Ferdinand de Saussure. Both language (*langue*) and verbal speech (*langage*) are kept distinct from utterances (*parole*). Saussure considered an utterance to be a uniquely individual event in contrast to the structural 'essence' of language. Abstract rationalism also informs more sociological, Durkheim-influenced trends in linguistic theory that emphasise language as a social fact, external to and compulsory for individual agents.

Each extreme is partly corrected by the other. Individualistic subjectivism rightly emphasises the creative aspect of the utterance but fails to grasp expression as a social act. Abstract objectivism rightly rejects the individualist theory of expression but reifies language into a frozen system cut off from generative processes of social communication. Against these two schools, individualism and rationalism, whose effects on social theory are still felt, Vološinov argued for a process and relational sociological theory of communication that takes the concrete utterance, not individual psychology or abstract systems (or ideal speech situations), as the point of departure for analysis.

Every word is a product of a reciprocal relationship between speaker and listener. Vološinov set out a sociological theory of language:

> The concrete utterance (and not the linguistic abstraction) is born, lives, and dies in the process of social interaction between the participants of the utterance. Its form and meaning are determined basically by the form and character of this interaction. When we cut the utterance off from the real grounds that nurture it, we lose the key to its form as well as its import – all we have left is an abstract linguistic shell or an equally abstract semantic scheme. (2012: 175)

The important point is that the word is the most sensitive index of social relations even if these are only dimly perceived processes of social change. Understanding is inherently dialogical in nature, produced in the relationship between speaker and listener. This is the staple position of pragmatic 'dialogical' social theory. To this, Vološinov contributes something else: the *evaluative accent*.

Every utterance is concrete, meaningful and evaluative. It always contains an evaluative judgement about the relative social significance of whatever is communicated.

Evaluations arise from and make assumptions about everyday life. Social evaluations are generated by a 'community of value judgements', formed by family, colleagues, friends, class, ethnic and other groups, to which individual emotions add personal 'overtones'. Not only the literal meaning of words but also the intonation used by speakers express value judgements: 'In actuality, we never say or hear words, we say and hear what is true or false, good or bad, important or unimportant, pleasant or unpleasant, and so on' (Vološinov, 1973: 70).

Evaluation is not therefore the secondary effect of meaning, as some critical social theory suggests when it privileges signs, texts, and objects over concrete processes of sense-making (Billig, 1996). Rather, the meaning of any sign is always accompanied by some kind of social evaluation. Meaning cannot be separated from value judgement without it becoming formal and empty:

> The separation of word meaning from evaluation inevitably deprives meaning of its place in the living social process (where meaning is always permeated with value judgement), to its being ontologized and transformed into ideal Being divorced from the historical process of Becoming. (Vološinov, 1973: 105)

Evaluation alters social meaning from the purview of group interaction at a specific time and place. Antagonist classes and groups use the same language but place different accents on the word from their different social class positions. Every utterance meets with a response and becomes the site for the collision of different evaluative accents: 'A word in the mouth of a particular individual person is a product of the living interaction of social forces' (Vološinov, 1973: 41).

In everyday life, dominant groups try to impose a stable ideological meaning on the sign to make it uni-accentual and monological, not multi-accentual and dialogical. The more that an utterance assumes hierarchical social organisation – as in courtrooms, interviews, bureaucracies, army barracks, lecture halls – the more that it resists being answered back. But every sign is refracted and distorted by conflicting social interests. A book or an article, any 'verbal performance in print', engages in 'ideological colloquy of large scale: it responds to something, objects to something, affirms something, anticipates possible responses and objections, seeks support, and so on' (Vološinov, 1973: 95). This 'inner dialectical quality' of incompatible social evaluation, responsiveness, and answerability is only fully exposed in periods of acute social crisis (Vološinov, 1973: 23). With crisis, unspoken assumptions are made subject to open dispute and challenge.

It is not the case, therefore, that sociology had to wait until 'the cultural turn' of the 1980s to develop a sophisticated understanding of the social significance of language. Much exaggeration and condescension towards earlier social theory may have been avoided had Vološinov's pioneering social theory of language, alongside his more reputable associate the Russian literary theorist Mikhail Bakhtin, been critically assimilated to later developments in social theory, cultural studies, psychology, and sociology – as some have attempted during the recent textual inflation induced by the so-called 'cultural turn' (Bakhtin, 1984; Bell and Gardiner, 1998; Bennett, 1979; Billig, 1997; McNally, 2001; Shotter, 2001).

CRITIQUE AND DEVELOPMENT

From Debord to Castoriadis to Baudrillard, the artistic critique of everyday life is stirring stuff. It rehearsed the vocabulary of May 1968 as a creative theatre of presence and autonomy before it was petrified by the forces of consumer capitalism. In the 1970s, Situationism's reversal of perspective influenced the disruption to everyday life of the initial shockwave of punk subculture. Punk rudely interrupted 'England's dreaming' and briefly regenerated the tired genre of rock music before it again descended into another stale formula (Marcus, 1989; Savage, 1991). Having long since abandoned Marxism after sustained critique, Castoriadis finally acquired a reputation in social theory with an abstract philosophy of autonomy that readily lends itself to a perpetual process of reinterpretation. With little empirical ballast to freight it to any particular time and place, Castoriadis' 'imaginary institution' of society is set to enjoy a long career in social theory.

In the context of what Stuart Hall called the 'theoretical fluency' of inflated language, endless elucidations and textual productions, the artistic critique is vulnerable to appropriation by the very structures of domination that it was meant to dispel. As Luc Boltanski and Eve Chiapello (2005) argue in their study *The New Spirit of Capitalism*, by responding to demands for authenticity, expressiveness, creativity, identity, and personal autonomy against the stifling constraints of bureaucracy and consumerism, neoliberal capitalism appropriated and commodified the right to difference and 'authenticity'. Floundering around for a way out of the crisis of accumulation, management theorists of the 1980s found in the artistic critique a cultural ideology for reorganising businesses that made work more flexible, networked, and meaningful, and management less cumbersome, impersonal, and hierarchical.

Cultural theories were more inclined to find the resources for resistance to cultural domination in micro-forms of what de Certeau called everyday 'tactics': small, unspectacular, temporary victories against strategically positioned power. Signs do not simply transmit self-contained, ideal meanings that create spectacles or simulations or cultural dopes as the uni-directional expression of power resources. As Vološinov argued, signification is a deeply sociological process. Signs enter into the 'evaluative purview' of particular social groups, generating social re-evaluations in the pragmatic context of everyday life. It is precisely this evaluative accent that risks being lost by social theory dazzled by the self-referential power of simulacra.

As Giddens noted with the idea of ontological security, as Georg Simmel (1997: 174–185) had done a century before in his famous essay on the blasé personality and urban modernity (when never-ending cultural change is demanded by a ravenous cycle of capitalist production and consumption), everyday routines can provide a source of resistance and a safeguard for personal autonomy and integrity. In the UK, Stuart Hall and 'the Birmingham School' of cultural sociology similarly identified 'resistance through ritual'. Here street subcultures create their own evaluative codes to mediate the dominant cultural codes. However, tactical subcultural rebellion is always recuperated in the end by the strategic weight of hegemonic power. A self-confirming prophecy of cultural devaluation functions to subordinate dominated groups even as they engage in the low-intensity tactics of subcultural resistance.

Debates about authenticity and conformism have a long pedigree in sociology, including worries about anomie, alienation, isolation, pseudo-individualism, artificial happiness, psychological repression and dependency on authority figures. Such concerns were articulated in the 1950s by David Riesman (1961) in his classic study *The Lonely Crowd*. Influenced by the critical theory of Erich Fromm (1900–1980), Riesman addressed the effects on 'character' of the post-war transition to effortless consumption, and observed how – as the middle classes in post-war America were being transformed into privatised consumers – it spelled the end of the autonomous 'inner-directed' personality under the rise of a flexible, 'nice', tolerant and conformist 'other-directed' personality.

It now became more important to be liked rather than esteemed, to seek approval from others; to cooperate, be amenable and take part; to appear non-judgemental and well-meaning; and to accumulate wider circles of 'friends'. Such flattening of emotion reinforces feelings of powerlessness and reduces political action to bloodless forms of lifestyle indignation (Meštrović, 1997). In an age of shallow, other-directed networks, flexible collaboration, information overload, and the incessant collecting of 'friends' and 'followers' in social media, the possibilities for political and personal autonomy appear even more confined than Riesman was able to anticipate.

Where social theory abandons any sense of the real, genuine, authentic, or true, or is seduced by the power of media spectacles, then it forsakes any perspective from which to launch a critique of the inauthentic, wrong or false (Habermas, 1987; Boltanski and Chiapello, 2005: 455). Yet, counterposing an 'authentic' to an 'inauthentic' life reintroduces the type of static conceptual opposition that so bedevils social theory. Boltanski and Chiapello's claim that the artistic critique of capitalism supplanted the social critique after 1968 depends on precisely the conceptual operation of binary dualisms (artistic critique–social critique, authentic–inauthentic, expression–domination) that social theory needs to overcome (Stiegler, 2014).

In any case, critique has lost any purpose if symbols and signs are all that there is. Textual inflation functions as a scholastic rationalisation of shifts in the social structure and as a substitute for substantive analysis. Having said this, cultural sociology did not entirely cede the power for radical political critique of cultural domination as, for example, the work of Paul Gilroy and Pierre Bourdieu among others shows. In such cases, the sociology of cultural relations, practices, and processes restores a critical edge and political significance in times of crisis.

14

RELATIONAL TURN: NORBERT ELIAS AND PIERRE BOURDIEU

Sociology would not be worth an hour of anyone's time if it were to be merely an expert knowledge reserved for experts.

Pierre Bourdieu

Recently an attempt has been made to move beyond the perceived 'crisis' in sociology by making what has been called the 'relational turn' in social theory (Dunning and Hughes, 2013: 2; Emirbayer, 1997). This promises to overcome the abstract and static categories of philosophy and the common-sense reduction of social relations, process, and structures to individual physical things. Individuals appear to be substances that can be seen and touched, while social relations are intangible, making them rather difficult to nail down. It seems obvious that the individual and society really are two separate things. In fact they are inseparably bound up with each other. There is no society without individuals and no individuals without society. Relational theory insists on the points of connection between things rather than things in themselves. All individual 'things' are fashioned by the mutual contact with each other.

A wide range of approaches are possible under the rubric of 'relational sociology'. For some, relational sociology is informed by the philosophical perspective of 'critical realism' (Donati, 2011). For others like Nick Crossley (2011) relational sociology concerns the phenomenological social world of interaction. Still others understand relational sociology in terms of social networks and network analysis (Scott, 2012). Claims have been made that such theoretical diversity can be woven together to establish a new paradigm for sociology as a whole that could result in an ontological and methodological consensus (Powell and Depelteau, 2013). Relational sociology is, however, a synthesis of much older pedigree that can be traced back to the sociology of Marx and Simmel and the philosophy of Ernst Cassirer.

In the twentieth century this legacy was developed in distinctive ways by the empirical and theoretical approaches of Norbert Elias and Pierre Bourdieu. Both are recognised today as among the greatest sociologists. When the popular psychologist Steven Pinker discovered that homicide had been in decline since the Middle Ages he consulted the ground-breaking work of Elias, whom he labelled as 'the most important thinker that you have never heard of' and 'the only major social thinker with a theory that could explain it' (2011: 59, 61). In the process, Pinker marshalled an impressive range of data that generally corroborated in the twenty-first century what Elias proposed in the 1930s, even though at that time civilisation was going in reverse direction.

At the time Elias described the properties of his new relational sociology: 'The understanding of a formation of this kind requires a breakthrough to a still little-known level of reality: to the level of the immanent regularities of social relationships: the field of relational dynamics' (2012: 347). His major study *On the Process of Civilisation* is now hailed as a masterpiece but languished in obscurity for thirty years after it was first published in 1939 (Walter Benjamin refused to review it on the mistaken grounds that it paid scant attention to class relations) (Elias, 1938; 2012: xiv; Goudsblom, 1977; Schöttker, 1998).

Pierre Bourdieu is perhaps the most influential sociologist of the past fifty years. If Elias sustained the fundamental framework of his relational sociology more or less consistently for almost six decades, Bourdieu constantly revised and reflected on his own substantial body of work in the light of changing social conditions and theoretical challenges. His huge output included studies of peasant society, education, culture, art and literature, science, media, housing, sport, gender, methodology, philosophy, language, and the state. In this body of work Bourdieu attempted to overcome the temptation to think about the social world in terms of substances, self-contained individuals, groups, classes, or populations. As he put it, 'one must *think relationally*' since 'the real is relational' (Bourdieu and Wacquant, 1992: 228).

This chapter outlines some of the central concepts and subject areas of Elias and Bourdieu. It shows that while there are some differences in emphasis between them, they were both concerned with how symbolic power mediates social relations over time. Their common accent was on a relational theory of practices over time. To think relationally is also to think historically. Both tried to bypass the arid dualisms in sociology like structure and agency by emphasising practical social relations. They shared certain concepts in common – habitus, field, and power – while examining a range of subjects at different levels of analysis and over different timeframes (Paulle et al., 2011; Dépelteau, 2013). Both shared a concern with similar substantive issues like body controls, socialisation, state formation, sports, group belonging, and science. Both saw theoretical *synthesis* as the beginning of a solution to crisis. Neither tried to build a finished theoretical system. They aimed to provide conceptual tools for the orientation of empirical sociology as a vital stage in the orientation of human societies. They developed sociological theory only to the extent that it develops alongside empirical research as part of a single process.

CIVILISING PROCESSES

Elias was exposed to the major currents of Western theory, German philosophy and sociology, including Marx and Comte (van Krieken, 1998; Mennell, 1992). He had some contact with the Frankfurt School between 1930 and 1933 when Elias worked as Mannheim's assistant, although there was limited intellectual exchange between them. Elias claimed to have been more influenced by Freud than 'any theoretical sociologist', though his classic study of the civilising process is deeply indebted to Johan Huizinga's (1998) classic study, *The Waning of the Middle Ages*, which exposed the tempestuous, violent character of pre-modern Europe. Counter-intuitively, Elias related the development in Europe of the psychic structure, or what he called 'habitus', to wider changes in social and political relationships.

What Elias called *sociogenesis* – meaning the social generation of relations – is necessarily linked to *psychogenesis* – processes of psychological development experienced as a second-nature habitus. Sociogenesis was preferred to alternative concepts such as 'social construction' or 'social shaping' since these give unplanned social processes an overly-subjective tinge. Sociogenesis enabled Elias to describe the shifting balance between compulsion and agency depending on the figuration under consideration (Dunning and Hughes, 2013: 81). It also circumvented any search for absolute beginnings for civilising processes. Elias considered speculation about starting points to be a futile diversion from acquiring socially useful knowledge of processes: 'This process has no beginning, and here we cannot trace it back indefinitely. Wherever we start, there is movement, something that went before' (2012: 68).

Volume one of his book on the civilising process examined changes in the conduct of the European upper classes. Increasingly the manners of the nobility became more delicate and refined and less aggressive and warrior-like. Elias drew examples from medieval manners books that instructed young nobles how to behave civilly, how to eat at the table, the correct use of knife and forks, 'natural functions', blowing one's nose, spitting, sleeping arrangements, relations between men and women, and emotional controls over aggression. All these controls stimulated a rising threshold of shame and embarrassment at outward signs of social incompetence. Violence, sex and bodily functioning were allocated to special spaces 'behind the scenes', the slaughterhouse, bedroom, and toilet. Everyday speech about bodily functions came to be seen as coarse and vulgar, with euphemisms filling in for unspeakable things like sexual organs and bodily waste (Inglis, 2001).

This process filtered down from those closest to the European courts to the middle classes and, eventually, to the great unwashed masses as the centuries passed. As people in Europe became progressively tied up with each other's affairs they needed increasingly to take account of each other. Feelings and emotions were put under greater social constraint, reducing the chances of wild swings of mood and violent outbursts against their neighbours (Elias, 2012). Social constraint was internalised as self-restraint. Manners and politeness negotiate the mean distance in the tension between social constraint and self-restraint.

Here Elias' relational sociology has some parallels to Schopenhauer's parable about porcupines. As a student of Freud, Elias may have known how Freud (1991a: 130) used Schopenhauer's parable to illustrate his claim that a balance needs to be struck between social intimacy and social distance:

> On a cold winter's day, a number of porcupines huddled together quite closely in order through their mutual warmth to prevent themselves from being frozen. But they soon felt the effect of their quills on one another, which made them again move apart. Now when the need for warmth brought them once more together, the drawback of the quills was repeated so that they were tossed between two evils, until they discovered the proper distance from which they could best tolerate one another. Thus the need for society which springs from the emptiness and monotony of men's lives, drives them together; but their many unpleasant and repulsive qualities and insufferable drawbacks once more drive them apart. The mean distance which they finally discover, and which enables them to endure being together, is politeness and good manners. Whoever does not keep to this is told in England to 'keep his distance'. By virtue thereof, the need for mutual warmth will be only imperfectly satisfied, but, on the other hand, the prick of the quills will not be felt. (Schopenhauer, 1974: 651–2)

Freud claimed that almost every intimate emotional relation between two people that lasts any length of time – marriage, friendship, parents, and children – leaves a sediment of feelings of disgust, aversion, and hostility that are repressed psychologically.

Elias would not have accepted that individuals could exist in a pre-social state, only driven together like porcupines for the warmth of association or the mystical idea that individuals might have enough inner contentment that they would have no need of society. Nor would he have thought much of the timeless, unchanging porcupine-nature of the parable in its search for an eternal truth about the need for society. Elias would, however, have recognised the functional need for humans to come together out of mutual necessity and that a certain power balance is negotiated through processes of interdependency, intimacy, and threat.

Volume two of the book describes the sociogenesis of the state and concludes with an overarching theory of the entire civilising process. Here the rise of the state and the rise of 'civilised' habits are shown to be interconnected. On the one hand, state power was centralised by the time of the absolutist states of seventeenth- and eighteenth-century Europe, draining much of the violence from everyday life. On the other hand, social functions became increasingly differentiated, competitive, and interdependent. Two 'logics' of social, political, and economic competition intersected: the 'monopoly mechanism' and the 'royal mechanism'. Like Marx's twin processes of centralisation and concentration for capital, Elias described the 'monopoly mechanism' as emerging out of the competition between a large number of comparable small social units until 'fewer and fewer will control more and more opportunities, and more and more units will be eliminated from the competition, becoming directly or indirectly dependent on an ever-decreasing number' (Elias, 2012: 303).

Second, a situation develops where the power of all functional groups is so evenly spread that none can strike a decisive blow against the others. Here the 'royal mechanism' is able to hold the balance of power within the 'multi-polar' tensions and ambiguities of dense interdependencies present at court society (Elias, 2012: 355). At the same time the royal ruler is forced to submit to the social pressures that holding competing groups in a constant state of tension creates. The central authority plays one side off against the other by adopting a certain ambivalent style about who is in and who is out of royal favour, itself dependent on a complex network of position-taking in court society. Social ambivalence becomes a defining characteristic of European society and a vital factor in shaping self-restraint.

No group or individual can become too close to the monarch, who tends to favour the second-most-powerful group to keep the most powerful in a position of tension, uncertainty, and cooperation. So long as the social tensions are more or less evenly dispersed the central authority can wield absolute power within a differentiated society. As the state monopolised the means of violence other ways of mutually measuring the power balance in social relations had to be found. Reflexive controls over human contact, including 'continuous reflection, foresight, and calculation, self-control, precise and articulate regulation of one's own affects, knowledge of the whole terrain, human and non-human, in which one acted' became indispensable preconditions of social recognition (Elias, 2012: 439). More indirect tactics than violently lashing out are required in situations where short-term action can have unknown long-term effects.

While the process in France seems paradigmatic, Elias (2012) also showed how the process differed across European state-societies. In England, longer and more sustained contact between the upper and middle classes made it difficult to separate class-specific behaviour from the more general blend of upper-class culture. In Germany, a large number of small and relatively poor courts could not maintain anything like the same interdependencies and opportunities for the upper and middle classes. A socially significant bourgeois class only developed in earnest late on in the development process, leaving state power in the hands of an authoritarian nobility (Elias, 1996). In France, state power was centralised by a powerful and wealthy royal court that over a long period drew on the bourgeoisie for finance (Elias, 2013a). Even the French Revolution did not represent an absolute break with aristocratic models of conduct, which the triumphant bourgeoisie had assimilated from its long contact with court society.

ELIAS AND CRISIS

While the work of Norbert Elias will be forever associated with the long-term moderation of physical violence as part of 'the civilising process' in Europe, this was founded on and returned repeatedly to the crisis of human interdependencies, what he called 'de-civilising spurts' (Fletcher, 1997). As Elias put it, 'The civilization of which I speak is never completed and always endangered' (2013a: 186).

By this Elias meant that civilisation is a social achievement that can be thrown suddenly into reverse in the direction of 'modern barbarism'. His study of the civilising process was above all an attempt to come to grips with how mutual tensions of social interdependencies stabilised over centuries but might unravel in crisis conditions, as happened in 1930s Europe.

When the bonds of interdependency are severed, then the concentration of coercive power in the state becomes literally a matter of life and death. Like millions of others identified as Jewish, Elias experienced this first-hand. He saw the horror of the 1914–1918 war, the chaos after it; experienced anti-Semitism, the rise of fascism; narrowly escaped the concentration camps (where his mother perished); was interned as an enemy alien by Britain; and became alarmed at the Cold War logic of the nuclear weapons race (Elias, 2013b). Such experiences inoculated Elias against the twin extremes of scholasticism and political dogmatism: 'To be sure, the onset of the great social crises had long ago driven me out of the ivory tower – more than three years of war and soldiering, the years in a factory in the depths of the great inflation and much else' (2013b: 12).

In the early 1930s, feelings of insecurity and anxiety and the need for illusory solutions for economic and political crises made Nazi annihilationism an immediate possibility. In his *Studies on The Germans*, Elias (2013a) described the 'de-civilising spurt' in the specific case of Germany as a state-society. A discontinuous and fragmented state formation process in Germany produced over the centuries an authoritarian national habitus. Yet, even here, in the midst of the worst barbarism, the Nazi leadership was concerned that the German people would find mass annihilation emotionally repulsive despite the uneven social conditioning of the national habitus by the civilising process. And when the facts were revealed later in the trial of Adolf Eichmann the atrocities were put down to a historical exception, as something peculiar to the Hitler regime or the Fuhrer's mental state (Elias, 2013a: 225). In this way a collective self-image of the highest national and personal values could be maintained despite all the evidence to the contrary, so dispelling the idea that modern barbarism arose from social conditions and could happen again.

Tragically, the rise of the Nazis revealed where self-deception can lead. By 1932, Elias (2013b: 107) realised that the Nazis posed a real threat as the levels of street violence escalated and the German army, the Reichswehr, sided openly with extreme right-wing militias. In this situation, the state's monopoly of the means of violence broke down as it lost control of the army to the right-wing, leaving a vacuum which was filled by escalating political and anti-Semitic violence. Elias tried in vain to explain the deteriorating situation to local trade unions and socialists in Frankfurt where he worked. Such groups found it difficult to adjust to the impending danger because they could not give up the illusion that the Weimer Republic was a constitutional state that protected the rights of all citizens equally.

In an early essay on the sociology of German anti-Semitism, written in 1929 before the catastrophe, Elias (2006b) located its causes, not in the aberrant beliefs of misguided individuals or groups who need to be enlightened, but as a function of economic and social development in Germany that produced points of friction between Jews and other social strata. Drawing the logical conclusion, Elias argued 'that a social order in which a group of gifted, often spiritually and intellectually rich and productive people is deliberately degraded and debased, and thus is violently crippled, does not deserve to exist and must be fought' (2006b: 83).

CRISIS AND THE STATE FORMATION PROCESS

As society undergoes a pacification process the capacity for violence does not disappear. Violence was centralised as the exclusive right of the state to use force against other states and its internal enemies. Organised state violence does not just threaten the individuals close at hand as inter-personal violence does. States accumulate weapons, materiel, and people because rival states are also acquiring their own capabilities for organised mass violence. Today states legitimate themselves by appealing to national populations as the sole protector of their welfare and well-being. This marks an important shift from pre-modern dynastic states, whose main aim was to protect the ruling elite by conquering rival dynasties and subjugating populations under their rule. So while the state form has changed, states remain a dangerous threat to each other's population.

Evidently, the modern state form presents a paradox. On the one hand, it displaces violence from society and, on the other, it concentrates violence in its own apparatus. This process presents a further paradox. On one hand, the state appears as the guardian of peace and stability and, on the other hand, it is the sole agent of mass lethal violence and suffering. Here the state system reproduces something of the relational dynamic between what Elias (Elias and Scotson, 1994) called the established and the outsiders. Within its territory the state classifies which groups are accepted as 'established' citizens, and those defined as 'outsiders', for instance Muslims, immigrants, or prisoners. At the borders of the state, this translates into an insider–outsider relation, with the state deciding who may pass over the threshold of its jurisdiction.

It is not that political leaders are particularly stupid or mendacious, though they can be both. For Elias the problem is that events become locked into an unplanned 'double-bind' logic that is difficult to control. Elias opposed the tendency in sociology that confuses wishes for reality, what is hoped for rather than what actually is the case. Sociologists must be careful what they wish for. His hope for sociology was that it could provide the big picture of interdependencies and enable humans to take control of the 'double-bind', tit-for-tat logic that so often consumes rival social groups. This double-bind becomes even more dangerous when it threatens humanity on a planetary scale. It is necessary, therefore, to try to face reality squarely and so counter fantasy images that serve to obscure the dangers of double-bind logic.

KNOWLEDGE AS A MEANS OF ORIENTATION

Elias refused to countenance any illusions in parliament, violence, liberalism, or communism. Instead he was committed to sober realism to try to understand the unfolding barbarism without deceiving himself about false solutions. The problem with facing up to reality is that it can be deeply unpleasant. Sociologists may prefer to turn away from it and seek gratification in philosophical puzzles or empirical descriptions. Elias' obdurate realism was such that he even attended a Hitler rally, an extremely dangerous thing for a Jew to do in 1932, in order to know firsthand what was going on. As Elias (2013b: 111–2) explained in an interview:

Why did you want to know what was going on?

Because I think that it is one of the most important tasks of human beings: if they want to arrange their lives better than they are now, they have to know how things are connected together. I mean that quite practically, since otherwise we act wrongly.

Sociologists are often intimately involved with their object of study but somehow need to fashion a degree of detachment to overcome the emotional satisfaction of social mythologies and fantasy images (Elias, 1987).

Elias (1987: 45–6) compared the need for qualified detachment to the tale of Norwegian fishermen being sucked into a whirlpool in Edgar Allan Poe's famous story, 'A Descent into the Maelström' (1982: 127–40). With their boat ravaged by a furious storm, the fishermen are placed at the mercy of violent tides beyond their control, and are swept closer to the deathly vortex. One fisherman resigns himself to his watery fate and begins to feel detached from the unfolding events even as he swirls into the abyss. Terror and paralysis is replaced by reflection and action. He gradually notices that objects of certain shape, mass, and size descend into the vortex at different rates. On the basis of these observations he lashes himself to a barrel that slowed the slide into the whirl. A new hope for survival was made possible by the pattern of the fisherman's becalmed observations allied to his past experience of floating materials found during his routine contact with the coast.

On the other hand, intellectual detachment runs the risk of scholasticism where reality is reified by abstract static concepts (Dunning and Hughes, 2013). Elias called this 'process-reduction': 'the process – the individual human being as a process in growing up, human beings together as a process in the development of humankind – [is] reduced in thought to a state' (2012: 514). It makes no sense for social theory to separate the individual and society.

As far as Elias (1978) was concerned, the sociologist should be a 'destroyer of myths'. If people feel a need for myths, then they should write poetry, Elias (2013b: 105) caustically remarked. From the same interview:

You do not like illusions.

What do you mean: You do not like illusions? I know that they are harmful. Why do you translate that into likes and dislikes? What kind of language is that? I am speaking of knowledge.

What counts as knowledge is not fixed for ever but develops over time in a cumulative direction. This is always a joint theoretical and empirical effort which neither the static methods of induction nor deduction in the philosophy of science capture adequately.

Theories of scientific revolutions, like Thomas Kuhn, tend to exaggerate the role of radical breaks in scientific theory while some theorists of scientific discovery, like Karl Popper, exaggerate the smooth logic of scientific deduction (Elias, 2009a; 2009b). Knowledge has a 'developmental order' in so far as it is premised on some previously well-established 'datum' but it is also subject to contingencies, arbitrary findings, guesswork, changing fashions, and so on. When the scientist plunges into the stream of knowledge, so to speak, it is into the 'relative autonomy' of the scientific community 'as a broad intergenerational grouping of knowledge carriers and knowledge-producers' (2009a: 93).

Polarised criteria such as 'true' or 'false', or verified and refuted, in the philosophy of science are too absolute, static, and final to grasp science as a process of theoretical and empirical work. Science is only relatively true, more or less secure and definite. Moreover, science does not develop as a closed system of instrumental rationality or in isolation from sociological processes. It arises out of and is in continual contact with pre-scientific worlds. On the other hand, sociological relativism treats knowledge as ideologies that directly serve social interests. If this is the case then how might sociology or any other science establish knowledge that doesn't serve the needs of social interests? Elias contended that only with increasingly detached social relations does science become possible as a relatively autonomous process of constructing theories and testing them against systematic observations and comparisons.

'Relative autonomy' is an important qualifying term for Elias. Knowledge is not absolutely autonomous but nor is it absolutely determined by non-scientific interests – political, economic, religious, or cultural. Such relative autonomy allows small scientifically oriented groups to struggle against the prevailing untested beliefs that more powerful groups accept uncritically. Elias held the deeply unfashionable view that science must progress cumulatively so that theory exerts more comprehensive coverage of newly emergent but poorly understood empirical material.

Sociology means for Elias the critical evaluation or rejection of the dominant and widely accepted ideas of society when they fail to correspond to the observable facts. Myths, religious or philosophical, make unprovable claims that guide human conduct and need to be countered with empirically testable theories (Elias, 1978: 52). Elias was also concerned about the opposite process where theories developed to explicate certain facts harden into belief systems that are extended to cover all sorts of things beyond its limited empirical grounding.

POWER BALANCES

Although it is a fundamental feature of society, power is a difficult issue for many people. Power smacks of something offensive and distasteful and is kept shrouded by 'a mist of fear and suspicion' (Elias, 1978: 93). Elias (1978: 69) suggests that this is due to extremely unequal relations of power for much of the development of human societies. As soon as any form of dependency on another being or thing is involved, as it is in all social relations, it is structured by the dynamics of power. Thinking of power in relative terms of a balance of dependency in a 'power ratio' allows some sense of the mutual constitution of power between parties even if they have unequal access to the sources of dependency. This is a function of the fact that power inequalities have diminished, but not disappeared, over the course of the past few hundred years or so. In terms of politics, oligarchic rule by small dynastic-military groups has given way to oligarchic rule by mass parties.

Explaining such shifts in the balance of power is the core problem of sociology ever since Durkheim examined changing differentials of regulation and integration in the social division of labour. Democratisation is not the result of a legal decision to extend the franchise but the reverse process: extension of the franchise expressed the reduction of the power differential between the rulers and the ruled. An increase in social interdependence meant that the ruled could not simply be ignored by the rulers. A similar shift is evident in relations between classes and groups. Compared to the dependence of the peasant on the landlord, wage labourers are far less dependent on any single employer. Power differentials have also been reduced between men and women, adults and children and, more unevenly, humans and animals.

Elias calls this process 'functional democratisation', to refer to the practical equalisation of social relations, something different from the 'institutional democracy' of formal political power. It is a result of the lengthening chains of interdependency created by an increased specialisation of functions. At the same time the chains of interdependency become longer and more opaque, making them more uncontrollable by any single group. Thus, groups and individuals need to anticipate the consequences of their action on other co-dependents even though the future balance of power cannot be known with complete certainty. This provides a more substantive and historical perspective of power as a social relation than formal models of power 'over' others, for instance that isolate overt, covert, and ideological dimensions of power (Lukes, 2005) or, like Foucault (2001), of power passing 'through' people as discourses of body discipline.

Long-term shifts from a large number of relatively small social units to a small number of increasingly larger social units, especially states, has implications for the problem of power differentials. Group charisma now takes its 'exemplary form' in the shape of nations 'united against outsiders by a common social belief in their unique national virtue and grace' (Elias, 2012: xli). Such shifts are obscured unless sociology steps back from the present and places power inequalities in long-term perspective. A focus on long-term processes of social development helps to lower the temptation to reduce human relations to fixed states or substances.

Sociology itself only becomes feasible with the increase in functional democratisation. This means that events can no longer be explained simply in terms of individuals or groups as the authors of large-scale change. An exclusive focus on a political leader like Thatcher or Blair hardly begins to explain the large-scale social changes that occurred while they were Prime Minister of the UK. They were participants in large-scale trials of strength, for instance with trade unions or foreign states, based not on a scientific understanding of 'relatively autonomous functional nexuses' but on an ideological orientation of 'relatively impersonal but emotionally charged belief systems and ideals' (Elias, 1978: 69).

Myths reify or personify power. Power is not a zero-sum issue where some groups somehow have power while others don't have any. Power is always a matter of balances established by 'functional interdependencies'. Elias gives a very clear statement of how dependency determines the ratio of power:

> In so far as we are more dependent on others than they are on us, they have power over us, whether we have become dependent on them by their use of naked force or by our need to be loved, our need for money, healing, status, a career, or simply excitement. (2012: 88)

Power is a relationship, not a thing in itself. Thus, like other social relations, power is always in the balance. The classic example of this is Hegel's idea of the master–slave dialectic. While the master has the power of life and death over the slave in so far as the master is dependent on the slave for the functions performed, then the slave has some power over the master. Elias also notes how a baby has power over parents in so far as the parents place value on it.

CONTRASTS AND VARIETIES

In his study of civilising processes Elias (2012) captured the double-sided process of 'diminishing contrasts and increasing varieties'. Social contrasts are continually being reduced while the range of social possibilities is continually being extended. It is important to note that Elias is not saying that class divisions have been abolished. One trend, for instance, is that lower-class values have spread to all classes. People are now expected to work for a living whereas in earlier societies physical labour of any kind was seen as dishonourable and fit only for the lowest orders. In the other direction, distinguishing features of the upper classes such as table manners or exclusive use of a private toilet have also spread throughout society. In this situation of narrowing contrasts, relatively small cultural differences can take on a magnified importance. Again this is not a uniform process and it is subject to fluctuations, especially when groups are engaged in fierce social competition for the same opportunities.

Upper-class habits of foresight and self-control are important instruments of domination. During European colonialism the upper class supervised each other's conduct and inflicted severe penalties on any of its members who 'let go' of their emotions as exposing a weakness that social inferiors might exploit. Such constant attention to the power balance has deep psychological effects:

> The fear arising from the situation of the whole group – from their struggle to preserve their cherished and threatened position – acts directly as a force maintaining the code of conduct and the cultivation of the super-ego in its members. It is converted into individual anxiety, into the individual's fear of personal degradation or

> merely loss of prestige in his own society. And it is this fear of loss of prestige in the eyes of others, instilled as self-compulsion, whether in the form of shame or a sense of honour, which assures the habitual reproduction of distinctive conduct, and the strict drive control underlying it. (Elias, 2012: 425)

Precisely these contrasts were mitigated and eroded as the upper class became dependent on the colonial system even as they spread their habits of conduct in the colonies, just as at an earlier stage in the state formation process the court nobility and the bourgeoisie reciprocally affected each other in the process of becoming increasingly interdependent.

Ambiguity and anxiety emerge from the twin process of diffusion and exclusion, repulsion and assimilation. In the first phase, lower social groups are 'colonised' or assimilated by higher ones as social inferiors. This raises social tensions and personal insecurities. A classic example is the pressure for the petty bourgeoisie 'to be what one is not' by copying the tastes and conduct of higher classes. Lacking the naturalised poise of their social superiors, social imitation gives rise to 'a peculiar falseness and incongruity of behaviour – which nevertheless conceals a genuine distress, a desire to escape the pressure from above and the sense of inferiority' (Elias, 2012: 473). Lower groups prevented from rising through the social scales do not feel the same compulsion to conform to standards of conduct alien to their social universe.

Group assimilation and imitation is followed by a phase of repulsion, differentiation, or emancipation of rising social groups as they gain in social power, and the upper class is forced into increased isolation and restraint. As their power increases, the mockery and disdain of upper groups begins to disappear. A specifically bourgeois ethos asserts itself, pitching the value of work against the idleness of the aristocracy, knowledge and morals over good manners and polite conversation, professional discipline over courtly formality, and open competition over hereditary privilege. Increasingly, a fusion of the old and the new social codes emerges.

ESTABLISHED–OUTSIDERS THEORY

Elias (2012: 475) began to talk about 'established–outsider relations' as offering a more comprehensive model of social oppression than class relations. A theory of established–outsider relations emerged from a joint study of a working-class community near Leicester, in the East Midlands of England (Elias and Scotson, 1994). The fact that the community was relatively homogeneous, white and working class meant that it could function as a pure laboratory since the power balance was not derived from typical sources of power such as class, religion, ethnicity, or nationality (1994: xvii). One part of the community felt themselves to be superior to the other part simply because they had lived there longer. This gave them greater group cohesion and control over social positions. Outsiders were experienced as a threat to the cohesion of the dominant group, the secret source of established power.

At the heart of this figuration is the uneven balance of power. Power balances need not be conceived as economic struggles for resources, through they often are. Beyond a certain level of material subsistence, group status plays an important function in power differentials. Fantasies about group status are not arbitrary but conform to a practical social figuration formed by individual human beings sharing a background world of emotional contact and unspoken assumptions. This gives it a certain, if limited, elasticity. Outsiders represent a three-sided threat to the established group: a threat to the monopoly of power, to group charisma, and to group norms.

Central to the socio-dynamics of stigmatisation is the way that extreme examples become the basis for categorising entire social groups. In the self-image of the established group, the 'minority of the best' of its members is held up as a mirror of social superiority for the whole group, while 'the minority of the worst' of the outsiders is attributed to all social inferiors. Here the dynamics of 'group charisma' (us) and 'group disgrace' (them) construct rigid emotional barriers for mutual contact. Group members must submit to the charisma of social superiority: 'The gratification received through one's share in group charisma makes up for the personal sacrifice of gratification in the form of submission to group norms' (Elias and Scotson, 1994: xxiii). This involves exclusion of individuals from the disgraced group since any contact would lower an individual's standing inside the charismatic group.

So long as the interdependencies between the established and outsiders are weakly developed, then the power to stigmatise remains undiminished. Even the names used for outsiders – for instance 'nigger', 'papist', 'yid', 'dike', 'chav' – connote disgrace and are intended to inflict humiliation and shame (Elias and Scotson, 1994: xxv). Here a strong cultural tradition, as in the case of Jews, might shield individuals from the psychological damage of disgraceful codes. In contrast, outsiders are deprived of the power to shame socially superior groups unless the power balance becomes more even.

Where a large power differential exists, processes of social inferiority that define groups in terms of lower human value may be internalised by the stigmatised themselves. Past experience of collective disgrace and humiliation may well become a self-fulfilling prophecy when the previously weaker group retaliate. As the power balance becomes more equal, outsiders find themselves with mounting confidence in their ability to strike back. If power differentials are great, tensions will remain suppressed; when power differentials decrease, tensions come into the open. Here is a case of a 'double-bind', a term often used by Elias for the contradictory logic of a situation, first coined in the 1950s by the anthropologist Gregory Bateson (1972).

A person's identity is not a matter of an internal mental state that produces an image of the self somehow separate from social processes. This form of individualisation is what Elias calls *homo clausus*, the closed person or 'thinking statue'. Not only are the processes of illness, ageing, and dying placed behind the scenes of everyday life (de Swaan, 1990; Elias, 1985); disability is also defined as lower in human values and placed on the other side of the threshold of repugnance (Hughes, 2012). Every individual is enveloped by a 'we-image' as well as an

'I-image'. All we-images are composites of fantasy and reality. As a changing combination of fantasy and reality, 'normality' is an incredibly difficult state for individual 'thinking statues' to attain and maintain.

When reality changes, fantasy we-images can assume a pronounced importance. Nations, like Britain for instance, that once basked in a charismatic we-image may find it difficult to adjust to their declining importance relative to other nations. Imagined national charisma outlives the power balance that once supported it and may encourage a false assessment of its present status in the world. The emotional equation of charismatic groups with the highest human values makes it difficult to surrender illusions since that also means a lower human value for the we-group. When reality finally breaks through the fantasy shield of a formerly powerful nation, the feeling of lost greatness can be traumatic.

BOURDIEU: SOCIOLOGY AS A CRAFT

Where Elias emphasises interdependent processes, Bourdieu has a reputation for concentrating on the structural logic that reproduces unequal positions in social space, leaving little scope for discontinuities, crisis, and change. This is too one-dimensional. Bourdieu's own epistemology is based on the need for critique and a break with received wisdom through empirical objectivation. He is an unforgiving critic of abstract 'social theories'. Where 'pure theory' logically specifies everything about everything in advance it puts sociology as a craft into suspended animation. Sociology represents a formidable instrument of freedom so long as it recognises the specific determinations that weigh on it as an institutional practice.

Bourdieu opens his methodological textbook, *The Craft of Sociology* (Bourdieu et al., 1991), with a long quote from Comte to the effect that method cannot be studied in isolation from the uses to which it is put. 'There would be nothing to add' to Comte's stipulation, Bourdieu argues, were it not for the fact that both the prophets of theory and 'the high priests of method' dissociate theory from method and isolate both from the impure practices of social research (1991: 1). Methodic sociological practice develops as a 'craft' habitus. Following the philosopher of science, Gaston Bachelard, sociological facts, in Bourdieu's (1992) words, are 'conquered, constructed and confirmed'.

Sociological facts are first conquered by an 'epistemological break' (Bachelard in Bourdieu 1991: 233–239) with everyday concepts already pre-given by the social world. 'Spontaneous sociology' too often absorbs into its practice social preconstructions, as when something defined by non-scientific authority as a 'social problem' – youth, crime, housing, and so on – is uncritically repackaged as a 'sociological problem'. Sociology uncovers the structure of relations presupposed and often concealed by the pre-given reality of common-sense notions. Yet common sense is also part of that reality:

> Challenging the 'truths' of common-sense has become a commonplace of methodo-
> logical discourse, which is thereby in danger of losing all its critical force. Bachelard and
> Durkheim show that a point-by-point challenge to the prejudices of common-sense
> is no substitute for a radical questioning of the principles on which common-sense is
> based. (Bourdieu et al., 1991: 93)

Durkheim's great merit for Bourdieu was to always begin by conceptually reconstructing the immediately given reality, say of religion or suicide, although
Durkheim's emphasis on social facts as things proved far too substantialist for
Bourdieu's approach to relational sociology (Robbins, 2006: 572). This is
because 'it is so difficult to know that one does not know, and what one does not
know' (Bourdieu et al., 1991: 111). Psychological explanations of social institutions like the family, for example, have the intuitive attraction of being
immediately self-evident from the perspective of individual reality. However, it
is common-sense intuition of an individual reality itself that needs to be
explained by social institutions.

Science proceeds to construct facts as theoretical objects. Theoretical construction develops on the basis of what Bachelard (in Bourdieu et al., 1991: 144) called
'polemical reason', by which he meant criticism of the assumptions contained in the
given object to produce 'critical objectification, of an objectivity which only retains
that part of the object which it has criticized'. The problem of theoretically reconstructing the problem cannot be resolved in advance according to hard-and-fast
rules. Reality is not somehow 'proved' by 'neutral' techniques of data collection that
'theory' would only contaminate.

For instance, simply because there is not an absolute line that separates
social classes, with the working class on one side of the line and the middle
class on the other, does not mean that classes do not exist. Classes are constructed as the object of a theory of relations: 'The different "cultures" that
coexist in a single stratified society are objectively situated in relation to one
another, because the different groups situate themselves in relation to one
another, especially when they make reference to their culture' (Bourdieu et al.,
1991: 48). Theoretical models are thus constructed that break with spontaneously given reality and are capable of generalisation.

Finally, an empirical theory of relations is confirmed by the exercise of 'applied
rationalism'. This measures sociology against the reality that it initially left behind
owing to the suspicion of its unconscious presuppositions as part of a unitary
process of fact-theory-validation: 'facts that validate the theory are only as good
as the theory they validate' (Bourdieu et al., 1991: 60). A coherent theory remains
vulnerable to the discovery of problematic facts, whereas spontaneous sociology
finds 'easy confirmation' since it accepts the facts at face value, one at a time. Facts
need to be accommodated by the constructed theoretical system, constantly moving between part and whole in a 'methodic circle' (1991: 65). Positivism restricts
itself to technical control of research instruments in order to counter the 'intui-
tionist' shortcuts of social philosophy freed from the laborious methodic circle.
Without this process, spontaneous sociology is condemned 'to oscillate, as it often
does at present, between a "social theory" without empirical foundations and a

theoretically rudderless empiricism, between the risk-free temerity of intuition-ism and the undemanding meticulousness of positivism' (1991: 68).

PRONOUNCED REFLEXIVITY

Because the frontier between common sense and science is particularly porous in sociology, Bourdieu argues that it is necessary to adopt an even more pro-nounced reflexivity – a sociology of sociology. Sociologists lean towards the poles of theoreticism or empiricism less by vocation, as they may think, than by the social position that they occupy in the sociological field and wider social space. Sociologists are themselves bound to a habitus formed by primary experi-ences and a logic that is bound to a position in the intellectual field. Failure to recognise this runs the grievous risk of reintroducing the dispositions of social class or gender into a scientific relationship to social space. For instance, an account of economic determinism is more likely to seem crude and vulgar to sociologists that intuitively identify with individual agency, freedom, creativity, and subjectivity. Intellectuals are susceptible to what Bourdieu calls a 'class eth-nocentrism' that generates 'the presupposition of the absence of presuppositions' (Bourdieu et al., 1991: 72).

Only a sociology of sociology can prevent the uncritical absorption of social dis-positions into scientific practices. Sociology needs to reflexively exercise the 'epistemological vigilance' of a well-defended self-critical scientific community – 'the scientific city' as Bachelard called it (Bourdieu et al., 1991: 233) – as a protection against intellectual fads and outside influences of the social world, or 'heteronomy' as Bourdieu called the external limiting of scientific autonomy. Reflexivity has a long pedigree in sociology as meaning something approaching ethical and intellectual self-awareness and self-monitoring. It is not enough however, Bourdieu contends, to have good intentions but to recognise that 'all kinds of distortions are embedded in the very structure of the research relationship' (Bourdieu, 1999: 608).

Unless consciously controlled, such distortions reproduce a pattern of sym-bolic violence in research, not least in the unequal power and social distance of the researcher and the researched. Loic Wacquant defines Bourdieu's form of reflexivity as 'the inclusion of a theory of intellectual practice as an integral component and necessary condition of a critical theory of society' (Bourdieu and Wacquant, 1992: 36). In Bourdieu's sense, then, reflexivity is less about thinking or reflecting about your own personal feeling or thoughts as the privi-leged author of reality. Within sociology, Bourdieu viewed individualised reflexivity as a form of narcissism and solipsism. Sociological practice becomes reflexive only when it tries to objectify itself in the same way that it objectifies the subject of study.

Sociology needs to control its own biases if it wishes to produce knowledge adequate to a divided social world. Typical biases include neglecting both the social origin and position of the sociologist in terms of class, gender, and ethnicity, and their relationship to academic and institutional hierarchies. Intellectuals are especially vulnerable to what John Dewey (1929: 23) called 'the spectator theory of knowledge' and Bourdieu (1998) 'the scholastic point of view' that confuse the practical logic of the world for the theoretical logic of science. Science as a 'serious game' is removed from the urgency of practical necessity. As such it is vulnerable to the scholastic temptation to raise speculative problems that gratify the theoretical disposition while forgetting the social conditions that make scholastic gratification possible. While Bourdieu (1999: 607) was loath to isolate 'theory' as a gratuitous object for 'pedantic disquisitions on hermeneutics or the "ideal speech situation"' he did reflect at great length on the theory and practice of the social sciences across a number of works.

CRISIS AND CONCEPTS

Many of Bourdieu's concepts were developed to explain various facets of crisis. His earliest fieldwork in Algeria was conducted when traditional nomadic society was convulsed by a social transformation against the background of a colonial war (Bourdieu, 2012). Something of this experience informed his study of the crisis of peasant society in Bearn, France, where he had grown up (Bourdieu, 2008a). Crisis was experienced by unmarried men as peasant society was transformed by their inability to attract a partner, which is expressed in the bodily emotions of the village dance:

> Standing at the edge of the dancing area, forming a dark mass, a group of older men look on in silence. All aged about 30, they wear berets and unfashionably cut suits … There they all are, all the bachelors. (2008a: 129)

Married men in the village of the same age no longer attend the dance, compounding the bodily discomfort of the bachelors at the edge of the dancefloor.

Bourdieu brings in to play his concepts of 'habitus' and 'hexis' to understand the crisis of traditional society as an embodied experience. Habitus, with field and cultural capital, is now in wide circulation as a characteristic concept of Bourdieu (though Marcel Mauss, Elias, and others also used the term). Habitus refers to the predispositions individuals acquire from childhood that structure their perceptions of the social world. It instils a certain 'bodily hexis' as the physical dispositions of social comportment, posture, and motility:

> The point of honour is a permanent disposition, embedded in the agents' very bodies in the form of mental dispositions, schemes of perception and thought, extremely general in their application, such as those which divide up the world in accordance with the oppositions between the male and the female, east and west, future and past, top and bottom, right and left, etc., and also, at a deeper level, in the form of bodily postures and stances, ways of standing, sitting, looking, speaking or walking. (Bourdieu, 1977: 15)

In the right setting, habitus makes us feel perfectly at home, like 'a fish in water'. In other settings, habitus draws out deep feelings of incompetence and shame.

Habitus is also collective. Since members of social groups share similar experiences of the world, they will tend to inhabit a similar habitus – a system of dispositions or a 'feel for the game' as necessary and generative social practices.

Bourdieu's (1988) study of the educational field in France, *Homo Academicus*, revealed the objective contradiction between habitus and field that underlay the crisis in May 1968 – the declining value of educational qualifications threatened privileged students with an indeterminate, even proletarian future. By 'field' Bourdieu means a discrete structure of institutional positions and networks in social space, like education, art, or science – a 'field of force' latent with power.

In May 1968 a crisis specific to the university field became a general crisis. Hence the revolt had less to do with the spontaneous expression of existential freedom as the ideologists of the movement asserted, than the operation of the objective structures of contiguous fields. Such a crisis represents a challenge to social scientists whose profession is 'to read the meaning of the world' (1988: 160). Political profits are to be made with an instant analysis of events packaged for the right market. Scientific research and analysis takes time, however.

Several latent crises conspired to raise a specific crisis of social reproduction in the educational field, what Bourdieu identified as the 'generalised downclassing' of university qualifications, to a general crisis of social space. In this case, young students from the dominant class found the expected reconversion of cultural capital into academic capital under threat. By 'capital' Bourdieu means things and attributes that attract profits in three main forms: *social capital* (privileged networks), *cultural capital* (qualifications, avant-garde art, novels, and music, 'proper' conduct and speech) and *economic capital* (money). What matters is the amount and composition of total capital. Different combinations of capital can be adjusted to harvest profits from specific fields, for instance greater cultural capital in the educational field, greater money capital in the financial field, or greater social capital in the employment field.

Spontaneous slogans, such as those demanding that elite universities be handed over to the workers, produced 'a magical denial of the factors causing the malaise' (Bourdieu, 1988: 186). Schemes of perception that belong to an earlier phase of social space, what Bourdieu (1988: 167) calls *allodoxia*, contrasts here with what he calls *doxa*, meaning a taken-for-granted misrecognition of the arbitrary conditions of the field. Pushed into revolt, bourgeois students threatened a key instrument for reproducing their own social privilege by calling its legitimacy into question. Crisis was felt most intensively in social spaces that encouraged 'maladjusted expectations', as in the ambiguous career expectations of sociology and psychology graduates, taught by junior academics with limited opportunities due to the rapid expansion of the disciplines. Seen as a 'pretentious' challenger to philosophy, sociology represented 'a deluxe refuge allowing all those who wish to flaunt grand ambitions in theory, in politics and in political theory, the maximum symbolic profit for the cheapest educational entry fee' (1988: 171).

In the conjuncture of May 1968, local crises in relatively autonomous fields coincided in their relative dependence – 'independence in dependency' – on the economic structure to produce a critical historical event. While the crisis included 'accidental' factors external to the field, like police violence, it was only generalised when the agents experiencing the crisis were subject to similar social conditions. Agents in different social fields occupied 'structurally homologous' positions to the positions in open crisis, and so came to identify with the movement as a way to also advance their own specific grievances. Here the producers and distributors of mass cultural goods seized the opportunity to protest against their own symbolic devaluation:

> A crisis specific to a field where the opposition between the dominant and the subordinate takes the form of unequal access to the attributes of legitimate cultural competence should tend to give preference to the burgeoning of subversive ideological themes, such as the denunciation of 'mandarin rule' and all forms of statutory authority founded on academically guaranteed competence. (Bourdieu, 1988: 178).

Crisis forces the compromises and concessions of routine existence into the open and announces the emergence of 'prophets' critical of social orthodoxies (Fowler, 2011: 48). Demands are made for principled decisions, especially in a 'predominantly symbolic crisis' like 1968. 'Symbolic reversals' are initiated, like calling a professor by their first name, while the irruption disoriented those most integrated into the field. Ordinary time was suspended by strikes and demonstrations, replaced by 'festive time', and privileged spaces like theatres were occupied by trespassers.

All this made the crisis live. When the immediate crisis dissipated, what remained was the symbolic revaluation of everyday life in a culturally transformed perception of hierarchies, habits, manners, and deference. Here Bourdieu reaches a conclusion similar to that developed by Elias and Cas Wouters (2007: 231) of the symbolic 'informalisation' of society through a 'controlled decontrolling of emotional controls'. Where they see the relaxation of formal controls over social conduct as part of the long-term civilising process, Bourdieu provides a conjunctural analysis that makes May 1968 a symbolic turning point, even if few of the movement's demands were realised.

OUT OF TIME

Bourdieu's (1984) study of patterns of cultural consumption in *Distinction* highlighted the existential crisis experienced by the growth of lower-middle-class groups trying to acquire familiarity with high cultural taste but finding themselves ill-equipped by the dispositions bequeathed by their class habitus. This creates a tendency to over-compensate and to make an ostentatious show of having good taste, what Bourdieu calls 'hyper-correction'. As the dispositions of habitus are overtaken by changes in the cultural field, such classes end up out of time with the new opportunities and possibilities, what Bourdieu calls 'hysteresis' or the 'Don Quixote effect' after the knight-errant of Cervantes' novel failed to adapt his traditional code of chivalry to the new era and futilely tilted at windmills. Something similar happens to revolutionaries in non-revolutionary times:

The hysteresis of habitus, which is inherent in the social conditions of the reproduction of the structures in habitus, is doubtless one of the foundations of the structural
lag between opportunities and the disposition to grasp them which is the cause of
missed opportunities and, in particular, of the frequently observed incapacity to
think historical crises in categories of perception and thought other than those of the
past, albeit a revolutionary past. (Bourdieu, 1977: 83)

Cultural capital is only acquired by those with the time and leisure to inhabit
prized cultural possessions and defer gratification to some distant point in the
future when cultural knowledge can be capitalised upon as symbolic profits.
Without the leisure or motivation for cultural deferment the working class engage
simply in direct and unpretentious conviviality. Everybody knows what they like.
They just can't say why. Workers look for a spontaneously self-evident literal
meaning in cultural representations like photographs, television or books, while
the cultural elite take up the detached, abstract aesthetic of the spectator.

In the 1990s, Bourdieu and colleagues examined the effect that neo-liberalism
was having on generating widespread insecurity and anxiety in everyday life.
Weight of the World (Bourdieu, 1999) was the result of a large research collaboration into new forms of social suffering and degraded social life. Through personal
interview testimonies Bourdieu's team exposed something of the intimacy of
'positional suffering' of cultural inferiority alongside material poverty. Here the
revised role of the state results in lived contradictions where people are caught
between the 'left hand' (social function) and the 'right hand' (economic function)
of the state in the political construction of reality. On the one hand, social, health,
education, housing, and community workers experience the contradiction
between impossible missions and scant resources. On the other hand, the most
disadvantaged young people experience their descent into the 'subproletariat' and
the prolonged experience of school as a 'failure': 'a subproletariat fated by lack of
power over the present give up on the future or constantly switch aspirations, is
rooted in an absolute uncertainty about the future and in the conflicting aspirations that school opens and closes at one and the same time' (1999: 185).

In response to the 'neo-liberal vulgate' Bourdieu (2008b) adopted a more public
form of sociology, what he called a 'realpolitik of reason' in support of social
movements, trade unions, migrants, dispossessed youth, and the welfare state.
While this was alternatively represented as either a radical or a conservative return
to the republican traditions of state sociology established in France by Durkheim,
Bourdieu saw the public responsibility of the sociologist as standing in the tradition in France of a 'specific intellectual', at least since Emile Zola's public
declaration of *J'accuse!* with the Dreyfus affair in 1898, as against the 'universal
intellectual' seeking to pass public judgement on every conceivable public issue.

Relational sociology

Sociology disenchants what philosophy still wants to enchant. A number of
attempts have been made to shelter social and moral philosophy from the claim
that relational sociology has superseded them. Elias and Bourdieu attempted to

establish the connections between things that appear on the surface to be disconnected. Both share an intellectual legacy of classical sociology and European
philosophical traditions. Bourdieu expressed his intellectual solidarity with Elias
in 'the historical psychosociology of an actual grand historical process' (Bourdieu
and Wacquant, 1992: 92) in the formation of the state and the function of symbolic violence. They derived fundamental principles from Durkheim and Weber
that Bourdieu considered constitutive of sociology.

Elias and Bourdieu engaged critically with the relational philosophy of phenomenology and the relational theory of the neo-Kantian philosopher Ernst
Cassirer as alternatives to 'substantialist theory' (Goudsblom, 1995). Bourdieu
took inspiration from Cassirer's (1923) *Substance and Function* to develop a 'relational mode of thought' as a 'break' with the 'substantialist mode of thought'.
Conceived structurally, relationism characterises each element in a system 'by the
relationships which unite it with all the others in a system and from which it
derives its meaning and function' (Bourdieu, 1990: 4). While Elias (2013b: 148)
was less susceptible to viewing relations in the static terms of 'structures', he was
exposed in his early philosophical training to the relational theory of Cassirer and
claimed 'some affinity with his work', although how much and what kind of
affinity is disputed (Goudsblom, 1995).

Bourdieu and Elias transposed Cassirer's relationism into a sociological idiom
wedded to empirical inquiry. As far as Elias was concerned, even Cassirer's relational theory remained far too close to the Kantian objective of uncovering
'timeless' metaphysical categories within variable historical processes, just as
Simmel attempted to banish substantive content from a supposedly invariant
principle of universal form. When Bourdieu claimed that Elias shared with him a
relational approach in common with Cassirer, Elias rejected the purely formalist
character of Cassirer's relational philosophy: 'It is highly misleading to use "rela-
tionalism" as a purely formalistic category, disguising fundamental differences of
substance' (in Kilminster and Wouters, 1995: 101).

Theory for Elias cannot be formal and abstract, as in philosophy, but must be
supported substantively. This further means that the relations of a social figuration
cannot be frozen synchronically at a single point in time but must be integrated
diachronically within a processual understanding of change over time. Relations
and processes are inseparable in Elias' conception of figurational sociology. For his
part, Bourdieu criticised Elias for failing to register 'critical breaks' in the civilising
process and for failing to identify which groups benefit from the state monopoly of
violence. Precisely these issues of discontinuity and the group dynamics of power
were addressed by Elias' (2013a) studies of state violence, established and outsiders,
and the 'critical break' represented by fascism in Germany.

Elias and Bourdieu are often presented as torn between two alternative camps
of uncritical sympathisers and dismissive critics. This schism fails to do justice to
their achievements. Neither produced anything like a finished theoretical system
that could be applied wholesale to every field of study. Instead, both attempted to
provide a broad set of conceptual tools to practise sociology as an open-ended
inquiry. Their work has been subject to considerable criticism, codification, and
caricature. Bourdieu became narrowly identified with the idea of 'cultural capital'
and Elias with 'the civilising process' without these conceptual tools necessarily

being located within a wider theoretical and historical understanding. Concepts like habitus cannot be isolated from the wider framework held together by other concepts like symbol, power, field, figuration, capital, sociogenesis-psychogenesis, social space, capital, doxa, relative autonomy, and so on, as well as the particularities of the subject being examined.

At the centre of their concerns is the problem of power as a social relation rather than a thing that some people have or possess. This focus on power may be uncomfortable and an inconvenience for approaches in sociology that view social subjects as things of more or less of equal value and the problem of unequal power relations a marginal concern. In such cases, discussions of identity, culture, emotions, or the body may reflect little on the state, violence, or the impersonal logic of economic compulsion (Adkins, 2011).

CRITIQUE AND DEVELOPMENT

A range of cultural theorists in the hothouse intellectual field in France denied that 'popular culture' was necessarily inferior to elite culture or purely functional, and accused Bourdieu of a 'miserabalist' rejection of popular culture as the site of domination that leaves no room for resistance, values, and creativity (Rigby, 1991). Bourdieu's former collaborator Luc Boltanski (2011: 18–23) argues that Bourdieu's sociology operates in the scientific register of objectivity and so neglects the normative sources of critique in morals and values. Bourdieu's self-reinforcing structuralism predominates over sense-making problems of phenomenology. Hence the relative uncertainty of worldly situations is undone by a logic of necessity attributed retrospectively to structures and dispositions. If all social subjects suffer from symbolic domination, blissfully unaware, then something must have hidden it from view.

Bourdieu's closed theoretical model, Boltanski claims, has the effect of squeezing the life out of everyday existence and with it any possibility of critique. Boltanski argues that his own 'meta-critical theory' both unmasks the institutional structures of domination and advances the sense of justice that already exists in the social world:

> Critique only becomes meaningful with respect to the order that it puts in crisis, but also, reciprocally, that the systems which ensure something like the preservation of an order only become fully meaningful when one realizes that they are based on constant threat, albeit unequally depending on epochs and societies, represented by the possibility of critique. (2011: 57)

Bourdieu, Boltanski claims, surreptitiously deploys emotive rhetoric within putatively objective analyses to inflame the reader's sense of injustice instead of clearly stating the problem of normative commitment and descriptive truth. Boltanski's pragmatic theory makes uncertainty more salient by isolating all moments of action as events in their own right to pinpoint moments of dilemma, decision, modifications, and so on.

A different critique was made by Jacques Ranciere (2003) that Bourdieu merely replaced Plato's philosopher-king to install himself as a 'sociologist-king', where science rather than metaphysics rules the roost. This sociology accepts the residual role that philosophy left it, that of describing the social causes of symbolic misrecognition of the poor's own predicament. Sociology is content to deal with doxa as the banal 'small change' of economic exploitation (2003: 169).

Bourdieu simply inverts Plato's myth of leisure and contemplation as the secret of educational success but, in fact, school is far from leisurely. As all students know, it is regulated by timetables, homework, exams, punishments, dress codes, and so on. If educational success is self-selecting, then sociology must assert that what is arbitrary must appear as necessary. Bourdieu's claim that only the middle class play the game of symbolic capital, while the poor do not have the time or motivation to invest, does not allow for social mingling, learning, or exchange of cultural taste whereby the rich enjoy 'working-class sports' and the poor acquire the 'taste' for cultural things (Ranciere, 2003: 189). Ranciere's (2012) own historical studies show how militant workers embraced bourgeois culture, becoming writers, poets and dandies. By denying social mingling Bourdieu's cultural arbitrary becomes an absolute, without contradiction, choice, or contingency.

While Ranciere charges Bourdieu with the oft-repeated claim that structures reproduce themselves with the collusion of its losers, Elias is similarly convicted of an old-fashioned evolutionism, where civilisation and progress are automatically reproduced, rendering de-civilising convulsions inexplicable. In his important study, *Modernity and the Holocaust*, Zygmunt Bauman (2000b) argues that there are two antithetical ways to explain the genocide: either it was an aberration to the usual progress of civilising processes or it is inscribed into modernity as an ever-present potential. Elias 'celebrates with a relish' the first myth-explanation while Bauman (2000b: 107) critically identifies with the second account. Elias allegedly supports an 'etiological myth' of civilisation as a symbol of Western superiority. In contrast, Bauman argues that violence has simply been removed from daily life and organised by technical specialists and bureaucracies lacking any social or moral controls. The pacification of daily life makes it defenceless against the machinery of organised violence in pursuit of a total rational state-society.

Like Boltanski's critique of Bourdieu, Bauman relies on essentially philosophical rather than sociological premises, that the 'natural' feeling of humans for each other is being distorted by the opaque rationality of modernity that obscures the consequences of social action (Dunning and Mennell, 1998). In fact, one of the key aspects of the civilising process that Elias identified sixty years before was exactly the point that Bauman claims as a new insight: that violence was displaced behind the scenes of daily life and kept in constant readiness for use by the state (Fletcher, 1997). Bauman also fails to register that Elias identified the possibilities for 'de-civilising spurts' such as genocidal fascism in Germany. However, such processes occur under definite sociological conditions, not as the demi-urge of instrumental rationality.

Rather than speculation about human nature or the political demands of 'universal intellectuals', both Elias and Bourdieu assumed that theoretical reconstruction, better description, and close observation are the necessary first stages in a 'detour of detachment' before returning, better informed by substantive theory for a public critique of the logic of social power.

CONCLUSION

Today, as in the past, crisis sits at the core of social theory. This is so in a double sense. Social theory responds to crisis in the social universe and is itself productive of a seemingly permanent theoretical crisis. This is reflected in the constant need every few years for theoretical 'turns'. Every such turn finds it necessary to dismiss what went before and to present itself as overcoming past deficiencies and aporia. In the serious game of theoretical turn-taking it is necessary to construct earlier theories as profoundly mistaken. It is all too easy for social theory to wage polemical struggles against waxwork adversaries of their own making, just as the brutality of the past or faraway places is easily denounced by the self-righteous moral tones of the present from places nearby. Denouncing 'brutal methods in the age of gentle methods' is one way to misrecognise contemporary forms of institutional domination (Bourdieu, 2008a: 196).

It is the contention of this book that placing reflexive controls over theory-baiting creates a chance that the crisis afflicting social theory might be alleviated. A necessary stage in theoretical progress is to understand adversaries in any theoretical dispute as potential allies, not enemies to be demolished, since they may well have uncovered genuine problems demanding substantive sociological analysis. It is essential to control the gratuitous misrepresentation of competing theoretical perspectives, especially ones that have come to be marginalised as barely worth a second thought. Certain types of social theory are overlooked or treated with disdain today while more familiar survivals in sociology, 'the big names', are returned to ritualistically for ever-increasing commentary that runs in ever-decreasing circles.

Too often the crisis of social theory has been a consequence of an internal, esoteric struggle to dominate the field rather than a response to social novelty. Domination is the power to define the reality of others from the standpoint of imposing particular norms as if they were universal ones. Institutional power allows opponents, past and present, to be cast as deluded fools who failed to recognise the fundamental theoretical errors uncovered by opponents whose conceptual faultlines will, in turn, also be exposed.

There is no more self-deluded a figure in sociological texts than Comte. Comte responded to post-revolutionary crisis in France by raising a fundamental challenge to metaphysical philosophy. While Comte's dreams for positive sociology failed to bring the crisis to a close it nonetheless exercised a grip on the socio-logical imagination from John Stuart Mill, Herbert Spencer, Emile Durkheim through to Norbert Elias. This did not prevent 'positivism' from becoming a car-toonish form of 'scientism' in the tradition of ill-informed theory-baiting. Even today, unfounded clichés and caricatures are routinely trotted out about Comte's project despite substantial scholarship demonstrating their speciousness. Indeed, the caricature of Comte's positivism is often the exact opposite of what he attempted to do.

Although Marx has been treated with more respect than Comte in social the-ory, indeed with uncritical reverence in some quarters, the tradition of Marxist social theory has, of course, been subject to more than a century of intense theory-baiting. Despite the profound crises of social survival that capitalism reproduces along with itself as a system, Marx's theory today is among the most vigorously denounced. It is described as a 'grand theory' indifferent to the varieties of social life, which is in any case reduced to the economic base and vulgar materialism. However, Marx saw his own social theory as concrete, specific and processual. Its focus was on definite social forms, social relations of class above all, not timeless abstractions. Marx developed an original constructive method that attempted to presuppose the concrete at every stage of theoretical abstraction. Marx insisted on locating social forms in terms of historically specific conditions and opposed all attempts to transcend definite social relations by theoretical worldplay and wish-ful thinking.

Theorists who claimed to be legitimate heirs drew diametrically opposed lessons from Marx's social theory. In one type of Marxism, therefore, objective historical structures determine the possibilities for action while, in the other type, subjective political action determines the fundamental structures. This tension persisted as Marxist theory went through various changes in post-war Europe, with a rediscov-ery of praxis and everyday life by the 'existential Marxism' of Merleau-Ponty, Sartre, and Lefebvre and, in opposition to the lingering influence of idealist philosophy in Marxism, emergence of the 'structuralist Marxism' of Althusser and the formal philosophical logic of 'analytical Marxism' (Callinicos, 1989).

Like Comte and Marx, Nietzschean social theory also broke with traditional notions of philosophy as a search for universal truth, beauty and morality. Nietzsche developed a new kind of theory, an anti-philosophy, which some saw as having important consequences for social theory and sociology, not least Simmel and Weber, but also Adorno, Horkheimer, Benjamin, Lefebvre through to Foucault and other 'post-structuralists'. At the furthest extreme of anti-philosophy was the social theory of Otto Neurath. Similarly, the relational sociology of Bourdieu and Elias aimed to control the excesses of prophetic speculation in social theory by synthesising theoretical traditions as 'tools for thinking' about substantive problems, not as scholastic exercises in constructing an abstract meth-odology or epistemology. Phenomenology, pragmatism, and feminist standpoint theory, for instance, insist that since theory is context-dependent it requires detailed, ethnographic studies of power relations in everyday life, although here also satisfaction is taken from abstract conceptual puzzles that obscure power relations behind static categories.

An examination of everyday life might be thought to produce the most concrete forms of social theory. With the micrological studies of Kracauer and Benjamin the ephemera of everyday life was uncovered as historically specific constructions. Although indebted to a unique form of theological Marxism that produced its fair share of obscurities about elusive categories such as 'aura', what Benjamin called 'delicate empiricism' proved itself to be a more adequate kind of social theory than formal theoretical system-building. At a far higher level of abstraction, Lefebvre remained indebted to existential philosophy for understanding the meaning of everyday life through a reflexive critique of social relations.

These represent different roads to substantive theory. Social theory has repeatedly turned away from the sociological constitution of problems to revisit the most general philosophical concepts, often with polemical and ideological intent. Problems in social theory are devised in philosophical terms around an apparently contradictory or mutually exclusive conceptual binary such as subject and object. Theory 'progresses' by emphasising now one side of the dualism, now the other, before introducing a third term to reconcile the abstract opposition. By producing a scholastic solution to a non-existent problem, a wedge is driven between theory and empirics in sociology. Priority is given to conceptual and ideological puzzles over theory developed in close contact with substantive problems of sociological inquiry. Human relations are so varied in practice that only a constant interrogation of language and concepts seems able to impose theoretical order on them.

Exposing fatal weaknesses in rival theories is a scholastic game that necessarily induces crisis. A number of solutions are possible to control the symptoms of crisis. First, sociologists may don the mantle of the prophet, free to comment on all manner of social problems made visible by crisis from the most general standpoint possible. While prophecy is evident with Comte and Marx, they themselves thought that they stood on firm scientific ground. Nietzschean social theory ranging from Simmel and critical theory to post-structuralism measured the social world negatively against the 'ought' of alternative images of the highest human capacities. Prophetic philosophical constructions serve the purpose of morally damning current realities from individual examples rather than the laborious process of substantive analysis. Prophecy can also be used to justify current policies, as with Giddens' promotion of Third Way politics, based on generalisations about social change drawn from selective illustrations.

Second, crisis may be evaded when sociologists confine theory to increasingly narrow areas of theoretical or methodological interest. Sociology has fragmented into the specialised activities of limited sub-disciplines, for example, organisational sociology, sociology of science, sociology of knowledge, cultural studies, criminology, and so on. More and more is known about less and less. Increased specialisation is bought at the expense of increased ignorance of other fields or other traditions in social theory. This encourages the glossing of social theory into easily digestible models, rendering them vulnerable to dismissive caricatures and limited judgements of social theory's 'relevance' to particular sub-fields. Social theory itself comes to be viewed in terms of technical expertise. It constantly runs the risk of becoming an esoteric specialism open to initiates steeped in narrowly

conceived theoretical problem solving without need of exoteric contact with substantive problems. It is easier to constantly discuss whether 'reality' or 'society'
exists than to study it. Theoretical generalisation accelerates away from empirical
studies to develop, almost unchecked, as a semi-autonomous game.

A third possible solution to crisis is a context-dependent 'critical' sociology sensitive to the way that conceptual language is used. Such a linguistically sensitive social
theory is suggested by Vološinov's sociology of the concrete utterance or, at a more
removed level, Habermas' 'ideal speech situation', as well as much of the 'linguistic
turn' associated with discourse analytics and post-modernism. Here social theory
might be formulated in such a way that it stands a chance of being understood and
discussed by all participants, even by dissenters and non-specialists. Raymond
Boudon (1980: 38), for instance, predicted in 1971 that by the year 2000 a general
theoretical vocabulary would be shared by sociologists, replacing the then-current
'impressionistic social philosophy' and 'the glossing of new sacred texts'. This has
not yet happened. If anything the tendency to theoretical fragmentation far out-
weighs the tendency to theoretical synthesis.

Finally, substantive social theory, or simply 'sociological theory', will temper
theory-baiting. In this conception, theory and empirical analysis are co-dependent,
as in the relational sociology of Bourdieu and Elias, Neurath's 'physicalism', or
Benjamin's 'delicate empiricism'. Theoretical synthesis provides a heuristic, guiding function for specific empirical content and generates more adequate
sociological knowledge. Beyond certain general categories essential for orientation, like habitus or figuration, this need not mean a standardised conceptual
vocabulary or methodology. Invariant categories rarely prove adequate to historically variable processes. Nor does it mean a return to naive empiricism since
theory and research necessarily function together as an iterative process. Here
concepts operate in ways similar to what Bourdieu referred to as 'thinking tools',
useful for specific forms of sociological research and analysis but not as autonomous categories that define reality in advance.

In this survey of social theory and crisis an attempt has been made to lessen the
temptation to engage in counter-productive 'theory-baiting' rooted in polemical
social and political philosophy. Social theory must become practical and specific.
As Holmwood and Stewart argue, 'Instead of a return to the drawing-board to
find appropriate methodological procedures and rational criteria, the specific and
located nature of problems ensures that creative solutions involve the resources
that the schemes in crisis otherwise hold within them' (1991: 178). Progress has
undoubtedly been made in the direction of substantive sociological theory, particularly with the refusal by relational sociology to play the chicken-or-egg game
of whether to prioritise social theory over social research or vice versa.

REFERENCES

Abromeit, J. (2011) *Max Horkheimer and the Foundations of the Frankfurt School*. Cambridge: Cambridge University Press.

Adkins, L. (2011) 'Practice as temporalisation: Bourdieu and economic crisis', in S. Susen and B.S. Turner (eds), *The Legacy of Pierre Bourdieu*. London: Anthem Press.

Adorno, T.W. (1936) 'Letter to Benjamin', 18 March, in T.W. Adorno, W. Benjamin, E. Bloch, B. Brecht and G. Lukacs (1977), *Aesthetics and Politics*. London: NLB.

Adorno, T.W. (1967) *Prisms: Cultural Criticism and Society*. London: Neville Spearman.

Adorno, T.W. (1973) *Negative Dialectics*. New York: Continuum.

Adorno, T.W. (1974) *Minima Moralia: Reflections from a Damaged Life*. London: Verso.

Adorno, T.W. (1977) 'Reconciliation under duress', in T.W. Adorno, W. Benjamin, E. Bloch, B. Brecht and G. Lukacs (1977), *Aesthetics and Politics*. London: NLB.

Adorno, T.W. (1980) *The Authoritarian Personality*. New York: Norton.

Adorno, T.W. (1991) *The Culture Industry: Selected Essays on Mass Culture*. London: Routledge.

Adorno, T.W. (1992) 'The curious realist: On Siegfried Kracauer', *Notes to Literature, Vol. Two*. New York: Columbia University Press.

Adorno, T.W. (1994) *The Stars Down to Earth and Other Essays on the Irrational in Culture*. London and New York: Routledge.

Adorno, T. (2000a) *The Adorno Reader*. B O'connor(ed). Oxford: Blackwell.

Adorno, T.W. (2000b) *Introduction to Sociology*. Stanford, CA: Stanford University Press.

Adorno, T.W. (2002) *Aesthetic Theory*. London: Continuum.

Adorno, T.W. (2003) *Can One Live After Auschwitz? A Philosophical Reader*. Stanford, CA: Stanford University Press.

Adorno, T.W. (2013) *Against Epistemology: A Metacritique*. Cambridge: Polity Press.

Adorno, T.W., Albert, H., Dahrendorf, R., Habermas, J., Pilot, H. and Popper, K.R. (1976) *The Positivist Dispute in German Sociology*. New York: Harper Row.

Allan Poe, E. (1982) *The Complete Works of Edgar Allan Poe*. London: Penguin.

Althusser, L. (2008) *On Ideology*. London: Verso.

Anderson, B. (1991) *Imagined Communities: Reflections on the Origin and Spread of Nationalism* (revised edition). London: Verso.

Anderson, P. (1976) *Considerations on Western Marxism*. London: NLB.

Anderson, P. (2009) *The New Old World*. London: Verso.

Antonio, R.J. (2001) 'Nietzsche: Social theory in the twilight of the millennium', in G. Ritzer and B. Smart (eds), *Handbook of Social Theory*. London: Sage.

Archer, M. (1995) *Realist Social Theory: The Morphogenetic Approach*. Cambridge: Cambridge University Press.

Aronowitz, S. (2011) 'Georg Lukács' *Destruction of Reason*', in M.J. Thompson (ed.), *Georg Lukács Reconsidered: Critical Essays in Politics, Philosophy and Aesthetics*. London: Continuum.

Atkinson, P. (1988) 'Ethnomethodology: A critical review', *Annual Review of Sociology*, 14: 441–465.

Baert, P. (2005) *Philosophy of the Social Sciences: Towards Pragmatism*. Cambridge: Polity Press.

Baker, K.M. (1989) 'Closing the French Revolution: Saint-Simon and Comte', in F. Furet and M. Ozouf (eds), *The French Revolution and the Creation of Modern Political Culture, Vol. III*. Oxford: Pergamon.

Bakhtin, M. (1984) *Rabelais and His World*. Bloomington, IN: Indiana University Press.

Barck, K. (2011) 'The Neurath–Horkheimer Controversy reconsidered: Otto Neurath's *Erwiderung* to Max Horkheimer's attack against the Vienna Circle', in J. Symons, O. Pombo and J. M. Torres (eds), *Otto Neurath and the Unity of Science*. Dordrecht: Springer.

Barker, M. (1981) *The New Racism: Conservatives and the Ideology of the Tribe*. London: Junction Books.

Barnow, D. (1994) *Critical Realism: History, Photography, and the Work of Siegfried Kracauer*. Baltimore: Johns Hopkins University Press.

Bateson, G. (1972) *Steps to an Ecology of Mind*. New York: Ballantine Books.

Baudrillard, J. (1975) *Mirror of Production*. St. Louis, MO: Telos Press.

Baudrillard, J. (1993) *Symbolic Exchange and Death*. London: Sage.

Baudrillard, J. (1994a) *Simulacra and Simulation*. Ann Arbor, MI: University of Michigan Press

Baudrillard, J. (1994b) *The Illusion of the End*. Cambridge: Polity Press.

Baudrillard, J. (1996) *The System of Objects*. London: Verso.

Bauman, Z. (2000a) *Liquid Modernity*. Cambridge: Polity Press.

Bauman, Z. (2000b) *Modernity and the Holocaust*. Cambridge: Polity Press.

Bauman, Z. (2007) *Consuming Life*. Cambridge: Polity Press.

Bauman, Z. and Bordini, C. (2014) *State of Crisis*. Cambridge: Polity Press.

Beck, U. (1992) *Risk Society: Towards a New Modernity*. London: Sage.

Beck, U. (2009) *World at Risk*. Cambridge: Polity Press.

Beck, U. (2013) *German Europe*. Cambridge: Polity Press.

Beck, U., Giddens, A. and Lash, S. (1994) *Reflexive Modernisation: Politics, Tradition and Aesthetics in the Modern Social Order*. Cambridge: Polity Press.

Bell, M.M. and Gardiner, M.E. (eds) (1998) *Bakhtin and the Human Sciences: No Last Words*. London: Sage.

Bendix, R. and Roth, G. (1971) *Scholarship and Partisanship: Essays on Max Weber*. Berkeley, CA: University of California Press.

Benford, R.D. and Snow, D.A. (2000) 'Framing processes and social movements: An overview and assessment', *Annual Review of Sociology*, 26: 611–639.

Benjamin, W. (1994) *The Correspondence of Walter Benjamin, 1910–1940*. Chicago, IL: University of Chicago Press.

Benjamin, W. (1996) *Selected Writings, Vol. 1: 1913–1926*. Cambridge, MA: The Belknap Press of Harvard University Press.

Benjamin, W. (1998) '"An outsider attracts attention" – On the *Salaried Masses* by S. Kracauer', in Kracauer, S. (ed.), *The Salaried Masses: Duty and Distraction in Weimar Germany*. London and New York: Verso.

Benjamin, W. (1999a) *Selected Writings, Vol. 2, Part 2: 1931–1934*. Cambridge, MA: The Belknap Press of Harvard University Press.

Benjamin, W. (1999b) *The Arcades Project*. Cambridge, MA: The Belknap Press of Harvard University Press.

Benjamin, W. (1999c) *Selected Writings, Volume 2, Part 1, 1927–1930*. Cambridge, MA: The Belknap Press of Harvard University Press.

Benjamin, W. (2002) *Selected Writings Vol. 3: 1935–1938*. Cambridge, MA: The Belknap Press of Harvard University Press.

Benjamin, W. (2003) *Selected Writings Vol. 4: 1938–1940*. Cambridge, MA: The Belknap Press of Harvard University Press.

Benjamin, W. and Adorno, T.W. (1999) *The Complete Correspondence, 1928–1940*. Cambridge: Polity.

Bennett, T. (1979) *Formalism and Marxism*. London: Routledge.

Benzer, M. (2011) *The Sociology of Theodor Adorno*. Cambridge: Cambridge University Press.

Berger, J. (1972) *Ways of Seeing*. London: Penguin.

Berger, P. and Luckmann, T. (1967) *The Social Construction of Reality*. Harmondsworth: Penguin.

Berlin, I., Ginsberg, M., Aron, R. and Ryle, G. (1964) *Auguste Comte Memorial Lectures, 1953–1962*. London: Athlone Press.

Berman, M. (1983) *All that is Solid Melts into Air: The Experience of Modernity*. London: Verso.

Bernstein, R.J. (1971) *Praxis and Action*. Philadelphia, PA: University of Pennsylvania Press.

Bernstein, R.J. (1976) *The Restructuring of Social and Political Theory*. Oxford: Blackwell.

Bernstein, R.J. (2010) *The Pragmatic Turn*. Cambridge: Polity Press.

Billig, M. (1995) *Banal Nationalism*. London: Sage.

Billig, M. (1996) *Arguing and Thinking: A Rhetorical Approach to Social Psychology*. Cambridge: Cambridge University Press.

Billig, M. (1997) 'From codes to utterances: Cultural studies, discourse and psychology', in P. Golding and M. Ferguson, (eds), *Beyond Cultural Studies*. London: Sage.

Blumer, H. (1986) *Symbolic Interactionism: Perspective and Method*. Berkeley, CA: University of California Press.

Boltanski, L. (2011) *On Critique: A Sociology of Emancipation*. Cambridge: Polity Press.

Boltanski, L. (2013) *The Foetal Condition: A Sociology of Engendering and Abortion*. Cambridge: Polity.

Boltanski, L. and Chiapello, E. (2005) *The New Spirit of Capitalism*. London: Verso.

Borkenau, F. (1936) *Modern Sociologists: Pareto*. London: Chapman and Hall.

Borkenau, F. (1937) *The Spanish Cockpit*. London: Phoenix.

Borkenau, F. (1938a) *Austria and After*. London: Faber and Faber.

Borkenau, F. (1938b) *The Communist International*. London: Faber and Faber.

Borkenau, F. (1938c) 'Review of Norbert Elias', *Ueber den Prozess der Zivilisation, vol. 1, Sociological Review,* .Borkenau, F. (1939a) *The New German Empire*. London: Penguin 30(3): 308–11.

Borkenau, F. (1939b) 'Review of Norbert Elias', *Ueber den Prozess der Zivilization, vol. 2, Sociological Review,* 31(4): 450–52.

Borkenau, F. (1940) *The Totalitarian Enemy*. New York: AMS Press.

Borkenau, F. (1976) *Der Übergang vom feudalen zum bürgerlichen Welt-bild: Studien zur Geschichte der Philosophie der Manufakturperiode*. Darmstadt: Wissenschaftliche Buchgesellschaft.

Borkenau, F. (1981) *End and Beginning: On the Generations of Cultures and the Origins of the West (European Perspectives)*. Columbia, NY: Columbia University Press.

Borkenau, F. (1987) 'The sociology of the mechanistic world-picture', *Science in Context*, 1(1): 109–127.

Boudon, R. (1980) *The Crisis in Sociology: Problems of Sociological Epistemology*. London: Macmillan.

Bourdieu, P. (1977) *Outline of a Theory of Practice*. Cambridge: Cambridge University Press.

Bourdieu, P. (1984) *Distinction: A Social Critique of the Judgement of Taste*. London: Routledge.

Bourdieu, P. (1988) *Homo Academicus*. Cambridge: Polity Press.

Bourdieu, P. (1990) *The Logic of Practice*. Stanford, CA: Stanford University Press.

Bourdieu, P. (1991) *The Political Ontology of Martin Heidegger*. Cambridge: Polity Press.

Bourdieu, P. (1992) 'Thinking about limits', *Theory, Culture & Society*, 9(1): 37–50.

Bourdieu, P. (1998) *Practical Reason: On the Theory of Action*. Cambridge: Polity Press.

Bourdieu, P. (1999) *Weight of the World: Social Suffering in Contemporary Society*. Cambridge: Polity Press.

Bourdieu, P. (2001) *Masculine Domination*. Cambridge: Polity Press.

Bourdieu, P. (2008a) *Bachelor's Ball: The Crisis of Peasant Society in Béarn*. Chicago, IL: University of Chicago Press.

Bourdieu, P. (2008b) *Political Interventions: Social Science and Political Action*. London: Verso.

Bourdieu, P. (2012) *Picturing Algeria*. New York: Columbia University Press.

Bourdieu, P. and Wacquant, L.J.D. (1992) *An Invitation to Reflexive Sociology*. Chicago, IL: University of Chicago Press.

Bourdieu, P., Chamberdon, J.-C. and Passeron, J.-C. (1991) *The Craft of Sociology: Epistemological Preliminaries*. New York: Walter de Gruyer.

Boyd White, I. and Frisby, D. (eds) (2012) *Metropolis Berlin: 1880–1940*. Berkeley, CA: University of California Press.

Bukharin, N. (1972) *Imperialism and World Economy*. London: Merlin Press.

Bukharin, N. (2011) *Historical Materialism: A System of Sociology*. Abingdon: Routledge.

Bukharin, N. and Preobrazhensky, E. (1969) *The ABC of Communism*. Harmondsworth: Penguin.

Bull, M. (2011) *Anti-Nietzsche*. London: Verso.

Burckhardt, J. (1979) *Reflections on History*. Indianapolis, IN: Liberty Fund.

Burkhard, B. (2000) *French Marxism Between the Wars: Henri Lefebvre and the 'Philosophies'*. New York: Humanity Books.

Burns, T. (1999*) Erving Goffman*. London: Routledge.

Butler, C. (2012) *Henri Lefebvre: Spatial Politics, Everyday Life and the Right to the City*. London: Routledge.

Butler, J. (1990) *Gender Trouble: Feminism and the Subversion of Identity*. London: Routledge.

Butler, J. (1993) *Bodies that Matter: On the Discursive Limits of 'Sex'*. London: Routledge.

Butler, J. (2009) *Frames of War: When is Life Grievable?* London: Verso.

Callinicos, A. (ed) (1989) *Marxist Theory*. Oxford: Oxford University Press.

Campbell, L. and Garnett, W. (1882) *The Life of James Clerk Maxwell: With a Selection from his Correspondence and Occasional Writings and a Sketch of his Contributions to Science*. London: Macmillan.

Canguilhem, G. (1994) *A Vital Rationalist: Selected Writings*. New York: Zone Books.

Capra, F. (1982) *The Turning Point: Science, Society and the Rising Culture*. London: Flamingo.

Carchedi, G. (2011) *Behind the Crisis: Marx's Dialectics of Value and Knowledge*. Chicago, IL: Haymarket.

Carnap, R. (1963) 'Intellectual autobiography', *The Philosophy of Rudolf Carnap*. La Salle, IL: Open Court.

Cartwright, N., Cat, J., Fleck, L. and Uebel, T.E. (1996) *Otto Neurath: Philosophy Between Science and Politics*. Cambridge: Cambridge University Press.

Cassirer, E. (1923) *Substance and Function and Einstein's Theory of Relativity*. Mineola, NY: Dover.

Castoriadis, C. (1984) *Crossroads in the Labyrinth*. London: Harvester.

Castoriadis, C. (1987) *The Imaginary Institution of Society*. Cambridge: Polity Press.

Castoriadis, C. (1997) *World in Fragments: Writings on Politics, Society, Psychoanalysis and the Imagination*. Stanford, CA: Stanford University Press.

Cat, J. (1995) 'The Popper–Neurath debate and Neurath's attack on scientific method', *Studies in History and Philosophy of Science*, 26(2): 219–250.

Charlesworth, S.J. (2000) A *Phenomenology of Working-Class Experience*. Cambridge: Cambridge University Press.

Cicourel, A. (1973) *Cognitive Sociology: Language and Meaning in Social Interaction*. Harmondsworth: Penguin.

Clarke, J., Hall, S., Jefferson, T. and Roberts B. (1976) 'Subcultures, cultures and class: A theoretical overview', in S. Hall and T. Jefferson (eds), *Resistance Through Rituals: Youth Subcultures in Post-War Britain*. London: Hutchinson.

Clawson, D., Zussman, R., Misra, J., Gerstel, N., Stokes, R., Anderton, D.L. and Burawoy, M. (eds) (2007) *Public Sociology: Fifteen Eminent Sociologists Debate Politics and the Profession in the Twenty-First Century*. Berkeley, CA: University of California Press.

Cohen, S.F. (1980) *Bukharin and the Bolshevik Revolution: A Political Biography, 1888–1938*. Oxford: Oxford University Press.

Collins, H. (2010) *Tacit and Explicit Knowledge*. Chicago, IL: University of Chicago Press.

Comte, A. (1858) *The Positive Philosophy*. New York: Calvin Blanchard.

Comte, A. (1998) *Early Political Writings*. Cambridge: Cambridge University Press.

Crossley, N. (2004) 'Phenomenology, structuralism and history: Merleau-Ponty's social theory', *Theoria*, 103: 88–121.

Crossley, N. (2011) *Towards Relational Sociology*. Abingdon: Routledge.

de Certeau, M. (1984) *The Practice of Everyday Life*. Berkeley, CA: University of California Press.

de Swaan, A. (1990) *The Management of Normality: Critical Essays in Health and Welfare*. London: Routledge.

Debord, G. (1983) *Society of the Spectacle*. Detroit, MI: Black and Red Press.

Dépelteau, F. (2013) 'Comparing Elias and Bourdieu as relational thinkers', in F. Dépelteau and T.S. Landini (eds), *Norbert Elias and Social Theory*. New York: Palgrave Macmillan.

Derrida, J. (1973) *Speech and Phenomena: And Other Essays on Husserl's Theory of Signs*. Evanston, IL.: Northwestern University Press.

Derrida, J. (1994) *Specters of Marx: The State of the Debt, the Work of Mourning and the New International*. Abingdon: Routledge Classics.

Derrida, J. (1999) 'Marx & Sons', in M. Sprinker (ed.), *Ghostly Demarcations: A Symposium on Jacques Derrida's Specters of Marx*. London: Verso.

Derrida, J. (2001) *Writing and Difference*. Abingdon: Routledge Classics.

Descombes, V. (1980) *Modern French Philosophy*. Cambridge: Cambridge University Press.

Dewey, J. (1929) *The Quest for Certainty: A Study of the Relation of Knowledge and Action (Gifford Lectures 1929)*. New York: Minton, Balch.

Dewey, J. (1973) 'Means and ends', in L. Trotsky (ed.), *Their Morals and Ours*. New York: Pathfinder Press.

Dewey, J. (2012) *The Public and its Problems: An Essay in Political Inquiry*. Pennsylvania: Penn State University Press.

Dews, P. (2007) *Logics of Disintegration: Post-Structuralist Thought and the Claims of Critical Theory*. London: Verso.

Döblin, A. (1929) *Berlin Alexanderplatz*. London: Penguin.

Donati, P. (2011) *Relational Sociology: A New Paradigm for the Social Sciences*. Abingdon: Routledge.

Dunning, E. and Hughes, J. (2013) *Norbert Elias and Modern Sociology: Knowledge, Interdependence, Power, Process*. London: Bloomsbury Academic.

Dunning, E. and Mennell, S. (1998) 'On the balance between "civilizing" and "decivilizing" trends in the social development of Western Europe: Elias on Germany, Nazism and the Holocaust', *British Journal of Sociology*, 49(3): 339–357.

Durkheim, E. (1933) *The Division of Labor in Society*. New York: Free Press.

Durkheim, E. (1952) *Suicide: A Study in Sociology*. London: Routledge & Kegan Paul.

Durkheim, E. (1962) *Socialism*. New York: Collier.

Durkheim, E. (1964) 'Sociology', in K.H. Wolff (ed.), *Emile Durkheim et al.: Essays on Sociology and Philosophy*. New York: Harper Torchbook.

Durkheim, E. (1980) *Contributions to L'Année Sociologique*. New York: Free Press.

Durkheim, E. (1982) *The Rules of Sociological Method and Selected Texts on Sociology and its Method*. Houndsmill: Macmillan.

Durkheim, E. (1983) *Pragmatism and Sociology*. Cambridge: Cambridge University Press.

Eagleton, T. (2003) *After Theory*. London: Allen Lane.

Eden, R. (1987) 'Weber and Nietzsche: Questioning the liberation of social science from historicism', in W.J. Mommsen and J. Osterhammel (eds), *Max Weber and His Contemporaries*. London: Routledge.

Eder, K. (1993) *The New Politics of Class: Social Movements and Cultural Dynamics in Advanced Societies*. London: Sage.

Elden, S. (2004) *Understanding Henri Lefebvre: Theory and the Possible*. London: Continuum.

Eldridge, J. (1983) *C. Wright Mills*. London: Ellis Horwood.

Elias, N. (1938) 'An exchange of letters with Walter Benjamin'. (Available at http://hyperelias.jku.at/HyperElias-1930–1949.htm, accessed 28 July 2014.)

Elias, N. (1978) *What is Sociology?* London: Hutchison. p.52.

Elias, N. (1985) *The Loneliness of the Dying*. Oxford: Blackwell.

Elias, N. (1987) *Involvement and Detachment*. Cambridge: Polity Press.

Elias, N. (2006a) *The Court Society: Collected Works, Volume 2*. Dublin: University College Dublin.

Elias, N. (2006b) 'The sociology of German anti-Semitism (1929)', in R. Kilminster (ed.) (trans. E. Jephcott), *Early Writings: Collected Works of Norbert Elias, Vol. 1*. Dublin: University College Dublin Press.

Elias, N. (2009a) 'Theory of science and history of science: Some comments on a recent discussion', in R. Kilminster (ed.) (trans. E. Jephcott), *Essays 1: On the Sociology of Knowledge and the Sciences, Collected Works of Norbert Elias, Vol. 14*. Dublin: University College Dublin Press.

Elias, N. (2009b) '"On the creed of a nominalist: Observations on Poppers", The logic of scientific discovery', in R. Kilminster (ed.) (trans. E. Jephcott), *Essays 1: On the Sociology of Knowledge and the Sciences, Collected Works of Norbert Elias, Vol. 14*. Dublin: University College Dublin Press.

Elias, N. (2012) *On the Process of Civilisation: Sociogenetic and Psychogenetic Investigations, Collected Works of Norbert Elias, Vol. 3*. Dublin: University College Dublin Press.

Elias, N. (2013a) *Studies on The Germans: Power Struggles and the Development of Habitus in the Nineteenth and Twentieth Centuries, Collected Works Vol. 11*. Dublin: University College Dublin Press.

Elias, N. (2013b) *Interviews and Autobiographical Reflections, Collected Works Vol. 17*. Dublin: University College Dublin Press.

Elias, N. and Scotston, J. (1994) *The Established and the Outsiders: A Sociological Enquiry into Community Problems*. London: Sage.

Elliott, A. (2002) 'The social imaginary: A critical assessment of Castoriadis's psychoanalytic social theory', *American Imago*, 59(2): 141–170.

Elliott, G. (1987) 'Further adventures of the dialectic: Merleau-Ponty, Sartre, Althusser', in A.P. Griffiths (ed.), *Contemporary French Philosophy*. Cambridge: Cambridge University Press.

Emirbayer, M. (1997) 'Manifesto for a relational sociology', *American Journal of Sociology*, 103(2): 281–317.

Engels, F. (1882) 'Letter to Eduard Bernstein, 2 November', in K. Marx and F. Engels (1986), *Marx and Engels Collected Works: 1880–1883, Vol. 46*. London: Lawrence & Wishart.

Engels, F. (1954) *Dialectics of Nature*. Moscow: Foreign Languages Publishing House.

Fallada, H. (1932) *Little Man, What Now?* Brooklyn, NY: Melville House.

Felski, R. (2000) *Doing Time: Feminist Theory and Postmodern Culture*. New York: New York University Press.

Ferguson, H. (2006) *Phenomenological Sociology: Insight and Experience in Modern Society*. London: Sage.

Fletcher, J. (1997) *Violence and Civilization: An Introduction to the Work of Norbert Elias*. Cambridge: Polity.

Foucault, M. (1974) 'Noam Chomsky and Michel Foucault: Human nature: Justice versus power', in F. Elders (ed.), *Reflexive Water: The Basic Concerns of Mankind*. London: Souvenir.

Foucault, M. (1984) 'Nietzsche, genealogy, history', in M. Foucault and P. Rainbow, *The Foucault Reader: An Introduction to Foucault's Thought*. London: Penguin.

Foucault, M. (1997) *Essential Works of Michel Foucault 1954–1984, Vol. 1: Ethics*. London: Penguin.

Foucault, M. (2001) *Essential Works of Michel Foucault 1954–1984, Vol. 3: Power*. London: Penguin.

Fournier, M. (2013) *Émile Durkheim: A Biography*. Cambridge: Polity Press.

Fowler, B. (2011) 'Pierre Bourdieu: Unorthodox Marxist?', in S. Susen and B.S. Turner (eds), *The Legacy of Pierre Bourdieu*. London: Anthem Press.

Frank, P. (1949) *Modern Science and Its Philosophy*. Cambridge, MA: Harvard University Press.

Fraser, N. and Nash, K. (2013) *Transnationalizing the Public Sphere*. Cambridge: Polity Press.

Freud, S. (1984) *On Metapsychology*. Harmondsworth: Penguin.

Freud, S. (1991a) 'Group psychology and the analysis of the ego', *Civilization, Society and Religion, Vol. 12*. Harmondsworth: Penguin.

Freud, S. (1991b) 'Civilization and its discontents', *Civilization, Society and Religion, Vol. 12*. Harmondsworth: Penguin.

Freudenthal, G. and McLaughlin, P. (eds) (2009) *The Social and Economic Roots of the Scientific Revolution: Texts by Boris Hessen and Henryk Grossmann*. Dordrecht: Springer.

Frisby, D. (1985) *Fragments of Modernity: Theories of Modernity in the Work of Simmel, Kracauer and Benjamin*. Cambridge: Polity Press.

Frisby, D. (1987) 'The ambiguity of modernity: Georg Simmel and Max Weber', in W.J. Mommsen and J. Osterhammel (eds), *Max Weber and His Contemporaries*. London: Routledge. pp. 68–101.

Frisby, D. (1992) *Sociological Impressionism: A Reassessment of Georg Simmel's Social Theory*. London: Routledge.

Frisby, D. (1994) 'The flaneur in social theory', in K. Tester (ed.), *The Flaneur*. London: Routledge.

Frisby, D. (2001) *Cityscapes of Modernity: Critical Explorations*. Cambridge: Polity Press.

Frisby, D. and Sayer, D. (1986) *Society*. Chichester: Ellis Horwood.

Gane, M. (1998) 'Lyotard's early writings, 1954–1963', in C. Rojek and B.S. Turner (eds), *The Politics of Jean-Francois Lyotard: Justice and Political Theory*. London: Routledge.

Gane, M. (2006) *Auguste Comte*. London: Routledge.

Garaudy, R., Cogniot, G., Caveing, M., Desanti, J.T., Kanapa, J., Leduc, V. and Lefebvre, H. (1956) *Mésaventures de l'anti-marxisme – Les malheurs de M. Merleau-Ponty, avec une lettre de Georg Lukacs*. Paris: Éditions Sociales.

Gardiner, M.E. (2000) *Critiques of Everyday Life*. London: Routledge.

Garfinkel, H. (1967) *Studies in Ethnomethodology*. Englewood Cliffs, NJ: Prentice-Hall.

Garfinkel, H. (2002) *Ethnomethodology's Program: Working Out Durkheim's Aphorism*. Lanham, MD: Rowman & Littlefield.

Geras, N. (1983) *Marx and Human Nature: Refutation of a Legend*. London: Verso.

Geras, N. (1990) *Discourses of Extremity: Radical Ethics and Post-Marxist Extravagances*. London: Verso.

Giddens, A. (1982) 'Historical materialism: Interview with Anthony Giddens', *Theory, Culture & Society*, 1(2): 63–77.

Giddens, A. (1984) *The Constitution of Society*. Cambridge: Polity Press.

Giddens, A. (1985) *A Contemporary Critique of Historical Materialism*. Cambridge: Polity Press.

Giddens, A. (1987a) 'Weber and Durkheim: Coincidence and convergence', in W.J. Mommsen and J. Osterhammel (eds), *Max Weber and His Contemporaries*. London: Routledge.

Giddens, A. (1987b) *Social Theory and Modern Sociology*. Cambridge: Polity Press.

Giddens, A. (1990) *The Consequences of Modernity*. Cambridge: Polity Press.

Giddens, A. (1991) *Modernity and Self-Identity: Self and Society in the Late Modern Age*. Cambridge: Polity Press.

Giddens, A. (1998) *The Third Way: The Renewal of Social Democracy*. Cambridge: Polity Press.

Giddens, A. (2000) *The Third Way and its Critics*. Cambridge: Polity Press.

Giddens, A. (2013) *The Politics of Climate Change*. Cambridge: Polity Press.

Gilloch, G. (1997) *Myth and Metropolis: Walter Benjamin and the City*. Cambridge: Polity Press.

Gilroy, P. (2000) *Against Race: Imagining Political Culture Beyond the Color Line*. Cambridge, MA: Harvard University Press.

Goffman, E. (1959) *The Presentation of Self in Everyday Life*. New York: Anchor.

Goffman, E. (1986) *Frame Analysis: An Essay on the Organization of Experience*. Boston, MA: Northeastern University Press.

Goldmann, L. (1964) *The Hidden God: A Study of Tragic Vision in the Pensees of Pascal and the Tragedies of Racine*. London: Routledge.

Goldmann, L. (1977) *Lukács and Heidegger: Towards a New Philosophy*. London: Routledge, Chapman & Hall.

Goonewardena, K., Kipfer, S., Milgrom, R. and Schmid, C. (eds) (2008) *Space, Difference, Everyday Life: Reading Henri Lefebvre*. London: Routledge.

Goudsblom, J. (1977) 'Responses to Norbert Elias's work in England, Germany, the Netherlands and France', in P.R. Gleichmann, J. Goudsblom and H. Korte (eds), *Human Figurations: Essays for Aufsätze für Norbert Elias*. Amsterdam: Stichting Amsterdams Sociologisch Tijdschrift.

Goudsblom, J. (1980) *Nihilism and Culture*. Totowa, NJ: Rowan and Littlefield.

Goudsblom, J. (1995) 'Elias and Cassirer: Sociology and philosophy', *Theory, Culture & Society*, 12(3): 121–126.

Gouldner, A. (1971) *The Coming Crisis of Western Sociology*. London: Heinemann.

Gramsci, A. (1971) *Selections from the Prison Notebooks*. London: Lawrence & Wishart.

Grossmann, H. (1987) 'The social foundations of mechanistic philosophy and manufacture', *Science In Context*, 1: 129–80.

Grossmann, H. (1992) *The Law of Accumulation and Breakdown of the Capitalist System: Being also a Theory of Crises*. London: Pluto Press.

Grossmann, H. (2006) 'The beginnings of capitalism and the new mass morality', *Journal of Classical Sociology*, 6(2): 201–213.

Grossman, H. (2009) 'The social foundations of the mechanistic philosophy and manufacture', in Freudenthal, G. and McLaughlin, P. (eds), *The Social and Economic Roots of the Scientific Revolution: Texts by Boris Hessen and Henryk Grossmann*. Dordrecht: Springer.

Grosz, E. (2004) 'Notes towards a corporeal feminism', in Aberdeen Body Group (eds), *The Body: Critical Concepts in Sociology, Vol. 1*. London: Routledge.

Habermas, J. (1973) *Theory and Practice*. Boston, MA: Beacon Press.

Habermas, J. (1976) *Legitimation Crisis*. London: Heinemann.

Habermas, J. (1983) *Philosophical-Political Profiles*. Cambridge, MA: MIT Press.

Habermas, J. (1984) *Theory of Communicative Action, Vol. One: Reason and the Rationalization of Society*. Boston, MA: Beacon Press.

Habermas, J. (1986) *Knowledge & Human Interests*. Cambridge: Polity Press.

Habermas, J. (1987) *The Philosophical Discourse of Modernity: Twelve Lectures*. Cambridge, MA: MIT Press.

Habermas, J. (1989) *The Structural Transformation of the Public Sphere: An Inquiry into a Category of Bourgeois Society*. Cambridge: Polity Press.

Habermas, J. (1996) *Between Facts and Norms: Contributions to a Discourse Theory of Law and Democracy*. Cambridge, MA: MIT Press.

Habermas, J. (2012) *The Crisis of the European Union: A Response*. Cambridge: Polity Press.

Hall, S. (1980a) 'Cultural studies: Two paradigms', *Media, Culture & Society*, 2(1): 57–72.

Hall, S. (1980b) 'Encoding/decoding', in S. Hall, D. Hobson, A. Lowe and P. Willis (eds), *Culture, Media, Language: Working Papers in Cultural Studies, 1972–79*. London: Hutchinson.

Hall, S. (1988) *The Hard Road to Renewal: Thatcherism and the Crisis of the Left*. London: Verso.

Hall, S. (1996) 'Cultural studies and its theoretical legacies', in D. Morley and K.H. Chen (eds), *Stuart Hall: Critical Dialogues in Cultural Studies*. London: Routledge.

Hall, S. (2011) 'The neo-liberal revolution', *Cultural Studies*, 25(6): 705–728.

Hall, S. and Jefferson, T. (eds) (1976) *Resistance Through Rituals: Youth Subcultures in Post-War Britain*. London: Hutchinson.

Hall, S., Critcher, C., Jefferson, T., Clarke, J. and Roberts, B. (1978) *Policing the Crisis: Mugging, the State and Law and Order*. London: Macmillan.

Hansen, M. (2012) *Cinema and Experience: Siegfried Kracauer, Walter Benjamin, and Theodor W. Adorno*. Berkeley, CA: University of California Press.

Harding, S. (1986) *The Science Question in Feminism*. Ithaca, NY: Cornell University Press.

Harvey, D. (2005) *A Brief History of Neoliberalism*. Oxford: Oxford University Press.

Hebdige, D. (1979) *Subculture: The Meaning of Style*. London: Methuen.

Hegal, G. W. F. (2003) *The Phenomenology of Mind*. Mineola, NY: Dover.

Heidegger, M. (1977) *The Question Concerning Technology and Other Essays*. New York: Harper & Row.

Heilbron, J. (1995) *The Rise of Social Theory*. Cambridge: Polity Press.

Hekman, S.J. (1990) *Gender and Knowledge: Elements of a Postmodern Feminism*. Cambridge: Polity Press.

Helle, H.J. (2001) *Georg Simmel: Introduction to his Theory and Method/ Einführung in seine Theorie und Methode*. Munich: Oldenbourg.

Heller, A. (2002) *The Time is Out of Joint: Shakespeare as Philosopher of History*. Lanham, MD: Rowman and Littlefield.

Heritage, J. (1984) *Garfinkel and Ethnomethodology*. Cambridge: Polity Press.

Herrick, T. (2005) '"A book which is no longer discussed today": Tran Duc Thao, Jacques Derrida, and Maurice Merleau-Ponty', *Journal of the History of Ideas*, 66(1): 113–131.

Hessel, F. (1929) 'The suspicious character', in A. Kaes, M. Jay and E. Dimendberg (eds) (1994), *The Weimar Republic Sourcebook*. Berkeley, CA: University of California Press.

Hill Collins, P. (1990) *Black Feminist Thought: Knowledge, Consciousness and the Politics of Empowerment*. London: Routledge.

Hinde, J.R. (2000) *Jacob Burckhardt and the Crisis of Modernity*. Montreal: McGill-Queen's Press.

Holmwood, J. (1995) 'Feminism and epistemology: What kind of successor science?', *Sociology*, 29(3): 411–428.

Holmwood, J. and Stewart, A. (1991) *Explanation and Social Theory*. New York: St. Martin's Press.

Honneth, A. (2008) *Reification: A New Look at an Old Idea*. Oxford: Oxford University Press.

Horkheimer, M. (1972) *Critical Theory: Selected Essays*. New York: Continuum.

Horkheimer, M. (1985) 'Die Rackets und der Geist', in A. Schmidt and G.S. Noerr (eds), *Gesammelte Schriften, Band 12: Nachgelassene Schriften 1931–1949*. Frankfurt: Fischer.

Horkheimer, M. (1989) 'The Jews and Europe', in S.E. Bronner and D. Kellner (eds), *Critical Theory and Society: A Reader*. London: Routledge.

Horkheimer, M. (1993) 'The present situation of social philosophy and the tasks of an Institute for Social Research', in G. Hunter (ed.), *Between Philosophy and Social Science: Selected Early Writings*. Cambridge, MA: MIT Press.

Horkheimer, M. and Adorno T. W. (1972) *Dialectic of the Enlightenment*. New York: Seabury.

Howard, D. (1977) *The Maxian Legacy*. London: Macmillan.

Howson, A. (2005) *Embodying Gender*. London: Sage.

Hughes, A. and Witz, A. (2004) 'Feminism and the matter of bodies: From de Beauvoir to Butler', in Aberdeen Body Group (eds), *The Body: Critical Concepts in Sociology, Vol. 1*. London: Routledge.

Hughes, B. (2012) 'Civilising modernity and the ontological invalidation of disabled people', in D. Goodley, B. Hughes and L. Davis (eds), *Disability and Social Theory: New Developments and Directions*. Houndmills: Palgrave Macmillan.

Hughes, H.S. (1958) *Consciousness and Society: The Reorientation of European Social Thought, 1890–1930*. New York: Knopf.

Huizinga, J. (1998) *The Waning of the Middle Ages: A Study of the Forms of Life, Thought, and Art in France and the Netherlands in the Fourteenth and Fifteenth Centuries*. London: Folio Society.

Hume, D. (2007) *An Enquiry Concerning Human Understanding: And Other Writings*. Cambridge: Cambridge University Press.

Husserl, E. (1970) *The Crisis of European Sciences and Transcendental Phenomenology: An Introduction to Phenomenological Philosophy*. Evanston, IL: Northwestern University Press.

Inglis, D. (2001) *A Sociological History of Excretory Experience: Defecatory Manners and Toiletry Technologies*. Lewiston, NY: Edwin Mellen Press.

Ives, P. (2004) *Language and Hegemony in Gramsci*. London: Pluto Press.

James, W. (1975) *Pragmatism: A New Name for Some Old Ways of Thinking*. Cambridge, MA: Harvard University Press.

James, W. (2002) *The Meaning of Truth*. Mineola, NY: Dover.

Jay, M. (1986) *Permanent Exiles: Essays on the Intellectual Migration From Germany to America*. New York: Columbia University Press.

Jay, M. (1973) *The Dialectic Imagination. A History of the Frankfurt School and the Institute of Social Research, 1923–1950*. Boston: Little Brown, and Co.

Jensen, H. (2012) *Weber and Durkheim: A Methodological Comparison*. London: Routledge.

Joas, H. (1985) *G.H. Mead: A Contemporary Re-Examination of his Thought*. Cambridge, MA: MIT Press.

Joas, H. (1989) 'Institutionalization as a creative process: The sociological importance of Cornelius Castoriadis's political philosophy', *American Journal of Sociology*, 94(5): 1184–1199.

Joas, H. (1993) *Pragmatism and Social Theory*. Chicago, IL: University of Chicago Press.

Joas, H. (1996) *The Creativity of Action*. Chicago, IL: University of Chicago Press.

Jones, W.D. (1992) 'Toward a theory of totalitarianism: Franz Borkenau's Pareto', *Journal of the History of Ideas*, 53(3): 455–466.

Jones, W.D. (1999) *The Lost Debate: German Socialist Intellectuals and Totalitarianism*. Urbana and Chicago: University of Illinois Press.

Kadavany, J. (2001) *Imre Lakatos and the Guises of Reason*. Durham, NC: Duke University Press.

Kilminster, R. (1998*) The Sociological Revolution: From the Enlightenment to the Global Age*. London: Routledge.

Kilminster, R. and Wouters, C. (1995) 'From philosophy to sociology: Elias and the Neo-Kantians (A response to Benjo Maso)', *Theory, Culture & Society*, 12(3): 81–120.

King, A. (2004) *The Structure of Social Theory*. London: Routledge.

Kloppenberg, J.T. (1996) 'Pragmatism: An old name for some new ways of thinking?', *Journal of American History*, 83(1): 100–138.

Koch, G. (2000) *Siegfried Kracauer: An Introduction*. Princeton, NJ: Princeton University Press. pp. 16–25.

Kolakowski, L. (1972) *Positivist Philosophy: From Hume to the Vienna Circle*. Harmondsworth: Penguin.

Kolakowski, L. (2005) *Main Currents of Marxism*. New York: Norton.

Kolakowski, L. and Lefebvre, H. (1974) 'Evolution or revolution', in F. Elders (ed.), *Reflexive Water: The Basic Concerns of Mankind*. London: Souvenir.

Korsch, K. (1938) *Karl Marx*. London: Chapman and Hall.

Korsch, K. (1970) *Marxism and Philosophy*. London: NLB.

Korsch, K. (1971) *Three Essays on Marxism*. London: Pluto Press.

Koselleck, R. (1988) *Critique and Crisis: Enlightenment and the Pathogenesis of Modern Society*. Cambridge, MA: MIT Press.

Koselleck, R. (2006) 'Crisis', *Journal of the History of Ideas*, 67(2): 357–400.

Kracauer, S. (1929[1998]) *The Salaried Masses: Duty and Distraction in Weimar Germany: Disorientation and Distraction in Weimar Germany* (trans. Q. Hoare). London: Verso.

Kracauer, S. (1930) 'The Blue Angel', in A. Kaes, M. Jay and E. Dimendberg (eds) (1994), *The Weimar Republic Sourcebook*. Berkeley, CA: University of California Press.

Kracauer, S. (1931a) 'Girls and crisis', in A. Kaes, M. Jay and E. Dimendberg (eds) (1994), *The Weimar Republic Sourcebook*. Berkeley, CA: University of California Press.

Kracauer, S. (1931b) 'Murder trials and society', in A. Kaes, M. Jay and E. Dimendberg (eds) (1994), *The Weimar Republic Sourcebook*. Berkeley, CA: University of California Press.

Kracauer, S. (1932a) 'The task of the film critic', in A. Kaes, M. Jay and E. Dimendberg (eds) (1994), *The Weimar Republic Sourcebook*. Berkeley, CA: University of California Press.

Kracauer, S. (1932b) 'Working women', in A. Kaes, M. Jay and E. Dimendberg (eds) (1994), *The Weimar Republic Sourcebook*. Berkeley, CA: University of California Press.

Kracauer, S. (1947) *From Caligari to Hitler: A Psychological History of the German Film*. Princeton, NJ: Princeton University Press.

Kracauer, S. (1960) *Theory of Film: The Redemption of Physical Reality*. Princeton, NJ: Princeton University Press.

Kracauer, S. (1995) *The Mass Ornament: Weimar Essays*. Cambridge, MA: Harvard University Press.

Kracauer, S. (1997) 'On employment agencies: The construction of a space', in N. Leach (ed.), *Rethinking Architecture*. London: Routledge.

Kracauer, S. (2002) *Jacques Offenbach and the Paris of His Time*. New York: Urzone.

Kracauer, S. (2012) *Siegfried Kracauer's American Writings: Essays on Film and Popular Culture*. Berkeley, CA: University of California Press.

Kuhn, R. (2006) 'Introduction to Henryk Grossmann's critique of Franz Borkenau and Max Weber', *Journal of Classical Sociology*, 6(2): 195–200.

Kuhn, R. (2009) 'Henryk Grossman: A biographical sketch', in Freudenthal, G. and McLaughlin, P. (eds), *The Social and Economic Roots of the Scientific Revolution: Texts by Boris Hessen and Henryk Grossmann*. Dordrecht: Springer.

Kuhn, T. (2012) *The Structure of Scientific Revolutions*. Chicago, IL: University of Chicago Press.

Kuypers, J.A. (2009) *Bush's War: Media Bias and Justifications for War in a Terrorist Age*. Lanham, MD: Rowman & Littlefield.

Laclau, E. and Mouffe, C. (2001) *Hegemony and Socialist Strategy: Towards a Radical Democratic Politics* (2nd edn). London: Verso.

Leck, R.M. (2000) *Georg Simmel and Avant-Garde Sociology: The Birth of Modernity, 1880–1920*. New York: Humanity Books.

Lefebvre, H. (1946) 'Retrospections', in S. Elden, E. Lebas and E. Kofman (eds) (2003), *Key Writings*. New York: Continuum.

Lefebvre, H. (1953) 'Perspectives on rural sociology', in S. Elden, E. Lebas and E. Kofman (eds) (2003), *Key Writings*. New York: Continuum.

Lefebvre, H. (1962) 'Myths in everyday life', in S. Elden, E. Lebas and E. Kofman (eds) (2003), *Key Writings*. New York: Continuum.

Lefebvre, H. (1968a) *The Sociology of Marx*. London: Allen Lane.

Lefebvre, H. (1968b) *Dialectical Materialism*. London: Jonathan Cape.

Lefebvre, H. (1969) *The Explosion: Marxism and the French Upheaval*. New York: Monthly Review Press.

Lefebvre, H. (1971) *Everyday Life in the Modern World*. London: Allen Lane.

Lefebvre, H. (1976) *The Survival of Capitalism: Reproduction of the Relations of Capitalism*. London: Allison and Busby.

Lefebvre, H. (1980) 'Triads and dyads', in S. Elden, E. Lebas and E. Kofman (eds) (2003), *Key Writings*. London: Continuum.

Lefebvre, H. (1987) 'The everyday and everydayness', *Yale French Studies*, 73: 7–11.

Lefebvre, H. (1989) 'The inventory', in S. Elden, E. Lebas and E. Kofman (eds) (2003), *Key Writings*. New York: Continuum.

Lefebvre, H. (1990) 'From the social pact to the contract of citizenship', in S. Elden, E. Lebas and E. Kofman (eds) (2003), *Key Writings*. New York: Continuum.

Lefebvre, H. (1991a) *The Production of Space*. Oxford: Blackwell.

Lefebvre, H. (1991b) *Critique of Everyday Life, Vol. I*. London: Verso.

Lefebvre, H. (1995) *Introduction to Modernity: Twelve Preludes, September 1959– May 1961*. London: Verso.

Lefebvre, H. (2002) *Critique of Everyday Life, Vol. II: Foundations for a Sociology of the Everyday*. London: Verso.

Lefebvre, H. (2003) *The Urban Revolution*. Minneapolis, MN: University of Minnesota Press.

Lefebvre, H. (2004a) *Rhythmanalysis: Space, Time and Everyday Life*. New York: Continuum.

Lefebvre, H. (2004b) 'Theses on modernism', in B.H.D. Buchloh, S. Guilbaut and D. Solkin (eds), *Modernism and Modernity: The Vancouver Conference Papers*. Halifax: The Press of the Nova Scotia College of Art and Design.

Lefebvre, H. (2005) *Critique of Everyday Life, Vol. III: From Modernity to Modernism (Towards a Metaphilosophy of Daily Life)*. London: Verso.

Lefebvre, H. (2009) *State, Space, World: Selected Essasys* (eds N. Brenner and S. Elden). Minneapolis, MN: University of Minnesota Press.

Lefebvre, H. and Guterman, N. (1933) 'Mystification: Notes for a critique of everyday life', in S. Elden, E. Lebas and E. Kofman (eds) (2003), *Key Writings*. New York: Continuum.

Lenin, I.L. (1909) *Materialism and Empirio-Criticism*. Moscow: Progress Publishers.

Lenzer, G. (ed.) (1998) *Auguste Comte and Positivism: The Essential Writings*. New Brunswick, N.J. : Transaction.

Leslie, E. (2000) *Walter Benjamin: Overpowering Conformism*. London: Pluto Press.

Leslie, E. (2006a) 'Ruin and rubble in the arcades', in B. Hansen (ed.), *Walter Benjamin and the Arcades Project*. London: Continuum.

Leslie, E. (2006b) *Walter Benjamin*. London: Reaktion.

Lethen, H. (2002) *Cool Conduct: The Culture of Distance in Weimar Germany*. Berkeley, CA: University of California Press.

Lévi-Strauss, C. (1966) *The Savage Mind*. Chicago, IL: University of Chicago Press.

Levine, D.N. (1985) *The Flight from Ambiguity: Essays in Social and Cultural Theory*. Chicago, IL: University of Chicago Press.

Lewin, K. and Korsch, K. (1939) 'Mathematical constructs in psychology and sociology', *Erkenntnis*, 8(1): 397–403.

Lichtheim, G. (1970) *Lukács*. Glasgow: Fontana/Collins.

Liebersohn, H. (1988) *Fate and Utopia in German Sociology, 1870–1923*. Cambridge, MA: MIT Press.

Lockwood, D. (1992) *Solidarity and Schism: The Problem of Disorder in Durkheimian and Marxist Sociology*. Oxford: Clarendon Press.

Love, N.S. (1986) *Marx, Nietzsche and Modernity*. New York: Columbia University Press.

Lowy, M. (1979) *Georg Lukacs: From Romanticism to Bolshevism*. London: NLB.

Lukacs, G. (1923[1971]) *History and Class Consciousness: Studies in Marxist Dialectics*. London: Merlin Press.

Luhmann, N. (1995) *Social Systems*. Stanford, CA: Stanford University Press.

Lukacs, G. (1972) *Political Writings, 1919–1929*. London: NLB.

Lukacs, G. (1980) *The Destruction of Reason*. London: Merlin Press.

Lukes, S. (2005) *Power: A Radical View*. London: Macmillan.

Luxemburg, R. (1903) 'Stagnation and progress of Marxism', in *Rosa Luxemburg Speaks*. New York: Pathfinder Press,.

Luxemburg, R. (2003) *The Accumulation of Capital*. Abingdon: Routledge Classics.

Lynch, M. (1993) *Scientific Practice and Ordinary Action: Ethnomethodology and Social Studies of Science*. Cambridge: Cambridge University Press.

Lyotard, J. F. (1984) *The Postmodern Condition: A Report on Knowledge*. Minneapolis, MN: University of Minnesota Press.

Lyotard, J.-F. (1991) *Phenomenology*. Albany: State University of New York Press.

MacIntyre, A. (1981) *After Virtue: A Study in Moral Theory*. London: Duckworth.

Mack, M. (2000) 'Film as memory: Siegfried Kracauer's psychological history of German "National Culture"', *Journal of European Studies*, 30(2): 157–181.

Mackie, J.L. (1965) 'Causes and conditions', *American Philosophical Quarterly*, 12 (4): 245–265.

Mannheim, K. (1936) *Ideology and Utopia: An Introduction to the Sociology of Knowledge*. New York: Harcourt, Brace & World.

Manuel, F.E. (1962) *The Prophets of Paris*. Cambridge, MA: Harvard University Press. pp. 268–274.

Marcus, G. (1989) *Lipstick Traces: A Secret History of the Twentieth Century*. Cambridge, MA: Harvard University Press.

Marcuse, H. (1941) *Reason and Revolution: Hegel and the Rise of Social Theory*. London: Routledge & Kegan Paul.

Marcuse, H. (1968) *Negations: Essays in Critical Theory*. Boston, MA: Beacon Press. pp. 98–124.

Marshall, T.H. (1936) 'Review of F. Borkenau *Pareto*', *Political Quarterly*, 7(3): 459–461.

Marx, K. (1842) 'Comments on the latest Prussian censorship instruction', in K. Marx and F. Engels (1986), *Marx and Engels Collected Works, 1835–1843, Vol. 1*. London: Lawrence & Wishart.

Marx, K. (1843–4) *Critique of Hegel's Philosophy of Right*, in K. Marx and F. Engels (1975), *Marx and Engels Collected Works, 1843–44, Vol. 3*. London: Lawrence & Wishart.

Marx, K. (1845) 'Theses on Feuerbach', in R. Tucker (ed.) *The Marx–Engels Reader* (2nd edn). New York: Norton.

Marx, K. (1999) *On Suicide*. Evanston, IL: Northwestern University Press.

Marx, K. (1856) 'Speech at the anniversary of the People's Paper', in R. Tucker (ed.) (1978), *The Marx–Engels Reader* (2nd edn). New York: Norton.

Marx, K. (1859) *A Contribution to the Critique of Political Economy*, in *Marx and Engels Collected Works: Karl Marx Economic Works 1857–1861, Vol. 29*. London: Lawrence & Wishart.

Marx, K. (1866) 'Marx to Engels, 7 July', in K. Marx and F. Engels (1986), *Marx and Engels Collected Works: 1864–1868, Vol. 42*. London: Lawrence & Wishart.

Marx, K. (1959) *Capital, Vol. 3: A Critique of Political Economy: The Process of Capitalist Production as a Whole*. London: Lawrence & Wishart.

Marx, K. (1973) *Grundrisse: Foundations of the Critique of Political Economy*. London: Pelican.

Marx, K. (1976) *Capital, Vol. 1: A Critique of Political Economy*. London: Pelican.

Marx, K. and Engels, F. (1844) *The Holy Family, or Critique of Critical Criticism*, in K. Marx and F. Engels (1986), *Marx and Engels Collected Works: 1844–1845, Vol. 4*. London: Lawrence & Wishart.

Marx, K. and Engels, F. (1845–6) *The German Ideology*, in K. Marx and F. Engels (1975), *Marx and Engels Collected Works: 1845–1847, Vol. 5*. London: Lawrence & Wishart.

Marx K. and Engels, F. (1975) *Marx and Engels Collected Works: 1845–1847, Vol. 5*. London: Lawrence & Wishart.

Marx, K. and Engels, F. (1998) *The Communist Manifesto: A Modern Edition*. London: Verso.

McDonough, T. (ed.) (2009) *The Situationists and the City*. London: Verso.

McLean, I. and Hewitt, F. (eds) (1994) *Condorcet: Foundations of Social Choice and Political Theory*. Cheltenham: Edward Elgar.

McLuhan, M. (2001) *Understanding Media: Extensions of Man*. London: Routledge.

McNally, D. (2001) *Bodies of Meaning: Studies on Language, Labor and Liberation*. Albany, NY: State University of New York Press.

McRobbie, A. (2009) *The Aftermath of Feminism: Gender, Culture and Social Change*. London: Sage.

McRobbie, A. (2011) 'Beyond post-feminism', *Public Policy Research*, 18(3): 179–184.

Mead, G.H. (1934) *Mind, Self, and Society*. Chicago, IL: University of Chicago Press.

Mead, G.H. (1964) *Mead on Social Psychology: Selected Papers*. Chicago, IL: University of Chicago Press.

Mehlman, J. (1993) *Walter Benjamin for Children: An Essay on His Radio Years*. Chicago: University of Chicago Press.

Meikle, S. (1985) *Essentialism in the Thought of Karl Marx*. London: Duckworth.

Memos, C. (2013) 'Axelos, Castoriadis, Papaioannou and Marx: Towards an anti-critique', *Philosophy & Social Criticism*, 39(10): 1029–1047.

Mennell, S. (1992) *Norbert Elias: An Introduction*. Dublin: University College Dublin Press.

Merleau-Ponty, M. (1964) *Sense and Non-Sense*. Evanston, IL: Northwestern University Press.

Merleau-Ponty, M. (1968) *The Visible and the Invisible*. Evanston, IL: Northwestern University Press.

Merleau-Ponty, M. (1970) *Themes from the Lectures at the College de France, 1952–1960*. Evanston, IL: Northwestern University Press.

Merleau-Ponty, M. (1973a) *The Prose of the World*. Evanston, IL: Northwestern University Press.

Merleau-Ponty, M. (1973b) *Adventures of the Dialectic*. Evanston, IL: Northwestern University Press.

Merleau-Ponty, M. (1974) *Phenomenology, Language and Sociology: Selected Essays* (ed. J. O'Neill). London: Heinemann.

Merleau-Ponty, M. (2000) *Humanism and Terror: An Essay on the Communist Problem*. New Brunswick, NJ: Transaction.

Merleau-Ponty, M. (2002) *Phenomenology of Perception*. London: Routledge Classics.

Merleau-Ponty, M. (2007) *The Merleau-Ponty Reader* (eds T. Toadvine and L. Lawlor). Evanston, IL: Northwestern University Press.

Merrifield, A. (2006) *Henri Lefebvre: A Critical Introduction*. New York: Routledge.

Merton, R.K. (1995) 'The Thomas theorem and the Matthew effect', *Social Forces*, 74(2): 379–424.

Meštrović, S.G. (1988) *Emile Durkheim and the Reformation of Sociology*. Lanham, MD: Rowman & Littlefield.

Meštrović, S. (1991) *The Coming Fin De Siècle: An Application of Durkheim's Sociology to Modernity and Postmodernity*. London: Routledge.

Meštrović, S. (1997) *Postemotional Society*. London: Sage.

Mészáros, I. (1995) *Beyond Capital: Toward a theory of Transition*. London: Merlin.

Mill, J.S. (1971) *A Logical Critique of Sociology*. London: Michael Joseph.

Mills, C.W. (1964) *Sociology and Pragmatism: The Higher Learning in America*. New York: Oxford University Press.

Mills, C.W. (2000) *The Sociological Imagination*. Oxford: Oxford University Press.

Montesquieu, B. de (1949) *Spirit of the Laws*. New York: Hafner Press.

Moran, D. and Steinacher, L. (2008) 'Husserl's letter to Lévy-Bruhl: Introduction', in B. Hopkins and J.J. Drummond (eds), *The New Yearbook for Phenomenology and Phenomenological Philosophy, VIII* (pp. 1–23). Durham: Acumen.

Mouzelis, N. (1995) *Sociological Theory: What Went Wrong?* London: Routledge.

Natanson, M. (1986) *Anonymity: A Study in the Philosophy of Alfred Schütz*. Bloomington, IN: Indiana University Press.

Negt, O. and Kluge, A. (1993) *Public Sphere and Experience: Toward an Analysis of the Bourgeois and Proletarian Public Sphere*. Minneapolis: University of Minnesota Press.

Nemeth, E. (1994) 'Empiricism and the norms of scientific knowledge: Some reflections on Otto Neurath and Pierre Bourdieu', in H. Pauder-Studer (ed.), *Norms, Values and Society*. Dordrecht: Kluwer.

Nemeth, E. and Stadler, F. (eds) (1996) *Encyclopedia and Utopia: The Life and Work of Otto Neurath (1882–1945)*. Dordrecht: Kluwer.

Neurath, O. (1940–41) 'Universal jargon and terminology', *Proceedings of the Aristotelian Society*, 41: 127–148.

Neurath, O. (1959) 'Sociology and physicalism', in A.J. Ayer (ed), *Logical Positivism*. Glencoe, IL: The Free Press.

Neurath, O. (1970) 'Foundations of the social sciences', in O. Neurath, R. Carnap and C. Morris (eds), *Foundations of the Unity of Science: Towards an International Encyclopedia of Unified Science, Vol. II*: 1–9. Chicago, IL: University of Chicago Press.

Neurath, O. (1973) *Empiricism and Sociology* (eds. M. Neurath and R.S. Cohen). Dordrecht: Reidel.

Neurath, O. (1983) *Philosophical Papers 1913–1946 Sociology* (eds M. Neurath and R.S. Cohen). Dordrecht: Reidel.

Neurath, O. (1996) 'Visual education: Humanisation versus popularisation', in E. Nemeth and F. Stadler (eds), *Encyclopedia and Utopia*. Dordrecht: Kluwer.

Neurath, O. (2004) *Otto Neurath: Economic Writings Selections 1904–1945*, (eds T.E. Uebel and R.S. Cohen). Dordrecht: Kluwer.

Neurath, O. (2011) 'Unity of science and logical empiricism: A reply', in J. Symons, O. Pombo and J.M. Torres (eds), *Otto Neurath and the Unity of Science*. Dordrecht: Springer.

Nietzsche, F. (1967) *The Will to Power*. New York: Random House.

Nietzsche, F. (1995) *Philosophical Writings*. New York: Continuum.

Nietzsche, F. (2003) *Genealogy of Morals*. Mineola, NY: Dover Thrift.

Norris, C. (1982) *Deconstruction: Theory and Practice*. London: Methuen.

O'Neill, J. (1972) *Sociology as a Skin Trade: Essays Towards a Reflexive Sociology*. London: Heinemann.

O'Neill, J. (1975) *Making Sense Together: An Introduction to Wild Sociology*. London: Heinemann.

O'Neill, J. (2003) 'Unified science as political philosophy: Positivism, pluralism and liberalism', *Studies in the History of the Philosophy of Science*, 34(3): 575–596.

O'Neill, J. (2007) 'Pluralism and economic institutions', in E. Nemeth, S. Schmitz and T. Uebel (eds), *Neurath's Economics in Context*. Dordrecht: Kluwer.

O'Neill, J. and Uebel, T. (2004) 'Horkheimer and Neurath: Restarting a disrupted debate', *European Journal of Philosophy*, 12(1): 75–105.

Oakes, G. (1987) 'Weber and the Southwest German school: The genesis of the concept of the historical individual', in W.J. Mommsen and J. Osterhammel (eds), *Max Weber and His Contemporaries*. London: Routledge.

Orwell, G. (1968) 'The English people', in S. Orwell and I. Angus (eds), *The Collected Essays and Letters of George Orwell, Vol. 3: As I Please*. London: Secker & Warburg.

Pascal, B. (1995) *Pensées and Other Writings*. Oxford: Oxford University Press.

Paulle, B., van Heerikhuizen, B. and Emirbayer, M. (2011) 'Elias and Bourdieu', in S. Susen and B.S. Turner (eds), *The Legacy of Pierre Bourdieu*. London: Anthem Press.

Perec, G. (1999) *Things: A Story of the Sixties*. London: Harvill Press.

Perkins, S. (1993) *Marxism and the Proletariat: A Lukacsian Perspective*. London: Pluto Press.

Petro, P. (1989) *Joyless Streets: Women and Melodramatic Representation in Weimar Germany*. Princeton, NJ: Princeton University Press.

Pickering, M. (1993) *Auguste Comte: An Intellectual Biography, Vol. 1*. Cambridge: Cambridge University Press. pp. 277–314.

Pickering, M. (1997) 'A new look at Auguste Comte', in C. Camic (ed.), *Reclaiming the Classics: The State of the Scholarship*. Oxford: Blackwell.

Pickering, M. (2009) *Auguste Comte: An Intellectual Biography, Vol. 3*. Cambridge: Cambridge University Press.

Pinker, S. (2011) *The Better Angels of Our Nature: A History of Violence and Humanity*. London: Penguin.

Polanyi, M. (1958) *Personal Knowledge: Towards a Post-Critical Philosophy*. New York: Harper Torchbooks.

Popper, K.R. (1992) *The Logic of Scientific Discovery*. London: Routledge.

Poster, M. (1977) *Existential Marxism in Postwar France: From Sartre to Althusser*. Princeton, NJ: Princeton University Press.

Postone, M. (1980) 'Anti-semitism and national socialism: Notes on the German reaction to "Holocaust"', *New German Critique*, 19(1): 97–115.

Postone, M. (1993) *Time, Labor, and Social Domination: A Reinterpretation of Marx's Critical Theory*. Cambridge: Cambridge University Press.

Powell, R. and Depelteau, F. (eds) (2013) *Conceptualizing Relational Sociology: Ontological and Theoretical Issues*. New York: Palgrave Macmillan.

Rabinbach, A. (1997) *In the Shadow of Catastrophe: German Intellectuals between. Apocalypse and Enlightenment.* Berkeley, CA: University of California Press.

Radkau, J. (2009) *Max Weber: A Biography.* Cambridge: Polity Press.

Ranciere, J. (2003) *The Philosopher and His Poor.* Durham, NC: Duke University Press.

Ranciere, J. (2012) *Proletarian Nights: The Workers' Dream in Nineteenth-Century France.* London: Verso.

Ranulf, S. (1964) *Moral Indignation and Middle Class Psychology.* New York: Schocken Books.

Rawls, A. (2000) 'Harold Garfinkel', in G. Ritzer (ed.), *Blackwell Companion to Major Social Theorists.* London: Blackwell.

Ray, L. (1999) *Theorizing Classical Sociology.* Buckingham: Open University Press.

Reeh, H. (2004) *Ornaments of the Metropolis: Siegfried Kracauer and Modern Urban Culture.* Cambridge, MA: MIT Press.

Reisch, G.A. (1997) 'How postmodern was Neurath's idea of unity of science?', *Studies in History and Philosophy of Science*, 28(3): 439–451.

Reisch, G.A. (2005) *To the Icy Slopes of Logic: How the Cold War Transformed Philosophy of Science.* New York: Cambridge University Press.

Richter, G. (2007) *Thought-Images: Frankfurt School Writers' Reflections from Damaged Life.* Stanford, CA: Stanford University Press.

Riesman, D. (1961) *The Lonely Crowd.* New Haven: Yale University Press.

Rigby, B. (1991) *Popular Culture in Modern France: A Study of Cultural Discourse.* London: Routledge.

Robbins, D. (2006) *On Bourdieu, Education and Society.* Oxford: Bardwell Press.

Roberts, I. (2004) 'Caligari revisited: Circles, cycles and counter-revolution in Robert Weine's "Das Cabinet Des Dr. Caligari"', *German Life & Letters*, 57(2): 175–188.

Roberts, J. (2006) *Philosophizing the Everyday: Revolutionary Praxis and the Fate of Cultural Theory.* London: Pluto Press.

Rochberg-Halton, E. (1986) *Meaning and Modernity: Social Theory in the Pragmatic Attitude.* Chicago, IL: University of Chicago Press.

Rockmore, T. (1992) *Irrationalism: Lukács and the Marxist View of Reason.* Philadelphia, PA: Temple University Press.

Roitman, J. (2014) *Anti-Crisis.* Durham, NC: Duke University Press.

Rojek, C. (2003) *Stuart Hall.* Cambridge: Polity Press.

Rojek, C. (2012) *Fame Attack: The Inflation of Celebrity and its Consequences.* London: Bloomsbury.

Rojek, C. and Turner, B.S. (eds) (1993) *Forget Baudrillard?* London: Routledge.

Rorty, R. (1982) *Consequences of Pragmatism: Essays 1972–1980.* Minneapolis, MN: University of Minnesota Press.

Rose, G. (1978) *The Melancholy Science: An Introduction to the Thought of Theodor W. Adorno.* London: Macmillan.

Rose, G. (2009) *Hegel Contra Sociology.* London: Verso.

Ross, K. (1997) 'Henri Lefebvre on the Situationist International: An interview', *October*, 79: 69–83.

Runciman, W.G. (2000) 'Can there be a Nietzschean sociology?', *European Journal of Sociology/Archives Européennes de Sociologie*, 41(1): 3–21.

Sacks, H. (1995) *Lectures on Conversation*. Oxford: Blackwell.

Saint-Simon, H. (1975) *Selected Writings on Science, Industry, and Social Organisation* (ed. K. Taylor). London: Croom Helm.

Sartre, J.-P. (2004) *Critique of Dialectical Reason, Vol. 1: Theory of Practical Ensembles*. London: Verso.

Saussure, F. De (1983) *Course in General Linguistics*. London: Duckworth.

Savage, J. (1991) *England's Dreaming: Sex Pistols and Punk Rock*. London: Faber and Faber.

Scharff, R.C. (1995) *Comte after Positivism*. Cambridge: Cambridge University Press.

Scheler, M. (1994) *Ressentiment*. Milwaukee, WI: Marquette University Press.

Schermer, W. and Jary, D. (2013) *Form and Dialectic in Georg Simmel's Sociology: A New Interpretation*. Houndsmill: Palgrave Macmillan.

Schlupmann, H. (1987) 'Phenomenology of film: On Siegfried Kracauer's writings of the 1920s', *New German Critique*, 40: 97–114.

Schmidt, J. (1985) *Maurice Merleau-Ponty: Between Phenomenology and Structuralism*. London: Macmillan.

Schneider, L. (ed.) (1967) *The Scottish Moralists on Human Nature and Society*. Chicago, IL: University of Chicago Press.

Schopenhauer, A. (1974) *Parerga and Paralipomena, Vol. 2: Short Philosophical Essays*. Oxford: Oxford University Press.

Schöttker, D. (1998) 'Norbert Elias and Walter Benjamin: An unknown exchange of letters and its context', *History of the Human Sciences*, 11(2): 45–59.

Schumpeter, J. (2010) *Capitalism, Socialism and Democracy*. London: Routledge Classics.

Schütz, A. (1967) *The Phenomenology of the Social World*. Evanston, IL: Northwestern University Press.

Scott, J. (2012) *What is Social Network Analysis?* London: Bloomsbury.

Scott, J. and Nilsen, A. (eds) (2013) *C. Wright Mills and the Sociological Imagination: Contemporary Perspectives*. Cheltenham: Edward Elgar.

Sennett, R. (2008) *The Craftsman*. New Haven, CT: Yale University Press.

Shields, R. (1999) *Lefebvre, Love and Struggle: Spatial Dialectics*. London: Routledge.

Shilling, C. and Mellor, C. (2001) *The Sociological Ambition: Elementary Forms of Social and Moral Life*. London: Sage.

Shotter, J. (2001) 'From within our lives together: Wittgenstein, Bakhtin, and Voloshinov and the shift to a participatory stance in understanding understanding', in L. Holzman and J. Morss (eds), *Postmodern Psychologies, Societal Practice and Political Life*. New York: Routledge.

Silverman, D. (1998) *Harvey Sacks: Social Science and Conversation Analysis*. Oxford: Oxford University Press.

Silverman, H.J. (1997) *Inscriptions: After Phenomenology and Structuralism*. Evanston, IL: Northwestern University Press.

Simmel, G. (1977) *The Problems of the Philosophy of History: An Epistemological Essay*. New York: Free Press.

Simmel, G. (1984) *On Women, Sexuality and Love*. New Haven, CT: Yale University Press.

Simmel, G. (1986) *Schopenhauer and Nietzsche*. Amherst, MA: University of Massachusetts Press.

Simmel, G. (1994) 'The picture frame: An aesthetic study', *Theory, Culture & Society* (February) 11: 11–17.

Simmel, G. (1997) *Simmel on Culture* (eds D. Frisby and M. Featherstone). London: Sage.

Simmel, G. (2005) *Rembrandt: An Essay in the Philosophy of Art*. New York: Routledge.

Simmel, G. (2008) 'Tendencies in German life and thought since 1870', in *Englischsprachige Veröffentlichungen 1893–1910, Georg Simmel: Gesamtausgabe, Band 18*. Frankfurt: Suhrkamp.

Simmel, G. (2009) *Sociology: Inquiries into the Construction of Social Forms*. Leiden: Brill.

Simmel, G. (2010) *The View of Life: Four Metaphysical Essays with Journal Aphorisms*. Chicago, IL: University of Chicago Press.

Simmel, G. (2011) *The Philosophy of Money*. London: Routledge Classics.

Smith, D.E. (1987) *Everyday World as Problematic: A Feminist Sociology*. Boston, MA: Northeastern University Press.

Smith, D.E. (1990) *Texts, Facts, and Femininity: Exploring the Relations of Ruling*. Abingdon: Routledge.

Smith, D.E. (2005) *Institutional Ethnography: A Sociology for People*. Lanham, MD: Rowman Altamira.

Sohn-Rethel, A. (1978) *Intellectual and Manual Labour: A Critique of Epistemology*. London: Macmillan.

Solms-Laubach, F. (2007) *Nietzsche and Early German and Austrian Sociology*. Berlin: Walter de Gruyer.

Sombart, W. (1998) *The Quintessence of Capitalism: A Study of the History and Psychology of the Modern Business Man*. London: Routledge Thoemmes.

Sorokin, P.A. (1985) *Social and Cultural Dynamics: A Study of Change in Major Systems of Art, Truth, Ethics, Law, and Social Relationships*. New Brunswick, NJ: Transaction.

Sorokin, P.A. (1992) *The Crisis of Our Age*. Oxford: Oneworld.

Spengler, O. (1991) *The Decline of the West*. Oxford: Oxford University Press.

Sprinker, M. (ed.) (1999) *Ghostly Demarcations: A Symposium on Jacques Derrida's Specters of Marx*. London: Verso.

Stanek, L. (2011) *Henri Lefebvre on Space: Architecture, Urban Research, and the Production of Theory*. Minneapolis, MN: University of Minnesota Press.

Starn, R. (1971) 'Historians and "Crisis"', *Past & Present*, 52(1): 3–22.

Stauth, G. and Turner, B.S. (1988) *Nietzsche's Dance: Resentment, Reciprocity and Resistance in Social Life*. Oxford: Blackwell.

Stern, J.P. (1978) *Nietzsche*. Glasgow: Fontana.

Stiegler, B. (2014) *The Lost Spirit of Capitalism: Disbelief and Discredit, Volume 3*. Cambridge: Polity.

Stirk, P.M.R. (1992) *Max Horkheimer: A New Interpretation*. Hemel Hempstead: Harvester Wheatsheaf. pp. 140–147.

Strydom, P. (2000) *Discourse and Knowledge: The Making of Enlightenment Sociology*. Liverpool: Liverpool University Press.

Szakolczai, A. (2000) 'Norbert Elias and Franz Borkenau: Intertwined lifeworks', *Theory, Culture & Society*, 17(2): 45–69.

Szondi, P. (1988) 'Walter Benjamin's city portraits', in G. Smith (ed.), *On Walter Benjamin: Critical Essays and Recollections*. Cambridge, MA: MIT Press.

Tarbuck, K.J. (1989) *Bukharin's Theory of Equilibrium*. London: Pluto Press.

Taylor, C. (1989) *Sources of the Self: The Making of the Modern Identity*. Cambridge, MA: Harvard University Press.

Thao, T. Duc (1986) *Phenomenology and Dialectical Materialism*. Dordrecht: Springer.

Therborn, G. (2008) *From Marxism to Post-Marxism?* London: Verso.

Thomas, W.I. (2002) 'The definition of the situation', in N. Rousseau (ed.), *Self, Symbols, and Society: Classic Readings in Social Psychology*. Lanham, MD: Rowman & Littlefield.

Thompson, J.B. (1984) *Studies in the Theory of Ideology*. Cambridge: Polity Press.

Tolstoy, L. (1962) *Fables and Fairy Tales*. New York: New American Library.

Tönnies, F. (2002) *Community and Society*. Newton Abbot: David & Charles.

Trotsky, L. (1975) *My Life: An Attempt at an Autobiography*. Harmondsworth: Penguin.

Turner, B.S. and Rojeck, C. (2001) *Society and Culture: Principles of Scarcity and Solidarity*. London: Sage.

Uebel, T.E. (1992) *Overcoming Logical Positivism from Within: The Emergence of Neurath's Naturalism in the Vienna Circle's Protocol Sentence Debate*. Amsterdam: Rodopi.

Uebel, T.E. (1996) 'Normativity and convention: On the constructivist element of Neurath's naturalism', in E. Nemeth and F. Stadler (eds), *Encyclopedia and Utopia: The Work of Otto Neurath*. Dordrecht: Kluwer.

Uebel, T.E. (2004) 'Introduction: Neurath's economics in critical context', in O. Neurath (eds T.E. Uebel and R.S. Cohen), *Otto Neurath: Economic Writings Selections 1904–1945*. Dordrecht: Kluwer.

van Elteren, M. (1992) 'Karl Korsch and Lewinian social psychology: Failure of a project', *History of the Human Sciences*, 5(2): 33–61.

van Krieken, R. (1998) *Norbert Elias*. London: Routledge.

Vandenberghe, F. (2009) *A Philosophical History of German Sociology*. London: Routledge.

Vaneigem, R. (1994) *The Revolution of Everyday Life*. London: Rebel Books.

Vološinov, V.N. (1973) *Marxism and the Philosophy of Language*. Cambridge, MA: Harvard University Press.

Vološinov, V.N. (2012) 'Discourse in life and discourse in art (concerning sociological poetics)', in *Freudianism: A Marxist Critique*. London: Verso.

Von Wright, G.H. (1974) *Causality and Determinism*. New York: Columbia University Press.

Vossoughian, N. (2008) *Otto Neurath: The Language of the Global Polis*. Rotterdam: NAI.

Weber, M. (1930) *The Protestant Ethic and the Spirit of Capitalism*. London: Unwin.

Weber, M. (1946) *From Max Weber: Essays in Sociology*. New York: Oxford University Press.

Weber, M. (2012) *Collected Methodological Writings* (eds H.H. Bruun and S. Whimster). Abingdon: Routledge.

Weingarter, R.H. (1960) *Experience and Culture: The Philosophy of Georg Simmel.* Middletown, CT: Wesleyan University Press.

Weiss, G. (1999) *Body Images: Embodiment as Intercorporeality.* London: Routledge.

Weitz, E.D. (2007) *Weimar Germany: Promise and Tragedy.* Princeton, NJ: Princeton University Press. pp. 41–79.

Wernick, A. (2001) *Auguste Comte and the Religion of Humanity.* Cambridge: Cambridge University Press.

Wheatland, T. (2009) *The Frankfurt School in Exile.* Minneapolis: University of Minnesota Press.

Whimster, S. (ed.) (1999) *Max Weber and the Culture of Anarchy.* London: Macmillan.

Whimster, S. (ed.) (2004) *The Essential Weber: A Reader.* London: Routledge.

Whimster, S. (2007) *Understanding Weber.* Abingdon: Routledge.

Wiggerhaus, R. (1994) *The Frankfurt School: Its History, Theories, and Political Significance.* Cambridge: Polity.

Wilkie, R. and McKinnon, A. (2013) 'George Herbert Mead on humans and other animals: Social relations after human–animal studies', *Sociological Research Online,* 18(4). (Available at www.socresonline.org.uk/18/4/19.html, accessed 7 June 2014).

Williams, R. (1965) *The Long Revolution.* Harmondsworth: Penguin.

Wilson, E. (1991) *The Sphinx in the City: Urban Life, the Control of Disorder, and Women.* Berkeley, CA: University of California Press. pp. 54–56.

Winch, P. (1990) *The Idea of a Social Science and its Relation to Philosophy* (2nd edn). London: Routledge.

Wolff, K.H. (1974) *Trying Sociology.* New York: Wiley.

Wood, E.M. (1986) *The Retreat from Class: The New 'True' Socialism.* London: Verso.

Wouters, C. (2007) *Informalization: Manners and Emotions since 1890.* London: Sage.

Young, I.M. (1998) 'Throwing like a girl': Twenty years later', in D. Welton (ed.), *Body and Flesh: A Philosophical Reader.* Oxford: Blackwell.

Young, I.M. (2005) *On Female Body Experience: 'Throwing Like a Girl' and Other Essays.* Oxford: Oxford University Press.

Yuval-Davis, N. (2011) *The Politics of Belonging: Intersectional Contestations.* London: Sage.

Zolo, D. (1989) *Reflexive Epistemology: The Philosophical Legacy of Otto Neurath.* Dordrecht: Kluwer.

INDEX